INTERNATIONAL SERVICE LEARNING

IUPUI Series on Service Learning Research

Series Editors
Robert G. Bringle and Julie A. Hatcher

INTERNATIONAL SERVICE LEARNING

Conceptual Frameworks and Research

Edited by

Robert G. Bringle, Julie A. Hatcher,
and Steven G. Jones

Vol 1: IUPUI Series on Service Learning Research

STERLING, VIRGINIA

COPYRIGHT © 2011 BY
STYLUS PUBLISHING, LLC.

Published by Stylus Publishing, LLC
22883 Quicksilver Drive
Sterling, Virginia 20166-2102

Library of Congress Cataloging-in-Publication-Data

International service learning : conceptual frameworks and research / edited by Robert G. Bringle, Julie A. Hatcher, and Steven G. Jones. – 1st ed.
   p. cm. – (IUPUI series on service learning research ; v. 1)
   Includes bibliographical references and index.
   ISBN 978-1-57922-338-0 (cloth : alk. paper) –
ISBN 978-1-57922-339-7 (pbk. : alk. paper)
 1. Service learning.   2. Service learning–Research.
3. Education and globalization.   I. Bringle, Robert G.
II. Hatcher, Julie A., 1953–   III. Jones, Steven G.
   LC220.5.I585 2011
   361.3′7–dc22   2010023010

Printed in the United States of America

All first editions printed on acid free paper
that meets the American National Standards Institute
Z39-48 Standard.

Bulk Purchases

Quantity discounts are available for use in workshops
and for staff development.
Call 1-800-232-0223

First Edition, 2011

10   9   8   7   6   5   4   3   2   1

CONTENTS

PART FOUR: AN INTERNATIONAL PERSPECTIVE

C hange does not come easily to higher education, but service learning has demonstrated its capacity to have an influence on areas of the academy that are among the most difficult to change: the curriculum, faculty work, organizational infrastructure, budget allocations, promotion and tenure, assessment of student learning, and campus-community partnerships. These changes have manifested themselves across institutional types and have demonstrated a tenacity that suggests that they are not mere fads but enduring trends. More than 1,000 institutions are now members of Campus Compact and service learning involves increasing numbers of students, faculty, and community partners (Campus Compact, 2008; Hartley & Hollander, 2005). Stimulated and guided by the model provided by service learning, institutions of higher education have examined how civic engagement can change the nature of faculty work, enhance student learning, better fulfill the complete campus mission, provide a basis for public accountability, and improve the quality of life in communities (e.g., Boyer, 1994, 1996; Bringle, Games, & Malloy, 1999; Calleson, Jordan, & Seifer, 2005; Colby, Ehrlich, Beaumont, & Stephens, 2003; Edgerton, 1994; Harkavy & Puckett, 1994; O'Meara & Rice, 2005; Percy, Zimpher, & Brukardt, 2006; Rice, 1996).

However, when the degree and nature of the changes associated with service learning, and more broadly, civic engagement, are assessed for their quality, breadth, and depth, the interpretation of change during the past 15 years is open to a variety of interpretations. Saltmarsh et al. (2009) analyzed dossiers from the Carnegie Elective Classification for Community Engagement that paints a "half full/half empty" portrait, with uneven evidence offered by institutions for institutional change associated with community engagement: change has occurred in all successful institutions, but there is also evidence of resistance to change (e.g., promotion and tenure) and some consistent shortcomings (e.g., authentic campus-community reciprocity). Butin's (2005) edited volume presents multiple perspectives that raise issues about the degree to which the assumptions, values, and operations of service learning are incompatible with the engrained culture of higher education and constrain the capacity of service learning to produce transformational institutional change. Saltmarsh, Hartley, and Clayton (in press) question the degree to which the depth of change associated with civic engagement has been democratic, fundamental, and systemic. Regardless of how full or how empty, service learning has produced change not only in the curriculum but also more broadly, which is not a trivial outcome. In the absence of a consensual goal, either among civic engagement practitioners or leaders in higher education in general, to produce deep systemic change across all institutional types in a decade, the amount of change so far in higher education can be viewed as an extraordinary accomplishment and the criticism that change has been too slow, too small, incomplete, or falls short of ideals is shortsighted in acknowledging what changes have occurred. Furthermore, the presence of these interpretations, analyses, critiques, and commentaries indicates that (a) scholars have some progress to review; (b) they care enough about it to invest their resources in studying it; (c) there are aspirations and standards against which incomplete, though significant, accomplishments can be evaluated; and (d) reflection on the extent and nature of change that has occurred can inform future work.

The development of service learning and civic engagement on the Indiana University-Purdue University Indianapolis (IUPUI) campus mirrors these national developments. Starting with opening an IUPUI Office of Service Learning in 1993 (now incorporated into the IUPUI Center for Service and Learning), the growth of service learning has been nurtured on a campus of more than 30,000 students with strong traditions of community involvement among its many professional schools. Through strategic decisions by executive leadership (Bringle & Hatcher, 2004; Bringle, Hatcher, & Holland, 2007; Plater, 2004), significant commitments to infrastructure were made to support the growth of service learning that was guided by the Comprehensive Action Plan for Service Learning (CAPSL) that identifies 10 tasks (planning, increasing awareness, developing a prototype of good practice, gathering resources, expanding programs, providing recognition, monitoring, evaluating, conducting research, and institutionalization) for four stakeholders (institution, faculty, students, and community) (Bringle & Hatcher, 1996). There is evidence of institutional progress across all areas of CAPSL at IUPUI, including infrastructure to support service learning and civic engagement (Bringle et al., 2007; Bringle & Hatcher, 2004: Bringle, Hatcher, & Clayton, 2006; Bringle, Hatcher, Hamilton, & Young, 2001; Bringle, Hatcher, Jones, & Plater, 2006).

In addition, independent external reviews support the assessment of significant institutional progress at IUPUI around service learning and civic engagement. Since 2003, for example, the campus' service learning program has been recognized as one of the top programs in the country by U.S. News and World Report. In 2006, IUPUI was recognized in the Saviors of our Cities national report by the New England Board of Higher Education as one of 25 urban colleges and universities that have dramatically strengthened the economy and quality of life of its neighboring communities. IUPUI was the highest ranked public university receiving this distinction, and IUPUI was again recognized in 2009. Most noteworthy, in 2006, the inaugural year for the award, IUPUI was selected by the Corporation for National and Community Service as one of three universities in the country, out of 510 campuses that applied, to receive the Presidential Award for exceptional accomplishments in General Student Community Service activities. The Carnegie Foundation in 2006 confirmed IUPUI's designation as a member of the first group of colleges and universities to receive the distinction of Community Engagement in the two categories of "Curricular Engagement" and "Outreach and Partnerships."

With the intention to improve on these accomplishments, the IUPUI Center for Service and Learning (CSL) received a designation in 2007 as an IUPUI *Signature Center* and established the CSL Research Collaborative. The mission of the CSL Research Collaborative is to:

- Increase the capacity of faculty to engage in research on service learning practice.
- Convene service learning scholars to develop new conceptual frameworks and methodological tools to improve the quality of service learning research.
- Disseminate high-quality scholarship through books, research briefs, annual monographs, a website that provides information on resources (e.g., grant opportunities, scales for research), presentations at scholarly conferences, and publications in peer-reviewed journals.

The CSL Research Collaborative has provided the basis for launching many new research activities for advancing scholarship on campus and nationally, including the *IUPUI Series on Service Learning Research.*

International Service Learning: Conceptual Frameworks and Research

As part of the IUPUI CSL Research Collaborative, themes were identified for developing scholarship on research that would advance the field and for their capacity to meet strategic goals for IUPUI. The initial theme, international service learning (ISL), grew out of institutional collaboration between CSL and the IUPUI Office of International Affairs to emphasize service learning as a distinctive aspect of the development of study abroad and strategic international partnerships. This volume is intentionally focused on North American students' involvement in ISL and how to conduct more and better research on their ISL experiences.

The volume is intended to be relevant to all students: undergraduates at all types of institutions, graduate students, and professional students. Authors who contributed to the volume do not analyze service learning across the globe and, therefore, this volume is not about service learning internationally. Service learning is growing in South Africa, aided by the Joint Education Trust-CHESP initiative (JET, 2006; Lazarus, 2004), in Australia (see Holland & Bennett, 2003), in Asia (see United Board for Christian Higher Education in Asia [International Christian University], 2002), and Ireland (McIlrath & MacLabhrainn, 2007) as well as Latin America, South America, Mexico, the Middle East, Europe, and South America (see Annette, 2003; Perold, 2005; Perold, Stroud, & Sherraden, 2003). These are important models that can enhance practice of American service learning both domestically and especially abroad. Furthermore, the possibility of American students being engaged in service learning alongside students from international institutions should augment cross-cultural experiences and learning. Nevertheless, this volume is limited to ISL of North American students and developing a research agenda that will provide a basis for increased opportunities for them to study abroad, engage in international service, and enhance their international education.

This volume is focused, in particular, on stimulating research on ISL. This analysis could not be done in the absence of considering the nature and purposes of ISL, conceptual frameworks that can guide the research, variations in implementation, and the relationships of ISL research to past research on study abroad, service learning, international learning, and teaching and learning. The chapters will have appeal to educators, researchers, and practitioners in study abroad, service learning, and international education as well as faculty who are interested in developing research projects on ISL. The contents of this volume have confirmed that there is great potential for the development of ISL in higher education and that there is a great need for scholarly analysis, assessment, and research of ISL. The growth in service learning and civic engagement, coupled with the Lincoln Commission's recommendation for one million American students to study abroad as a matter of national policy (NAFSA, 2008), confirms that now is the time for closer attention to ISL.

This volume benefited greatly from collaborations with Susan Sutton, Associate Vice President for International Programs at Indiana University and

Associate Vice Chancellor of International Affairs at IUPUI, who has been willing to explore, discuss, plan, implement, and assess activities related to developing service learning and ISL on the IUPUI campus. In 2006, in collaboration with her IUPUI Office of International Affairs and the International Partnership of Service Learning and Leadership, IUPUI hosted a workshop: *Engaging the World: Developing a Campus-Wide Approach to International Service Learning.* The workshop was structured for institutional teams of faculty and administrators from colleges and universities to develop campus plans for ISL programs and courses for their students. To gain maximum benefit from participating in the workshop, team members could include key leaders and campus administrators from study abroad programs, international affairs, and service learning programs as well as key faculty members. Plenary and breakout sessions focused on essential elements in constructing and operating ISL courses and programs abroad. Topics included:

- Developing a strategic plan for the campus—broadening the civic engagement mission from local to global
- Defining and organizing international partnerships
- Curriculum design, including reflection, for ISL courses
- Legal, visa, safety, and other administrative challenges
- Uses of technology for orientation, reflection, and program development
- Cross-cultural issues
- Scholarships and financial aid programs for students
- Faculty development strategies
- Engaging the disciplines

To develop this book, **International Service Learning: Conceptual Frameworks and Research,** national experts were identified for their scholarship, expertise, and relevance to that theme. Because one of the deficiencies that too frequently occurs in edited books is a lack of coherence, each collaborator participated in two symposia at IUPUI to discuss key issues that guided their writing, without sacrificing the distinctiveness of their individual contributions. Many of the authors also participated in the Third Annual Conference on **International Service Learning: Advancing Research and Practice** held on the IUPUI campus in spring 2007 and jointly sponsored by the International Partnership for Service Learning and Leadership and Indiana Campus Compact. The authors devoted significant time and attention to forging new areas of work associated with ISL. In doing so, they have demonstrated persistence and dedication to all of the activities that were associated with the production of this volume, including their willingness to discuss, review, listen, and share ideas as a means for improving all of the chapters. Mabel Erasmus, who traveled from South Africa to be part of the Third Annual Conference on *International Service Learning: Advancing Research and Practice* and the second Symposium on International Service Learning, warrants a special note of gratitude. The authors also benefited from the participation of colleagues who provided feedback to them as they wrote their chapters: Andrew Furco, Frederick Bein, Robert Osgood, Kathleen Sideli, Dawn Whitehead, Armando Soto, Julie Reed, Sarah Woiteshek, and Stephanie Leslie.

Dean Uday Sukhatme, Executive Vice Chancellor and Dean of the Faculties at IUPUI, provided support for the CSL Research Collaborative through the Signature Center initiative. A special note of appreciation is extended to William M. Plater, who served as Executive Vice Chancellor and Dean of the Faculties at IUPUI from 1987 to 2006, and is currently Director of the Office of International Community Development. Dean Plater has been the architect for advancing IUPUI's work on civic engagement and service learning (Bringle & Hatcher, 2004; Bringle et al., 2006, 2007). He has provided persistent and pervasive support to the CSL and its work, national initiatives, and the work associated with the CSL Research Collaborative.

RGB
July 2009

References

Annette, J. (2003). Service-learning internationally: Developing a global civil society. In S. Billig & J. Eyler (Eds.), *Deconstructing service-learning: Research exploring context, participation and impacts.* Greenwich, CT: Information Age.

Boyer, E. L. (1994). Creating the new American college. *Chronicle of Higher Education,* A48.

Boyer, E. L. (1996). The scholarship of engagement. *Journal of Public Service and Outreach, 1*(1), 11–20.

Bringle, R. G., Games, R., & Malloy, E. A. (1999). Colleges and universities as citizens: Issues and perspectives. In R. G. Bringle, R. Games, & E. A. Malloy (Eds.), *Colleges and universities as citizens* (pp. 1–16). Needham Heights, MA: Allyn & Bacon.

Bringle, R. G., & Hatcher, J. A. (1996). Implementing service learning in higher education. *Journal of Higher Education, 67,* 221–239.

Bringle, R. G., & Hatcher, J. A. (2004). Advancing civic engagement through service-learning. In M. Langseth & W. M. Plater (Eds.), *Public work and the academy: An*

academic administrator's guide to civic engagement and service-learning. (pp. 125–145)
Boston, MA: Anker Press.

Bringle, R. G., Hatcher, J. A., & Clayton, P. H. (2006). The scholarship of civic
engagement: Defining, documenting, and evaluating faculty work. *To Improve the
Academy, 25*, 257–279.

Bringle, R. G., Hatcher, J. A., Hamilton, S., & Young, P. (2001). Planning
and assessing campus/community engagement. *Metropolitan Universities, 12*(3),
89–99.

Bringle, R. G., Hatcher, J. A., & Holland, B. (2007). Conceptualizing civic engagement: Orchestrating change at a metropolitan university. *Metropolitan Universities,
18*(3), 57–74.

Bringle, R. G., Hatcher, J. A., Jones, S., & Plater, W. M. (2006). Sustaining civic
engagement: Faculty development, roles, and rewards. *Metropolitan Universities,
17*(1), 62–74.

Butin, D. W. (Ed.). (2005). *Service-learning in higher education: Critical issues and
directions.* New York: Palgrave.

Calleson, D. C., Jordan, C., & Seifer, S. D. (2005). Community-engaged scholarship:
Is faculty work in communities a true academic enterprise? *Academic Medicine,
80*(4), 317–321.

Campus Compact. (2008). *2008 Service statistics: Highlights and trends of Campus
Compact's annual membership survey.* Providence, RI: Campus Compact. Retrieved
November 9, 2009, from http://www.compact.org/wp-content/uploads/2009/10/
2008-statistics1.pdf

Colby, A., Ehrlich, T., Beaumont, E., & Stephens, J. (2003). *Educating citizens:
Preparing America's undergraduates for lives of moral and civic responsibility.* San
Francisco, CA: Jossey-Bass.

Edgerton, R. (1994). The engaged campus: Organizing to serve society's needs. *AAHE
Bulletin, 47*, 2–3.

Harkavy, I., & Puckett, J. L. (1994). Lessons from Hull House for the contemporary
urban university. *Social Science Review, 68*, 299–321.

Hartley, M., & Hollander, E. L. (2005). The elusive ideal: Civic learning and higher
education. In S. Fuhrman & M. Lazerson (Eds.), *The public schools* (pp. 252–275).
New York: Oxford University Press.

Holland, B. A., & Bennett, H. (Eds.). (2003, November). Civic engagement in
Australia. *Metropolitan Universities, 14*(2).

JET Educational Trust. (2006). *JET educational services: Annual report 2006.* Braamfontein, South Africa: JET Educational Trust.

Lazarus, J. (2004). Community engagement. In *South African higher education in
the first decade of democracy* (chapter 7). Cape Town: The South African Council
on Higher Education. Retrieved August 13, 2009, from http://www.che.ac.za/
documents/d000081/index.php

McIlrath, L., & MacLabhrainn, I. M. (2007). *Higher education and civic engagement:
International perspectives.* Surrey, UK: Ashgate.

NAFSA (Association of International Educators). (2008). *Public policy benefits of study abroad.* Retrieved November 10, 2008, from http://www.nafsa.org/public_policy.sec/study_abroad_2/benefits_of_study_abroad

O'Meara, K., & Rice, R. E. (Eds.). (2005). *Faculty priorities reconsidered: Rewarding multiple forms of scholarship.* San Francisco, CA: Jossey-Bass.

Percy, S. L., Zimpher, N., & Brukardt, M. (Eds.). (2006). *Creating a new kind of university.* Bolton, MA: Anker.

Perold, H. (2005). *Civic engagement in higher education: An overview of participating universities.* Retrieved September 12, 2005, from http://president.tufts.edu/conference/trend.shtml

Perold, H., Stroud, S., & Sherraden, M. (Eds.). (2003). *Service enquiry. Service in the 21st Century* (pp. 47–58). Cape Town, South Africa: Compress.

Plater, W. M. (2004). Civic engagement, service-learning, and intentional leadership. In M. Langseth & W. M. Plater (Eds.), *Public work and the academy: An academic administrator's guide to civic engagement and service-learning* (pp. 1–22). Bolton, MA: Anker.

Rice, R. E. (1996, January). *Making a place for the new American scholar.* Paper presented at the AAHE Conference on Faculty Roles and Rewards, Atlanta, GA.

Saltmarsh, J., Giles, D. E. Jr., O'Meara, K. A., Sandmann, L., Ward, E., & Buglione, S. M. (2009). The institutional home for faculty engagement: An investigation of reward policies at engaged campuses. In B. E. Moely, S. H. Billig, & B. A. Holland (Eds.), *Creating our identities in service-learning and community engagement. Advances in service-learning research* (pp. 3–32). Greenwich, CT: Information Age.

Saltmarsh, J., Hartley, M., & Clayton, P. (in press). Democracy and higher education: The future of engagement. *Journal of Higher Education, Outreach, and Engagement.*

United Board for Christian Higher Education in Asia and International Christian University. (2002). *Service learning in Asia: Creating networks and curricula in higher education.* Tokyo, Japan: International Christian University.

PART ONE

CONCEPTUAL FRAMEWORKS FOR INTERNATIONAL SERVICE LEARNING

1

INTERNATIONAL SERVICE LEARNING

Robert G. Bringle and Julie A. Hatcher

I f a medical researcher discovered a cure for cancer, or some other serious illness, there would be great enthusiasm about the development and a sense of urgency for publicizing its availability to the benefit of as many patients as possible. By analogy, what if higher education identified a pedagogical approach that had educational outcomes that are extensive (influences a broad array of desirable educational outcomes), robust (are evident across a variety of conditions and for a wide range of students), transformational (produces deep, permanent changes in present and future lives), and distinctive (produces educational outcomes that are not as effectively attained using other pedagogies)? International service learning (ISL) holds this potential and may be a pedagogy that is best suited to prepare college graduates to be active global citizens in the 21st century.

The purposes of this edited book, *International Service Learning: Conceptual Frameworks and Research*, are to bring greater attention to ISL in higher education and to provide insight on conducting research on this learning experience. We anticipate that this focus on research will contribute to greater understanding of the nature of ISL, greater quality in its implementation, and greater confidence in its potential to produce measurable outcomes. Given a climate in which higher education has directed increased attention over the past decade to assessment and accountability, civic engagement and service learning, and internationalizing the curriculum and study abroad, these conditions are conducive to support the expansion of and more rigorous study of ISL.

The contributing authors of each chapter in this volume are focused on different facets of ISL. Each chapter provides not only information that supports the design and implementation of ISL but also information that guides research to improve practice and contribute to an understanding of why and under what conditions ISL is an effective pedagogy. Therefore, the book will be useful to both practitioners and scholars. The purpose of this chapter is to frame the nature of ISL.

Conceptualizing International Service Learning

ISL can be conceptualized as the intersection of three different educational domains: (a) service learning, (b) study abroad, and (c) international education (see Figure 1.1). The intersection of these three domains borrows important elements from each and creates a pedagogy that has the added value of its own combination of unique qualities. Each of the three domains will be introduced as a basis for developing an understanding of ISL and what potential it has as a powerful pedagogy that warrants increased attention by practitioners and researchers in higher education. Based on this analysis of three overlapping domains, the chapter presents a definition of ISL and this definition provides the guiding framework for the book.

FIGURE 1.1
International service learning as the intersection of service learning, study abroad, and international education.

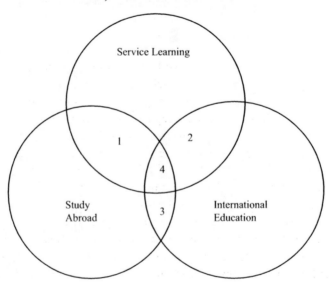

Service Learning

Over the past two decades, the prevalence of service learning courses has increased dramatically in higher education. This has occurred for all types of institutions of higher education and across the spectrum of disciplines with a reported rate of 12% of faculty involved in teaching service learning classes (Campus Compact, 2007). Service learning is a form of experiential education that has gained prominence in higher education as one type of high-impact educational practice (Kuh, 2008) and an active learning strategy that provides a rich set of opportunities for educators to explore teaching and learning (Eyler, Giles, Stenson, & Gray, 2001). Service learning is defined as

> A course-based, credit-bearing educational experience in which students (a) participate in an organized service activity that meets identified community needs, and (b) reflect on the service activity in such a way as to gain further understanding of course content, a broader appreciation of the discipline, and an enhanced sense of personal values and civic responsibility. (Bringle & Hatcher, 2009, p. 38)

This definition identifies four important qualities that are relevant to defining ISL. First, service learning is an academic activity. This differentiates service learning from volunteering, which is cocurricular and not intentionally linked to the curriculum (Furco, 1996). Faculty assume a pivotal role in service learning by identifying and assessing learning outcomes and collaborating with community partners to structure experiences both in and outside of the classroom that contribute to the academic goals of the course. Second, the community service activities are selected with two necessary conditions: (a) they provide educationally meaningful service activities that contribute to the educational objectives of the course and situate student learning in the course and the discipline and (b) they are reciprocally identified with community partners to ensure that the activities are agreed to be of value to both parties.

Third, service learning course design includes integrating structured reflection activities that contribute to the intended educational outcomes by linking the community service activities to the course content and vice versa (Hatcher & Bringle, 1997). Thus, reflection activities bridge the community service activities and the educational content of the course in a way that produces new learning not delivered solely by the course content or the community service alone. Reflection activities should be designed by educators to provide new interpretations of events and the activities provide a means through which the community service can be studied, analyzed, and interpreted much like a text is read and studied for deeper understanding.

Well-designed reflection activities should (a) intentionally link the service experience to course-based learning objectives, (b) be structured, (c) occur regularly, (d) allow feedback and assessment, and (e) include the clarification of values (Bringle & Hatcher, 1999; Bringle, Hatcher, & Muthiah, 2004; Hatcher & Bringle, 1997). Critical reflective thought adds new meaning to service experiences, enriches the academic content of the course, and develops students' ability to take informed actions in the future (Ash & Clayton, 2004; Ash, Clayton, & Atkinson, 2005; Dewey, 1916, 1933; Hatcher, 1997; Whitney & Clayton, chapter 8).

Finally, this definition of service learning establishes that the civic responsibility of students is one of the unique objectives of a service learning course. Civic learning is composed of civic knowledge, skills, and habits (Battistoni, 2002; Billig & Eyler, 2003; Eyler & Giles, 1999; Eyler et al, 2001; Zlotkowski, Longo, & Williams, 2006). Kahne and Westheimer (2003) identified three distinct domains that align with the objective of a service learning course: (a) the personally responsible citizen, (b) the participatory citizen, and (c) the justice-oriented citizen. Battistoni (2002) conducted an analysis of the different dimensions of citizenship with reference to the content domains and paradigms of the disciplines and professions. His analysis identifies the following approaches to civic education as distinctive: (a) civic professionalism, (b) social responsibility, (c) social justice, (d) connected knowing and the ethic of caring, (e) public leadership, (f) public intellectual, and (g) engaged or public scholarship. Service learning has the potential to contribute to these civic outcomes for higher education and the civic-minded graduate.

Study Abroad

Study abroad is another form of experiential education and an increasing number of college students are participating in study abroad during their undergraduate years. The Institute for International Education estimates that 240,000 college students studied abroad in 2006–2007, and although this represents an annual growth rate of 8%, no more than 1–2% of American college students study abroad each year (Blumenthal & Gutierrez, 2009). Organizations such as the Institute for International Education, the Forum on Education Abroad, and the newly established Center for Capacity Building in Study Abroad advocate for increasing the quality within study abroad programs, building the capacity of colleges and universities to support study abroad, and tracking participation rates and types of study abroad programs. The majority of study abroad programs (55%) are short-term experiences of eight weeks or less, with the one-semester, mid-length programs (40%), and full academic year programs (5%) no longer being the most common length of stay (Blumenthal & Gutierrez, 2009). Study abroad programs that involve students in educationally meaningful community service in the host country are not yet formally tracked by these organizations.

Students traveling to study in other nations is centuries old. The European tradition of study abroad was the Grand Tour, which took typically aristocratic men to capital cities to study the country's arts, literature, and culture as they related to a classical education (Lewin, 2009b). North American traditions initially followed this model, with shifts over time from emphasizing the classics to linking study abroad to the liberal arts and now to professional education (Association of American Colleges and Universities [AAC&U], 2007; Hovland, McTighe Musil, Skilton-Sylvester, & Jamison, 2009), from involving the rich elite to a broader spectrum of students who can afford the experience, from American students studying in European locations to studying in more diverse locations around the world (Che, Spearman, & Manizade, 2009), and from a study abroad experience that lasts an academic year to shorter duration of eight weeks or less (Blumenthal & Gutierrez, 2009; Chin, 2003). Female students now participate in study abroad more frequently than males (Kim & Goldstein, 2005) with steady increases in numbers of students studying abroad during the past decade (Institute of International Education, 2008).

The Commission on the Abraham Lincoln Study Abroad Fellowship Program, a bipartisan commission appointed by Congress and the President in 2005, set forth the ambitious goal that within a decade there would be one million American students studying abroad each year. The Lincoln Commission, and resulting legislation through the Paul Simon Foundation Study Abroad Act, has heightened attention to study abroad and the measures necessary to increase capacity both here and abroad to provide study abroad opportunities for undergraduates, particularly to underrepresented minorities. Preliminary results from the *Beyond Immediate Impact: Study Abroad for Global Engagement* (SAGE) research project being conducted at the University of Minnesota, and funded by the U.S. Department of Education, indicates that students who participated in study abroad, even short-term programs with duration of between two and eight weeks, reported significant gains in terms of their global engagement and global values (Fry, Paige, & Stallman, 2009). Results from both quantitative and qualitative research in the SAGE project indicate that

> This study provides strong empirical evidence that undergraduate students who study abroad during their college years become globally engaged in a variety of ways in subsequent years. Moreover, many of them attribute their global engagement to their having studied abroad. An investment in study abroad then, at the federal and state levels, is a much broader investment in the long term well-being of society and the globe: socially, environmentally, and politically. (Fry et al., 2009)

In ways similar to the Morrill Land Grant Act of 1862 and 1892 that resulted in the establishment of land-grant universities and extension services, and to the GI Bill of 1944 that resulted in doubling the enrollment in higher education between 1943 and 1946 (Thelin, 2004), this national initiative to support the expansion of study abroad programs has been described as the next step in the evolution of American higher education (Commission on the Abraham Lincoln Study Abroad Fellowship Program, 2005).

Although the rationale for study abroad might appear obvious, there are analyses that present a variety of perspectives, some anchored in particular historical periods in American history (e.g., the Cold War, post-September 11, 2001). First and foremost in the rationale for study abroad, though, is that it is primarily for the benefit of the student. The presumption is that all study abroad experiences provide students with academic credits that they can apply to their degrees upon their return to colleges and universities. Other usually implicit rationales that accompany analyses of study abroad include developing appreciation for culture, language proficiency gained by international experience, critical thinking and other cognitive skills, interpersonal skills, enhanced communication skills, intercultural empathy and understanding, and marketable job skills that are increasingly valued in a globalized economy. Recently, Lewin (2009a) develops the rationale that study abroad can contribute to global citizenship and Fry et al. (2009) provide the conceptual framework for study abroad having a long-term impact on global engagement and global values. The rationale for increased government support of study abroad rests on issues such as improved diplomacy with other nations, American national security, international peace, and economic competitiveness of America (Kiely, chapter 11). In addition, a rationale of profit is evident in the field as third-party providers (e.g., International Education Programs; ProWorld) enter the market to promote custom-designed study abroad programs to students, faculty, and staff.

This mix of motives complicates issues of goals and objectives, program design, and assessment. This results in a broad spectrum of program types (Engle & Engle, 2003). Study abroad can too easily be viewed as an activity that is "good for its own sake," without regard to clarifying and analyzing why it is good and in what ways it is beneficial for participants. Practitioners and educators may have very firm convictions about the purposes of study abroad, but they may also have limited control on how the design or implementation of the study abroad experience contains program elements that produce the desired outcomes, and little evidence about the degree to which those outcomes are reached. Principles of good practice for study abroad exist. For example, the Institute for International Education of Students Abroad MAP provides guidelines for program planning and development. In 2008, the Forum on Education Abroad published *Standards of Good Practice for Education Abroad*, and followed this with *Standards of Good Practice for Short-Term Education Abroad Programs* in 2009. However, compliance with these principles of good practice is varied across programs and across institutions.

Furthermore, even though faculty and staff who design study abroad experiences may have clear ideas about their rationale and objectives, these may be missed by the students. Based on interviews of a limited sample of study abroad students, Zemach-Bersin (2009) concluded,

> Some students actively and critically dismissed global citizenship in advertising and mission statements as empty and meaningless, reflective of a rhetorical ideology rather than an educational reality. Because they both do not understand and have not experienced *global citizenship*, these students understand the term as a mere buzzword. (p. 315)

This state of confounded rationales, program goals, and program types complicates assessing study abroad outcomes to the point that there is limited high-quality evidence on its outcomes that has been gathered across programs. Although Akande and Slawson (2000) report that 95% of study abroad alumni stated that study abroad affected their worldview and their career paths, there is limited independent evidence to corroborate these self-report findings and anecdotal accounts. The research underway through the SAGE project at the University of Minnesota will provide valuable empirical evidence of the outcomes of study abroad (Fry et al., 2009). Furthermore, most evidence does not compare study abroad to alternative curricula (e.g., international studies at home) (Jones & Steinberg, chapter 5; Kiely & Hartman, chapter 13).

Large-scale studies by the Institute for International Education of Students permit analyses of program characteristics (e.g., model, duration, housing arrangements) on student outcomes (Dwyer, 2004a, 2004b; Dwyer & Peters, 2004; Norris & Dwyer, 2005). Bolen (2007) published *A Guide to Outcomes Assessment in Education Abroad*. Deardorff (2009) and Gillespie, Braskamp, and Dwyer (2009) provide comprehensive models for linking program assessment to program design. These approaches provide useful resources for ISL researchers. Nevertheless, the status of compelling evidence about independent evaluation of specific outcomes, either as changes in students or in comparison to domestic curricular experiences, is still meager.

International Education

American higher education continues to direct increased attention to the international education of college students. Over time, this endeavor has been referred to by many different names. Many of these terms are overlapping, but some have subtle or substantive differences or emphases. Terms used to describe international education include *global awareness, global education, global learning and development, intercultural competence, world studies, cross-cultural competence, cross-cultural empathy*, and *cross-cultural understanding* (Davies & Pike, 2009; Deardorff, 2009; Gillespie et al., 2009; Hovland et al., 2009). Developing skills and knowledge that are associated with action in an international world can be focused on either (a) technical aspects of a major (e.g., how one executes a business contract with a labor union in South Africa, how healthcare is provided in developing nations) or (b) topical issues within a discipline associated with cultural, political, and social systems in other countries (e.g., geography, gender roles, transparency of government) (Toh, 1993). A subset of objectives associated with international education, and one that will be particularly relevant to the subsequent discussions of ISL, is referred to as global citizenship (Lewin, 2009a).

[Aspects of global citizenship can be extrapolated from the North American analyses of civic involvement; however, extrapolating American conceptions of citizenship (Battistoni, 2002; Kahne & Westheimer, 2003) to a global scale can run the risk of inappropriately imposing North American views in a context in which they lose their relevance.] As Schudson (2003) notes, there are different types of citizenship skills needed for different forms of government and cultural traditions, and American students study abroad in many countries that are not representative democracies. Thus, the nature of civic learning objectives is context specific and is different in locales such as Southern Africa, Eastern Europe, Southeast Asia, North America, and Australia (Annette, 2003). In addition, conceptions of active involvement as a citizen in the international arena can be described by the degree of involvement. McTighe Musil (2003) describes six levels of involvement that are applicable to global citizenship: (a) exclusionary, (b) oblivious, (c) naïve, (d) charitable, (e) reciprocal, and (f) generative. Boyte and Kari (2000) identify three forms of involvement applicable to international involvement: (a) civic (involvement as a citizen, such as voting), (b) communal (involvement in civil society and the nonprofit sector), and (c) commonwealth (actions that improve the common good). Finally, Nussbaum (1997) presents the goal of students to become world citizens, with the primary point of reference of their identity, interdependency, and action being the world, rather than a national or provincial place. Nevertheless, the analysis of ISL in this book is focused on educational experiences for North American students, and the dynamic relationship between American notions of civic education and international perspectives on civic education can be a focus of international education of these American students.

Although international education could appear to be synonymous with study abroad, that is not always the case (although the overlap will be discussed subsequently), as indicated in Figure 1.1. International education of American students can occur by internationalizing the curriculum within American classrooms, although such a strategy would be viewed by most educators as incomplete. Nevertheless, study of the commerce, law, health practice, culture, history, language, and political and social issues associated with a country or a region of the world, as well as discipline-based studies with an international component, can result in meeting many of the educational objectives delineated in sets of objectives for international education. Brockington and Wiedenhoeft (2009), after reviewing curricula, note that "study abroad seems to be optional for the global or international studies major" (p. 122).

The American Council on Education (ACE), through its Center for International Initiatives, has created resources that analyze the importance of international education, including study abroad. For example, Sutton, Miller, and Rubin (2007) specified global knowledge, skills, and attitudes for international education. Similarly, the *Shared Futures: Global Learning and Social Responsibility* initiative, sponsored by the AAC&U, highlights the importance of making the undergraduate experience have increased international content and preparation (Hovland et al., 2009). However, reports generated by ACE also document how the internationalization of American higher education falls far short of aspirations and still influences relatively few students (Green, Luu, & Burris, 2008; Siaya & Hayward, 2003).

Intersection #1: Service Learning and Study Abroad

The combination of service learning and study abroad has interesting implications for designing successful internationally based educational experiences for students. Students do more than study in another nation; they are also engaged in organized service activities that (a) complement and augment their classroom learning, (b) contribute to the community in the host country, (c) support face-to-face interaction with others, (d) increase cross-cultural understanding of others, and (d) challenge students to clarify and reconsider their role as a citizen. As a result, the international service experience provides opportunities for additional learning goals, activities, and relationships that are not available in the same domestic service learning course or in a traditional study abroad course. The service experience sheds light on and provides an added dimension to the curricular component of the study abroad course.

Service learning brings structured reflection to study abroad. Whitney and Clayton (chapter 8) demonstrate that the nature of reflection is not a loose, freewriting exercise, but a very deliberate and intentionally designed set of learning activities that are guided by the learning objectives. Good reflection generates learning, documents learning, provides a basis for assessing learning, and can contribute evidence to research that studies ISL. The use of reflection as a pedagogical tool is less well developed in study abroad than in service learning, where it is acknowledged as integral to the pedagogy (Ash & Clayton, 2004; Ash et al., 2005; Bringle & Hatcher, 1999; Chisholm, 2000; Eyler & Giles, 1997; Eyler, Giles, & Schmiede, 1996; Hatcher & Bringle, 1997). One example of reflection in the study abroad literature is provided by Gillespie et al. (2009). Within their holistic approach to analyzing student growth and development, they structure their approach around three key questions for college students: Who am I (corresponding to the intrapersonal dimension of learning and development)? How do I know (related to the cognitive dimension)? How do I relate to others (aligned with the interpersonal dimension)? (Braskamp, 2007). Another strategy is to provide students with a set of writing prompts based on targeted learning outcomes, for example intercultural competence (Deardorff, 2008), and ask participants to select a prompt to respond to based on the events of the day.

Intersection #2: Service Learning and International Education

Adding a community service component to any course broadens the range of educational objectives. In addition to being able to enhance the depth of learning associated with the existing content in a course, a well-designed service component integrated into the course content through structured reflection can enhance critical thinking and other cognitive skills, personal development, motivations for civic involvement, a sense of self-efficacy, and the civic development of students (Eyler, chapter 10). This can be the case for any curriculum associated with international education, including language and culture courses, international studies, global comparative perspectives course, immigrant and citizenship issues, cross-cultural communication, public health and social issues, or internationally oriented courses in the discipline or professions. As Plater (chapter 2) points out, the service component in a service learning course can be with immigrant communities in the United States, when available. A service component integrated into an international education course provides an experiential component that allows students to practice, apply, test, evaluate, and criticize course content in ways that cannot occur in the classroom (Brown, chapter 3). International education broadens the perspective of a service learning course and provides opportunities to compare and contrast North American and international perspectives on course content and civic education issues.

Intersection #3: International Education and Study Abroad

At the risk of oversimplifying a very complicated and varied set of experiences in study abroad, Hovey and Weinberg (2009) suggest that there may be "low road" study abroad experiences and "high road" study abroad experiences anchoring the ends of the spectrum of programs. They describe the low-road experiences in the following way:

> Under low road models, universities and programs send college students into the world, with little preparation, for culturally thin experiences. Students make minimal effort to learn local languages or customs, travel in large groups, and are taught in American-only classrooms. They live and go to bars with other Americans, often drinking too much and getting into trouble. They see local sights through the windows of traveling buses. Far from experiencing another culture deeply and on its own terms, these students (at best) simply get the American college experience in a different time zone. (p. 36)

The prevalence of the low-road study abroad experience is unknown. However, its existence is the reason that study abroad does not necessarily overlap with international education, as indicated in Figure 1.1. Students who are studying calculus, biology, and accounting at an international location run the risk of not having an *intentionally designed* educational experience that results in an international education. Nor do they have the opportunity to engage in regular and structured reflection activities about the international experiences in a way that permits them to explore and attain feedback on the relevance of the international experiences to their learning and their personal, career, educational, or civic goals. Do those students in low-road study abroad experiences have an international experience and learn from it? Probably so. This may happen through interactions with local students, living in an international community, housing with local families, or travel. However, all of these experiences are outside the curriculum, and they are not designed to produce specific educational outcomes that are assessed and represented in formal records of learning (i.e., transcript). For Hovey and Weinberg (2009), high-road study abroad experiences are designed "to ensure deep cultural and linguistic immersion," and to "understand and respect local customs" (p. 37).

Although the presumption of international education is associated with study abroad, the evidence for these outcomes is largely anecdotal. As Wanner (2009) notes,

> In the end, a justification of the practice of study abroad must come from a commonly shared belief, based on concrete evidence, that this is an excellent way to foster the a priori goal of international competency and globalized consciousness, and that it therefore belongs to the foundational ingredients of education in the 21st century. (p. 88)

The presumption is based on an immersion model that if the study is in an international setting, then international learning must be occurring. International education without study abroad may be lacking, but study abroad without a deliberate plan for how it will result in international learning that is tied to curricular goals and is assessed in some way does not necessarily guarantee that study abroad produces intended international learning.

Gillespie et al. (2009) present a comprehensive and extensive model that begins with a holistic view of student development that focuses on cognitive, intrapersonal, and interpersonal aspects of the experience and relates them to the culture of the educational experience, the curriculum, cocurricular activities, and community (both narrowly and broadly construed). This framework is then related to direct and indirect measures of outcomes. Applied to study abroad, the framework gives "purpose and clarity to the principles of program planning that are established by the IES Abroad MAP" (Gillespie et al., 2009, p. 463). This approach focuses attention on the ways in which a study abroad experience can produce intended international learning that is described by others in Lewin (2009a).

The Triple Intersection: International Service Learning

From this analysis of the three component parts, we argue that ISL is the combination of service learning, study abroad, and international education, and that ISL draws from the strengths of each strategy. This section will examine these attributes and describe how they each contribute to defining ISL.

Understanding local culture, customs, mores, history, and language are contextually important elements of predeparture orientation and preparation for ISL. Study abroad practitioners have given significant attention to both departure and reentry issues (Kiely, chapter 11), and this practice needs to be part of well-designed ISL (Brown, chapter 3; Whitney & Clayton, chapter 8) as well. Study abroad practice, then, also makes more salient for service learning practitioners the importance of cross-cultural competence, cross-cultural communication skills, and cross-cultural empathy as learning objectives in preparation for, during, and upon completion of an ISL experience. Service learning practitioners probably spend too little time preparing students for interacting with communities in domestic service learning. Hopefully, when confronted with sending students to an international destination, service learning educators would acknowledge the importance of adequate predeparture preparation and plans for student reentry—issues that are of great importance to study abroad practitioners (Kiely, chapter 11).

Service learning brings to study abroad and international education the experiential immersion of students into international communities in ways that are absent from traditional study abroad (i.e., intentionally designed, implemented, assessed). In doing so, the nature of study abroad moves from the low road to the high road by providing authentic and educationally meaningful opportunities for students to interact with, learn from, and contribute to an international community (Hovey & Weinberg, 2009). Sutton (chapter 7) and Kahn (chapter 6) demonstrate ways in which adding a community service component to two study abroad anthropology courses changes the content of the courses, the nature of instruction, the nature of the student interactions with residents and staff in community-based organizations, the engagement of students in their learning, and the relationship of the students to the community. However, more importantly, the values associated with well-designed service learning shape how these interactions and relationships are established and how they are maintained in the international setting.

Educators need to establish these relationships as mutually beneficial exchanges that are reciprocal, nonexploitive, democratic, and respectful (Longo & Saltmarsh, chapter 4), which establishes an entirely different relationship between the study abroad students and their international communities. As Plater (chapter 2) notes, ISL provides opportunities for students to participate in communities in face-to-face interactions that Dewey (1916) saw as integral to democratic processes. As Sutton (chapter 7) documents, this is not easy with partnerships in distant sites, but it is a requirement of optimally designed ISL. The emphasis in study abroad to primarily consider the students' outcomes is expanded through ISL to include an equally important standard of community benefits through the participation of the students in the community service activity. Service learning practitioners regularly struggle with the counterproductive connotations that the word *service* carries with it, implying a charity model of helping (Morton, 1995). Yet, most practitioners conceptualize and approach community service in a manner that emphasizes working *with* the community.

Working *with* the community is not easy in ISL because there are many constituencies to be considered when working with international partners. Sutton (chapter 7) started with community leaders (e.g., mayor) to gain direction, leverage, and credibility with the rest of the community. Other relationships to support ISL may be with or developed through faculty or staff at partner colleges or universities in the international setting. Gillespie et al. (2009) provide many examples of partnerships between Bard College and global partner institutions.

Many American service learning practitioners rely heavily (too heavily?) on the staff of community-based organizations. This practice may not work in international settings where staff and resources are likely to be much more constrained. Lewin and van Kirk (2009) identify several difficulties in developing partnerships with community-based organizations in international settings. First, there is the difference in agenda. The representatives from the academy have the interests of the students as dominant; community-based organizations have as their mission serving members of their community. Second, community-based organizations often do not have the same infrastructure and resources as American counterparts. These restrictions may limit the organization committing resources (e.g., staff time) to ISL students in spite of the benefits that the students provide to the organization and its clients. This leads to a third problem identified by Lewin and van Kirk (2009), the inherent power differential that exists between the academic constituencies and the community-based organization, and how this is managed in negotiating the nature of the relationship during its initiation and its maintenance (Bringle, Clayton, & Price, 2009; Bringle & Hatcher, 2002). These are all issues that are echoed in Erasmus's analysis in chapter 15 of North American ISL in developing countries.

The difficulties of establishing relationships for ISL are even more complicated when considering residents of international communities. As mentioned earlier, service learning practitioners in the United States often deal exclusively with staff from community-based organizations in establishing relationships to identify community needs and to support the service activities of students. Staff at agencies may be good proxies for residents of communities for the same purposes, but they may not. Professional staff may have goals (e.g., personal or career, sustainability of their organizations, political context, competition with other community-based organizations, funding issues) that interfere with or are at odds with their capacity to represent the interests of residents (or clients) in their community. These issues may be more extreme in international settings. Because of the risk that agency staff might not be adequate representatives of communities, the work in South Africa on the

Community–Higher Education–Service Partnership program intentionally expanded the campus–community dyad and delineates a campus–resident–service provider triad for capturing the important relationships (Lazarus, 2004). This model required that faculty, service providers from nongovernmental organizations, and residents be at the table when the service learning course was being designed. This is an excellent model to consider for developing ISL courses, acknowledging that one resident is probably not an adequate representative of different community interests. Kahn (chapter 6) and Sutton (chapter 7) illustrate how service learning can be used as a research tool to gain additional representation and information to redesign and modify subsequent offerings of an ISL course. In addition, Whitney and Clayton (chapter 8) describe how reflection can be conducted with community residents to contribute to their growth and to the quality of the educational experience.

To extend the use of reflection across all three domains (i.e., service learning, study abroad, international learning) provides a powerful method for thinking systematically about the learning objectives for each domain and for their integration in ISL. As Plater, Jones, Bringle, and Clayton (2009) note, "using reflection maximally toward these ends requires a precise understanding of the learning and service objectives at stake in the ISL activity" (p. 494). The reflection activities should be varied and can include written products, group discussion, oral presentations, multimedia presentations, and other forms of expression (Eyler et al., 1996; Hatcher & Bringle, 1997). For written reflection, how the writing is structured is important to guiding student learning and development. Whitney and Clayton (chapter 8) contend that all written reflection should be guided by prompts and these can be focused on the academic content, the personal growth of students, or their civic growth.

A focus on civic education is found in all three domains (i.e., service learning, study abroad, international education). Service learning practitioners view civic education as integral to what defines the nature of the pedagogy. According to Longo and Saltmarsh (chapter 4), democratic skills are best learned through democratic practice, and service learning aspires to providing students with opportunities to engage in and develop democratic action through community activities. Although less central and less well developed, study abroad practitioners are exploring the opportunities that study abroad can provide for developing civic or global citizenship in students (Lewin, 2009a). Zemach-Bersin (2009)notes from her interviews with study abroad students that traditional study abroad failed to convince students that "they had become global citizens by studying abroad because they felt that *they had not developed the skills of a global citizen*" (p. 316) during their study abroad experience. Adding a service learning component provides study abroad students with opportunities to practice citizenship skills through community service activities.

Some educators also include civic education and global citizenship in curricula focused on international education. However, there is a difference for students between the didactic presentation of information about international civic skills and knowledge, and being involved in real-life situations in which students practice civic skills and apply knowledge in an international setting. What study abroad and international education bring to the civic education practice of service learning is an international and global dimension. Hovey and Weinberg (2009) note that "civic education and study abroad need each other" (p. 33) and the best means for enhancing civic education in study abroad and in international education is through service learning. Not only is this important to enhancing student engagement in their learning while abroad but it also holds the greatest promise (Astin & Sax, 1998; Eyler, chapter 10) for developing lifelong civic habits. Through ISL,

> student[s] learn that they return to the United States with an obligation to stay active, help others learn from their experiences, and push for better understanding from their academic institutions, future workplaces, and political representatives with regard to the world beyond our borders. (Hovey & Weinberg, 2009, p. 37)

Definition of International Service Learning

This analysis demonstrates how the three domains of service learning, study abroad, and international education combine and contribute to form a unique pedagogy. What should it be labeled? Should it refer to *global*, *world*, *intercultural*, or *international*? The American Council on Education (2005) distinguishes between three types of learning goals: (a) global (denoting the systems and phenomena that transcend national borders), (b) international (focusing on the nations and their relationships), and (c) intercultural (focusing on knowledge and skills to understand and navigate cultural differences). How should it succinctly represent the three pedagogical domains? There are many possibilities that were considered or have been offered by others. Longo and Saltmarsh (chapter 4) elect to use *global service learning*. Another candidate is *global citizenship study abroad* (Lewin & van Kirk, 2009). We recommend *international service learning* because it makes salient all three components of the pedagogy. However, ISL is more than just service learning in a different setting because ISL's international settings provide new and unique opportunities for learning, especially in ways that contribute to the international education of students. Because ISL involves reflection, it is much more than just study abroad plus a community service component. ISL is a purposive integration of community activities that are selected to contribute in specific ways to educational objectives of the course(s) and community issues. Therefore, ISL is defined as

> A *structured academic experience in another country* in which students *(a)* participate in an organized service activity that addresses identified community needs; *(b) learn from direct interaction and cross-cultural dialogue with others*; and *(c)* reflect on the *experience* in such a way as to gain further understanding of course content, a deeper understanding of *global and intercultural* issues, a broader appreciation of the *host country* and the discipline, and an enhanced sense of their own responsibilities as citizens, locally and *globally*.

The words and concepts that are italicized are those that have been added to or have modified Bringle and Hatcher's (2009) definition of service learning, based on the analysis of how service learning benefits from being integrated with study abroad and international education.

International Service Learning: Conceptual Frameworks and Research

This volume, ***International Service Learning: Conceptual Frameworks and Research***, was framed around this definition of ISL. As a curricular experience, the development of ISL can be focused on an individual course or a set of courses (Jones & Steinberg, chapter 5). A set of courses might have a particular group of students as the focus, such as underrepresented students (Picard, Bernardino, & Ehigiator, 2009) or first-generation students (Martinez, Ranjeet, & Marx, 2009). They could also focus on a particular aspect of the curriculum, such as liberal arts (Brockington & Wiedenhoeft, 2009), professional training (e.g., see Currier, Lucas, & Saint Arnault, 2009, for nursing; Cushner, 2009, for teacher education), or language study (Wanner, 2009). In all of these cases, the development of ISL is academic work and involves faculty to redesign the curriculum to create ISL courses or programs. As such, in addition to inheriting the strengths of each of the three domains, ISL borrows issues and obstacles from each. Faculty are typically unfamiliar with service learning as a pedagogy because very few faculty were students in a service learning class. In addition to lack of knowledge and concrete experience, many faculty fail to see how service learning is relevant to their courses

(Abes, Jackson, & Jones, 2002) and they fail to appreciate how community service can enrich the learning of their students. Nolan (2009) and Gore (2009) discuss how international education and study abroad often linger at the periphery of the academy, are not viewed as serious academic work, accrue little credit in the promotion and tenure process, do not stimulate policies and infrastructure to support them, and have suffered from lack of rigorous attention to program design and assessment. All of these issues also exist for service learning.

Like service learning, ISL is frequently a pedagogy with which faculty have no direct, personal experience. Faculty development activities will need to be planned to help faculty become familiar with each of the pedagogical domains: study abroad, service learning, and international education. The institutional capacity to combine expertise and resources across various offices (e.g., study abroad, international affairs, service learning, centers for teaching and learning, assessment) will need to occur and personnel will need to be willing to collaborate and learn (Plater, chapter 2). Although the chapters in this volume do not deal directly with these issues, they are important institutional issues that need to be addressed, and resources need to be committed to develop the capacity of institutions to offer ISL experiences that are successful and rewarding for faculty, students, and international partners. In addition, each of these issues presents the opportunity for research.

In addition to local obstacles and borrowing principles of good practice from each domain, the design and implementation of ISL raises many important ethical issues. Issues related to the ethics of doing ISL (not the ethics of conducting research on ISL, which is covered in Wells, Warchal, Ruiz, & Chapdelaine, chapter 14) are embedded in several chapters (e.g., Kahn, chapter 6; Kiely & Hartman, chapter 13; Tonkin, chapter 9; Whitney & Clayton, chapter 8). What justification is there for American colleges and universities to send their students to international destinations to be involved in someone else's community and the personal lives of residents of those communities, especially when they are not invited by the residents (Illich, 1968)? Answering the fundamental question of, "What right do you have to enter this community?" must be addressed by each practitioner of ISL. Any student in an ISL experience is likely to be privileged in many ways (e.g., education, wealth) that are in stark contrast to those with whom they are interacting and working with during the community service activities. How these differences are approached, embraced, analyzed, or questioned provides educators with opportunities to help students explore issues related to community, human rights, citizenship, values, social responsibility, and social justice.

We anticipate that as ISL pedagogy becomes more prevalent, there is the need for a set of checks and balances through a process that can review new initiatives not only for their pedagogical integrity but also for their moral and ethical decisions and consequences (Tonkin, chapter 9). At one level, this must encourage all faculty and staff associated with ISL activities to be conscientious, ethical, and reflective practitioners about their own work. However, review should also include input and feedback from colleagues from appropriate departments and professionals from campus offices (e.g., service learning, teaching and learning, international office, international education, external affairs). This review process will be helped by mechanisms that permit capturing knowledge about ISL across campuses so that it results in a unique set of ISL Principles of Good Practice.

This volume and its contributing scholars chose to focus predominantly on students in ISL. Tonkin (chapter 9) notes the lack of balance that is potentially created if ISL has its center of gravity on study abroad (i.e., students), with a community service component simply added in. Community service tacked onto study abroad has many shortcomings, including failing to view ISL as an integrated whole that warrants more purposive attention to design across multiple constituencies, failing to take advantage of the integral role of reflection when designing and assessing the course, and failing to understand the importance of reciprocal relationships with the communities in which the education and community service are carried out. This latter point, clearly articulated by Erasmus (chapter 15), shifts the focus of ISL to a more balanced answer to the question "Why ISL?" and focuses appropriate attention on the role that the community constituencies (i.e., organizations, residents, clients, consumers) should assume as cocreators of the curriculum, coeducators in the delivery of the curriculum, and coinvestigators in the evaluation of and study of ISL. All authors understood that the primary emphasis on students is an incomplete picture of ISL, both in practice and in conducting research on it. Some chapters (e.g., Erasmus, chapter 15; Kahn, chapter, 6; Kiely, chapter 11; Kiely & Hartman, chapter 13; Sutton, chapter 7; Tonkin, chapter 9; Whitney & Clayton, chapter 8) provide discussions about community relationships and institutional issues as well as suggestions for conducting research with community residents on community outcomes and benefits. This volume's focus on students mirrors the distribution of attention and research related to domestic service learning (Eyler et al., 2001). The emphasis on students also acknowledges the importance of understanding the educational justification of ISL from the point of view of the academy and what it cares most about—the academic, personal, and civic benefits to students. Service learning, more so than the other two educational domains (study abroad, international education), brings to the forefront the importance of the relationship of any pedagogy to its communities. Thus, even though the focus on students is dominant across the chapters of this volume, we expect that the addition of service learning to discussions about study abroad and international education will be accompanied by a concomitant sensitivity to the integrity of partnerships, reflection, reciprocity, and community benefits (Plater et al., 2009).

Summary

We initiated this volume because of the tremendous potential that we foresee for ISL to contribute to student education and the desire to promote rigorous research on ISL to further its development. As such, the focus is on ISL as a pedagogical intervention and recommendations for strategies to conduct good research on key issues. We expect that subsequent research will demonstrate an *intensification effect*—that ISL will have the capacity to intensify any previously documented outcome from study abroad, service learning, or international education in isolation. That is, we expect that even short-term ISL results in greater improvement in intercultural skills, more rapid language acquisition, better demonstration of democratic skills, deeper understanding of global issues, greater transformation of students' lives and careers, more sensitivity to ethical issues, and more lifelong interest in global issues (to identify only a few possible outcomes) than domestic service learning, international education without study aboard or service learning, and traditional study abroad. We further predict that this *intensification effect* will exceed an additive effect of combining the simple effects of the components (study abroad, service learning, international education) taken two at a time. Finally, we expect that ISL will produce results that are more extensive, robust, transformational, and distinctive than any one of the components. And we invite subsequent researchers to evaluate these predictions.

However, based on our experience with domestic service learning, we know that there are broader implications, both explicit and implicit, in promoting ISL and research on ISL. We have already seen how a consideration of ISL results in communication, sharing, and implementing activities between and among units on campuses that may have had limited interactions prior to the development of ISL. We have seen how many ISL courses grow from the passion of an individual faculty or staff member, but we have also seen how ISL can lead to growth of projects beyond the particular ISL class that resulted in a multifaceted international partnership. This includes inter-disciplinary collaboration among departments, strategic use of institutional resources to support strategic partnerships, and the expansion of work across the domains of teaching, research, and service (including clinical services).

We firmly expect that the development of ISL through good research will lead to an enhanced network of international partnerships, better academic work, the enhanced growth of colleges and universities as global citizens, greater productivity and satisfaction among professionals, and the development of cities, both locally and in other countries, as global communities. Thus, we expect ISL to be a transformational force that can change not only the trajectory of the lives of individual students but also institutions of higher education and communities, including their constituencies who are associated with high-quality civic engagement. And, again, we invite researchers to evaluate these hypotheses. We are realistic enough to understand that research on the potency of ISL to develop expected and desired outcomes is a limited type of evidence; nevertheless, we hope that it will contribute to a broader base of advocacy that provides evidence to convince executive leadership in the academy, external funders, and key community leaders on the value of further commitments to ISL. If ISL is the most powerful pedagogy available to higher education, then it deserves a more diligent level of commitment.

Acknowledgment

We greatly appreciate Patti Clayton's comments and feedback on an early draft of this manuscript.

References

Abes, E. S., Jackson, G., & Jones, S. R. (2002). Factors that motivate and deter faculty use of service-learning. *Michigan Journal of Community Service Learning,* *9*(1), 5–17.

Akande, Y., & Slawson, C. (2000). A case study of 50 years of study abroad alumni. *International Educator, 9*(3), 12–16.

American Council on Education. (2005). *Global learning for all*. Retrieved May 14, 2008, from www.acenet.edu/AM/Template.cfm?Section=fipse1&TEMPLATE=/CM/ContentDisplay.cfm&CONTENTID=19125

Annette, J. (2003). Service-learning internationally: Developing a global civil society. In S. H. Billig, & J. Eyler (Eds.), *Deconstructing service-learning: Research exploring context, participation and impacts* (pp. 241–249). Greenwich, CT: Information Age.

Ash, S. L., & Clayton, P. H. (2004). The articulated learning: An approach to reflection and assessment. *Innovative Higher Education, 29,* 137–154.

Ash, S. L., Clayton, P. H., & Atkinson, M. P. (2005). Integrating reflection and assessment to capture and improve student learning. *Michigan Journal of Community Service Learning, 11*(2), 49–60.

Association of American Colleges and Universities. (2007). *College learning for the new global century.* Washington, DC: Association of American Colleges and Universities.

Astin, A. W., & Sax, L. J. (1998). How undergraduates are affected by service participation. *Journal of College Student Development, 39,* 251–263.

Battistoni, R. (2002). *Civic engagement across the curriculum: A resource book for service-learning faculty in all disciplines.* Providence, RI: Campus Compact.

Billig, S. H., & Eyler, J. (Eds.). (2003). *Deconstructing service-learning: Research exploring context, participation, and impacts.* Greenwich, CT: Information Age.

Blumenthal, P., & Gutierrez, R. (Eds.). (2009). *Meeting America's global education challenge: Expanding study abroad capacity at U.S. colleges & universities.* New York, NY: Institute of International Education.

Bolen, M. C. (Ed.). (2007). *A guide to outcomes assessment in education abroad.* Carlisle, PA: Forum on Education Abroad.

Boyte, H. C., & Kari, N. N. (2000). Renewing the democratic spirit in American colleges and universities: Higher education as public work. In T. Ehrlich (Ed.), *Higher education and civic responsibility* (pp. 37–59). New York, NY: National Council on Education/Oryx Press Series.

Braskamp, L. A. (2007). Developing global citizens. *Journal of College and Character, 10*(1), 1–5.

Bringle, R. G., Clayton, P. H., & Price, M. (2009). Partnerships in service learning and civic engagement. *Partnerships: A Journal of Service-Learning and Civic Engagement, 1*(1), 1–20.

Bringle, R. G., & Hatcher, J. A. (1999, Summer). Reflection in service learning: Making meaning of experience. *Educational Horizons, 77*(4), 179–185.

Bringle, R. G., & Hatcher, J. A. (2002). University-community partnerships: The terms of engagement. *Journal of Social Issues, 58,* 503–516.

Bringle, R. G., & Hatcher, J. A. (2009). Innovative practices in service learning and curricular engagement. In L. Sandmann, A. Jaeger, & C. Thornton (Eds.), *New directions in community engagement* (pp. 37–46). San Francisco, CA: Jossey-Bass.

Brockington, J. L., & Wiedenhoeft, M. D. (2009). The liberal arts and global citizenship: Fostering intercultural engagement through integrative experiences and structured reflection. In R. Lewin (Ed.), *Study abroad and the making of global citizens: Higher education and the quest for global citizenship* (pp. 117–132). New York, NY: Routledge.

Campus Compact. (2007). *2006 Service statistics: Highlights and trends of Campus Compact's annual membership survey.* Providence, RI: Campus Compact.

Che, M. S., Spearman, M., & Manizade, A. (2009). Constructive disequilibrium: Cognitive and emotional development through dissonant experiences in less familiar destinations. In R. Lewin (Ed.), *Study abroad and the making of global citizens: Higher education and the quest for global citizenship* (pp. 99–116). New York, NY: Routledge.

Chin, K. K. (2003). *Open doors: Report on international educational exchange*. New York, NY: Institute of International Education.

Chisholm, L. A. (2000). *Charting a hero's journey*. New York, NY: International Partnership for Service-Learning.

Commission on the Abraham Lincoln Study Abroad Fellowship Program. (2005). *Global competence & national needs: One million Americans studying abroad*. Washington, DC: Congress of the United States.

Currier, C., Lucas, J., & Saint Arnault, D. S. (2009). Study abroad and nursing: From cultural to global competence. In R. Lewin (Ed.), *Study abroad and the making of global citizens: Higher education and the quest for global citizenship* (pp. 133–150). New York, NY: Routledge.

Cushner, K. (2009). The role of study abroad in the preparation of globally responsible teachers. In R. Lewin (Ed.), *Study abroad and the making of global citizens: Higher education and the quest for global citizenship* (pp. 151–169). New York, NY: Routledge.

Davies, I., & Pike, G. (2009). Global citizenship education: Challenges and possibilities. In R. Lewin (Ed.), *Study abroad and the making of global citizens: Higher education and the quest for global citizenship* (pp. 61–77). New York, NY: Routledge.

Deardorff, D. K. (2008). Intercultural competence: A definition, model, and implications for study abroad. In V. Savicki (Ed.), *Developing intercultural competence and transformation: Theory, research, and application in international education* (pp. 297–321). Sterling, VA: Stylus.

Deardorff, D. K. (2009). Understanding the challenges of assessing global citizenship. In R. Lewin (Ed.), *The handbook of practice and research in study abroad: Higher education and the quest for global citizenship* (pp. 61–77). New York, NY: Routledge.

Dewey, J. (1916). *Democracy and education*. New York, NY: MacMillan.

Dewey, J. (1933). *How we think: A restatement of the relation of reflective thinking to the educative process*. Boston, MA: DC Heath and Company.

Dwyer, M. M. (2004a). Charting the impact of studying abroad. *International Educator, 13*(1), 14–20.

Dwyer, M. M. (2004b). More is better: The impact of study abroad program duration. *Frontiers: The Interdisciplinary Journal of Study Abroad, 10,* 151–163.

Dwyer, M. M., & Peters C. K. (2004, March-April). The benefits of study abroad. *Transitions abroad*. Retrieved July 1, 2009, from http://www.transitionsabroad .com/publications/magazine/0403/benefits_study_abroad.shtml

Engle, L., & Engle, J. (2003, Fall). Study abroad levels: Toward a classification of program types. *Frontiers: International Journal of Study Abroad, 9,* 1–20.

Eyler, J., & Giles, D. E., Jr. (1997). The importance of program quality in service-learning. In A. S. Waterman (Ed.), *Service-learning: Applications from the research* (pp. 57–78). Mahwah, NJ: Lawrence Erlbaum.

Eyler, J., & Giles, D. E., Jr. (1999). *Where's the learning in service-learning?* San Francisco, CA: Jossey-Bass.

Eyler, J., Giles, D. E., Jr., & Schmiede, A. (1996). *A practitioner's guide to reflection in service-learning.* Nashville, TN: Vanderbilt University.

Eyler, J. S., Giles, D. E., Jr., Stenson, C. M., & Gray, C. J. (2001). *At a glance: What we know about the effects of service-learning on college students, faculty, institutions and communities, 1993–2000* (3rd ed.). Nashville, TN: Vanderbilt University.

Forum on Education Abroad. (2008). *Standards of good practice for education abroad.* Carlisle, PA: Dickinson College.

Forum on Education Abroad. (2009). *Standards of good practice for short-term education abroad programs.* Carlisle, PA: Dickinson College.

Fry, G. W., Paige, R. M., & Stallman, E. M. (2009, August). *Beyond immediate impact: Study abroad for global engagement.* Presentation at the International Academy for Intercultural Research, Honolulu, Hawaii.

Furco, A. (1996). Service-learning: A balanced approach to experiential education. In *Expanding boundaries: Service and learning* (pp. 2–6). Washington DC: Corporation for National Service.

Gillespie, J., Braskamp, L., & Dwyer, M. (2009). Holistic student learning and development abroad: The IES 3-D Program Model. In R. Lewin (Ed.), *The handbook of practice and research in study abroad: Higher education and the quest for global citizenship* (pp. 445–465). New York, NY: Routledge.

Gore, J. E. (2009). Faculty beliefs and institutional values: Identifying and overcoming these obstacles to education abroad growth. In R. Lewin (Ed.), *The handbook of practice and research in study abroad: Higher education and the quest for global citizenship* (pp. 282–302). New York, NY: Routledge.

Green, M. F., Luu, D. T., & Burris, B. (2008). *Mapping internationalization on US campuses: 2008 edition.* Washington, DC.: American Council on Education.

Hatcher, J. A. (1997). The moral dimensions of John Dewey's philosophy: Implications for undergraduate education. *Michigan Journal of Community Service Learning, 4,* 22–29.

Hatcher, J. A., Bringle, R. G., & Muthiah, R. (2004). Designing effective reflection: What matters to service learning? *Michigan Journal of Community Service Learning, 11*(1), 38–46.

Hatcher, J. A., & Bringle, R. G. (1997). Reflection: Bridging the gap between service and learning. *College Teaching, 45*(4), 153–158.

Hovey, R., & Weinberg, A. (2009). Global learning and the making of citizen diplomats. In R. Lewin (Ed.), *Study abroad and the making of global citizens: Higher education and the quest for global citizenship.* (pp. 33–48) New York, NY: Routledge.

Hovland, K., McTighe Musil, C., Skilton-Sylvester, E., & Jamison, A. (2009). It takes a curriculum: Bringing global mindedness home. In R. Lewin (Ed.), *The handbook of practice and research in study abroad: Higher education and the quest for global citizenship* (pp. 466–484). New York, NY: Routledge.

Illich, I. (1968). *The hell with good intentions.* New York, NY: The Commission on Voluntary Service & Action.

Institute of International Education. (2008). *Open doors: Report on international student exchange*. New York, NY: Institute of International Education.

Kahne, J., & Westheimer, J. (2003). Teaching democracy: What schools need to do. *Phi Delta Kappa, 85*(1), 34–40.

Kim, R. I., & Goldstein, S. B. (2005). Intercultural attitudes predict favorable study abroad expectations of U.S. college students. *Journal of Studies in International Education, 9*, 265–278.

Kuh, G. D. (2008). *High-impact educational practices: What they are, who has access to them, and why they matter*. Washington, DC: Association of American Colleges and Universities.

Lazarus, J. (2004). Community engagement. In *South African higher education in the first decade of democracy* (chap. 7). Cape Town: The South African Council on Higher Education. Retrieved August 13, 2009, from http://www.che.ac.za/documents/d000081/index.php

Lewin, R. (2009a). Introduction: The quest for global citizenship through study abroad. In R. Lewin (Ed.), *The handbook of practice and research in study abroad: Higher education and the quest for global citizenship* (pp. xii–xxii). New York, NY: Routledge.

Lewin, R. (2009b). *The handbook of practice and research in study abroad: Higher education and the quest for global citizenship*. New York, NY: Routledge.

Lewin, R., & Van Kirk, G. (2009). It's not about you: The UConn Social Entrepreneur Corps global commonwealth study abroad model. In R. Lewin (Ed.), *Study abroad and the making of global citizens: Higher education and the quest for global citizenship* (pp. 543–564). New York, NY: Routledge.

Martinez, M. D., Ranjeet, B., & Marx, H. A. (2009). Creating study abroad opportunities for first-generation college students. In R. Lewin (Ed.), *The handbook of practice and research in study abroad: Higher education and the quest for global citizenship* (pp. 527–542). New York, NY: Routledge.

McTighe Musil, C. (2003, Spring). Educating for citizenship. *Peer Review, 5*(3), 4–8.

Morton, K. (1995). The irony of service: Charity, project and social change in service-learning. *Michigan Journal of Community Service Learning, 2*, 19–32.

Nolan, R. W. (2009). Turning our back on the world: Study abroad and the purpose of US higher education. In R. Lewin (Ed.), *The handbook of practice and research in study abroad: Higher education and the quest for global citizenship* (pp. 266–281). New York, NY: Routledge.

Norris, E. M., & Dwyer, M. M. (2005). Testing assumptions: The impact of two study abroad program models. *Frontiers: The Interdisciplinary Journal of Study Abroad, 11*, 121–142.

Nussbaum, M. C. (1997). *Cultivating humanity: A classical defense of reform in liberal education*. Cambridge, MA: Harvard University.

Picard, E., Bernardino, F., & Ehigiator, K. (2009). Global citizenship for all: Low minority student participation in study abroad: Seeking strategies for success. In R. Lewin (Ed.), *Study abroad and the making of global citizens: Higher education and the quest for global citizenship* (pp. 321–345). New York, NY: Routledge.

Plater, W. M., Jones, S. G., Bringle, R. G., & Clayton, P. H. (2009). Educating globally competent citizens through international service learning. In R. Lewin (Ed.), *Study abroad and the making of global citizens: Higher education and the quest for global citizenship* (pp. 485–505). New York, NY: Routledge.

Schudson, M. (2003). How people learn to be civic. *Campus Compact Reader*, Winter, 14–21.

Siaya, L., & Hayward, F. (2003). *Mapping internationalization on US campuses: Final report*. Washington, DC: American Council on Education.

Sutton, R., Miller, A. N., & Rubin, D. L. (2007). Research design in assessing learning outcomes in study abroad programs. In M. Bolen & P. Martin (Eds.), *A guide to outcomes assessment in education abroad* (pp. 23–59). Carlisle, PA: The Forum on Education Abroad.

Thelin, J. R. (2004). *A history of American higher education*. Baltimore, MD: Johns Hopkins University.

Toh, S. (1993). Bringing the world into the classroom, global literacy and a question of paradigms. *Alberta Global Education*, *1*(1), 9–17.

Wanner, D. (2009). Study abroad and language: From maximal to realistic models. In R. Lewin (Ed.), *Study abroad and the making of global citizens: Higher education and the quest for global citizenship* (pp. 81–98). New York, NY: Routledge.

Zemach-Bersin, T. (2009). Selling the world: Study abroad marketing and the privatization of global citizenship. In R. Lewin (Ed.), *Study abroad and the making of global citizens: Higher education and the quest for global citizenship* (pp. 303–320). New York, NY: Routledge.

Zlotkowski, E., Longo, N. V., & Williams, J. R. (Eds.). (2006). *Students as colleagues*. Providence, RI: Campus Compact.

2

THE CONTEXT
FOR INTERNATIONAL
SERVICE LEARNING

An Invisible Revolution Is Underway

William M. Plater

As the 19th century turned into the modern era, John Dewey wrote perceptively for his time in 1899 and prophetically for our own time,

> One can hardly believe there has been a revolution in all history so rapid, so extensive, and so complete. Through it the face of the earth is making over, even as to its physical forms; political boundaries are wiped out and moved about as if they were indeed only lines on a paper map; population is hurriedly gathered into cities from the ends of the earth; habits of living are altered with startling abruptness and thoroughness. (Dewey, 1899, p. 22)

In the still early part of this century, we can only marvel that the revolution has accelerated to the point it has. With abundant clarity, Americans now know that we cannot possibly live apart from the world because it intrudes every day into our private lives with such startling abruptness that events in China, India, Iraq, or Venezuela have personal and daily consequences in every dimension of our lives from the drugs we take, or the toys we buy, to the loans we secure, to the gasoline we burn in our cars, to the wine we sip at night, to the teachings of religious leaders, to the prophecies of politicians. Reciprocally, decisions Americans make about farm subsidies, biofuels, trade agreements, immigration, and carbon emissions ripple across whole populations with unforeseen consequences.

The altered habits of living are certainly economic, but they are also much more. Instantaneous global communications bring natural disasters, famine, cultural conflict, and intolerances as well as acts of heroism, persistence, and philanthropy from around the world into our living rooms and to our breakfast tables just as our growing awareness of climate interdependence makes us recognize that this summer's glacial melt may swell the flood in our neighborhood next winter. We can contribute micro-loans in Bangladesh online as easily as we can give to the local United Way. And diseases traverse the globe as rapidly as passengers on planes moving ceaselessly from continent to continent.

Almost everyone in the United States is now aware of global interdependence and the need not only to know about what is happening elsewhere but to manage intentionally and thoughtfully the role *we* play in these interactions because we now understand that our practices cause reactions that cannot be ignored. As Dewey's prescient observation so clearly shows, there is nothing new in our global connectedness, but there is a difference in the depth and extent of our understanding and our interdependence. Without considering the merits of America's engagement in the wars of the last century, there can be no doubt that the experience of those wars has had an intensifying and even cumulative impact on a broader social consciousness about other peoples and the expression of collective action through governments, ethnic groups, or religions. A broad swath of America ventured out into the world and came home with stories that transcended generations. And at the same time, waves of immigration have each brought their own challenges and responses as questions of identity, values, and assimilation resurface with new implications on each successive wave.

In the century since Dewey's assessment, America has been preparing itself for world engagement on a new scale with each generation, and we are now at a heightened stage of awareness—and readiness, we might hope—perhaps a new tipping point, not unlike that which Dewey encountered in the early 20th century. In 2006, 12.5% of the U.S. population was foreign born, a significant increase over 11.1% in 2000 (U.S. Census Bureau, 2008) and reflecting a trend that has some demographers speculating that within a decade America will have the highest percentage of foreign-born residents in its history. By the midpoint of the 21st century, the United States Census Bureau estimates that only 50% of the population will be Caucasian and a very high percentage will speak languages other than English (U.S. Census Bureau, 2004).

In our present awareness of the world, we see the most recent patterns of immigration, the wars in Iraq and Afghanistan, the politics of energy or climate change, the rights of national sovereignty, the globalization of business, and—alas—the threats of terrorism as inherently complex and beyond the interests of only a small elite of this nation's more worldly citizens. Irrespective of degrees, wealth, or titles, we are all shoeless at the portal of the departure gate. As the recent American presidential elections have so poignantly demonstrated, people in the United States are now aware of their responsibility for electing a president who, if not a "president of the world," takes actions that affect not only America's interests abroad but the rest of the world's interactions with us. There is something different about the changes in our habits of living from those Dewey so clearly understood more than a century ago. It is these differences, the more personal and pervasive awareness of the world's intrusion into our private lives, that lends urgency and relevance to international service learning (ISL).

The definition of ISL by Bringle and Hatcher in chapter 1 guides the overall framework of this volume and underlies the variety of theoretical and practical approaches represented by the authors of the different chapters. There is considerable divergence—and richness—in the way service learning has been adapted to international settings (Jones & Steinberg, chapter 5) and, in turn, to the purposes and goals attributed to service learning conducted abroad by the colleges and universities who self-consciously use this peda-gogy to achieve institutional mission. Yet, there is a shared recognition of what constitutes service learning and its core elements as a result of the work of Campus Compact, the American Association of Higher Education, and even the *US News & World Report*, whose ratings have presumed compara-tive commonalities. There is an inherent philosophical underpinning to the international dimension of service learning.

There is also a clear understanding of the linkage of ISL to study abroad and an appreciation for the grounding that centuries of travel to other places bring to it. For thousands of years—in China, Greece, India, and Africa—leaders have pushed their students beyond the borders of their own learning to seek out new insights and discoveries, certainly to enhance the student's erudition but also to return—transformed—with experiences that can be shared and adapted to those who remained behind. Study abroad not only was a way to find out the new, discover something that was not yet known or understood at home, but also it was a way to test home-based ideas and practices in new cultural settings and physical environments. Religions traversed the globe in such expeditions, but so did democracy, literacy, and—for awhile—enlightenment.

When Dewey made his comments about the global revolution of the new 20th century, he had in mind the implications of new technologies such as electricity, of industrialization that led to urbanization, of changes in community brought about by the telegraph and then (much later) the telephone, and of the influx of immigrants to North America's cities and farms in such numbers as to challenge—even threaten—social norms. But he also noted that these factors were changing education as well: "That this revolution should not affect education in other than formal and superficial fashion is inconceivable" (Dewey, 1899, p. 22).

Given the impact Dewey has had on American social thought and educational practice—especially experiential learning—it is fitting that consideration of the role and importance of ISL begins with acknowledging the connections Dewey made among learning, citizenship, and community as the foundation of democracy. Dewey argued profoundly and well that even if communication at a distance (via electronic means now) might create some forms of community that were not otherwise possible, there could be no substitute for face-to-face interaction. Dewey concluded that "[w]e lie, as Emerson said, in the lap of immense intelligence. But that intelligence is dormant and its communications are broken, inarticulate, and faint until it possesses the local community as its medium" (Benson, Harkavy, & Puckett, 2007, p. 57). Despite all the power of the Internet, global telephone connections, and worldwide television, the creation of community depends on physical, face-to-face interaction. It may be possible to maintain a sense of community (even if not community itself) via distance means once established, but it is not possible unless that sense of community has been created by people being together in the same place and the same time with a recognized shared experience. The intellectual foundation for service learning and, by extension, ISL lies in this distillation of Dewey's reflection on education as engaged experience. You have to be there to be in a community.

In a recent book, *Dewey's Dream: Universities and Democracies in an Age of Education Reform*, Benson, Harkavy, and Puckett (2007) have carefully analyzed Dewey's contribution to concepts of civil society and democracy. They observe that "Dewey brilliantly and correctly identified the central problem of constructing democratic, cosmopolitan neighborly communities in the age of the global economy, global communication systems, supranational corporations, and global terror" (Benson et al., 2007, p. 58). That problem, they state, is that "democratic, cosmopolitan, face-to-face, neighborly communities are *necessary* for a democratic society" (Benson et al., 2007, p. 58).

Although the purpose of ISL may not be to create communities of any kind, let alone democratic cosmopolitan societies, its central purpose is to advance learning and the understanding of how particular forms of knowledge can be applied to social ends in a cosmopolitan or international context. When community creation or development is a goal of ISL, it ordinarily depends on collaboration with an existing or defined community, and the resulting sense of community may last no longer than the project or program. Reciprocally, ISL is also intended to show how the experiences, practices, and knowledge resident in a specific community can inform and reform theory and expertise. How do learning and understanding in one community transfer—or not—to another community where the language, beliefs, culture, political structures, resources, and other social factors are different—and why does our appreciation of differences and similarities make a difference? How does the experience of a particular community help the learner reframe and interpret what was presumed to be known?

The essential point is that service learning abroad draws its power and relevance and utility from the same source as domestic service learning: it occurs within the lived experience of a community and depends on a bond of mutual benefit and interaction between the students and the community itself. Service learning is not performed *for* or done *to* a community. It is enacted *in* and with the community through communication and shared activity among people who can articulate the mutual benefit and the reciprocity of interest that makes the service shared. Service learning requires the "local community as its medium," as Dewey said (Benson et al., 2007, p. 57). And, of course, students must articulate the learning that has occurred through the communal activity, through the service and the application of knowledge to the issues of the community.

We can learn *about* a community without ever visiting it, but that learning is less than what can be learned in and through the community itself, through the community as medium. This volume is dedicated to understanding through research on ISL how, in what ways, and why the learning through the medium of the community is deeper, richer, and more enduring.

Thus, the implications for ISL are profound. ISL can achieve what other forms of distance or mediated learning may not, despite the increasing intimacy and pervasiveness of the Internet and video and even the pseudo, or haptic, senses of touch and feeling and smell that technology simulates. At a time when the world is intensely more aware of itself because of global systems of communication and interaction, the face-to-face engagement of students with a community not their own makes the experience personal, real, and consequential.

The Urgency of Internationalization and the Role of Service Learning

The parallels between the beginnings of the 20th and 21st centuries are intriguing, and numerous social commentators for the earlier period such as Henry Adams or Charles Sanders Peirce as well as John Dewey have an eerie familiarity with our own circumstances. They surely felt urgency; yet, nothing could compare to the headlong rush toward globalization underway currently. More specifically, the present internationalization movement among schools, colleges, and universities as reflected in the work of national educational associations is surely unprecedented. There are several threads to be woven together, but for many people outside the academy, Friedman's (2005) thesis of global competition and interaction is widely perceived as the underlying motivation because of the sense of urgency he has created in revealing the nature both of the competition and of the stakes that are at risk.

The idea Friedman (2005) advances that universities are the global supply chain of human capital—and like other supply chains are subject to higher efficiency, lower cost, and equal or better quality from other competitors—needs to be considered in light of the civic purpose of universities and colleges and the preparation of graduates for civic purposes. Nonetheless, there is no doubt that education is a primary if not principal means for advancing the human condition as well as individual prosperity within local, national, and global communities.

Widely circulated reports of the investments being made by other nations in educational systems and individual student academic achievement are inviting comparisons and predictions that cast the United States in a less than favorable light at both K-12 and postsecondary levels. There are many such reports and analyses, but some of the most frequently cited are the periodic reports of the Organization for Economic Cooperation and Development (Organization for Economic Cooperation and Development, 2007). There is a growing sense among policy makers, legislators, corporate executives, and nonprofit leaders that America is falling behind in its levels of educational attainment, especially as it has failed to close achievement gaps among its own economic and social classes, with recent immigrants from South and Central America and Mexico posing a major and growing challenge to educational supremacy—especially at the K-12 levels (U.S. Census Bureau, 2008). Reports comparing student achievement in math and science (Organization for Economic Cooperation and Development, 2006), in particular, paint an alarming picture at the same time that America's productivity in graduating students with baccalaureate degrees is declining in comparison with others (e.g., see Postsecondary Education Opportunity, 2007; and Usher & Cervenan 2005, for various aspects of international comparisons). Congressional hearings and reports such as that prepared by the National Academy of Science, *Rising Above the Gathering Storm* (National Academy of Sciences, 2007), all contribute to a public call for action by schools, colleges, and universities.

But the response of U.S. higher education has taken on its air of urgency not only because of the heightened awareness of threats *from* abroad but also because of an opportunity to provide educational services *to* nations abroad. There is a rush to export U.S. higher education as another commodity with market value and a market share to be claimed. Campuses and programs are being opened in those parts of the world where there is presumed to be sufficient wealth and demand to pay the premium necessary to cover costs of overseas operations. U.S.-style classrooms, residences, recreation centers, and course credit systems are being replicated from Doha to Kolkata to Shanghai. Universities may not be opening campuses or study centers abroad but they are considering global initiatives to use the growing effectiveness of learning technologies to offer classes over the Internet.

Preoccupied with prestige, many American universities have shifted their attention from competing on the pages of the *US News & World Report* to the Internet rankings of Shanghai Jiao Tong University or the *London Times Education Supplement* where a world pecking order of the elite universities is being forged annually according to criteria that, at best, are highly suspect. The pressure on presidents from trustees and others who are anxious about the prestige and quality of their own institution at a time when reputations are in flux has created a flurry of activity that has moved internationalization of higher education to the front pages of the *Wall Street Journal*, the *New York Times*, and *USA Today* as well as the prime-time spots on network news channels. Those universities that have elected not to engage so directly in competitive activity abroad cannot help but be affected as questions are raised by policy makers and alumni about international activities and programs. There is now a presumption that education at higher levels (at least) must be involved internationally. Nothing less than America's prestige and global ranking is at risk in a way not challenged since Sputnik sprang full-blown and unexpectedly out of a presumed second-world educational system.

Accordingly, the more common approach from community colleges, liberal arts schools, comprehensive universities, and the research elites alike has been to think about how they are preparing their students, on one hand, for citizenship in an increasingly interdependent world (Lewin, 2009b) and, on the other, for competition in a job market that places a premium on global experience or knowledge—especially as the job market flattens and supranational corporations can hire their workforce from anywhere because work can be carried out anywhere across the world. All colleges must have programs, initiatives, and public relations to explain how they and their students are shaping global change—not merely being affected by it.

Among the possible responses, study abroad and ISL offer two of the most effective ways to serve students and to satisfy public interest. Enrolling students from other nations, engaging faculty from abroad on a continuing or visiting basis, and offering a wide variety of courses, languages, and degree programs with international components are similarly important—as they have been for decades going on to centuries. When most universities and colleges talk of the internationalization of the institution or the curriculum, they have in mind all of these means of increasing the exposure of their students to the world through an appreciation of its rich diversity and history in art, religion, history, culture, and languages. Unlike study abroad and ISL, these other activities and modes of learning are at home—they do not require going out into the world. And it is this feature that sets study abroad and ISL apart because they take the students out of their own familiar contexts into a place that is recognizably different.

Nearly the same thing can occur without leaving the United States, since many communities contain neighborhoods that are linguistically and culturally different. Regrettably, too many Americans do not know or visit the communities of their own nation and sometimes of their own cities. Effective service learning courses are based in these locally accessible communities, and many of the same benefits accrue as they might were the students actually to leave America. Indeed, one of the models for ISL explored in this volume combines domestic service learning for extended periods with an ethnic or cultural community at home and a shorter, intensive experience abroad where there is a linkage of the people with families and social groupings who maintain cultural ties (Jones & Steinberg, chapter 5). But the imperative for an experience outside the United States has grown dramatically because of the perceived need to be international—even if only for a week or two.

The urgency of global competition has infected higher education, and the best inoculation for living with such urgency without its disrupting the system may lie in being clear about the ends and purposes of education as well as the means. The repertoire of internationalization is large and diverse, and the use of one type of pedagogy or learning objective or experience over another can best be made in the context of the mission of the institution and the results it seeks to achieve in graduating its students. Student interest, engagement, voice, and style of learning need to be considered fully and seriously to ensure effective programs, but the articulation of learning objectives and the assessment of achievement remain faculty responsibilities consistent with institutional mission. No matter how personally meaningful or enjoyable the experience, international involvement separated from articulated learning goals and reflection is incomplete.

Graduating Globally Competent Citizens

Although secondary to the self-imposed institutional commitment to internationalization and to responding to a public perception of the need to engage students in understanding how the global world works and, more specifically, how the graduate fits into that world, colleges and universities have recognized the obvious connection between two long-established goals for most college graduates: understanding other cultures while appreciating or respecting diversity, on the one hand, and preparing graduates for the responsibilities of citizenship, on the other hand.

In most institutions, the liberal education objectives have treated appreciation of the world cultures and citizenship as separate requirements, as they have been codified in general education requirements. The former might have historically been checked off by completing several years of foreign language or taking a few courses from an approved list in a variety of subjects where other countries or periods in time were discussed—political science, art, sociology, history, comparative literature, and other subjects might well have satisfied the expectations as long as the title of the course had a nod to other nations. Many professional schools from social work and nursing to business and engineering have accepted the premise that global awareness is now a necessity for effective practice and have become, in many instances, even more insistent and creative in their expectations for graduates than the liberal arts with regard to internationalization as a part of the job-readiness toolkit.

Citizenship, on the other hand, has been much harder to define and, although recognized as a goal for all graduates, the requirement has not been so easily fulfilled by selecting courses from a list of political science or civics courses. The skills and knowledge of an effective citizen have more typically been assumed in the overall education of all students and characterized by skills of critical thinking, effective communication, and a breadth of knowledge. Participation in the life of the community through political and social action was assumed—or at least the graduate was ready for such involvement, if so motivated personally.

The rapid translation of public concern about internationalization into curricular and programmatic forms has highlighted the natural relationship of knowledge of the world and citizenship (Lewin, 2009b). A few universities, such as Fairleigh Dickinson University, have integrated the two and specified distinct graduation requirements that anticipate how graduates will be prepared to operate effectively as both citizens of their own communities and nation as well as to relate to the world. Most other universities have not (yet) moved to such an integration of the goals of undergraduate learning even as they seek to find ways to relate them as, for example, in ISL or study abroad. Indeed, the recent rapid development of these pedagogies has heightened our collective thinking about what citizenship must mean for the future as our global interdependence intensifies (Lewin, 2009b).

There are multiple conceptual frameworks for thinking about the role of colleges and universities in preparing graduates for their responsibilities as citizens in a global context, to be globally minded citizens as some have called this quality (Hovland, McTighe Musil, Skilton-Sylvester, & Jamison, 2009), while others have gone further to expect globally competent citizenship skills and preparation (Gillespie, Braskamp, & Dwyer, 2009). Only a few have declared their intent to educate global citizens. These distinctions are soft and overlapping. For faculties used to debating nuance, the distinctions may lie in semantics but the differences can be powerfully substantive when setting course, major, and degree requirements or accepting specific ways in which learning outcomes can be documented. In most cases, however, the expectations for citizenship are designed to avoid having to make doctrinaire or philosophical distinctions. But it may be useful to understand some of the distinctions and to appreciate how ISL fits into the conceptual alternatives for preparing citizens.

It is at this point, in fact, that the different roles and functions of study abroad and ISL become meaningful (Bringle & Hatcher, chapter 1). In all but its most superficial forms, ISL is (almost) always study abroad (Jones & Steinberg, chapter 5). The exception is the special case when students can have a foreign experience at home because they enter into a neighborhood whose language, culture, and practice of community are so different as to be revelatory by their differences. As noted, effective ISL can combine such engaged domestic experiences with shorter experiences abroad. Study abroad, however, becomes ISL only when the community is the medium and service activities are the mode of communication and interaction with the community. Study abroad is *of* the community (and maybe some of it is even *in* the community) while ISL is *through* and *with* the community. These are substantive distinctions—not semantic.

There are two basic philosophical perspectives for considering citizenship education. These have been explored thoughtfully by Nussbaum (1996) in an edited anthology of contrasting views in *For Love of Country*, which begins with Nussbaum's concept of one's being, first, a citizen of the world, and includes the countervailing perspective of devotion or loyalty to one's country or group. The rich discussions in her volume warrant careful consideration and the distinctions are important, but they can be boiled down to the focal point of conceiving a person as belonging to a cosmopolitan worldview wherein the highest allegiance is to the world community and some basic conditions of humanity shared across all religions, nations, languages, ethnicities, or cultures. In this view, the citizen has a first duty to the collective whole of humanity as opposed to a nation or state or group or even the individual and family.

In the framework established by Nussbaum and others who share this sense of personal responsibility for the world as a whole, every individual is valued equally and education must be directed toward capacities that can elevate the whole of society, not merely the individual. Although not necessarily a determining condition for the cosmopolitan view, Nussbaum would say the goal of such education is a minimally just society.

Put crudely and in its baldest terms, the contributions of Nussbaum (1996) and those arguing for a cosmopolitan or global sense of citizenship is to highlight the differences between an instrumental and applied social science perspective of educating graduates for being successful in global competition by possessing more potent skills and knowledge in contrast to forms of education that develop the human potential through enhanced capacity for reflection and self-awareness developed through critical thinking, moral reasoning, and the humanities (as those disciplines that help us understand the human condition . . . not as specializations of erudite knowledge). In the former view, the familiar course-completion pattern of graduation requirements can be adjusted by requiring certain courses and skills. The goals and ends of such learning are focused less on citizenship than skill, more on the individual than the whole of societies connected across ethnicities, religions, and geography. In this instance, learning is more of an end than a means. In the latter cosmopolitan view, the evidence of attainment is more difficult to measure or certify since course completion by itself does not assure critical thinking, moral reasoning, or critical self-assessment (i.e., effective and engaged reflection). The ends and goals of such learning are more on what it means to be part of a group and to see one's self as sharing a basic equality that comes from being human. Learning is thus a means to an end and includes the process of continuously seeing one's self in the role of others.

It is not the purpose or even the potential of a discussion of ISL to solve this conceptual difference. However, ISL must be practiced within this tension of purpose. The administrators, advisors, faculty, international partners, and students who are so engaged will be more effective the clearer they are about how ISL can contribute to the preparation of both globally competent, or aware, citizens *and* highly skilled individuals who can succeed in a globally competitive environment precisely because they have an informed understanding of interdependence.

As will be discussed subsequently, many of the national higher education associations as well as governmental and nonprofit organizations concerned with learning in the global context have been careful to avoid pitting one extreme view against the other. Instead, they have seen value in both perspectives and, in general, have seemed to say that preparing globally competent citizens does not limit the capacity—or drive—of an individual to act out of self-interest or for short-term gain. The differences can be sidestepped, but they are ignored at the peril of effective learning and achieving an institution's mission. Graduation expectations set narrowly in a course check-off system or abstractly in ambitious but unmeasured principles miss the cumulative impact of thoughtfully aligning course and program (or major) requirements with the more comprehensive expectations for what a degree from a specific institution might mean and might enable a graduate not only to do but also to understand what needs to be done.

More frequently, institutions themselves have resolved the conceptual tension by noting the immediate and practical tension that exists between the local and the global with regard to such matters as the everyday consequences of world events on lives led in a particular place and time. While felicitous phrasing has not yet entered common parlance, colleges and universities are increasingly talking about the convergence of global and local issues, and showing the interconnections and reciprocal consequences of actions taken near and far (see Lewin, 2009b, for examples). Once ethereal and abstract, issues such as free trade, tariffs, capital formation, trade deficits, corporate ownership, language hegemony, farm subsidies for biofuels, and immigration become concerns to be discussed over the dinner table and in the editorial section of the hometown newspaper as well as in the classroom. The pall of terrorism—once a foreign issue—has brought religious, ethnic, and cultural conflict home, just as rapid climate change and threats to health from disease, defective products, and greed have intensified awareness of the world's role in daily life. Even humanitarian aid and spontaneous responses to natural disaster have been subject to questions about the purposes and means of philanthropy.

While less acute, there is a reciprocal awareness of how local issues affect other parts of the world as cities take actions to self-impose environmental standards even as federal agencies equivocate on issues of climate change, as states take up immigration legislation, and even a few special communities adopt local ordinances on such matters as nuclear proliferation and human rights. The ability to think globally has already reached a point where many citizens are searching for the means to act globally as well as think about the consequences of their individual acts.

In this environment of heightened awareness and with a growing sense of urgency, public community colleges and private research universities alike are all considering both their collective role as corporate citizens of a city or state or region and as society's most effective institution for preparing people to deal with the world as a whole.

ISL Responds

The underlying concept, pedagogy, and practice of service learning have been so thoroughly established across institutional types and across the nation as to require little explanation or justification. The very fact that service learning offers a pathway to national rankings by the *US News & World Report*, among others, implies that the practice is so widespread and so well understood as to be a useful benchmark. A number of organizations—Campus Compact principal among them along with the American Association of Higher Education before its demise—have usefully illustrated the effectiveness of service learning as an engaging pedagogy that positively affects everything from undergraduate retention to alumni giving (Eyler, chapter 10). Even hyperbole about the attributes of service learning may be warranted (Astin, 1999).

Nonetheless, there are risks and concerns. These less positive aspects of ISL are explored in several chapters in this volume (e.g., Erasmus, chapter 15; Kahn, chapter 6; Tonkin, chapter 9). These concerns need to be acknowledged, anticipated, and addressed, especially in the context of their local implementation where good ideas and good intentions can collide with reality. Knowledge and experience acquired in the United States may not transfer to other nations in any but superficial forms. The unintended consequences of poorly conceived, implemented, or supervised ISL can be harmful to the communities where the failures occur, and occasionally disastrous since the innocence or good intentions of the American foreigners can quickly become insults and incidents in unfamiliar settings that magnify similar domestic shortcomings.

As we now know, as a result of increasingly convincing cognitive sciences research, there are multiple ways of learning and no single approach works for everyone. The active learning pedagogies of service learning can no more be standardized than language acquisition or quantitative reasoning. Although brain and neural sciences are still informing learning theories, developmental psychologists like Gardner (1993) have already had a profound impact on recognizing a range of learning styles and rates of learning matched with a range of pedagogies to achieve the same ends. As the tensions between developing citizenship awareness for greater, even global, responsibility and the contrasting development of skills for personal advancement and enrichment play out in the minds and aspirations of students as well as the faculty who set graduation expectations, we need to acknowledge that service learning can play a critical, even central, role in international education (Bringle & Hatcher, chapter 1; Plater, Jones, Bringle, & Clayton, 2009). Yet, it is not a cure-all nor is there a single formula suitable for everyone.

The following definition of ISL guided the development of this volume (Bringle & Hatcher, chapter 1):

> A *structured academic experience in another country* in which students (a) participate in an organized service activity that addresses identified community needs; (b) learn from *direct interaction and cross-cultural dialogue* with others; and (c) reflect on the experience in such a way as to gain a deeper understanding of *global and intercultural* issues, a broader appreciation of the *host country* and the discipline, and an enhanced sense of their own responsibilities as citizens, locally and *globally*.

As defined, ISL is a particularly well-suited response to the urgency attached to preparing graduates to be effective in their communities—wherever they might be—because they have the ability to act *in* the world and *for* the world. Throughout the essays that comprise this volume, the attributes that make ISL such a strong and positive way of responding to internationalization are laid out with convincing clarity. But underlying them all is a sense of *immediacy* that ISL brings to a topic that is as immense and as large as the world with all of its complexity and seeming remoteness—despite the urgency:

- By its purpose and nature, ISL involves and immerses students in a community of action, and the experience in other nations has intensity as well as immediacy because of the novelty and unfamiliarity of the place and its peoples; although the service aspect of ISL may be restricted in time (to specified hours in a day and for a known period), the experience of living abroad is constant and inescapable;

- Students are required to apply their curricular knowledge and preparation to issues and circumstances in real time; there is little opportunity to delay action until a more convenient or certain time;
- Action necessitates dialogue and interaction with others—whether in their language or English—in such a way as to create a shared understanding, definition, approach, or plan;
- As dialogue becomes more familiar and purposeful, it requires a negotiated and defined basis for acting in concert as the learners and community mentors enact a project or activity;
- Because of the necessity of drawing on prior knowledge, experience, and preparation as a condition of action, ISL inherently encourages students to connect their sense of local as they have lived it at home with their hosts' sense of local as they display it in their actions and as students observe it being enacted; the comparisons are constant, personal, and inescapable; and
- ISL is about learning, first and foremost, which means that it is a reflexive, self-aware process—learning occurs in the moment, and while not everything experienced may be learned immediately, learning requires a realization of the here and now.

Often—more often than might be wished—learning occurs with a sense of investment in the future and a near-blind acceptance of a presumption that required courses or fulfilling important learning goals will pay off sometime in the future. Service learning, on the other hand, offers immediate feedback and reinforces the value of adapting the learning through the service to meet today's challenges. Although these are aspects of service learning in general, when carried out in the international context and for the sake of developing international civic skills, the immediacy of both the experience and the learning offers students a direct measure of satisfaction (even when shrouded in frustration) that is simply unavailable in learning *about* the world instead of *in* it. When the students are engaged in a meaningful way in real time with consequential responses to the application of their learning, internationalization is direct, tangible, and personal. Reflection is the primary means of achieving the sense of awareness and immediacy described here, and as a continuous process concurrent with both the service and the learning, it serves as the bridge between the prior accumulation of knowledge and its potential application for future action (Chisholm, 1997; Whitney & Clayton, chapter 8).

While the essays of this volume analyze and discuss ISL from a variety of perspectives and thus offer multiple classifications, pedagogical strategies, and typologies, there are perhaps three ways in which ISL fulfills the institutional expectations for internationalization. The three broad classifications referenced here are framed from the perspective of how there might be ISL even when the students' time in a setting outside the United States is limited or perhaps even nonexistent. All three types can help institutions develop and enrich their commitments to international education and address the growing demand from students for international experiences that help them anticipate their futures in a global context.

1. Service Learning Abroad: This most familiar and widespread form of ISL extends the experiences of domestic service learning to other nations and to their respective communities and organizations. Most often, such programs are established because of the prior work of faculty in international settings, frequently based on research projects that may include collaborations with international colleagues or with organizations. One of the most common and effective means of establishing ISL is to re-conceive and redesign a study abroad course into a more significantly engaged service learning course, building on previously established relationships, familiarity with a place, and the potential to contribute to a community. In such instances, faculty draw on their personal contacts and the trust or respect established through prior engagement to involve students in meaningful work in the host nation (Kahn, chapter 6; and Sutton, chapter 7, for examples of this process). Alternatively, many colleges and universities have had long-standing relationships with other universities, learning centers, or organizations abroad that can serve as a point of contact and departure for developing specific service learning projects. In both instances, the fact of prior association provides a context that facilitates the introduction of American students into a community for a short period of time with minimal disruption to the local community because of the preparation and planning enabled through the colleagues abroad. Moreover, such collaborations enable successive iterations of the course offering to extend beyond the original setting or purpose to include more and wider ranges of possibilities as communities or organizations become familiar with the capacities and reliability of the Americans. Although it is easy to talk of trust and reciprocity, the key to most successful ISL is based on trust built carefully over several years.

Further, established relationships often permit collaborations between the American institution's faculty member and a college or university abroad. Using distance learning technologies, two groups of students can work together to prepare for a service project through shared learning and planning. By implementing the project together, the learning is multiplied through the peer-to-peer relationship and often the subsequent international learning on site is significantly enhanced because of the personal ties among students. And perhaps most importantly, the opportunity for collective reflection and shared learning throughout the experience and its completion may offer a much deeper and lasting appreciation for all aspects of the learning. Occasionally, these experiences can lead to follow-up courses, collaborations, or even friendships. When there is a long-standing relationship, the possibility of the host community being more actively involved in defining and broadening the service opportunities is enhanced markedly; the community itself can become a partner—perhaps even the leading partner—in conducting the service project. While there are many variants on the traditional form of ISL (Jones & Steinberg, chapter 5), the key point is that the faculty and the college or university are able to establish a relationship of mutuality that enables and builds trust.

When service learning courses are offered for the first time in a setting in other nations without prior involvement of the faculty or institution or when such courses are offered in settings that are unstable due to community circumstances, there are special risks that must be considered. While most experienced faculty or college administrators will defer and decline either study abroad or ISL programs in countries where there is political or economic uncertainty, some of the most attractive opportunities—for students—occur in places where world events have intruded into their consciousness. These places attract interest because of the significance of events that may be unfolding. The most common form of this type of involvement is in responding to a natural disaster or to some acute need for humanitarian aid following an earthquake, tsunami, flood, famine, pandemic, or any other large-scale man-made or natural disaster that puts people at risk. When courses—including individual study—are developed in response to such conditions, special care must be taken not only for the safety of the participants but to establish—or maintain—the trust and sense of reciprocity.

Finally, it is important to make a distinction between service learning and internships or other forms of work abroad that are not based on service. The differentiating characteristic of service learning, as made clear in the definition of ISL being used in this volume (Bringle & Hatcher, chapter 1), is the added and particular value that philanthropic service—voluntary action for the public or common good—adds to international learning. As noted earlier in the discussion of the motivations for internationalizing education, both the citizenship and personal enrichment approaches to international education can recognize the inherent values of service as distinct from work and preprofessional training (Longo & Saltmarsh, chapter 4).

2. ISL at Home: As mentioned earlier, the United States has its own communities that are distinct with regard to language, culture, and ethnicity, creating special opportunities for many students to experience a very different social setting in the United States. There is no denying the value of such service learning courses, but unless they also engage the country of origin for the American community where the experience takes place (or its equivalent, in the case of service learning situated on Native American tribal lands or reservations), the learning is constrained and perhaps not sufficient to develop international understanding. Many faculty have found ways to combine domestic service learning in ethnic communities by either using distance technologies to engage directly with a matched community abroad or by having a shorter-term, intensive service project in the community abroad through preparation in the nearby community in America (see, for example, Jones & Steinberg, chapter 5). Such projects are most easily designed when there are specific activities that link a neighborhood or community in the United States with a community abroad through fundraising for building a community service facility (e.g., a school, hospital, elder care home, or other social services program) or through political action, since many persons living in the United States may still vote or remain politically active in their home village, town, or city. Through carefully established linkages with appropriate counterparts abroad, effective ISL projects can be created and sustained over time. As the visits to the host community overseas are repeated, the level of familiarity and trust increases along with the depth of the learning experience for the students.

Some of the positive aspects as well as the limitations of ISL at home are considered elsewhere in this volume (e.g., Jones & Steinberg, chapter 5; Kiely, chapter 11), but the one necessary component is a clear statement of the intended learning goals—what is it about the experience that develops the students' understanding of the world and the relation of America as well as themselves as individuals in that world. Still, the value of such arrangements in increasing the access for many students whose work, family, or economic circumstances preclude longer-term visits abroad require that institutions consider how to take advantage of such arrangements.

3. Service Learning in the United States by Students from Abroad: While not as familiar or widespread as it may become, students enrolled in service learning courses in colleges and universities in other nations are seeking opportunities for service learning in the United States for the same reasons that students in America wish to study, work, or serve abroad. The Hurricane Katrina disaster motivated faculty and students from Indonesia (and other nations) to seek comparative learning opportunities while providing service through rebuilding houses and lost infrastructure based on their own experiences with tsunami, earthquakes, and cyclones. Just as faculty or institutions in the United States develop sustained relationships abroad, colleges in other countries seek to do the same. When a North American university receives students from abroad, there is an opportunity to create an international learning experience for their own students, especially if they are purposefully paired with the group of students coming from another country and the joint service project is prepared in advance through collaboration of the type already suggested when American students go abroad. The experience of hosting students from abroad for service in the American communities or organizations can be made international for the American students by having them subsequently visit their counterparts abroad for a similar, intense but perhaps short-term, ISL experience. If the service aspects are focused in the United States, the learning experience abroad may be based more on comparative and analytic studies to create a context for how the service experience of the international students fits into their own social, cultural, and economic context.

The value of differentiating these three types of ISL is to stimulate innovation and variation for the purpose of accommodating more students and to suggest that they be the focus of subsequent research. As evidence of growing student interest (even demand) and of directed public policy indicates the need for greater student international *experience and skills*—not merely knowledge about world events and places—community colleges, liberal arts colleges, comprehensive universities, and research universities alike will need to be more creative and resourceful in incorporating actual time and exposure abroad into their curricula and learning goals. A 2008 survey of American employers and CEOs documented the greater importance of assessed experiential learning—including study abroad and service learning—over grades and transcripts (American Association of Colleges and Universities, 2008). The inherent values of service learning make it the most comprehensive and satisfying form of international experience: immediacy of experience, enacting learning by doing through the medium of a community, reflection on the learning, and being most highly valued by employers as an assessed—as well as documented—achievement.

Colleges and Universities' Response to Student Demand and Public Interest

This volume is one response to the heightened awareness of the necessity of enhanced and—most likely expanded—international education. The variety of forms it can take are many, and recent studies have begun to take a comprehensive look (Lewin, 2009a). Appropriately, colleges and universities will involve the whole institutional community—not only faculty—in supporting these activities. Student affairs personnel, librarians, information technology staff, instructional designers, alumni and development offices, advisors, and others all have roles to play in contributing to and sustaining partnerships to support international education abroad. However, some components, and certainly ISL, require a clear definition and coordination of responsibilities. As universities and colleges respond to student and public demand, they need to consider, at least: (a) the role of executive leadership; (b) the academic purpose and framework for situating ISL within the goals for the whole institution; (c) the organizational responsibilities that will reduce competition and duplication; (d) opportunities to involve the local community in ISL courses or programs abroad; and (e) coping with demand within resource constraints and national trends, including competitiveness.

In most colleges and universities, individual faculty have considerable latitude in developing service learning courses—including ISL—because their courses continue to meet the departmental, college or school, and campus requirements for graduation. Many institutions have encouraged service learning because of its imputed success in improving retention and deep student learning. Individual faculty initiative and their offering ISL courses remain the bedrock of effectiveness, but student interest and public policy are moving consideration of ISL to a broader plane of institutional policy and, most specifically, mission.

The leadership role of presidents, provosts, deans, and department chairs in articulating the institution's mission with respect to internationalization is probably the single most important means of implementing meaningful campus-wide programs because the institutional conversation controlled by these leaders develops the context and priority for service learning generally and ISL specifically. The respective roles of these administrative leaders with respect to service learning has been extensively addressed in "Civic Engagement, Service Learning, and Intentional Leadership" in *Public Work and the Academy* (Plater, 2004). The same analysis applies to advocating on behalf of internationalization and then the role of service learning within the broader institutional commitment to international learning and action. If the academic leaders are unwilling or unable (out of lack of knowledge, familiarity, or experience) to articulate the value of ISL, it is nearly impossible for such programs to reach a scale and level of activity that is pervasive and sustainable—unless there is deliberate collective action as an alternative to the inaction of senior administrators (Plater, in press). Individuals may be able to develop their courses, but the practice of ISL will not be recognized as a means to achieve mission-driven priorities.

As colleges and universities take a step back from immediate demands and reactions to the rush toward internationalization, it may be useful for institutional leaders to conceptualize a framework for the overall learning objectives and the ways in which the administrative units of a campus might interact for common purpose in strengthening international education (Brustein, 2009). One such framework builds on the increasing complexity and cumulative experience of learning most common to liberal and general education programs, and this framework underlies several of the initiatives of national associations discussed subsequently:

1. **Cognitive and Intellectual Learning:** Attention should be given to the courses and opportunities to learn about a place or country—its culture, history, languages, religions, politics, and economy. The goals of internationalizing the overall curriculum provide abundant opportunities to introduce such global knowledge into many if not most courses. The importance of learning about other places in the world—as well as our own nation and our own community—are clear and compelling (Hovland et al., 2009).

2. **Skills Acquisition and Development:** There are many skills and applied or practice-based learning outcomes that can be developed well if not ideally in the context of study abroad and ISL. Certainly, language acquisition and enhancement is obvious, but so are skills or opportunities to apply knowledge in practice setting such as those related to political and organizational theory, group dynamics and teamwork, communication practices, environmental understanding, health practices, nutrition, tourism management, engineering technologies, and so forth. When given the opportunity to develop both skills and professional practice in settings abroad, students will often become more intensively and reflectively engaged.

3. **Identity Development:** For most colleges and universities, the capacity to develop one's sense of self and identity as both a citizen of one's own community and nation as well as the world can be substantially enhanced and refined by the opportunity to see one's self in the world—interacting with others and engaging in activities shared with persons in other nations and cultures (Braskamp, 2007). While there need be no advocacy toward specific ends—such as seeing an end of learning as developing an identity as a citizen of the world with all of its implications, being cosmopolitan in the way Nussbaum (1996)

and others suggest—the intentional development of opportunities for reflecting on one's identity must surely be important to every college or university regardless of its mission.

The purpose of a framework such as this is to contextualize the role of ISL within the institution's own objectives by articulating broad learning goals. In such a way, the roles and responsibilities of administrators, faculty, and support staff are implicitly organized according to the priority of academics within the mission of the university or college.

Not that effective study abroad programs are easy, they are nonetheless comparatively easier to arrange, to implement, and to complete than ISL because study abroad does not necessarily include engagement with the community on terms of mutual benefit and reciprocity. Moreover, study abroad does not necessarily require faculty-supervised learning (Lewin, 2009a). It is possible to be passive, an observer, through study abroad—but not when the learner is also engaged in service in a community or organization abroad. This demand-side development of international learning affords those interested in ISL many opportunities for creativity and innovation, including developing service learning with optional additional study abroad that might be sponsored by or coordinated with student affairs programming, alumni offerings, or community organizations that sponsor voluntary service. Before or after the service learning component, there might be travel and study through a region or to nearby nations with the goal of enriching and contextualizing the specific service experience. Alert presidents, provosts, and deans will take full advantage of the growing public interest in international experiences to seek collaborations and joint ventures, including asking for scholarships and other forms of philanthropic, corporate, or foundation support for activities that are perceived to be of heightened value and mutual benefit, especially given the employers' clear preference for experiential learning.

As international education advances to higher levels as a campus priority, care needs to be taken in assigning responsibility for coordinating and managing the range of activities. The offices of international affairs, service learning, and student affairs—by whatever their respective names on specific campuses—all can properly play a role in both study abroad and ISL. The call for coordination is not sufficient reason for merging these offices or creating unwieldy management relationships, but there must be clearly defined roles and assigned responsibility that permit more extensive collaboration. Both study abroad and ISL carry risks that must be assessed and accepted as an institutional responsibility, and the duty incumbent on the university or college to manage these commitments is serious and necessary. Similarly, setting priorities for maximizing the institutional goals, as noted above, most likely belongs to the provost or chief academic officer.

This is an era when the more encompassing concept of student success is gaining momentum, sometimes at the expense of student learning, because success in learning is much harder to measure than satisfaction. There are two overriding concerns that should influence the administrative management of ISL. As a form of learning, the service experience abroad must have faculty oversight and involvement when credit is awarded; learning is paramount, and thus ISL must be the responsibility of academic affairs, even if it engages student affairs and other administrative and support units creatively and effectively. As a form of study abroad, ISL requires engaging several units, including such administrative units as risk management, financial affairs, and legal counsel to ensure that the college or university is meeting all of its due diligence responsibilities when taking students to other countries, especially those where there may be some risk from political, health, environmental, or social conditions. Even as others are involved, academic affairs remains the responsible party.

With moderately well-coordinated administrative roles inside the institution, the opportunities for collaboration with community organizations are unusually high with regard to ISL. In many communities, there are voluntary service organizations (e.g., Rotary, Kiwanis, Lions clubs), churches, and social service nonprofits (e.g., Red Cross, CARE, World Health Organization) with international outreach programs. In most instances, there is a role for the college or university to work with such existing international community relationships to form supplemental and meaningful projects that allow ISL courses to draw on these established relationships and to contribute in specific ways to the larger goals of the community or organizations abroad. Colleges and schools with existing religious affiliations will have little conflict in developing such relationships consistent with their missions, and public institutions can similarly develop relations with multiple religious organizations by carefully articulating the differences between the learning experience and the religious activities. Although not as obvious, similar bright lines may need to be drawn with service clubs and nondenominational nonprofits. But the point is, as communities themselves reach out to the world in interesting and varied ways, colleges and universities can both add value to this work and benefit from working with local groups on ISL.

Students are increasingly interested in international experiences—both for more international material in courses and for increased numbers of courses, more cocurricular experiences, and new degree programs. In one poll, more than 55% of entering students expressed interest in international learning experiences (American Council on Education, the Art and Science Group, & College Board, 2008). This will create a need for new and expanded resources to support course design, faculty development, institutional research, and student aid. The need for new funding is well understood and the advocacy is strong. Yet, most colleges and universities face similar demands in other—and equally compelling—new areas of intellectual and social development, without a compelling rationale to privilege ISL above all else, even despite its probable positive impact on cognitive and intellectual learning, skills acquisition, and identity formulation, to say nothing of increased retention and enhanced prospects for alumni giving in the future. The very real need for resources may best be addressed within the context of a national imperative, a need to make America successful as other nations catch up in economic development, development of human potential through education, and social innovation and compassion.

Study abroad and ISL are both experiencing increased demand, but the greatest attention has been focused on study abroad for good and sufficient reasons. There are few comprehensive sources of data other than aggregated anecdotal accounts from individual institutions to document either increased student demand for or greater institutional involvement in international education or ISL, but the work of the Lincoln Commission culminating in its recommendation—issued in November 2005—that funding be found for a million students to study abroad, funded by multiple sources, exemplifies the growing tide of public interest (Commission on the Abraham Lincoln Study Abroad Fellowship Program, 2005). This form of learning is well established with many national and international organizations—as well as federal agencies—to support study abroad; the relationships with universities in other nations are deep and wide; and the variety of forms, including increasing types of short-term visits, can satisfy many different perceived needs and budgets.

As ISL makes its case for a privileged place on the list of international initiatives, its champions may do well to join with advocates for study abroad, such as the Lincoln Commission, in order to create a unified and comprehensive case to the public for a national priority. ISL can prosper within an expanded and enriched study abroad environment because of its special characteristics and its impact on student learning. As the research on and assessment of ISL yields more and more results, the case can only be strengthened. In the meantime, a number of the national higher education associations have taken an interest.

National Higher Education Associations: Creating a Movement

Most of the national associations for higher education have developed initiatives or have offices dedicated to international education. These include those serving institutions as well as individuals, large research universities, community colleges, independent colleges, and specialized organizations, including one that specializes in ISL (e.g., International Partnership for Service Learning and Leadership, see Brown, chapter 3). Several associations, notably the American Council on Education (ACE), the Association of American Colleges and Universities (AAC&U), and the Association of Public and Land-grant Universities (APLU), have dedicated staff and offices to support international education and their members. These three organizations, along with a few others, such as NAFSA: Association of International Educators, have played key roles in developing international education for many years, and they are at the forefront of current developments (see Lewin, 2009b). There are a few associations focused on civic engagement, such as Innovations in Civic Participation or Campus Compact, with particular interests in international education and service. And there are a growing number of collaborative associations formed to achieve shared purposes, such as the Talloires Network, "a collective of individuals and institutions committed to promoting the civic roles and social responsibilities of higher education," (Talloires Network, 2009) or the International Consortium on Higher Education, Civic Responsibility, and Democracy. It is not possible or useful to list all of the relevant associations, especially since many of them shift their priorities periodically. Nonetheless, many of these collaborate on special initiatives, such as the Lincoln Commission's work, or on shared issues such as visa applications. The issue is, could they do more?

There is no lack of interest or effort among these associations to promote international education, but they collectively represent something greater than anyone of them might achieve on its own. Innovations in Civic Participation has perhaps summarized it best, declaring that "an invisible revolution is underway in higher education on all continents—a growing movement to educate active citizens and to apply university resources to community needs" (Innovations in Civic Participation, 2007). When the education and preparation of citizens for their responsibilities in an interconnected world is combined with the concept of applying the intellectual resources of universities to community needs worldwide, ISL is an obvious means for powering this revolution. Of course, universities and students are not alone in this work and apparently no one association is sufficient to provide the necessary focus and leadership for a revolution or for a powerful pedagogy like ISL that combines service learning, study abroad, and international education. The associations have enormous resources, experience, and commitment to assist institutions and individuals in developing ISL and in learning from others.

Given resource constraints in a time of increased demand for access and innovation, the time may have come for colleges and universities to ask their respective associations to work together to form a national movement toward support for ISL within the study abroad framework. The research being undertaken on the impact and value of this particular pedagogy can best be aggregated and mobilized through the concerted action of the several associations concerned with student learning, the development of globally prepared citizens, and the wise use of knowledge for the improvement of the world. Will these research studies and the invisible revolution be sufficient catalyst to mobilize the associations to act on our collective behalf?

Conclusion

Over a century ago, at a time with parallels similar to our own regarding new communication capabilities, immigration, urbanization, global strife and uncertainty, and a heightened awareness of what value communities hold for civic purposes, Dewey imagined that education could enact democracy. With the benefits of hindsight and of an optimism energized by a realization of urgent necessity, our time calls for something like a revolution that affects all of education. ISL is not likely to be a panacea or universal solution, but it has the promise of being a transformative pedagogy if it can only come to scale and affect enough of the world's future leaders. The chapters in this volume begin an exploration of this potential, and they have launched us on an expedition whose goal is nothing less than having every college graduate understand and accept the responsibilities of citizenship in communities that are always both local and global.

References

American Association of Colleges and Universities (2008). *How should colleges assess and improve student learning: Employers' views on the accountability challenge.* Washington, DC: Peter D. Hart Research Associates.

American Council on Education, the Art and Science Group, & College Board. (2008, January). *College bound students' interest in study abroad and other international learning activities.* Retrieved September 8, 2009, from http://www.artsci.com/data/files/news/StudentPOLLNews/studentPOLL_International_Issue.pdf

Astin, A. W. (1999). Promoting leadership, service, and democracy: What higher education can do. In R. G. Bringle, R. Games, & E. A. Malloy (Eds.), Colleges and universities as citizens (pp. 31–47). Needham Heights, MA: Allyn & Bacon.

Benson, L. L., Harkavy, I., & Puckett, J. (2007). *Dewey's dream: Universities and democracies in an age of education reform.* Philadelphia, PA: Temple University Press.

Braskamp, L. A. (2007). Developing global citizens. *Journal of College and Character, 10*(1), 1–5.

Brustein, W. (2009). It takes an entire institution: A blueprint for the global university. In R. Lewin (Ed.), *The handbook of practice and research in study abroad: Higher education and the quest for global citizenship* (pp. 249–265). New York: Routledge.

Chisholm, L. A. (1997). International service-learning: For a world of difference. *Black Collegian, 27*(2), 149–151.

Commission on the Abraham Lincoln Study Abroad Fellowship Program. (2005). *Global competence & national needs: One million Americans studying abroad.* Washington, DC: Congress of the United States.

Dewey, J. (1899). *The school and society.* Chicago, IL: The University of Chicago Press.

Freidman, T. (2005). *The world is flat: A brief history of the twenty-first century.* New York, NY: Farrar, Straus, & Giroux.

Gardner, H. (1993). *Multiple intelligences: The theory in practice.* New York, NY: Basic Books.

Gillespie, J., Braskamp, L., & Dwyer, M. (2009). Holistic student learning and development abroad: The IES 3-D Program Model. In R. Lewin (Ed.), *The handbook of practice and research in study abroad: Higher education and the quest for global citizenship* (pp. 445–465). New York, NY: Routledge.

Hovland, K., McTighe Musil, C., Skilton-Sylvester, E., & Jamison, A. (2009). It takes a curriculum: Bringing global mindedness home. In R. Lewin (Ed.), *The handbook of practice and research in study abroad: Higher education and the quest for global citizenship* (pp. 466–484). New York, NY: Routledge.

Innovations in Civic Participation. (2007). Retrieved February 9, 2007, from www.icicp.org/

Lewin, R. (2009a). *The handbook of practice and research in study abroad: Higher education and the quest for global citizenship.* New York, NY: Routledge.

Lewin, R. (2009b). Introduction: The quest for global citizenship through study abroad. In R. Lewin (Ed.), *The handbook of practice and research in study abroad: Higher education and the quest for global citizenship* (pp. xii–xxii). New York, NY: Routledge.

National Academy of Sciences. (2007). *Rising above the gathering storm: Energizing and employing America for a brighter economic future.* Washington, DC: National Academies Press.

Nussbaum, M. C. (1996). Patriotism and cosmopolitanism. In J. Cohen (Ed.), *For love of country: Debating the limits of patriotism* (pp. 3–20). Boston, MA: Beacon.

Organization for Economic Cooperation and Development. (2006). *PISA 2006 science competencies for tomorrow's world leaders volume one analysis.* Retrieved February 25, 2009, from http://www.pisa.oecd.org/dataoecd/30/17/39703267.pdf

Organization for Economic Cooperation and Development. (2007). *Education at a glance 2007.* Retrieved September 8, 2009, from http://www.oecd.org/dataoecd/22/51/39317423.pdf

Plater, W. M. (2004). Civic engagement, service-learning, and intentional leadership. In M. Langseth & W. M. Plater (Eds.), *Public work and the academy: An academic administrator's guide to civic engagement and service-learning* (pp. 1–22). Bolton, MA: Anker.

Plater, W. M. (in press). Collaborative leadership for engagement. In J. Saltmarsh & M. Hartley (Eds.), *Democratic civic engagement: Institutional change for reclaiming the purpose of higher education.* Philadelphia, PA: Temple University Press.

Plater, W. M., Jones, S. G., Bringle, R. G., & Clayton, P. H. (2009). Educating globally competent citizens through international service learning. In R. Lewin (Ed.), *The handbook of practice and research in study abroad: Higher education and the quest for global citizenship* (pp. 485–505). New York, NY: Routledge.

Postsecondary Education Opportunity. (2007). *Postsecondary education opportunity website.* Retrieved February 25, 2009, from www.postsecondary.org/

Talloires Network. (2009). *What is the Talloires Network?* Retrieved May 18, 2008, from www.tufts.edu/talloiresnetwork/

U.S. Census Bureau. (2004). *U.S. interim projections by age, sex, race, and hispanic origin: 2000–2050.* Retrieved February 25, 2009, from http://www.census.gov/population/www/projections/usinterimproj/

U.S. Census Bureau. (2008). *American community survey.* Retrieved August 28, 2008, from http://www.census.gov/acs/www/index.html

Usher, A., & Cervenan, A. (2005). *Global higher education rankings 2005.* Toronto, ON, Canada: Education Policy Institute.

3

A 360-DEGREE VIEW
OF INTERNATIONAL
SERVICE LEARNING

Nevin C. Brown

A s universities and others in the academic world strive to define the content and purpose of academic programs to engage students with communities, a key question remains how to connect student learning in the classroom with opportunities for observing and practicing engagement skills in intercultural and/or international settings. This chapter will discuss one pedagogical approach, service learning, that has been used in many disciplines in colleges and universities located in both developed and developing nations. This chapter will focus on one example of this approach to international service learning (ISL), reflected particularly through the many years of experience in nations, cultures, and postsecondary institutions involved with the International Partnership for Service Learning and Leadership (IPSL).

Service learning, particularly in its international form, is essential for the preparation of engaged citizens (Plater, Jones, Bringle, & Hatcher, 2009). It is experiential; ISL directly links theory with practice in communities and contexts in which such citizenship is an essential skill that can be practiced. It is reflective; ISL always has at its core the use of reflection activities (e.g., writing and discussion) to analyze theory in the light of lived experiences, and vice versa, so that learning in the classroom and in the field become mutually reinforcing. It is multicultural and multinational; ISL exposes students in deep, transformative ways to cultures and nations other than their own, resulting in a much richer understanding of the contexts in which a life of engaged citizenship must be carried out.

ISL: Implications for Good Practice

Service learning links academic study with the practical experience of community service. It has become an international movement (Annette, 2003; Lazarus, 2004; Holland, 2003; Perold, 2005; Perold, Stroud, & Sherraden, 2003; Thomson, Smith-Tolken, Naidoo, & Bringle, 2008; United Board for Christian Higher Education in Asia and International Christian University, 2002) that offers new approaches to teaching and learning and to the civic engagement of institutions of higher education. It provides students with an education that meets the highest academic standards and delivers meaningful service that makes a difference to the well-being of society, particularly for communities and persons on the socioeconomic margins. Service learning aims to develop in students a lifelong commitment to service and leadership. Since service learning is an international movement, it promotes not only local commitment, but also an understanding of the interrelatedness of communities and societies across the world.

Service learning unites academic study and volunteer community service in such a way that the one reinforces the other. The service makes the study immediate, applicable, and active; the study, through knowledge and reflection, informs the service. The service may involve teaching, health care, community development, environmental projects, construction, and a host of other activities that contribute to the well-being of individuals, communities, nations, or the world as a whole. The academic study may be related to one or more of many disciplines, especially the liberal arts, the humanities, and environmental science, and to professional training, including medicine, law, social work, engineering, and business.

In service learning programs, students and instructors use the experience of service as one source of information and ideas, along with the classroom, laboratory, library, and the Internet. They are asked to analyze critically what they learn from the service through structured reflection (Whitney & Clayton, chapter 8), just as they analyze the information and ideas garnered from the sources of traditional academic study. When academic credit is awarded, it is not for the service alone, but for the learning that the student demonstrates through written papers, classroom discussion, examinations and/or other means of formal evaluation. In service learning programs that are not offered for credit, the learning must be intentional, structured, and evaluated.

Service learning is different from community service unconnected to formal study in two important ways. First, it demands that the student understand the service agency—its mission, philosophy, assumptions, structures, and governance—and the conditions of the lives of those who are associated with the community activities. Second, it is characterized by a relationship of partnership: the student learns from the service agency and from the community and, in return, gives energy, intelligence, commitment, time, and skills to address human and community issues.

Service learning is different from field study, internships, and practica, although it may have elements of all of these (Furco, 1996). Unlike field study, service learning makes the student not only an observer but an active participant. Although the student may gain from service learning many of the benefits of an internship or practicum, service learning has two goals: student learning and service to the community. The success of a program is measured not only by what the student learns but also by the usefulness of the student's work to relevant constituencies in the community.

ISL can be especially rich, as it exposes North American educators and students to many conditions, ideas, assumptions, and people that are substantially different from those with whom they are familiar. ISL may be designed to link one course or subject to service or it may join several disciplines. It may be offered to a group of students or for an individual through independent study. The students may serve together in a single agency or village, or they may be individually placed in a variety of service positions. The pattern may be that of study, followed by a period of service and concluding with reflection and examination, or the service and study may be intertwined throughout the period of service learning (Jones & Steinberg, chapter 5).

Building on models for service learning, our experiences at IPSL demonstrate that well-designed ISL addresses simultaneously two important needs of societies both in developed and developing nations: the education and development of young persons, especially their international civic skills, and the provision of increased resources to contribute to individuals and communities. In particular, ISL:

- Enriches students' learning of academic subjects. Theory is field-tested in practice and is seen and measured within a host country's cultural context. Because the learning is put to immediate use, it tends to be deeper and to last longer (Tonkin, 2004). The learning is rigorous, sound, and appropriate to the academic level of the students. The studies do not offer foregone conclusions but rather, in the spirit of academic inquiry, expose students to a wide range of points of view, theories, and ideas, asking that they critically examine these ideas and their experience in service, reaching their own well-considered conclusions.

- Promotes intercultural and international understanding. The service, whether local, domestic, or international, almost always occurs with persons whose lives are very different from that of the students. By working with them, the students come to understand and appreciate their different experiences, ideas, and values, and to work cooperatively with them. Service learning nurtures global awareness and socially responsible citizenship.

- Fosters in students personal growth, maturity, the examination of values and beliefs, and civic responsibility, all within the context of a community and its issues and needs. Students explore how they may use their education for the benefit of the community and the well-being of others. Opportunities for personal reflection on the meaning of the experience in relation to the student's values and life decisions is built into the program in a structured way (Whitney & Clayton, chapter 8).

- Provides help to nongovernmental organization service agencies and to communities, addressing issues and needs that would otherwise remain unmet. Service learning does not replace paid work. Rather, it supplements and extends such work, contributing in ways that would otherwise not occur. The students' community activities must be useful to the community or agency. Experience has shown that the agency or community is best qualified to define what is useful. The time and quality of the community activities must be sufficient to offset the time spent in planning and evaluation; otherwise, the institution and student are exploiting those they intend to assist.

- Advances understanding of societies, cultures, and world issues by testing academic ways of knowing and formal scholarship against indigenous epistemologies, immediate practical experiences, and theory within a unique cultural context.

- Develops in students leadership skills as they learn to work collaboratively among themselves and with the host community. They learn that the most effective leadership is that which encourages and develops the participation—and indeed leadership—of others. Students are allowed and encouraged to develop and demonstrate leadership skills, using their own initiative when appropriate, bearing in mind that they should first listen to the community and be responsive to its values and needs (Kahn, chapter 6; Whitney & Clayton, chapter 8).

- Establishes reciprocity between the community served and that of the college or university, and their relationship is built on mutual respect and esteem.

- Provides opportunities for establishing clear connections between the studies and the community-based activities. The studies may focus on the general culture or be more specific in relating subject matter and the community service experience.
- Provides support services to students to ensure that they are prepared for their international experience, their community activities, and their return. Provisions need to include access to health care, should it be needed, and issues related to safety.

Finally, ISL is most effective when it is long-term rather than short-term in duration. Whether local or international, service learning is most effective when it is long enough (at least a summer, preferably a semester or longer) to provide both a genuine immersion in a local culture and language as well as a level of service that may have some long-lasting value to the communities being served.

Recognizing the desirability of developing international perspectives on academic learning, and wanting to provide the most stimulating and valuable education to their students, educators around the world have discovered during the past two decades the richness of ISL. They are applying the pedagogy of service learning in a wide variety of situations and through various models (Jones & Steinberg, chapter 5). In developing ISL, they are not following the lead of any one nation or system, although the models have been based on North American approaches (Erasmus, chapter 15). In adapting the pedagogy to international contexts, American educators are creating their own versions, compatible with specific cultures and national systems of education, the prevailing educational philosophies, the mission, curricula, and structures of their own institution, as illustrated by Erasmus (chapter 15). This work is also beginning to draw from examples of service learning being developed at institutions outside North America. Growth of service learning is taking place in South Africa, aided by the Joint Education Trust-CHESP initiative (JET, 2006; Lazarus, 2004); in Australia (see Holland, 2003); in Asia (see United Board for Christian Higher Education in Asia and International Christian University, 2002); in Ireland (McIlrath & MacLabhrainn, 2007); as well as Latin America, Mexico, and Europe (see Annette, 2003; Perold, 2005; Perold, Stroud, & Sherraden, 2003; International Partnership for Service Learning and Leadership). These institutions of higher education that are initiating and developing service learning include old and prestigious colleges and universities, as well as young and less-established ones. North American educators need to be aware of these international models for service learning and civic engagement and learn from them as they design ISL experiences for their students.

The International Partnership for Service Learning and Leadership

One organization that has been active for a quarter century in promoting service learning and its application worldwide has been the International Partnership for Service Learning and Leadership (IPSL). IPSL is a network of colleges, universities, and nongovernmental and service organizations united to foster service learning. The mission of IPSL is twofold: (a) to promote service learning through publications, conferences, research, and training opportunities for faculty and service agency staff; and (b) to offer international programs for undergraduate and graduate students from institutions of higher education primarily in the United States, but also including small numbers of students from other nations. Each year IPSL publishes and distributes books and newsletters related to service learning, leadership, and international education. A periodic conference, which has been held in Europe, Asia, and the Americas, draws participants from around the world. Ongoing research evaluates the impact of service learning on students, institutions of higher education, and on the agencies and communities in which the students serve.

Since the mid-1980s, IPSL has offered as many as 15 undergraduate ISL programs in 13 nations: Czech Republic, Ecuador, England (UK), France, India, Italy, Jamaica, Mexico, Philippines, Russia, Scotland (UK), Thailand, and the Lakota Nation within the United States. Currently, IPSL offers 13 ISL programs (see International Partnership for Service Learning and Leadership, 2009). IPSL's undergraduate programs combine full-time academic study for credit (including language study in nations where English is not the primary language), placement in a service agency for a significant number of hours of service per week, homestay accommodation in most cases, and a variety of cultural events and field trips related to the local culture. Since 1984, approximately 2,500 undergraduate students from 300 colleges and universities in the United States and several other nations have participated in programs ranging in duration from a month to an academic year. The great majority of IPSL's students have been women, a pattern that increasingly characterizes all international and study-abroad education programs in the United States.

IPSL also manages, in cooperation with universities in Mexico, Jamaica, and the United States, a Master's Degree in International Service, an 18-month cohort-based program that prepares graduates for careers in international non-governmental relief and development agencies. Over 100 students have earned degrees in the program since 2001. Other special programs have been designed and managed to fit the needs of particular institutions and organizations, particularly for college- and university-based service learning and community service units (particularly affiliates of Campus Compact) new to the field of ISL.

The IPSL Student Experience

Although a student's experience of ISL through the undergraduate and graduate programs of IPSL varies from country to country, there are a number of common elements that together work to deepen immersion in the national culture and language as well as to challenge preconceptions about residents and communities. Academic courses and readings are chosen to provide a wide range of scholarly perspectives on local history, society, economy, and human ecology; many of these courses are offered in English, but a student with greater language proficiency (particularly in Spanish- and French-speaking nations) is also encouraged to take courses in those languages. In addition, the student in each IPSL program takes a common course, "Institutions in Society," a multidisciplinary social science course designed to link the student's service assignment with an academic understanding of the role of service agencies and nongovernmental organizations in the host nation, culture, and society.

For all students in non-English speaking settings, intensive instruction in the local language is provided; although in some cases only a minimal level of proficiency can be gained in a summer or semester, a student is expected to use the language as much as possible in the community service activities. In most cases, a student is also living in a homestay environment, often with a family most of whose members are not proficient in English; this too helps to speed the student's acquisition of the local language.

While taking a relatively full load of academic courses, the ISL student is also working 15 to 20 hours per week in the community service activities, usually with a local community service agency or nongovernmental organization. The range of service settings is quite broad (e.g., day-care centers and homes for unwed mothers; shelters and schools for street children and abandoned girls; health clinics serving squatter communities, programs providing services to recently released prisoners; initiatives providing housing and microfinance opportunities for poor urban residents). Students' community service activities are also broad (e.g., tutoring in English, providing health clinic intake interviews, manual labor in housing projects, assisting with strategic planning, serving as a teacher's aide, assisting with a sustainable agriculture initiative in an environmentally sensitive island community). Service agencies may initially assign students to relatively low-level tasks, but as trust between agency staff and the student grows, the opportunities for more significant service experiences—and engagement with local communities—grow as well.

Students in IPSL's programs have often taken significant leadership roles in their service settings. A student serving in a mission school on a Lakota Nation reservation organized for the school (and for the reservation) its first museum of local artifacts that had been stored for many years in a dusty basement. Another student working on another Lakota Nation reservation applied his background in journalism to the founding of the reservation's first regular newspaper. Another student took a leading role in organizing the response of the local Red Cross in Jamaica to victims of a serious hurricane in the community in which she did her service. Other students have taken leadership roles in developing new strategies for teaching English to local children, leading an effort to develop the documentation needed to resolve a local border dispute, and assisting a local ministerial association in reorganizing its administrative procedures.

One of the most important dimensions of ISL for IPSL students is in the reflection in which they engage, particularly about the connections (or disconnections) between what students are learning in the academic courses and what students are observing and experiencing in the service activities. IPSL students keep a reflective written journal, discussed on a weekly basis with a faculty advisor and often using as a source of questions the book, *Charting a Hero's Journey* (Chisholm, 2000), as a guide to reflecting on the stages of the ISL experience. At the same time, the students are also writing a study of the service agency in which they are working, with a particular focus on how the agency serves its particular clientele in the context of the national culture in which it is located. Through reflection and writing, the ISL students are challenged to examine their assumptions about other national or local cultures, about the capacities and resources of local communities, and about the nature and causes of change, stability, and/or decline in a given social and economic setting.

Evaluating IPSL's ISL: An Initial Look

Since its inception in the early 1980s, IPSL has sought to support research and evaluation on the impact of service learning programs. IPSL has been particularly concerned about the ways in which ISL can (a) deepen the quality of undergraduate and graduate student learning and understanding; (b) support long-lasting change in the quality of teaching in colleges and universities; and (c) broaden the effectiveness of service agencies in meeting community needs.

IPSL has provided forums for discussing service learning research issues at its international conferences since the late 1980s; during the past 10 years, the organization has published books and curricular materials intended to help service learning and ISL practitioners deepen their effectiveness.

Beginning in 2001, IPSL undertook its first formal effort to answer two major questions, both about its own ISL programs and about postsecondary service learning in general. First, what do we know about the students who engage in service learning, particularly in international and intercultural contexts, and how effective are programs such as those offered by IPSL for these students? Secondly, do IPSL programs bring about change in the students who participate and in the communities they serve?

The evaluation is reported in *Service Learning Across Cultures: Promise and Achievement* (Tonkin, 2004). Funded by the Ford Foundation, the book reports on the effects of IPSL programs not only on students, but also on the service agencies and nongovernmental organizations where the students work and on the colleges and universities that host IPSL programs. The report also includes a profile of IPSL's students—the institutions they came from, their background, and their interests—and a research agenda for both future research on IPSL's own programs and other programs that have a significant ISL component. Among the study's major findings on the impact of ISL on IPSL's students are the following:

- ISL is a more radical educational experience than conventional study abroad and is likely to have a long-term effect on participating students. IPSL students underwent transformative intellectual and moral change, developed a pluralistic worldview, and often made career choices on the basis of the IPSL experience.
- Students participating in IPSL programs were adaptable, highly motivated, and eager to test theory against practice. They were comfortable with ambiguity and often displayed a strongly civic-minded personality.
- Students in IPSL programs achieved intense engagement with their host societies. All students going abroad suffered culture shock to some degree, but IPSL students, because of their level of engagement, found reentry to American society especially difficult.
- Students in IPSL programs developed significant qualities of leadership, including adaptability and resourcefulness, ability to look at old problems with fresh eyes, and recasting familiar issues in light of broader experience—all characteristics fundamental to a lifetime of leadership and community engagement.

Regarding colleges and universities, the study found that:

- IPSL programs were most successful at host colleges and universities where a campus-wide service learning philosophy and pedagogy address a specific institutional opportunity or priority, especially in institutions in developing nations or when the development of such programs coincides with the arrival of new campus leadership. Less responsive are large institutions in developed nations with a weaker tradition of community involvement and a stronger adherence to traditional academic procedures and pedagogy.
- Successful IPSL depended heavily on creative institutional leadership, and such factors as careful planning, creation of accommodating administrative structures, engagement and buy-in from administrators and faculty at many levels, and linkages of institutional mission with its implementation through service learning.

As for service agencies and nongovernmental organizations:

- IPSL students were particularly useful to service agencies and nongovernmental organizations because of their high degree of commitment over a long period of time, their special skills and experiences, the cultural diversity they brought, and the close relationships they built with service users. In return, agencies were effective in looking after and protecting students, and agency staff members often built strong bonds with students that were hard to break at the conclusion of a program.
- Service agencies and nongovernmental organizations in which IPSL students served often increased their regard for the value of volunteer help. The agencies experienced a strong sense of reciprocity with the student volunteers and their host colleges and universities.
- Service agencies and nongovernmental organizations would like to be involved in planning the service learning activities and in the academic work the students did as part of their service learning program.

An Evaluation Outcome: A New Focus on Leadership and Engagement

The IPSL study (Tonkin, 2004) did not begin with a focus on the link between service learning and student leadership and community engagement skills. Nonetheless, college, university, and service agency leaders interviewed for the study, as well as students themselves, repeatedly mentioned how valuable the IPSL experience had been in developing leadership skills and in shaping students' career and vocational aspirations toward public service, non-profit organizations, or later experiences in AmeriCorps or the Peace Corps. In addition, some students reported that they had sought out leadership and engagement opportunities after returning to their home colleges and universities, and/or graduate programs in leadership-related fields, as a result of their IPSL experiences.

One consequence of the evaluation study has been a renewed commitment by IPSL to making explicit in its own programs and advocacy the ways in which ISL contributes to the education of future leaders and citizens— particularly those who will enter careers in nongovernmental organizations focused on international work. An initial step for IPSL's work in leadership and engagement is at the undergraduate level, in which IPSL has begun to work with its partner programs to incorporate leadership and engagement into the existing service learning course, "Institutions in Society," now offered at each program site. Designed to make the explicit linkage for students between academic study of the society, culture, and history of the host nation and the service agency in which the students are placed, the course includes reflective journal (in consultation with the faculty member[s] teaching the course) and a major written study of the service agency in its national or cultural context. IPSL is working over the next several years with its program directors and faculty members to incorporate leadership and engagement topics in the course as well as a written study by each student of the ways in which leadership is practiced in a service agency or nongovernmental organization.

References

Annette, J. (2003). Service-learning internationally: Developing a global civil society. In S. Billig & J. Eyler (Eds.), *Deconstructing service-learning: Research exploring context, participation and impacts* (pp. 241–249). Greenwich, CT: Information Age.

Chisholm, L. A. (2000). *Charting a hero's journey.* New York: The International Partnership for Service-learning.

Chisholm, L. A. (2004). *Declaration of principles.* New York: The International Partnership for Service-learning and Leadership (Rev. 2007).

Furco, A. (1996). Service-learning: A balanced approach to experiential education. In *Expanding boundaries: Service and learning* (pp. 2–6). Washington DC: Corporation for National Service.

Holland, B. (2003). Civic engagement in Australia [Special issue]. *Metropolitan Universities, 14*(2).

International Partnership for Service-Learning and Leadership. (2009). *Semester service-learning study abroad programs.* Retrieved August 31, 2009, from http://www.ipsl.org/programs/programs.aspx

JET. (2006). *JET educational services: Annual report 2006.* Braamfontein, South Africa: JET Educational Trust.

Lazarus, J. (2004). Community engagement. In *South African higher education in the first decade of democracy* (chapter 7). Cape Town, South Africa: The South African Council on Higher Education. Retrieved August 13, 2009, from http://www.che.ac.za/documents/d000081/index.php

McIlrath, L., & MacLabhrainn, I. M. (2007). *Higher education and civic engagement: International perspectives.* Surrey, UK: Ashgate.

Perold, H. (2005). *Civic engagement in higher education: An overview of participating universities.* Retrieved September 12, 2005, from http://president.tufts.edu/conference/trend.shtml

Perold, H., Stroud, S., & Sherraden, M. (Eds.). (2003). *Service enquiry. Service in the 21st century* (pp. 47–58). Cape Town, South Africa: Compress.

Plater, W. M., Jones, S. G., Bringle, R. G., & Clayton, P. H. (2009). Educating globally competent citizens through international service learning. In R. Lewin (Ed.), *The handbook of practice and research in study abroad: Higher education and the quest for global citizenship* (pp. 485–505). New York, NY: Routledge.

Thomson, A. M., Smith-Tolken, A., Naidoo, T., & Bringle, R. G. (2008, July). *Service learning and civic engagement: A cross-cultural perspective.* Paper presented at the 8th International Conference of the International Society for Third Sector Research (ISTR) and 2nd European Conference of the EMES European Research Network and ISTR, Barcelona, Spain.

Tonkin, H. (Ed.). (2004). *Service-learning across cultures: Promise and achievement. A report to the Ford Foundation.* New York: International Partnership for Service-Learning and Leadership.

United Board for Christian Higher Education in Asia and International Christian University. (2002). *Service-learning in Asia: Creating networks and curricula in higher education.* Tokyo, Japan: International Christian University.

4

NEW LINES OF INQUIRY IN REFRAMING INTERNATIONAL SERVICE LEARNING INTO GLOBAL SERVICE LEARNING

Nicholas V. Longo and John Saltmarsh

"[O]ur systems of education have long given us far too little information about lives outside our borders, stunting our moral imaginations."

(Nussbaum, 2002, p. xiv)

... how students understand "America" has implications for future practices of citizenship. Citizens with an exclusionary, closed notion of the relationship between the national and state may seek to create one type of world, while citizens who have a more open, inclusive, sense of citizenship may struggle to create another. Thus, the perspectives that students bring back with them are part of public discourse in the United States and have implications for the future of American democracy, the public good, and the constant renegotiation of the material and imaginative space that is America. (Dolby, 2004, p. 173)

Service Learning as Global Education

During the last decade, globalization has had an impact on every sector of American society. For American higher education, the social, economic, cultural, and political interconnections of the world, along with the increasing ease of sharing ideas and knowledge, have highlighted the importance of bringing global perspectives into the undergraduate experience. Yet, as Bok (2006) contends, "It is a safe bet that a majority of undergraduates complete their four years with very little preparation either as citizens or as professionals for the international challenges that are likely to confront them" (p. 233).

Although the percentage of undergraduates participating in international education experiences is small, it is growing rapidly. A survey conducted by the American Council on Education (Siaya, Porcelli, & Green, 2002) found that at a time when 90% of the American public agreed that knowledge about international issues is important to careers of younger generations, just over 241,000 U.S. students studied abroad for credit in 2006/2007—just over 1% of all students enrolled in American higher education. Yet, according to *Open Doors*, the Institute for International Education's annual survey (2008) of student mobility, funded by the U.S. Department of State, this represents an increase of 8% over the prior year's figures. This latest increase builds on steady growth over the past few decades. In the last decade, study abroad increased by 150%, up from under 100,000 in 1996/1997, part of the trend that saw study abroad participation increase 9% annually over the past 10 years. But interestingly, much of the increase over the past ten years has come from short-term programs (8 weeks or less), while long-term programs of a year have fallen to less than 5% of total study abroad participation and semester programs have remained relatively flat at 40% (Institute of International Education, 2008).

Service learning has grown over the past two decades as a pedagogy that effectively produces a number of educational outcomes (e.g., learning course content in a discipline, to civic learning and leadership development; see Eyler, chapter 10). In this chapter, we consider its impact on education for global citizenship.

> Service learning in an international context, for the purposes of this discussion, refers to a *structured academic experience in another country* in which students (a) participate in an organized service activity that addresses identified community needs; (b) learn from *direct interaction and cross-cultural dialogue* with others; and (c) reflect on the experience in such a way as to gain a deeper understanding of *global and intercultural* issues, a broader appreciation of the *host country* and the discipline, and an enhanced sense of their own responsibilities as citizens, locally and *globally*. (Bringle & Hatcher, chapter 1)

Within this context, we want to emphasize the pedagogical complexity that surfaces, along with the implications of that complexity for service learning, in an increasingly diverse domestic environment.

Service learning in an international context requires practitioners and researchers to consider a diverse set of global outcomes that expand upon the design and goals of domestic service learning programs and courses. It also prompts the service learning practitioner and researcher to consider not only outcomes associated with civic engagement, but the parameters of citizenship defined by globalization, migration, national identity, regionalism, nationalism, and human rights. As Falk (1993) wrote,

> Citizenship, in general, expresses membership and the quality of participation in a political community. Its conditions can also be specified by law, but its reality is a matter of politics and the rigors of the experience. Thus, citizenship can be understood both formally as a status and, more adequately, existentially as a shifting set of attitudes, relationships, and expectations with no necessary territorial delimitation. (Falk, 1993, p. 39)

An exploration of the multiple dimensions of service learning in an international context opens doors to new areas of literature, new questions about program design and learning outcomes, and new perspectives on citizenship and intercultural understanding. All of these perspectives have direct relevance for the design and implementation of domestic service learning programs, and a global perspective necessitates a change in the way educators understand and engage with their local communities. Thus, research on international service learning (ISL) also contributes new perspectives on service learning in communities surrounding campuses. Scholarship suggests the importance of connecting a type of cosmopolitan education called for by Nussbaum (2002) and others (e.g., Appiah, 2006; Lewin, 2009; Schattle, 2008; Tarrow, 2006), who argue for educating students to be citizens of the world, with the practice of citizenship in local communities. In short, an examination of ISL, including studying it through research, invites examination about the global dimensions of service learning and civic practice in relation to the local, including designing education and practice for "cosmopolitan/local knowledge" (Battistoni, Longo, & Raill, 2009; Rhoades, Kiyama, McCormick, & Quiroz, 2008). This connection of the local and the international suggests that the framing of ISL may itself be limiting in its focus on the location of the service. The partnerships are international, but the service generates learning that is global. We want to argue here for a shift to an emphasis on outcomes that connect the local and international into the global. Instead of ISL, we prefer the framing of global service learning (GSL).

This chapter will explore some central conceptual frameworks related to the richly textured perspectives that GSL provides, including the implications these frameworks have for the design of programs, and then offer suggestions for research that can deepen understanding of the outcomes of GSL courses and programs. First, we will examine the competencies of global citizenship introduced through GSL, including the possibilities for seeing global citizenship as a core competency of civic professionalism. Second, we examine the significance of focusing on *reciprocity* as a core value of GSL. Although relations with international community partners are complex, as they are politically, economically, and socially contextualized (Sutton, chapter 7), mutuality in partnerships must always be the foundation for this work. Finally, we conclude with the implications of a global perspective on service learning programs and research. We assert that a global framework introduced through GSL has relevance for how the service experience is perceived and the outcomes that are articulated, regardless of where the service takes place. We also believe that interrogating these frameworks can have implications for domestic service experiences and the design of education opportunities for students engaged in local community-based learning and research.

Competencies of Global Citizenship

In an age of global migration and extensive high-speed communications, with people of different cultures and ethnicities engaging in a variety of social, political, and economic relationships, introducing students to the knowledge, skills, and values needed for civic engagement becomes a vital necessity. As Banks (2004) argues, "citizenship education should also help students acquire the attitudes, knowledge, and skills needed to function in communities other than their own, within the national culture and community, as well as within the global community" (p. 7).

However, Bok (2006) laments not only the lack of preparation of students for global citizenship, but he is also critical of the lack of ways to measure the extent to which campuses are becoming internationalized, noting that most measures rely on assessing inputs, like the number of students studying abroad and international students on campuses, rather than outcomes (e.g., skills, knowledge, and values). To address the lack of preparation for global citizenship, Bok proposes, among other things, at least a two-course sequence to prepare students for a global society, "a basic course on America's role in the world to help equip undergraduates to be reasonably informed citizens and a course on how to understand another culture that prepares them for lives characterized by increasing contact with other societies" (Bok, 2006, p. 252). The competencies for these courses—knowledge of America's role in the world and real-world opportunities for the understanding of another culture—are appropriate measures of global citizenship that should emerge from GSL.

Increasing attention has been paid to the development of civic learning outcomes through service learning (Battistoni, 2002; Howard, 2001; Saltmarsh, 2005; Westheimer & Kahne, 2004), drawing on the work of Sullivan. Sullivan (1995) reframes professional practice and social responsibility through the concept of civic professionalism. The concept of civic professionalism captures the understanding that "there is finally no successful separation between the skills of problem solving and those of deliberation and judgment, no viable pursuit of technical excellence without participation in those civic enterprises through which expertise discovers its human meaning" (Sullivan, 1995, p. xix)—and it provides a framework for designing global learning outcomes. What are the dimensions of civic professionalism in a global context? That is, what are the qualities of a civic professional when professional practice is increasingly conducted in a global context? Are there global competencies necessary for civic professionals? If so, how do we design ISL courses and programs that make explicit learning *outcomes* linked to the development of these global competencies?

Global competencies for students typically include outcomes commonly found in study abroad programs, such as language skills, knowledge of the host country, and intercultural sensitivity (Kahn, chapter 6; Kiely, chapter 11; Sutton, chapter 7). Global outcomes could also include competencies more common in service learning programs, such as civic agency. Boyte (2008) refers to civic agency as, "the broader set of capacities and skills required to take confident, skillful, imaginative, collective action in fluid and open environments where there is no script."

The American Council on Education (2005a), with support from the Ford Foundation, for example, initiated a project called "Global Learning for All" in which institutions provided examples of good practice in setting international learning goals. The American Council on Education (2005a) distinguishes between three types of learning goals, (a) global (denoting the systems and phenomena that transcend national borders), (b) international (focusing on the nations and their relationships), and (c) intercultural (focusing on knowledge and skills to understand and navigate cultural differences). Thus, they define global learning as "the knowledge, skills, and attitudes that students acquire through a variety of experiences that enable them to understand world cultures and events; analyze global systems; appreciate cultural differences; and apply this knowledge and appreciation to their lives as citizens and workers" (American Council on Education, 2005a). This definition of global learning weaves together the local and the international into a holistic view of global citizenship.

One of the participating campuses in the project, Kennesaw State University, has identified the following global learning outcomes for international education: "global perspectives [knowledge], intercultural communication/cross-cultural adjustment [skills], and social justice and sustainable development [values]" (American Council on Education, 2005b). At the Pacific Lutheran University, global learning outcomes are formulated as learning objectives throughout a curricular pathway that links first-year inquiry seminars, international core courses, short off-campus January term courses, the major, semester abroad, internships, undergraduate research, and a disciplinary or interdisciplinary capstone experience. The learning objective categories are (a) knowledge and intellectual skills, (b) cultural knowledge and skills, (c) global perspectives, and (d) personal commitment (Kelleher, 2005).

Colleges and universities have responded to the need for global competencies not only through program development, but also through institutional restructuring. For example, Macalester College recently launched an Institute for Global Citizenship with the mission "to encourage, promote, and support rigorous learning that prepares students for lives as effective and ethical "global citizen-leaders"; innovative scholarship that enriches the public and academic discourse on important issues of global significance; and meaningful service that enhances such learning and/or scholarship while enriching the communities within which Macalester is embedded" (Institute for Global Citizenship, 2008).

In order to achieve these ideals, the Institute has formed a new administrative unit that brings together the Civic Engagement Center and International Studies and Programming, which encompasses the International Studies department and the International Center, all of which is overseen by a Dean of Global Citizenship. Macalester has created an institutional structure that combines the local and the international with the goal of global citizenship as an educational outcome.

Because Macalester has a high proportion of international students and more than half of the students studying abroad for at least one semester in over 63 countries, education for global citizenship means applying principles of engagement in international, national, and local initiatives alike. Trail-Johnson, Associate Dean of the Institute, explains that the Institute is especially timely in a changing world that is more global and more interdependent, and that it hopes to help students to be "engaged citizens wherever [they] may find [themselves]" (Trail-Johnson, 2006). She outlines three primary characteristics of global citizens that the institute promotes, (a) a broad knowledge of social context and history of social issues; (b) creative skills around engagement and action, especially in working across differences; and (c) a vision oriented toward the common good (Trail-Johnson, 2006). These are all goals that have relevance in both local and international communities.

Macalester offers a course in Thailand focusing on educational and political reform activities, including community-based teaching experiences in Thai schools. To support a course like this, the Institute is developing a "Globalization in Comparative Perspective" seminar in the spring semester for students returning from international experiences. Furthermore, longer term plans include creating a certificate program in global citizenship and incorporating an introductory and capstone course as well as electives from the various academic divisions.

The focus on internationalism and globalization in the college curriculum has led to a tremendous growth of academic majors and minors in global studies over the past 10 years, along with a series of new academic journals, such as *Globalizations, New Global Studies,* and *global-e.* Programs are developing at schools as diverse as the University of California—Santa Barbara, the University of Wisconsin—Milwaukee, Providence College, and Hamline University. Although still somewhat ill-defined, many of the programs in global studies incorporate experiential education, including language requirements, study abroad, and integrated domestic and international experiences (Redden, 2008). These programs, and countless others, are elaborating definitions of competencies in global citizenship and drawing on best practices for domestic engagement, such as using reciprocity as a guiding principle in international partnerships.

Reciprocity in an International Context

"If you're going to take risks and be a democratic educator, you have to know the situation you are working in," explains Horton (1998, p. 193), who founded the Highlander Folk School that did some of the most innovative cross-cultural work in the United States, especially with Blacks and Whites working together during the civil rights movement. Horton tells the story of how, when asked to do work in communities outside the continental United States, he was hesitant because he "didn't know the situation" (Horton, 1998, p. 193). Highlander's approach to partnerships, which has served as a foundation for service learning in higher education today (Longo, 2007), was based on a deep and grounded knowledge of the culture of the people in communities. Although Horton was aware that he might gain understanding by reading and talking with people, international education was "all foreign to my experience" (Horton, 1998, p. 194). Horton said of his international work, "I don't know anything about your situation and I'm not going to be here long enough to learn" (Horton, 1998, p. 194). At Highlander, reciprocity was valued through equal respect for the knowledge and experience that everyone brought addressing community issues. Horton knew enough about the importance of reciprocity to approach international community work cautiously.

Horton's experiences were prior to the flattening of the world and rapid globalization, and he did develop international partnerships and do workshops in Nicaragua, Peru, Brazil, New Zealand, Australia, and other countries during his 58-year career at Highlander. But he still offers an important insight for GSL, the core value of reciprocity and the challenge that it presents to good practice.

The work at Highlander emphasized the power of creating a safe and open environment where people could become acquainted with another culture through a mutual exchange of ideas and experiences. As with all of Horton's cross-cultural work, in international settings he began by using questions to give voice to local knowledge and experience. In a dialogue with the Brazilian educator Paolo Freire, Horton (Horton & Freire, 1990) points to the value of asking questions as a core for cross-cultural exchange because it helps to put a value on local, as opposed to expert, knowledge. As Horton says plainly, "one of the best ways to educate is to ask questions" (Horton & Freire, 1990, p. 147).

Horton and Freire both agree about the importance of respect for the backgrounds, experiences, and cultures of learners, a point that Freire expands upon by telling a story about an academic and a fisherman. He explains that being an academic is not a bad thing, it just depends on "what kind of academic" (Horton & Freire, 1990, p. 150). He tells about an academic who was out in a fishing area doing research when he meets a fisherman. After the academic asks, "Do you know who is the president of the country?" he followed up by asking if the fisherman knew "the governor of the state or at least the name of the local authority?" After getting a *no* to each of the questions, the fisherman began to ask questions to the academic. Did the academic know the name of the different fish he had caught? The academic was forced to concede to the fisherman that he did not. Freire concludes, "You see? Each one with his ignorance" (Horton & Freire, 1990, p. 150).

If reciprocity is thought of in terms of a relationship that is defined by a mutually beneficial exchange between students who participate in ISL courses or programs and individuals who are part of the communities that North American students enter into, then deeper inquiry needs to be made into the dimensions of reciprocity in an international service context. GSL asks for a humility that is often absent in academic, expert culture, a humility that underscores Freire's story of local knowledge and cross-cultural exchange.

An essay on the lessons from the Zapatistas in Chiapas focuses on global solidarity provide guidance for reciprocity in GSL. Olesen (2004) points to the Zapatista phrase "asking we walk" as an approach that makes listening, rather than giving orders or proposing solutions, the guiding feature for international partnerships. Olesen (2004) further explains:

> The principle of "asking we walk" clearly reflects the essentially democratic character of the Zapatistas. Democracy is seen not only as an end, but also an integral part of the process of social change and it is a perspective that makes it impossible to predefine the path of social struggle or revolution and to think of a defined point of arrival. (p. 261)

In analyzing the concept of mutuality, Olesen also brings important lessons for GSL. He explains that when people visit Chiapas, they "aren't going as teachers, but as students" (Olesen, 2004, p. 260). And yet, the experience most often calls upon people to "want to apply what they've learned in Chiapas to community organizing [in their home communities]" (Olesen, 2004, p. 260). Thus, to be in solidarity with the Zapatistas, Olesen (2004) quotes American supporters as saying, "does not mean to simply write letters to your congressperson" (Olesen, 2004, p. 260). A focus on mutuality also means fighting against racism, sexism, homophobia, and economic inequality everywhere.

In GSL, then, reciprocity requires students who enter new communities, most often very different from their home communities, to go beyond an approach that emphasizes "doing no harm." Students participating in international partnerships should be prepared not to have expectations for meaningfully contributing to community change, but they can be prepared to participate in reflective inquiry on the origins and intent of the projects in which they participate, the relationship of the projects to the social and power structures of the host community and country, and the degree to which their projects and activities might either perpetuate or liberate political, social, and economic structures.

Students can engage in reflective inquiry related to the nature of service as a cultural construction in the community they have entered into (Whitney & Clayton, chapter 8). Interrogating the culture of service in a country other than the United States, for instance, can reveal insights into understanding various purposes and meanings of service, which can then open up the possibilities for a deeper analysis and understanding of service in the U.S. context (Sutton, chapter 7).

Implications of Global Perspectives on Practice and Research

The phases of a service learning experience grounded in domestic practice can have application for GSL. Deliberate design of curricular pathways for engagement closely connected to pre-service preparation and post-service reflection and reentry seem likely to lead to deeper outcomes, particularly outcomes associated with professional practice and civic capacity. GSL suggests that pre-service preparation can and should be connected to domestic service learning and that post-service reflection also be woven into local service. GSL design weaves together the domestic and international experiences, enriching both and fostering deeper learning. Future research on each of these propositions should be conducted.

Although preparation is normally a key component of any service learning experience, preparation for GSL suggests greater attention to many of the logistical elements, including finances, travel, visa requirements, and other more mundane issues like figuring out what to pack. Students, in some circumstances, can begin conversations with people in their host communities using the Internet. Preparation should include academic work, such as reading about and reflecting upon the political, economic, cultural, historical, and social issues of the cultures and country of the people students will work with. The preparation, ideally, could include learning from immigrant members of the local community, when possible. Students can interview community members about their home countries, and utilize the rich international and cultural resources in their home communities and campuses. The efficacy of each of these interventions provides opportunities for research that can contribute to an understanding of the best ways to reach their respective goals.

Preparation might include reading and discussions about service, community, and citizenship in different contexts. And any preparation for GSL that is centered upon reciprocity should also include readings on challenges to providing service in an international context. For instance, students might read Illich's (1993) provocative speech, "To Hell with Good Intentions," to provide them with an insightful critique that calls into question the very possibility of finding common ground in GSL. Illich makes known his opposition to North American "do-gooders" in Latin America and challenges the idea that the service by international volunteers is relevant or helpful to the communities they hope to serve. Illich concludes that international visitors are welcome as travelers or students, but not as volunteers. He writes: "Come to look, come to climb our mountains, to enjoy our flowers. Come to study. But do not come to help" (Illich, 1993, p. 460). Illich challenges international groups to think not only about the training of international visitors, but also about "spending money to educate poor Mexicans in order to prevent them from the culture shock" of meeting with Western students (Illich, 1993, p. 459).

Additionally, as with all international experiences, issues of reentry must be addressed by home institutions for students who have been involved in service learning projects abroad (Kiely, chapter 11). Reentry issues are likely to be greater for GSL because students will be invited to engage with people from very different backgrounds (in many study abroad experiences, on the other hand, students can avoid interaction with the local cultures). Intensive opportunities for critical reflection, along with opportunities to continue to support international community partners and address global issues that surface in local ways are core considerations for returning students.

A series of ideas for reentry are presented by Kiely (2004; chapter 11), one of the most prominent advocates for GSL. Kiely's longitudinal research on students involved in an ISL course in Nicaragua documents the transformational aspects of community-based learning in international settings. He also finds a "chameleon complex" upon reentry where students often have difficulty translating their transformations into action in the very different settings to which they return. As a result, Kiely suggests a series of strategies for faculty "to help students turn their emerging global consciousness . . . into meaningful action" (Kiely, 2004, p. 17). These include asking students to develop a contract specifying actions they hope to take when they return home. Other ways to create a community of support for students upon reentry include creating a post-program course for further reflection and to help them follow through on action plans, along with an alumni network.

One rich and sophisticated example of a GSL design that incorporates pre-service preparation, linkages between domestic immigrant communities and international experiences, curricular integration, post-service reentry, and outcomes shaped by civic professionalism is "Global Multicultural Track on Cultural Competence of Preclinical Medical Students" at the University of Massachusetts Medical School. Medical students can choose between a traditional medical school curriculum or an enhanced cultural competence track aimed at developing "the linguistic and cultural competence of preclinical medical students" (Godkin & Savageau, 2001). The specific learning goals of the Global Multiculturalism Track are, "(1) develop abilities to speak the language of a prevalent newcomer population (i.e., immigrant, refugee, and undocumented) in Massachusetts; (2) develop sensitivity, through first-hand experiences, to the difficulties people experience living in a new country; (3) develop understanding of the culture and health beliefs of a newcomer group and the problems they face in obtaining health care and other services in the United States; and (4) promote a career preference to serve underserved and multicultural populations" (Godkin & Savageau, 2001, p. 179).

The centerpiece of the curriculum is the integration of domestic and international learning experiences during the preclinical years. The professional context for the program is the need in medical education for cultural diversity training to serve multicultural and underserved populations. The demographic context for the program is that Massachusetts is the seventh leading state for immigrants, with significant populations coming from Southeast Asia, the former Soviet Union, China, Central America, the Dominican Republic, and Portuguese-speaking countries. Forty percent of the state's residents are recent newcomers or the children of immigrants or refugees. In the city of Worcester, where the Medical School is located, 15% of the population is foreign-born and just under 30% speak a language other than English at home (Godkin & Savageau, 2001, p. 178; Godkin, n.d., p. 1).

The curriculum begins with the "Family Curriculum" in which students in the fall of their first year of medical school work with a local family of a culture whose language the student is interested in learning. In the summer after their first year, students in the track complete a six-week language and cultural immersion experience—"Language Immersion Abroad"—in "a country in the developing world that is linguistically and culturally reflective of populations in Massachusetts" (Godkin & Savageau, 2001, p. 179). In the fall of the second year of medical school, students participate in a required "Domestic Community Service Project" that serves a group whose native culture/language is being studied by the student (Godkin, Savageau, & Fletcher, 2006). As part of the students' "Fourth-Year Elective," they are encouraged "to go to a country where their experiences were likely to support a desire to serve underserved populations, including recent immigrants" (Godkin, et al., 2006, p. 228). Finally, students in the Global Multiculturalism Track attend a "Seminar Series" every month that "focuses on topics such as cultural issues in the doctor–patient relationship, spirituality in the doctor–patient relationship, and the art of reflective practice in personal growth" (Godkin & Savageau, 2001, p. 179).

The development of civic professionalism and civic agency is apparent in the practice of the students involved in the curriculum. One student reflected on the experience by noting,

> a common thread between my experiences working to provide health care access to underserved populations patients in Worcester and the goal of successful tuberculosis treatment for patients in the Amazon. It was exciting to recognize that with my training I can be part of these common threads of health care delivery at an international level and a local level, in English and now in Spanish, in Boston, or in Ecuador. (Godkin et al., 2006, p. 231)

Students participating in the cultural competency track also initiated a series of community service projects for residents in the local community. After a domestic community service experience at a community health center, students started an obesity prevention project. After language training abroad, students started a weekly free clinic for Portuguese- and Spanish-speaking immigrants. After a community-based course on refugee health, students started a school mentoring program for recent refugees. These students found ways to connect their local and international experiences, bringing each to bear on their work in community.

The program at the University of Massachusetts Medical School also surfaces an appreciation of the varieties of global citizenship. Just as Westheimer and Kahne (2004) ask the question, "What kind of citizen do we need to support an effective democratic society?" when they evaluated the dimensions of citizenship reflected in school programs, studies of global citizenship indicate that there are varieties of global citizenship (p. 242). Falk (1993), for instance, distinguished five categories of global citizenship: (a) the global reformer who advocates for a world government or world state, (b) the transnational citizen engaged in global business activities, (c) the global citizen focused on managing global environmental and economic issues, (d) supporters of regional governance structures such as the European Union, and (e) transnational activists involved in grassroots organizations fighting for human rights and political democracy.

Some of these varieties of global civic engagement represent what Falk (1993) calls "globalization-from-above, reflecting the collaboration between leading states and main agents of capital formation" (p. 39). Others, particularly the last, represents "globalization-from-below" that consists of "an array of transnational social forces animated by environmental concerns, human rights, hostility to patriarchy, and a vision of human community based on the unity of diverse cultures seeking to end poverty, oppression, humiliation, and collective violence" (Falk, 1993, p. 39). Cognizance of the varieties of global civic involvement can, and should, influence the design of GSL and articulated outcomes. The Global Multicultural Track at the University of Massachusetts Medical School has characteristics that align strongly with Falk's fifth category and the impetus for globalizations-from-below. Other programs may be more aligned with other types of global citizenship. Advocates for GSL need to ask the question Westheimer and Kahne (2004) asked, "What political and ideological interests are embedded in varied conceptions of citizenship?" (p. 246).

An Emerging Research Agenda

Programs like the one at the University of Massachusetts Medical School suggest a research agenda that explores the characteristics of effective GSL that focus on competencies and the learning outcomes of GSL programs and courses. As appropriate, researchers will need to create instruments that measure and evaluate the development of these different kinds of global civic competencies (Bringle, Hatcher, & Williams, chapter 12; Gillespie, Braskamp, & Dwyer, 2009) and qualitative methods (Kiely & Hartman, chapter 13) that use various sources of evidence (e.g., reflection products, see Whitney & Clayton, chapter 8).

Although research on community outcomes is difficult due to the complexity of confounding variables—perhaps even more complex in an international setting—research can be pursued that employs the model offered by Cruz and Giles (2000). Studies can focus on the campus–foreign community partnership as the unit of analysis and examine the properties or characteristics of the partnership and the effects on the service provided to the community (Bringle, Clayton, & Price, 2009; Clayton, Bringle, Senor, Huq, & Morrison, 2010). This research asks the question: " . . . are service and/or learning better because of the quality of the partnership" (Cruz & Giles, 2000, p. 31). Evidence from these kinds of studies is essential for understanding effective GSL course or program design for community improvement and building effective, reciprocal, and equitable international partnerships.

Research can also explore student outcomes for students who participate in GSL experiences. What is the impact on students who do service in international contexts that represent the nationalities and cultures of the local immigrant populations, who also participate in complementary service learning with those communities domestically? Are these students more effective civic agents domestically and internationally? In what ways do they take their international experiences with them into new domestic service experiences? How does the connection of the local and international shape professional practice?

Finally, research can look deeply at the question of the connections and differences between international and domestic service learning. How can global outcomes be better incorporated into local service learning activities? And how can local outcomes become better incorporated into GSL? If we reframe the distinction between ISL and domestic service learning into a single framework of *global service learning*, are there a set of processes and outcomes that are universal? Are there some elements that are unique to international or domestic service?

GSL may allow an expansion of the maxim from the environmental movement to the service learning movement to "think globally and act locally." Perhaps research into the practice of GSL will call upon democratic-minded educators with an interest in global citizenship to engage with the "local" in new and different ways, to attempt to "be local" and "think and act globally" regardless of context. The more constituencies involved in GSL can critically reflect on international service experiences, develop global competencies, and act with respect for local wisdom and reciprocity, the more likely it is that service learning will be reframed and enriched and exciting lines of inquiry will be opened.

References

American Council on Education. (2005a). *Global learning for all*. Retrieved May 14, 2008, from www.acenet.edu/AM/Template.cfm?Section=fipse1&TEMPLATE=/CM/ContentDisplay.cfm&CONTENTID=19125

American Council on Education. (2005b). *Statements of international learning outcomes*. Retrieved August 6, 2009, from http://www.acenet.edu/AM/Template.cfm?Section=goodPractice&Template=/CM/HTMLDisplay.cfm&ContentID=1583#kennesaw

Appiah, K. (2006). *Cosmopolitanism: Ethics in a world of strangers*. New York, NY: Norton.

Banks, J. A. (Ed.). (2004). *Diversity and citizenship education: Global perspectives*. San Francisco, CA: Jossey-Bass.

Battistoni, R. (2002). *Civic engagement across the curriculum: A resource book for service-learning faculty in all disciplines*. Providence, RI: Campus Compact.

Battistoni, R., Longo, N., & Raill, S. (2009). Acting locally in a flat world: Global citizenship and the democratic promise of service-learning. *Journal of Higher Education Outreach and Engagement, 13*(2).

Bok, D. (2006). *Our underachieving colleges: A candid look at how much students learn and why they should be learning more*. Princeton, NJ: Princeton University Press.

Boyte, H. (2008). Against the current: Developing the civic agency of students. *Change, 40*(3). Retrieved July 23, 2009, from http://www.changemag.org/Archives/Back%20Issues/May-June%202008/full-against-the-current.html

Bringle, R., Clayton, P., & Price, M. (2009). Partnerships in service learning and civic engagement. *Partnerships: A Journal of Service-Learning and Civic Engagement*. Elon, NC: North Carolina Campus Compact.

Clayton, P., Bringle, R., Senor, B., Huq, J., & Morrison, M. (2010). Differentiating and assessing relationships in service-learning and civic engagement: Exploitative, transactional, or transformational. *Michigan Journal of Community Service Learning, 16*(2).

Cruz, N. I., & Giles, D. E. (2000, Fall). Where's the community in service-learning research? *Michigan Journal of Community Service Learning: Special Issue on Strategic Directions for Service Learning Research*, 28–34.

Dolby, N. (2004). Encountering an American self: Study abroad and national identity. *Comparative Education Review, 48*(2), 150–173.

Falk, R. (1993). The making of global citizenship. In J. Brecher, B. Childs, & J. Cutler (Eds.), *Global visions: Beyond the new world order*. Boston, MA: South End Press.

Gillespie, J., Braskamp, L., & Dwyer, M. (2009). Holistic student learning and development abroad: The IES 3-D Program Model. In R. Lewin (Ed.), *The handbook of practice and research in study abroad: Higher education and the quest for global citizenship* (pp. 445–465). New York, NY: Routledge.

Godkin, M. (n.d.). International medical education at UMass Medical School.

Godkin, M., & Savageau, J. A. (2001). The effect of a global multicultural track on cultural competence of preclinical medical students. *Family Medicine, 33*(3), 178–186.

Godkin, M. A., Savageau, J. A., & Fletcher, K. E. (2006). Effect of a global longitudinal pathway on medical students' attitudes toward the medically indigent. *Teaching and Learning in Medicine, 18*(3), 226–232.

Horton, M. (1998). *The long haul: An autobiography*. New York: Teachers College.

Horton, M., & Freire, M. (1990). *We make the road by walking: Conversations on education and social change*. Philadelphia, PA: Temple University Press.

Howard, J. (2001). *Michigan journal of community service learning, Service learning course design workbook*. Ann Arbor, MI: University of Michigan.

Illich, I. (1993). To hell with good intentions. In B. R. Barber & R. M. Battistoni (Eds.), *Education for democracy: Citizenship, community, service: A sourcebook for students and teachers* (pp. 456–460). Dubuque, IA: Kendall Hunt Publishing. (Original work published in 1968).

Institute for Global Citizenship. (2008). *Global citizenship*. Retrieved May 16, 2008, from www.macalester.edu/globalcitizenship/index.html.

Institute of International Education. (2008). *Open doors: Report on international student exchange*. New York, NY: Institute of International Education.

Kelleher, A. (2005). Global education continuum: Four phases. *Diversity Digest, 8*(3), 10.

Kiely, R. (2004). A chameleon with a complex: Searching for transformation in international service learning. *Michigan Journal of Community Service Learning, 10*(2), 5–20.

Lewin, R. (2009). *The handbook of practice and research in study abroad: Higher education and the quest for global citizenship*. New York, NY: Routledge.

Longo, N. (2007). *Why community matters: Connecting education with civic life*. Albany, NY: SUNY Press.

Nussbaum, M. (2002). *For love of country?* Boston, MA: Beacon Press Books.

Olesen, T. (2004). Globalizing the Zapatistas: From third world solidarity to global solidarity? *Third World Quarterly, 25*(1), 255–267.

Redden, E. (2008, February 21). Growing-and-defining global studies. Retrieved July 15, 2009, from http://www.insidehighered.com/news/2008/02/21/global

Rhoades, G., Kiyama, M., McCormick, R., & Quiroz, M. (2008). Local cosmopolitans and cosmopolitan locals: New models of professionals in the academy. *The Review of Higher Education, 31*(2), 209–235.

Saltmarsh, J. (2005). The civic promise of service learning. *Liberal Education 91*(2), 5–55.

Schattle, H. (2008). *The practices of global citizenship.* New York, NY: Rowan & Littlefield.

Siaya, L., Porcelli, M., & Green, M. (2002). *One year later: Attitudes about international education since September 11.* Washington DC, American Council on Education.

Sullivan, W. (1995). *Work and integrity: The crisis and promise of professionalism in America.* New York, NY: Harper Collins.

Tarrow, S. (2006). *The new transnational activism.* New York, NY: Cambridge University Press.

Trail-Johnson, K. (2006, March 15). Interview as part of Macalester Faculty Talks. Retrieved May 14, 2008, from www.macalester.edu/whatshappening/audio/archive/2006/macfac_031506.mp3

Westheimer, J., & Kahne, J. (2004). What kind of citizen? The politics of educating for democracy. *American Educational Research Journal, 41*(2), 237–269.

PART TWO

HOW COURSE DESIGN CAN INFORM RESEARCH ON INTERNATIONAL SERVICE LEARNING

5

AN ANALYSIS OF INTERNATIONAL SERVICE LEARNING PROGRAMS

Steven G. Jones and Kathryn S. Steinberg

R esearch on service learning suffers from a lack of clarity in defining *service learning* as an independent variable (Billig & Eyler, 2003; Bringle, Hatcher, & Williams, chapter 12). In practice, many community-based activities that carry the label *service learning* run the range of one-time service events as part of a course with little reflection and academic integration to service experiences of several hours per week during a semester with frequent and deep reflection. This lack of clarity can be multiplied in research on international service learning (ISL), the definition of which may have even greater variability than domestic service learning.

As a first cut to create greater clarity with respect to what ISL is, particularly when casting it as an independent variable in research, we make a distinction between ISL courses and ISL programs. ISL *courses* are individual courses, the content of which is at least partially completed in another country and in which some or all of the service is conducted in another country. We will discuss the variations of ISL courses in more detail below.

ISL *programs* integrate several courses, all of which are completed in another country, which last at least one academic term, and in which there is a service component for at least one of the courses. ISL programs can be offered through a college or university, or they may be coordinated by an intermediary organization. Examples of the latter type include those offered through the International Partnership for Service Learning and Leadership (IPSL), described by Brown (chapter 3), and the Amizade Global Service Learning Consortium, described by Kiely and Hartman (chapter 13).

The degree to which ISL occurs as part of a single-course or a program may be a factor in identifying the community, partnership, or student learning effects of ISL. These issues are explored in more detail below, after an analysis of the degrees of variation among ISL courses.

Variability in ISL Course Structure

Table 5.1 describes 20 types of variability that are possible in designing ISL courses, based on the locality of the course, whether the course is taught by host-country faculty or home-country faculty, the amount of service contact (H equals a high level of contact, L equals a low level of contact), and whether the course is content-focused or skill-focused (e.g., practica, competency-based curricula). In the sections that follow, these structural variations are analyzed in more detail.

All in the Host Country

ISL courses or programs that occur entirely in the host country have the potential advantage of providing students with greater contact with the host culture. However, a program can involve the completion of only a single course, and such courses tend to be of limited duration, generally six to eight weeks. The amount of service provided by the student may also vary, from a single service project to providing several hours of service per day during the duration of the course. In addition, whether students are taught by faculty from their home institution or a local institution may have an impact on students' learning, particularly their appreciation of teaching and learning

TABLE 5.1
Types of International Service Learning Course Structures

	All in Host Country		Sandwich 1		Sandwich 2		Practicum		Competency-Based Service	
Foreign Faculty	H	L	H	L	H	L	H	L	H	L
Domestic Faculty	H	L	H	L	H	L	H	L	H	L

H: a high level of service contact; L: a low level of service contact styles and strategies. Chisholm (2003) contends that faculty from host-country institutions are likely to be more knowledgeable about the local culture and current events and that students' learning will be enhanced by employing host-country expertise. Studies at a host institution can also provide students with exposure to a different type of educational system. Chisholm (2003) also warns that avoiding the use of host-country faculty may unintentionally suggest home-country superiority to students.

There are several case studies of service learning courses of this type. Wessel (2007) describes a sociology course taught in Mexico by a home-country professor. Students also enrolled in Spanish-language courses taught by host-country faculty at a local university. The service component of the course involved eight hours of service per week at one of three community sites. Wessel focuses on student outcomes related to participants' cultural adaptation and increases in cross-cultural understanding, but the study did not address academic outcomes related to the course or the discipline. Wessel acknowledges relying solely on students' reflections as the data source and the limitations of reflection products as a data source, particularly when students are not provided with structured instructions and expectations for writing reflection (see Whitney & Clayton, chapter 8, for suggestions for structuring reflection in ISL).

Smith-Paríolá and Gòkè-Paríolá (2006) describe a short-term ISL course taught for more than two weeks in Jamaica, with a variety of predeparture orientation activities. In addition to classroom instruction provided by home-country faculty, students in the program completed research-based service projects in local schools. The authors describe several shortcomings related to their short-term ISL course, including inconsistency in reflection activities, but did not directly address the degree to which the structure of the course might have affected student outcomes.

In contrast to case studies of individual courses, Tonkin and Quiroga (2004) describe the results of a focus-group study with participants in an ISL program organized through IPSL. As Brown describes (chapter 3), students enrolled in IPSL programs live at least one semester in the host country, take courses taught by host-country faculty, and are required to engage in 15–20 hours of service per week. As a result, student engagement with the host country and with service is more intense than in the types of host-country courses described by Wessel (2007) and Smith-Paríolá and Gòkè-Paríolá (2006). Because the Tonkin and Quiroga (2004) focus-group study was designed to assess the impact of only IPSL programs, the researchers did not compare their subjects' responses with participants in other types of ISL programs or courses. Although Tonkin and Quiroga do not report quantitative changes in students' attitudes as a result of their experiences, students did report changing their attitudes with respect to their ideas of service, their ability to cope with new cultures and with dealing with situations "outside of their comfort zone," their willingness to examine North American culture and foreign policy from the perspective of non-Americans, and their sense that their experiences profoundly shaped their future career choices, either by confirming their commitment to a chosen path or by identifying new paths.

Engle and Engle (2004) focus on a study abroad program for which community service with the host community is a requirement. Consequently, their study is concerned with the impact of the program as a whole as opposed to a single course component of the program. Program characteristics included a minimum stay of one semester, instruction in the target language by host-country faculty, homestays, structured reflection in a required intercultural competency course, and community service. They were primarily interested in the impact of the program on foreign language skills and intercultural sensitivity. The authors used standardized tests to assess pre- and postprogram competencies in language skills and intercultural sensitivity for program participants over the course of eight subsequent semesters. Despite already high preprogram scores on the cultural sensitivity measure, the authors report that over the period in question, students' postprogram scores improved on average by 33%. Engle and Engle did not compare student results in their program with students in other programs, but their study does provide a framework for future comparative studies given their use of standardized instruments and their discussion of specific program characteristics.

Peterson (2002) also examines ISL programs rather than courses by comparing three independent programs: the Center for Global Education at Augsburg College, the Higher Education Consortium for Urban Affairs, and the University of Minnesota Studies in International Development. This study focuses more on similarities and differences in program structures rather than the impact of the programs on students' learning. Peterson identifies core features of the programs that were believed to exemplify best practices: semester and year-long programs; host-country faculty instruction; service-based internships explicitly linked to academic learning objectives; a focus on addressing issues of power and privilege, not only within countries but also across countries; significant time for orientation, both predeparture and in-country; mission-driven programming; application of Freirian pedagogical techniques (Freire, 1970/2000); and structured, critical reflection assignments.

The key difference among the programs identified by Peterson is the degree to which each program emphasizes group cohesiveness among the participants versus increasing opportunities for cultural immersion for individual students. The value of Peterson's descriptive study of three similar, yet independent, programs is that it calls attention to program structure and characteristics. Unfortunately, it does not provide the researcher with any tools for more direct comparisons of program characteristics and their impact on student learning outcomes. The most valuable insight from Peterson's article is that program characteristics should be consistent with program goals.

Sandwich 1

As defined by Chisholm (2003), a sandwich structure occurs when there is a "pattern of several weeks of full-time study followed by full-time service" (p. 280) and concluding with another period of continued study, reflection, and examinations. One variation on the sandwich pattern is when the academic study occurs in the home country, with appropriate predeparture orientation to the host country, followed by a relatively brief period of service in the host country (e.g., during a fall or spring break period), and then a return to the home country for the conclusion of the course.

The review of the literature resulted in several single-case studies. For example, Lewis and Niesenbaum (2005) assessed the impact of a short-term (two-week) study abroad experience that was integrated into a full-semester course taught in the home country. They conducted an online survey of students who had completed the course between 1998 and 2003 to test the hypothesis that the benefits of short-term study abroad would be similar to those of longer term study abroad experiences if significant community-based experiences were part of the host-country experience. Although the authors report gains for students participating in the course, their study is limited in that there are no control groups, nor do they directly compare their students' results with results from studies of long-term study abroad.

Porter and Monard (2001) present another single-case study of a semester-long education course in which an ISL project occurred during the spring break. The service experience itself was organized by Amizade. The authors engaged in a qualitative evaluation of students' pre- and postservice written reflections, the field notes of one of the instructors, and interviews with community participants. Although the authors report that students were able to internalize the course concepts, their evidence consists of selected quotes from students' journals and the authors do not include comparisons of preservice reflections with postservice reflections. Results of the computer-aided analysis were not included in the article. Consequently, it is difficult to evaluate either the degree to which the short-term international service experience contributed to changes in students' attitudes and perceptions or the degree to which this experience would have produced significantly different results from domestic service learning or an extended community-based study abroad program or course.

Parker and Dautoff (2007) report on a variation of the sandwich structure in which the bulk of the course precedes the ISL component. They describe a business management course taught over a 13-week period in which the first 10 weeks occurred on the home campus and the final weeks were spent participating in an ISL project. Parker and Dautoff's qualitative analysis of student reflections seeks to separate students' learning that can be directly attributed to the service learning project versus what can be attributed to other learning activities and student experiences. Their conclusions demonstrate that the service learning project had a direct impact on 8 of 11 coded cognitive learning outcomes and all 4 affective learning outcomes. This study is useful in that it demonstrates how rigorous content analysis can identify where learning occurs as a result of a course, particularly when reflection is used for a wide range of learning activities, not just the service learning component. However, this study suffers from the same weakness as all single-case studies—lack of comparative analysis and small sample size.

Sandwich 2

This sandwich pattern also involves academic study at home with service abroad, but domestic service is also integrated with the service abroad. For example, a course on immigration issues may include domestic service with immigrant groups in the home community, followed by service work in "sending" communities, followed by follow-up service in the home country. This approach has the advantage of providing students with a comparative framework for analyzing an issue from different national perspectives. As beneficial as this variation might be, particularly in providing students with deep learning experiences in terms of analyzing social issues from a comparative perspective, no examples of this type appeared in the literature review.

Practicum

Another variation on the ISL course is the international service-based practicum or internship. In this structure, individual students study abroad as part of an intensive preprofessional learning experience. For example, some schools of education will allow students to complete student teaching in an international setting. Likewise, social work students might complete a bachelor's or master's level practicum or internship in another country. What defines such experiences as ISL depends on whether students are involved in community-based work that is linked to, but goes beyond, their practicum or internship requirements, and the degree to which students are required to reflect on such experiences. The potential benefit of this type of experience is that it provides students with a broader perspective on their chosen profession as well as providing them with an opportunity to explore the service orientation of the profession in a cross-cultural setting.

Several researchers and practitioners in professional disciplines (e.g., Currier, Lucas, & Saint Arnault, 2009; Cushner, 2009; Cushner & Mahon, 2002; Lindsey, 2005; Taylor, 1969; Wilson, 1982) have noted the need for international education and cross-cultural experiences for preprofessional students. A number of studies have attempted to identify what specific outcomes ISL practicum experiences have had on preprofessional teaching students, and in some cases, what long-term consequences such experiences had on their professional practice.

For example, Roberts (2003) analyzed an ISL course for preservice teachers conducted in Costa Rica. The course was taught over a four-week period at two sites in the host country. The service component involved English lessons provided by U.S. students to elementary-aged students. Roberts used a case-study methodology with multiple data sources, including student reflection products and videotapes of students giving lessons and giving presentations on their experiences upon return to the United States. The Roberts study focused primarily on the degree to which the ISL experience helped students develop "perspective consciousness," which she defined as "the active decision to realize issues through the eyes and minds of individuals representative of other cultures who maintain contrasting worldviews" (Roberts, 2003, p. 255). Based on the analysis of 30 students who participated in the course over a three-year period, Roberts identified three types of students according to the degree to which they demonstrated perspective consciousness (high, medium, and low).

The result of Roberts's open-ended qualitative approach is a student typology that provides a range of cultural competencies and adaptability. However, the study does not provide any analysis or attempt to explain why students who had similar learning experiences had dissimilar cultural responses other than to suggest that for students to benefit from ISL experiences, they must be predisposed to learn from and adapt to new cultural settings.

Cushner and Mahon (2002) also conducted an open-ended, qualitative study of participants in international student teaching experiences and the outcomes that emerged from those experiences. However, unlike Roberts (2003), Cushner and Mahon's study was grounded in several theoretical constructs related to cultural immersion and student development. In addition, their students had experiences of varying duration in several different countries, in contrast to Roberts's subjects who all had relatively similar experiences in the same country. Cushner and Mahon sent questionnaires to 50 in-service teachers who had completed overseas student teaching through the Consortium for Overseas Student Teaching.

Qualitative analysis of the responses to the questionnaire revealed that the respondents reported gains in cultural awareness, self-efficacy, and professional development. The analysis suggested that student narratives reflected the three highest stages in Bennett's (1993) model of intercultural sensitivity (acceptance, adaptation, integration). The authors concluded that respondents' international student teaching experiences contributed to these outcomes and that the respondents' increased cultural understanding and sensitivity carried over into their in-service teaching practices. The authors also concluded that these outcomes would not have emerged through traditional domestic student teaching. A weakness of Cushner and Mahon's study is that it does not take into account differences in students' prestudent teaching international and/or cultural experiences, or the quality of their predeparture orientations. Neither did they account for gender, age, or other personal variables.

Stachowski and Visconti (1997) conducted a study of participants in Indiana University's Overseas Student Teaching Project whose international student teaching had been arranged through the Consortium for Overseas Teaching. Although the students had varying placements, they all underwent similar predeparture orientation. Stachowski and Visconti examined not only the impact of the student teaching on student outcomes but also the contribution of the orientation to those outcomes. They also focused on a narrow range of student outcomes—"participants' ability to adapt to new ways of teaching, living, and generally doing, in a variety of cross-cultural situations and circumstances" (Stachowski & Visconti, 1997, p. 5). The authors used an open-ended questionnaire, which was administered following participants' third week in the host country. Stachowski and Visconti found that the most frequent responses to the questionnaire related to topics that were all covered in the orientation: adaptation to the host countries' educational system and classroom expectations, difficulties in adapting to living conditions in the host country, and adaptations with respect to interpersonal relations in the host country.

One of the benefits of the Stachowski and Visconti (1997) study is that it identified a structural element to international student teaching and its impact on student outcomes, in this case, the impact of predeparture orientation on students' ability to adapt to the host culture. The authors then used the results to make recommendations for improving predeparture orientation to prepare future student teachers better to adapt to new cultural environments. The weakness of their approach was that there was no attempt to control or account for other variables that might have affected students' adaptability, such as prior international or intercultural experiences, or whether the students were from urban or rural backgrounds, or their academic content specialization.

Stachowski, Richardson, and Henderson (2003) conducted another study of participants in Indiana University's Overseas Student Teaching Project, together with students who completed their student teaching on a Navajo Indian Reservation. Both projects required participants to have completed a full semester of local student teaching, a number of predeparture orientation activities, living with host families, completion of a service learning project, and participation in community events. In this study, the authors examined the degree to which exposure to host culture values, beliefs, and traditions affected participants' own values, classroom teaching, and community involvement.

The authors' analysis showed that participants were most likely to have reported applying local values to their professional practice and less likely to have reported applications of local values and beliefs to their personal and social actions. Overall, the authors concluded that the Overseas Teaching and Navajo Reservation programs had a positive impact on participants' understanding and application of host communities' cultures and beliefs, and that the participants actively sought to apply local cultural beliefs and traditions into their professional practices.

This study provides rich anecdotal evidence of the value of international student teaching in helping to improve preservice teachers' cultural understanding and sensitivity, particularly with respect to classroom teaching. Reflections cited in the study demonstrated that students actively sought to incorporate host values, beliefs, and traditions into lesson plans and learning activities. However, the authors did not complete an analysis of other variables that could have affected students' cultural awareness and practice, such as the impact of pre–student teaching requirements on the student teaching experience.

The studies of international student teaching described above share many commonalities. All are interested in how the international student teaching experiences were related to students' cultural understanding, sensitivity, and adaptability, and the degree to which these attributes are translated into teaching practice. These studies lend some support to the argument that preservice teachers would be more likely to develop cultural competence and global awareness were they to have more international experiences, preferably through international student teaching.

Another commonality of these studies is their reliance on qualitative methodologies. Each study used student narratives as their primary data source for qualitative analysis. Although such qualitative approaches provided rich data in terms of eliciting participants' descriptions of and reactions to their experiences, the studies also lacked the comparative power that emerges from the use of quasi-experimental design, quantitative measures of outcomes, and the identification of control variables (Bringle et al., chapter 12). This is not to say that qualitative approaches do not yield rich data or valuable examples of what and how students learn. Rather, qualitative approaches can be supplemented by techniques common to quantitative approaches, such as the use of quantitative measurement and control.

Competency-Based Service

Competency-based service learning occurs when the experience is part of the formal educational experience of the student but is not necessarily offered for credit. Rather, the experience is designed to allow students to meet required disciplinary or professional competencies. Such experiences are most common in the health science disciplines, such as dentistry, medicine, and nursing. Usually, these experiences are designed to provide students with opportunities to develop intercultural competencies related to their disciplines. For example, Dyjack, Anderson, and Madrid (2001) argued that Master of Public Health students should have international experiential education experiences such as ISL to meet professional competencies in an increasingly globalized world. Similarly, nursing educators Walsh and DeJoseph (2003) have argued for the necessity of cultural competencies in the nursing profession. Longo and Saltmarsh (chapter 4) provide an example from the University of Massachusetts School of Medicine.

Another argument for integrating international, competency-based programming into the health science disciplines is to make sure that participants have adequate medical knowledge to address the types of illnesses and social conditions they will likely encounter (Heck & Wedemeyer, 1991). Studies of international clinical experiences for medical students have demonstrated that students who have these international experiences are more likely to select primary care specializations (Gupta, Wells, Horwitz, Bia, & Barry, 1999; Pust & Moher, 1992; Ramsey, Haq, Gjerde, & Rothenberg, 2004); devote significant portions of their careers to provide medical care to underserved populations (Godkin & Savageau, 2003; Haq et al., 2000; Ramsey et al., 2004; Thompson, Huntington, Hunt, Pinsky, & Brodie, 2003); develop a greater understanding of global health issues and policies (Federico et al., 2006; Haq et al., 2000; Ramsey et al., 2004; Thompson et al., 2003); pursue public health–oriented career opportunities (Ramsey et al., 2004); and return to nonindustrialized countries to provide care and/or engage in research (Miller, Corey, Lallinger, & Durack, 1995; Ramsey et al., 2004). Such studies have contributed to calls for not only increasing international learning opportunities for medical students but also formally integrating international components into the core medical school curriculum (Drain et al., 2007). However, we should point out that, beyond international clinical practice broadening the scope of practice and experience, ISL entails working *with* the international community and focusing not only on the technical education of students but also their civic education.

Studies in medical education.   Our review of the medical education literature surfaced dozens of studies on the impact of international health experiences on medical students and their subsequent professional careers. Although few of these studies used the term ISL, the courses and programs being investigated were always service-oriented and frequently addressed specific clinical and/or cultural competencies. Consequently, these studies do address ISL as we define it. We review only the small proportion of those studies most relevant to this discussion.

Miller et al. (1995) studied the impact of Duke University's International Health Program (IHP), which provides overseas rotations for medical residents, on students' decisions about participating in the program; their understanding of international health issues and tropical medicine; their future career plans; and their comparative assessments of health care in the United States and other parts of the world. The authors conducted a single survey of all current and past residents between the years 1988 and 1996. Groups included residents who participated in the IHP, residents who did not participate in the program, and current residents who were preparing to participate in the program.

Compared with nonparticipants, students who completed international residency rotations were more likely to work overseas in the future, were more likely to forego private practice for academic medicine or public health careers, and were more likely to report a deeper understanding of tropical medicine. The authors concluded that the IHP did produce desired benefits for its participants.

Gupta et al. (1999) completed a similar study of the IHP at Yale University. They conducted a one-time survey of all students who completed their residencies between 1982 and 1996 and examined differences between

IHP participants and nonparticipants. Like Miller et al. (1995), Gupta et al. wanted to determine the impact of the IHP on participants' career choices and their attitudes toward American health care from a comparative perspective (p. 1020). Gupta et al. also wanted to determine how participation in the IHP affected participants' clinical practices, particularly with respect to providing care to underserved populations (p. 1021).

Overall, the authors concluded that the IHP at Yale University provided important personal benefits to participating physicians and social benefits to underserved communities and the medical profession as a whole. They noted the difficulty in eliminating the self-selection bias in such studies given that overseas clinical experiences have been elective experiences. However, they also concluded that the availability of international experiences for future physicians reinforces the desires of those who are motivated by a desire to provide care to underserved populations.

Haq et al. (2000) studied a single group of medical students who participated in an International Health Fellowship Program that involved students from multiple medical schools. Unlike the Miller et al. (1995) and Gupta et al. (1999) studies, Haq et al. did not survey a comparison group, but rather surveyed their target student population at four distinct intervals: on the first day of the fellows' predeparture course, immediately after the course, immediately following the completion of their international experience, and one to two years after the completion of their fellowship. The authors used a scaled survey instrument administered at the first three intervals and an open-ended questionnaire administered during the follow-up. The follow-up assessment also included a 10-item instrument measuring the impact of the international experience on respondents' clinical skills.

The authors identified statistically significant changes between the predeparture course and the postfield experience in participants' attitudes about issues such as providing health care in culturally diverse settings, enhanced clinical and communication skills, and changes in career plans. Although the authors recognized the limitations of their study (absence of a comparison group, highly selective nature of the target group), they contended that the value of the study was in supporting the case for providing more international programming for medical students.

Godkin and Savageau examined the impact of the University of Massachusetts Medical School's preclinical and clinical international experiences on participants' cultural competence (Godkin & Savageau, 2001) and attitudes and intentions related to serving underserved, culturally diverse populations (Godkin & Savageau, 2003). The 2001 study looked at the impact of the Medical School's Global Multiculturalism Track (GMT) on the cultural competencies and knowledge of preclinical medical students. The study was based on a pre–post, quasi-experimental design, comparing the students who completed the GMT to all other first-year medical students during the 1997 and 1998 academic years.

The authors used the Cultural Competence Self-Assessment Questionnaire (Mason, 1995) to assess respondents' cultural competence and knowledge. The authors' analysis of postexperience results showed that GMT students had statistically significant higher mean scores on 14 of the 43 items compared with non-GMT students. For seven of those items, there were statistically significant differences between the GMT students' pre- and post-experience scores, indicating that even though they had higher levels of cultural competence than their peers prior to the experience, their own cultural competence improved as indicated by those seven items. However, the authors also found that for some items, statistical significances in the pre-experience scores disappeared in the post-experience scores, indicating convergence between the test and control group students. These areas of convergence included attitudes about "limiting care for illegal immigrants, patients' responsibility for scheduling interpreters, desire to learn a new language even if interpreters are available, ability to treat all patients the same way, and knowledge about the cultural beliefs of the mentally ill" (Godkin & Savageau, 2001, p. 183).

In their conclusions, the authors noted the self-selection bias of the CMT participants and their comparatively high levels of cultural competence before completing the program. Nevertheless, they also argued that, "The Track appears at the very least to reinforce those traits of cultural competence," as well as contributing to participants' "higher levels of respect and compassion toward patients" (Godkin & Savageau, 2001, p. 185).

In another study, Godkin and Savageau (2003) investigated the impact of all international electives for preclinical and clinical students' attitudes about serving underserved populations. The authors included as their test group the cohort of all University of Massachusetts medical students who completed international electives between 1997 and 2003. As a comparison group they included all medical students from the 2002 academic year who did not complete an international elective experience. To measure the impact of international electives on medical students, the authors administered an instrument of their own design as a pre-travel/post-travel survey to all students with an international rotation and a start-of-year/end-of-year survey to the 2002 cohort of students who did not have an international rotation. The instrument included items to measure cultural competence, understanding the community context of medicine, humanistic self-awareness, and career interests.

The authors found statistically significant evidence that students who completed international electives demonstrated greater levels of cultural competency, humanistic values, and understanding of the community contexts of health care. The evidence tended to support the claim that medical students who complete international learning experiences would be more likely to pursue careers in primary medicine. The authors concluded that the value of international electives was that they reinforced the inclination toward primary care rather than directing students in that direction.

Comments. In spite of differences in research design and characteristics of the programs being investigated, the studies cited above reported a number of similar outcomes related to international learning experiences for medical students. Observed outcomes include enhanced cultural competencies, even when students had relatively high cultural competence prior to their international learning experiences; improved clinical skills, particularly with respect to using low-tech diagnostic techniques; increased commitment to public health careers; higher commitments to provide medical care to underserved populations; and generally improved medical knowledge. The replication of findings among different studies carried out at different points in time among different populations and across different programs lends greater credibility to the robustness of the findings.

However, another similarity, and a weakness, among the studies is the presence of self-selection bias. All of the programs under review involved elective or competitive program admission, which depended on applicants' demonstrating the very attitudes and competencies being measured by the subsequent studies. This was particularly true for the fellowship program examined by Haq et al. (2000) and the GMT investigated by Godkin and Savageau (2001, 2003). Thus, the researchers were led to conclude that international learning experiences did not necessarily "cause" greater commitments to public health careers, but rather reinforced preexisting inclinations held by participants. The degree to which international learning experiences would contribute to similar outcomes for students without such inclinations is still an unanswered question.

Along with the problem of self-selection, all of the studies reported that the majority of students had already participated in prior international experience and/or prior community service. This fact created difficulties in controlling for the effects of prior experience versus the effects of program involvement in the attitudes and competencies being measured. Furthermore, because the number of program participants without prior international travel and/or community service experience was so small, incorporating internal controls on the basis of prior experience would not have produced statistically significant results (Godkin & Savageau, 2001).

Given our interests in improving the quality of research on the impact of ISL course and/or program design on student outcomes, one of the collective shortcomings of the studies cited above was their failure to examine discreet program characteristics on student outcomes. For example, some of the programs had integrated curricular requirements (Godkin & Savageau, 2001, 2003; Haq et al., 2000), whereas others did not (Gupta et al., 1999; Miller et al., 1995). We cannot tell from these studies what influence, if any, the curricular component had on the measured outcomes relative to the international experience. In addition, no evidence could be found in the studies we examined about the degree to which length of experience contributes to the outcomes under investigation.

Still, compared to several other studies also cited in this chapter, these studies on medical students used higher quality research design and measurement. For example, most of the studies employed quasi-experimental research designs with pre–post surveys among test and comparison groups. In addition, some of the designs incorporated a combination of quantitative and qualitative instruments to assess the longitudinal effects of the programs being studied. These research design characteristics, plus the fact that several of the studies explored similar outcomes, provide a greater degree of generalizability of the findings than the single-case studies that tend to be prevalent in the ISL literature.

Studies in nursing education. Advocates of ISL in nursing education contend that not only does it improve future nurses' cultural competence but it also contributes to personal growth and professional practice in ways not available through domestic education alone (Cotroneo, Brunzwieg, & Hollingsworth, 1986; Frisch, 1990; Zorn, Ponick, & Peck, 1995). The studies described below seek to provide empirical evidence to support this contention.

Zorn (1996) sought to establish the long-term impact of international experiences on professional nurses who graduated from the University of Wisconsin-Eau Claire School of Nursing between 1979 and 1993, and who had participated in study abroad experiences during the undergraduate years. Zorn controlled for year of graduation, highest level of education, marital status, setting of nursing employment, academic year of the study abroad experience, and length of respondents' study abroad experiences. Using a survey instrument specifically designed for the study, Zorn surveyed all alumni for whom there was contact information. The survey measured the impact of study abroad across four dimensions: nurses' professional practice, cultural and international perspectives, personal development, and intellectual development.

Zorn concluded that study abroad experiences had long-term consequences for the nursing students. Although the outcomes were stronger for recent graduates, they persisted long after the study abroad experience. The most significant long-term outcomes were in the areas of respondents' international perspectives, global understandings, and personal development. Zorn also concluded that longer term study abroad programs had a deeper impact than short-term programs on the long-term effects of international study. She attributed this to "longer programs [allowing] for longer immersion into the host culture resulting in longer sustained influence" (Zorn, 1996, p. 109).

Unfortunately, one of the major shortcomings of this study is the failure to control for the intensity of the study abroad experience (i.e., amount of service contact) as well as the duration of the experience. On the other hand, Zorn's study does provide evidence for the long-term impacts of international learning experiences on nursing students, particularly as those experiences affect nursing practice.

Hurtado and Thompson (1998) also sought to identify the impact of study abroad experiences on nursing students. They examined whether the experiences occurred in a developing or a developed country and whether students had the opportunity to practice clinical skills during the experience. They expected that students whose study abroad experiences occurred in developing countries would demonstrate different outcomes than those whose experiences occurred in developed countries.

To test this assumption, Hurtado and Thompson conducted open-ended interviews with 14 nursing students who had participated in study abroad programs related to their respective community nursing programs. Ten of the 14 students completed their study abroad in the Dominican Republic or in Nicaragua; the remaining students completed their study abroad in the Netherlands. A content analysis of the interview transcripts revealed three major themes related to learning outcomes: "personal and professional growth, empirical knowledge, and learning experience" (Hurtado & Thompson, 1998, p. 15).

The authors drew three conclusions from their analysis of students' responses. First, that across many outcomes, the location of students' study abroad experiences did not have much impact on personal knowledge, self-confidence, communication skills, or sensitivity to being a minority. Second, whether students' experiences were in a developed or developing country did matter with respect to helping students internalize the ethic of care that is integral to the profession. Third, contrary to the conclusion drawn by Zorn (1996), Hurtado and Thompson concluded that "Length of time for the experience may be less critical to the learning outcomes than the specific design and type of experience . . . Factors such as the pre-trip preparation and the actual intensity of the learning for the nursing students during the experience may have a greater influence on the outcomes than the length of time" (Hurtado & Thompson, 1998, pp. 19–20). They also concluded that not only did the short-term study abroad experiences combined with intensive, hands-on clinical learning lead to outcomes similar to students with longer time abroad but the short-term programs also provided opportunities for study abroad that otherwise would not have been available to their respondents. Indeed, many of their respondents reported that had the programs been longer, they would not have been able to participate due to family, school, or work obligations.

The Hurtado and Thompson (1998) study provides support not only for the integration of study abroad into nursing education but also for the integration of intensive, direct service clinical opportunities in study abroad. Furthermore, their study suggests that when such experiences are integrated into a short-term study abroad program, more nursing students are able to receive the benefits of international study, both personally and professionally. Their study also suggests that for students to be able to internalize the professional ethic of care, they should have opportunities to complete their study abroad in developing countries.

In spite of its positive implications for advancing ISL in nursing education, the Hurtado and Thompson (1998) study is limited by its relatively small sample size ($n = 14$). Although the authors noted differences in the location of the study abroad programs and in the nature of their predeparture and in-country requirements, they did not explore the degree to which those differences contributed to student outcomes.

Walsh and DeJoseph (2003) conducted a single-case study analysis of an ISL course that paired nursing students with local midwives in a rural, indigenous community in Guatemala. Their study also relied on qualitative analysis of student interviews and journals. In their study, Walsh and DeJoseph conducted open-ended interviews with the study abroad participants prior to, during, and after the experience was completed. Three themes emerged from the content analysis of the interviews: development of empathy for minority patients, increased confidence in nursing skills, and expansion of worldviews. The primary conclusion reached by the authors is that short-term, intensive immersion programs can be a powerful tool for increasing students' cultural awareness and sensitivity. They noted that all of the students in their study had participated in community-based learning experiences with minority groups in their home community. Still, concluded the authors, "Not until the immersion experience did participants report they truly felt they were living and working in a community different from their communities of origin" (Walsh & DeJoseph, 2003, p. 271).

This is an interesting finding, particularly with respect to the goal of increasing cultural competence among nursing students. If the authors' conclusion is correct, providing nursing students with the types of intensive learning experiences described in their study will create deeper cultural competence than providing students with experiences working with diverse individuals and communities in a domestic setting. Unfortunately, the research design employed by the authors does not warrant this conclusion. The study included a sample of only 10 students, all of whom were from a selective, private, faith-based institution. Furthermore, the authors did not directly test this conclusion through replicating their methodology with students who had intensive clinical experiences working with diverse populations in a domestic context.

Advantages and Limitations of Each Variation

In general, research indicates that ISL can add value to study abroad experiences by increasing students' contact with the host culture, providing opportunities for reflection, and providing opportunities for the development of global citizenship competencies through the provision of meaningful service. As we have shown, ISL experiences can be structured in multiple ways, each variation possessing its own relative advantages and disadvantages. The advantage of the All-in-Host-Country approach is that it most closely resembles the traditional semester abroad program; the length of the experience, in theory, allows students to become more comfortable with and knowledgeable about the host country. Adding an intensive service component intensifies the contact between the student and the host community. The disadvantage is that this approach is not widely accessible, particularly with the growing number of commuter students (those who do not reside at or within walking distance of campus), who rely on part-time or full-time employment to pay for their college education.

The Sandwich approaches offer the advantage of greater accessibility. Because the time away from the home country is relatively short, this approach provides opportunities for overseas learning to a larger number of students. The service component can, to a degree, compensate for the shortened length of the experiences by allowing students to engage in meaningful and reflective interaction with host communities. The disadvantage of these approaches is that we do not know the degree to which the service truly adds value to shorter experiences abroad, particularly with respect to intercultural communication and understanding outcomes.

The practicum and competency-based models add a dimension to pre-professional training not available in the host country. Such programs offer students a comparative context in which to observe and practice their chosen professions. In addition, the service component allows them to adopt a global, civic, and cross-cultural perspective on their profession that they might not otherwise have the opportunity to develop. The disadvantage, like the All-in-Host-Country model, is that they often require time and financial commitments that are not available to the majority of students.

As we have already observed, the design of ISL experiences depends on a number of factors including the nature of the student population, the presence of prior contacts in the host country, the specific learning outcomes for the course, the specific learning outcomes for the institution, and the capacity of the higher education partner to provide desired services. Like any promising approach, the practice of ISL should be informed by rigorous research and assessment to know what works well and what does not, particularly with respect to improving students' intercultural and global competencies.

Suggestions for Future Research on the Impact of ISL Course or Program Structure

Our review of much of the ISL literature demonstrates that many questions with respect to how ISL experiences are structured have been left unexplored, underexplored, or only very tentatively answered. We contend that devoting greater attention to issues related to design, both quantitative (Bringle et al., chapter 12) and qualitative (Kiely & Hartman, chapter 13), theory, and measurement will improve clarity of information in future research.

One topic area for future research might be termed the dosage effect: Is more contact through community service in the host country better than less service contact? Is there a critical amount of time, or a critical number of contact or service hours, that is needed to optimize the impact of ISL? For example, if students complete one week of service internationally during spring break, is there as much impact on those students as there would be if they completed a month of service internationally over the summer? Is there a critical amount of time for community service to realize significant gains in affective development in students, in civic development, and in cross-cultural communication skills? Are there diminishing returns in terms of impact on students, after a critical amount of time spent on international service is completed? What about the impact on community partners?

Some of the studies cited above (Lewis & Niesenbaum, 2005; Parker & Dautoff, 2007) make the case that a short-term international experience with a high degree of contact with the host culture, particularly through the service experience, can produce similar outcomes as longer term international learning experiences with lower degrees of contact between students and the host culture. However, those studies were single-case studies without a comparison group against which to evaluate that claim. Future studies should compare the outcomes of students who participate in short-term, service-intensive programs with those of students who participate in longer term, traditional study abroad programs and ISL semester courses with varying amounts of service. In addition, future studies should also examine the longitudinal effects of shorter term, service-intensive study versus longer term study abroad.

Another question that warrants further research is, to what degree does instruction or service abroad contribute to different learning outcomes than home-country instruction and service? For example, are learning outcomes different for All-in-Host-Country programs than for students in Sandwich programs? One could expect that there would be different outcomes, assuming that learning the curriculum about a topic or country when in that country, even when taught by the same instructor, will contribute to different outcomes than when the curriculum is taught in the home country, with the service being done in the host country. However, no studies could be found that tested this hypothesis.

Do Sandwich 2 structures lead to greater understanding of social issues than Sandwich 1 structures? In Sandwich 2 structures, the service component occurs both domestically and internationally, providing students with a direct comparative framework from which to examine a particular social issue. For example, if an ISL course were designed for students to understand the impact of culture on health-care provider–patient relations and communications, does their understanding improve if they have only an international experience, if they have a domestic service experience plus an international experience, or if they have only a domestic service experience with a particular cultural group? Although cultural competence and intercultural communication skills are highly valued, particularly among educators in professional fields, no studies could be found that compared the results of domestic service versus international service versus a combination of domestic and international service with a target population. Given that not all students in professional programs are inclined to or can afford to participate in an ISL experience, determining the degree to which international service produces measurably different outcomes than domestic service with a similar population should be an issue worth study.

Do any of the structures defined above have greater impact on particular student outcomes than domestic learning, particularly domestic learning that is not service-based? Many of the studies cited above suggest that this should be the case, particularly with respect to cross-cultural competencies. However, in the studies in which there are comparisons between the outcomes of students who have participated in organized international service and their domestic counterparts who have not (e.g., Godkin & Savageau, 2001, 2003; Gupta et al., 1999; Miller et al., 1995) the problem of self-selection bias emerged—students who participated in international service already had relatively high levels of cultural competence. Indeed, Roberts's (2003) study suggests that students should have certain predispositions with respect to cultural adaptation and cross-cultural communication in order to benefit from ISL. For researchers who want to demonstrate that ISL can be beneficial for all students, more research-based evidence will be needed to counter the implications of Roberts's findings and to provide better understanding of moderator variables that differentiate outcomes for students with distinct backgrounds (Bringle et al., chapter 12; Tonkin, chapter 9).

Finally, do students who participate in ISL programs—whether through an intermediary organization such as IPSL or the Amizade Global Service Learning Consortium, or through a university program such as Duke University's IHP—gain more than students who participate in a single ISL course? Does it matter in terms of student outcomes whether course instructors are directly involved in making the arrangements with key community partners in the host country? What impact do long-term relationships with key community partners have on the participating agencies and the communities themselves?

Looking at the types of ISL course structures (all-in-host-country, Sandwich 1 or 2, practicum or competency-based service) allows us to view ISL experiences as independent variables for research purposes. Examining the various permutations of ISL course structure, foreign versus domestic faculty, and intensity of the service experience (high versus low contact) leads to a variety of research questions, such as those described above. Investigations of these and many other questions will help us more fully understand the effects of ISL and thereby help us provide more efficacious experiences for students.

References

Bennett, M. (1993). Towards ethnorelativism: A developmental model of intercultural sensitivity. In M. Paige (Ed.), *Cross-cultural orientation* (pp. 27–69). Lanham, MD: University Press of America.

Billig, S. H., & Eyler, J. (Eds.). (2003). *Deconstructing service-learning: Research exploring context, participation, and impacts*. Greenwich, CT: Information Age.

Chisholm, L. A. (2003). Partnerships for international service-learning. In B. Jacoby & Associates (Eds.), *Building partnerships for service-learning* (pp. 259–288). San Francisco, CA: Jossey-Bass.

Cotroneo, M., Brunzwieg, W., & Hollingsworth, A. (1986). All real living is meeting: The task of international education in a nursing curriculum. *Journal of Nursing Education, 25*, 384–386.

Currier, C., Lucas, J., & Saint Arnault, D. S. (2009). Study abroad and nursing: From cultural to global competence. In R. Lewin (Ed.), *Study abroad and the making of global citizens: Higher education and the quest for global citizenship* (pp. 133–150). New York, NY: Routledge.

Cushner, K. (2009). The role of study abroad in the preparation of globally responsible teachers. In R. Lewin (Ed.), *Study abroad and the making of global citizens: Higher education and the quest for global citizenship* (pp. 151–169). New York, NY: Routledge.

Cushner, K., & Mahon, J. (2002). Overseas student teaching: Affecting personal, professional, and global competencies in an age of globalization. *Journal of Studies in International Education, 6*(1), 44–58.

Drain, P. K., Primack, A., Hunt, D., Fawzi, W. W., Holmes, K. K., & Gardner, P. (2007). Global health in medical education: A call for more training and opportunities. *Academic Medicine, 82*, 226–230.

Dyjack, D., Anderson, B., & Madrid, A. (2001). Experiential public health study abroad education: Strategies for integrating theory and practice. *Journal of Studies in International Education, 5*, 244–254.

Engle, L., & Engle, J. (2004, Fall). Assessing language acquisition and intercultural sensitivity in relation to study abroad program design. *Frontiers: The Interdisciplinary Journal of Study Abroad, 10*, 219–236.

Federico, S. G., Zachar, P. A., Oravec, C. M., Mandler, T., Goldson, E., & Brown, J. (2006, February). A successful international child health experience: The University of Colorado Department of Pediatrics experience. *Archives of Pediatric and Adolescent Medicine, 160*, 191–196.

Freire, P. (2000). *Pedagogy of the oppressed*. (Ramos, M. B., trans.) New York, NY: The Continuum Publishing Company. (Original work published in 1970).

Frisch, N. (1990). An international nursing student exchange program: An educational experience that enhanced student cognitive development. *Journal of Nursing Education, 29*(1), 10–12.

Godkin, M. A., & Savageau, J. A. (2001). The effect of a global multiculturalism track on cultural competence of preclinical medical students. *Family Medicine, 33*(3), 178–186.

Godkin, M. A., & Savageau, J. A. (2003). The effect of medical students' international experiences on attitudes toward serving underserved multicultural populations. *Family Medicine, 35*, 273–278.

Gupta, A. R., Wells, C. K., Horwitz, R. I., Bia, F. J., & Barry, M. (1999). The international health program: The fifteen-year experience with Yale University's internal medicine residency program. *American Journal of Tropical Medicine and Hygiene, 61*, 1019–1023.

Haq, C., Rothenberg, D., Gjerde, C., Bobula, J., Wilson, C., Bickley, L., et al. (2000). New world views: Preparing physicians in training for global health work. *Family Medicine, 32*, 566–572.

Heck, J. E., & Wedemeyer, D. (1991). A survey of American medical schools to assess their preparation of students for overseas practice. *Academic Medicine, 66*(2), 78–81.

Hurtado, E. P., & Thompson, M. A. (1998). A comparison of international learning experiences for baccalaureate nursing students: Developed and developing country. *Journal of Nursing Education, 37*(1), 13–21.

Lewis, T. L., & Niesenbaum, R. A. (2005). Extending the stay: Using community-based research and service learning to enhance short-term study abroad. *Journal of Studies in International Education, 9*, 251–264.

Lindsey, E. W. (2005). Study abroad and values development in social work students. *Journal of Social Work Development, 41*, 229–249.

Mason, J. (1995). *Cultural Competence Self-Assessment Questionnaire: A manual for users.* Portland, OR: Portland State University Research and Training Center on Family Support and Children's Mental Health.

Miller, W. C., Corey, G. R., Lallinger, G. J., & Durack, D. T. (1995, September). International health and internal medicine residency training: The Duke University experience. *The American Journal of Medicine, 99*, 291–297.

Parker, B., & Dautoff, D. A. (2007). Service-learning and study abroad: Synergistic learning opportunities. *Michigan Journal of Community Service Learning, 13*(2), 40–53.

Peterson, C. (2002, Winter). Preparing engaged citizens: Three models of experiential education for social justice. *Frontiers: The Interdisciplinary Journal of Study Abroad, 8*, 165–206.

Porter, M., & Monard, K. (2001). *Ayni* in the global village: Building relationships of reciprocity through international service-learning. *Michigan Journal of Community Service Learning, 8*(1), 5–17.

Pust, R. E., & Moher, S. P. (1992). A core curriculum for international health: Evaluating ten years' experience at the University of Arizona. *Academic Medicine, 67*, 90–94.

Ramsey, A. H., Haq, C., Gjerde, C. L., & Rothenberg, D. (2004). Career influence of an international health experience during medical school. *Family Medicine, 36*, 412–416.

Roberts, A. (2003). Proposing a broadened view of citizenship: North American teachers' service in rural Costa Rican schools. *Journal of Studies in International Education, 7*, 253–276.

Smith-Paríolá, J., & Gòkè-Paríolá, A. (2006). Expanding the parameters of service learning: A case study. *Journal of Studies in International Education, 10*(1), 71–86.

Stachowski, L. L., Richardson, J. W., & Henderson, M. (2003). Student teachers report on the influence of cultural values on classroom practice and community involvement: Perspectives from the Navajo reservation and abroad. *The Teacher Educator, 39*(1), 52–63.

Stachowski, L. L., & Visconti, V. (1997, Spring). Adaptations for success: U.S. student teachers living and teaching abroad. *International Education, 26*, 5–20.

Taylor, H. (1969). *The world as teacher.* New York, NY: Doubleday.

Thompson, M. J., Huntington, M. K., Hunt, D., Pinsky, L. E., & Brodie, J. J. (2003). Educational effects of international health electives on U.S. and Canadian medical students and residents: A literature review. *Academic Medicine, 78*, 342–347.

Tonkin, H., & Quiroga, D. (2004, Fall). A qualitative approach to the assessment of international service-learning. *Frontiers: The Interdisciplinary Journal of Study Abroad, 10*, 131–149.

Walsh, L. V., & DeJoseph, J. (2003). "I saw it in a different light": International learning experiences in baccalaureate nursing education. *Journal of Nursing Education, 42*, 266–272.

Wessel, N. (2007). Integrating service learning into the study abroad program: US sociology students in Mexico. *Journal of Studies in International Education, 1*(1), 73–89.

Wilson, A. H. (1982). Cross-cultural experiential education for teachers. *Theory Into Practice, 21*, 184–192.

Zorn, C. R. (1996). The long-term impact on nursing students of participating in international education. *Journal of Professional Nursing, 12*(2), 106–110.

Zorn, C. R., Ponick, D. A., & Peck, S. (1995). An analysis of the impact of participation in an international study program on the cognitive development of senior baccalaureate nursing students. *Journal of Nursing Education, 34*(1), 67–70.

6

OVERCOMING THE CHALLENGES OF INTERNATIONAL SERVICE LEARNING

A Visual Approach to Sharing Authority, Community Development, and Global Learning

Hilary E. Kahn

As soon as he aims the camera, the ethnologist disturbs the life he is recording. In *Moi Noir* the actors played their everyday existence in front of the camera. I did not hide in order to film them. We were partners. (Jean Rouch, in Ruby 2000, p. 195)

International service learning (ISL) is a partnership, one that is more arduous, time-consuming, and pedagogically complex than most curricular methods. Few would deny how demanding it can be for students, directors, instructors, researchers, as well as for local community members and service providers. This chapter focuses on the least tangible challenges of these international collaborations, particularly those introduced by the cultural complexities and inequalities that foreground many ISL practices and supporting ideologies. This includes the basic and often unquestioned definitions of what are community, service, knowledge, and development, as well as the inherent politics and potential paternalism of scholarship and observation.

I will argue that goals of global engagement, local politics, cultural significances, individual voices, structural inequalities, biases, and community needs must be integrated and made visible in all aspects of ISL, including programming and research. I will demonstrate how vital it is to bring to the surface the often invisible networks (e.g., cultural systems, powers, ideologies) that give ISL its meaning as well as its profound challenges in practice and theory. To make these undercurrents approachable and applicable, I employ methods and theories that are particularly suited for making visible what is typically left less tangible. This *visual approach*, which is equally methodological and theoretical, has the potential to reveal and overcome many of the complexities and ideological barriers for students, directors, locals, and researchers of ISL. Visual approaches have diverse applications, such as in teaching, research, and even development projects (Wickett, 2007), but here I consider them as a metaphor of the embodied collaboration and shared authority that I argue is mandatory for ISL in the twenty-first century. This is not "collaboration" as semantics or rhetorical justification (Ginsburg, 1995); rather, it is partnership in its most phenomenological, lived, and truest sense.

Visual approaches are not the only way to achieve such rapport, respect, and reciprocity, but this type of thinking helps us understand the value of sharing authority and incorporating multiple voices in ISL. Therefore, consider this visual approach in three ways: (a) where cameras (i.e., authorities) are shared among diverse individuals; (b) where complex partnerships tap into deep knowledge and gain cultural insight in ways not possible through one set of (often Westernized, observing) eyes; and (c) where observers become those observed. Only with this shared vision and reflection does ISL have the ability to enhance student learning to profoundly deep levels and to engage students and spur civic-mindedness in local and global contexts. Only then can it be a conduit into communities and cultures, as well as a form of social advocacy and a life-changing and empowering experience. Only then, also, can research on ISL complement the pedagogy, echo community voices, and get to the heart of communities.

Why International Service Learning Needs Vérité

Cinéma vérité is a style of filmmaking that uses the camera as a protagonist, as a catalyst for action (Barnouw, 1993, pp. 51–71). The interactive process of filming and the camera itself provoke subjects to reveal inner selves, emotions, and the invisible elements of culture (Ruby, 2000, p. 12). Internalized feelings and the essences of social relationships are made evident through interference from the filmmaker and camera (MacDougall, 1998, p. 67). Insight and intimacy are achieved through the reflexive inclusion of the process of filming, where the filmmaker and camera become actors who contribute to the community or culture being represented.

Vérité can be used as an ethnographic tool of engagement and analysis, such as when I initiated a community video project in Livingston, Guatemala, handing over a video camera to a Q'eqchi' Mayan indigenous community to tap into perceptions and intangible identities. The multiple sets of eyes, as well as the reflexive analysis of my own participation and dialogue with the community members, were instrumental in my research on how the Q'eqchi' people identify themselves and others. Awareness of researchers' presence and biases is similarly necessary in ISL, which becomes a potent form of learning when the observer hands the metaphoric "camera" over and steps out from behind the distanced lens of academic authority. In other words, those learning through service must share their gazes and shift their eyes away from the "others" with whom they are working, to themselves. They will then become members of the casts they analyze, alongside the communities where service is provided. They will become objects of their gazes and that of others.

Vérité, through active participation and awareness, undoes the politics of a camera where the authority to reproduce images typically rests with the filmmaker and within the technology of the camera. Likewise, it overcomes a colonialist and Cartesian perspective often found in Western scholarship where viewers observe objects through distanced surveillance and by constructing objective notions of knowledge. In fact, it embodies a potential to unsettle "the very divisions upon which such an epistemology is founded" (Grimshaw, 2001, p. 91). Vérité techniques applicable to ISL—collaboration, self-reflection, reciprocity, defining service by local needs, and stepping into cultures—disrupt "the boundaries between the self and the world, mind and body . . ." (Grimshaw, 2001, p. 91). They decolonize and challenge typically unquestioned assumptions about ourselves and others.

And do not be deceived into thinking that decolonization is not needed in ISL. Neocolonialism need not be limited to situations where so-called independent states are directed by or dependent on more powerful nations; it also lurks within imperialistic attitudes that seep into ways of defining, observing, and practicing development and educational programs in international contexts. Because ISL brings together various frameworks where colonialistic ideologies still linger, such as community service, international development, study abroad, and academic definitions and paradigms of observation, it is vital that all participants acknowledge and work through and against these imperialistic ideas and actions.

Consider study abroad, where twenty-first-century students too often re-create knowable comfortable living and learning environments on a "veranda." From a privileged vantage point, like eighteenth-century colonists, they observe their international educations, the cultures in which they are learning and living, and the experience itself from a distance (Ogden, 2007). They are not participants in another culture as much as they are educated spectators who observe more than participate from the protection of their privileged positions and assumptions. Likewise, it is no understatement that many contemporary development programs and the institutions that support them are still in need of decolonization. Today, we distinguish our practices from the mid-twentieth century "development" paradigm that had little to do with collaboration, listening, and responding and more to do with politics and fortifying the international structural relationships between world powers "with" and those "without." However, "development from above" programs that are paternalistic, imperialistic, and typically "devised by those who are relatively well off to improve the lot of those who are not" remain (Kintz, 1999, p. 32). The "civilizing discourses" of empire and expansion are still evident in contemporary development projects (Lutz, 2006, p. 595) and international aid can effortlessly shift between "development" and "neo-colonialism" (Paragg, 1980). Further, the way we understand cultures, communities, and individuals in educational contexts typically involves transforming social phenomena and people into objects for academic scrutiny; this is not unlike cameras that "reproduce the world . . . based on a single and unified point of view" (Henley, 1998, p. 42), which many liken to the patriarchal, colonizing eye of the Enlightenment (Spanos, 2000, p. 14). Even our academic certainty is often rooted in arrogance and paternalism (Colligan, 2001, p. 18).

I am not suggesting that we (e.g., students, practitioners, professors, program directors) are imperialists. However, I do propose that we sincerely consider if any whispers of colonialistic thinking enter into ISL practices and perceptions. Are ISL programs truly collaboratively created? Are "partnerships" semantic ones or integrated and practiced in all aspects of a program? How often are community goals prioritized over programmatic concerns or "our" student learning? Do we truly share authority and listen and respond to various viewpoints, including those of our own students? Or do we rely on one or two individuals or one organization rather than a diverse, multivocal community? Do locals lecture, lead discussions, grade papers, and help design programs? Can we ensure that we are providing service that is culturally appropriate and warranted? Do we consider community feedback in modes of assessment? If so, do we make accommodations? Do we integrate concerns about sustainability in our programs? How often are service learning programs wholly reliant on personnel, funds, and institutions in the United States? Are we re-creating new forms of dependency? Simply, can we ever engage in ISL without succumbing in part to neocolonialist models of development that involve powerful and wealthy foreigners from one world providing for those in need in another?

Fox (2002), an anthropologist who directed a service learning program in Jamaica, struggles with the implications of international development and the inability for her to eschew this paradigm. She ultimately finds that the development archetype in which we find ourselves sets us up for undeliverable expectations. She suggests emphasizing service as a two-way street. She even goes as far as to define "learning as a form of service rather than on learning by way of service" (Fox, 2002, p. 7). By so doing, she defines the inevitable musings on "who is really benefiting here?" as a process of learning and service in itself. She, like a true, though unknowing practitioner of vérité, acknowledges that ISL is about a reciprocal flow of ideas that leads participants on both ends, through self-reflection, to cross institutional divides (i.e., between cultures and self/other) and begins a lifelong quest for cultural understanding. For her, this is how service learning silences those lurking attitudes about development and service as imperialistic missions of civilization.

Sometimes it is difficult to shake off those ideologies, as hard as one tries. For instance, I have encountered situations where locals, whether organizations or individuals, continue to define international-service programs through the development archetype. I have seen communities assume that international service programs are supported by endless financial resources, and I have also seen nonprofit representatives who are taken aback when they are asked for their input, opinions, and suggestions. Perhaps these individuals were unprepared for attempts at listening, learning, and collaboration because they expected international institutions to adhere to typical paradigms of development programs that are designed, supported, and implemented from afar.

Practicing Vérité: A Critical Pedagogy

With disparate definitions of collaboration, it is certainly an understatement that designing programs, including ISL curricula that resonate with local needs, ideas, and practices, is challenging. In some ways, it demonstrates the ongoing nature of program development—that a program is an entity constantly being remade—because service must be adaptable to changes, community activities, and local politics. Like a camera changing apertures or focal lengths due to shifting lights and movement, ISL programs must be pliable enough to accommodate to the nuances of local requirements and contexts.

I have experienced the need for such responsiveness. Like Fox (2002), I also direct an ISL program in Jamaica. We initially designed the program based upon community needs as stated in a comprehensive community survey completed two years earlier. However, even with such a useful guide (replete with community voices), there are problems. First, one cannot be guaranteed that answers are reliable or accurate representations of community wishes; that is, community members might provide answers they think the interviewers want to hear (interviews were conducted by undergraduate anthropology majors from a university in the United States). More importantly, when a survey reveals a particular service is needed, the way we define it through our cultural lenses can differ significantly from the way locals interpret the means to filling this need.

Through discussions with the community and a local nonprofit, my students and I decided to help coordinate a day camp for the local youth in the area, which was a stated need in the results of the community survey. The overarching theme would be "building community respect" and we would integrate instruction and activities about antilitter, environmental sustainability, and literacy, all of which were items listed as vital to community development in the survey. My students and I consistently requested input from the nonprofit, but we ended up designing most of the camp format, determining and delivering the content, and running the camp ourselves. It was a tremendous amount of work, and the community organization did not take the role we had anticipated. It was frustrating at first. We had to acquire new skills of communication and collaboration across cultural differences and varying definitions of what is service. We did adapt and learn and, in fact, the local nonprofit took a greater role in helping us design the format and coordinating the camp the following year. Each year the collaboration grows and intensifies. Nonetheless, by working through what was an arduous process of cross-cultural communication—which has much to do with our differing assumptions about what collaboration and service entails—we learned quite a number of things about Jamaican culture and ourselves.

For one, we encountered two very different definitions of a summer day camp. From our U.S. perspective, summer day camps are opportunities to teach children about subjects not necessarily covered during the school year, in a fun, entertaining, and engaging manner. We had various activities and lectures about such topics as the environment, civic engagement, global awareness, respecting differences, natural resources, and healthy living. Children were to learn skills through meaningful but enjoyable activities, so that they could build community respect and become the caretakers of the community. You can therefore imagine how shocked we were when we discovered on the second day of camp that the local representative from the nonprofit had a classroom of children doing mathematical equations! "This was not what children do at day camp," we thought indignantly and perhaps proprietarily. We quickly requested that the children not do any more mathematical equations, at least without relating the activity to one of the camp's themes focused on building community respect. My students and I discussed the children doing mathematical equations when we compared the educational contexts in Jamaica and the United States, and viewed this rote skill-building as defeating the purpose of the camp. However, by the next year, it was becoming increasingly clear why this woman had the children doing all those seemingly tedious mathematical equations: simply, this is what is expected at day camps in Jamaica. Day camps are opportunities to have fun, yes, but they are also opportunities to build skills that children will call upon during the school year. I was informed that some parents had inquired to see if we would be providing writing or mathematical skills and instruction. A few parents did not enroll their children when they heard that we would not. How could I have made such an assumption? I was appalled at my own ethnocentrism. Even though we thought we were doing everything right, we were failing to provide the community with what they had asked for. But, how could we have known better? Only by fumbling through the program and working in dialogue with the nonprofit and community did we realize our ignorance in this area. We listened to a variety of voices, became particularly aware of our own ingrained biases, and eventually learned that there is not one type of summer day camp. Today, we continue to integrate math and literacy skills into the curriculum.

Collaboration does not necessarily imply accord. Relationships, decision making, and determining division of tasks with the nonprofit in Jamaica was at times trying, but the process of working through our differences provides my students and me with much educational fodder. It bolsters our understanding of Jamaican culture and the value of service within. This progression of knowledge production and our roles within it is part of the educational situation we analyze. Anyway, the nonprofit organization is only one small portion of the community with whom we work in Jamaica. Students and I are culturally immersed. We live with local families, attend church, dance at local clubs (I opt out of this activity), hang our clothes on lines to dry, and play volleyball with the community youth. The students and I, therefore, are able to hear far more varied perspectives than those offered only by the staff of the nonprofit organization. These often disparate viewpoints are also foundations to the analyses of our experience. They remind us that a few people, or one nonprofit organization or service unit, do not represent a community. Communities, like cultures, are diverse and have multiple voices. Communities themselves are not neatly bound by geography, particularly in the twenty-first century, when identities are transnational phenomena. In fact, it is naïve of ISL practitioners to think that they can help or develop a community, since *communities* and *cultures* spill out across borders and are composed of various individuals who do not necessarily think like their neighbor. Do you think like your neighbor? Do we assume community members in developing countries inherently do? Is this another form of imperialist thinking that must be dismantled, and that encourages us to listen to only a few voices or organizations as representatives of the greater community? Again, would this be adequate in your communities? Would not it be best if we shared the camera with many others?

To deeply learn through ISL, students must become aware of this heterogeneity within communities and the global scope within local contexts. They must be able to see their own cultures in the foreign and the foreign in themselves. More so, they must attain an awareness that implicates their own values, biases, senses of entitlement, and previous training and upbringings in the entire educational process itself. ISL, as a collaborative form of educational and cultural vérité, leads to this type of metacognitive knowledge of self that creates the opportunity for a true international education (Anderson & Krathwohl, 2000).

Clearly, international education is far more than knowing facts about Jamaica, being able to ask directions in Chinese, or learning about the role of the United States in Latin America (though these are important parts of the foundation). In the spirit of vérité, global competency involves undoing the paradigm of the typical colonial student who studies with a sense of awe and entitlement from a veranda. These students are nothing more than tourists, with an international education instead of a camera (both, ironically, involve studying from a distance). Vérité, however, leads to a form of awareness—facilitated through community engagement, application of theories and methods to one's own experience, cultural immersion, contextual relativism, and reflection—where students implicate themselves, and their positions on that veranda, within their own acquisition of knowledge. Vérité is a critical pedagogy that encourages students to look at themselves, question their positions, and ultimately jump off the veranda with willingness, ease, and pride (Anderson & Krathwohl, 2000).

Not only should locals, consequently, be involved in the design of service and research, but so should students be actors in this production. This will help them take the necessary steps off the veranda of privileged sight. In Jamaica, my students sit in on numerous camp planning meetings that provide them with firsthand experience in working through cultural differences. Their contribution is always a benefit. Programs should be developed such that students are involved in the collaboration rather than just rote providers of service. Students must be actively drawn into partnerships and encouraged to recognize their multiple identities as viewers, providers, participants, listeners, and the ones viewed. They must also see how the process of doing ISL is in fact part of the product. Like vérité filmmaking, where the process is embedded in the product, the fumblings, dialogues, misgivings, biases, and critical reflections are the foundation of the learning product we aim to provide. When we hand cameras over to communities, metaphoric or not, we share ownership in the production of knowledge and the processes that substantiate it.

Through vérité, we hear and are heard; we see and are seen. Students and researchers learn to become objects, and locals become empowered and are given voice through collaboration. Identities are re-created, switched, reconsidered. Selves become others, and others become selves. Kiely (2005) considers this contextual border crossing as one of the critical elements of transformative ISL. Students are encouraged to cross borders (e.g., political, personal, economic, geographic, emotional) in order to process, connect, and acquire a global consciousness (Plater, chapter 2). The critical pedagogy of vérité, in fact, relies on the emotions and dissonance of displacement. The struggle with emotions, the objection to walking in tropical heat, the inability to properly hail taxis, and the irritation by early-rising roosters (i.e., all the initial components of culture shock) are integral to the deeper learning that is facilitated through vérité. Like the "reverse gaze" in tourism—when locals look directly at cameras when shutters are snapped—which causes discomfort, unease, and shifts in identity (Gillespie, 2006), vérité attacks basic assumptions that students harbor about themselves and others.

All this is what Colligan (2001) refers to as "building a multi-sited imaginary," where ISL humbles students, puts theory into practice, provides a global scope, and makes students realize and accept that they do not have all the answers. This prepares students to act out of conviction with a bit of welcomed uncertainty and to accommodate rather than inscribe differences (Colligan, 2001, p. 18). Leaning away from objectification involves a critical awareness of the multitude of biases and identities that students bring to service and learning. Not only is there heterogeneity within organizations and communities, but ISL reveals a multiplicity of identities of the students themselves, who become not only students but researchers, tutors, and advocates (Hathaway & Kuzin, 2007, p. 60). ISL students become cultural brokers who have the privilege of carrying "knowledge back and forth over seemingly rigid cultural barriers, elevating visibility of each social sphere." (Hathaway & Kuzin, 2007,

p. 59). ISL students do not necessarily carry or share real cameras, but their intimate collaboration is a form of ethnographic vérité that allows them access, insight, and multiple contexts of deep learning and self-reflection. Of course, many characteristics of vérité are inherent in contemporary ethnographic research, which typically involves cultural immersion; a breakdown of identities and authorities (teachers become learners and observers become participants); multiple voices and visions; a keen curiosity as to what lurks below the surfaces of cultures; consideration of the links between the local and global; an understanding of the diversity within cultures and communities; contextual relativism; and an acute emphasis on rapport, respect, and reciprocity.

Conclusion: *Seeing Ourselves and Others*

Sight is a principal metaphor for the objectification of knowledge that is at the heart of most Western research paradigms. Vérité's contribution to ISL and ISL research has the potential to overcome intangible and often unconscious political differences and institutional inequalities. Sharing cameras and authorities, as well as revealing multiple perspectives, can produce profound academic insight. When students implicate themselves or see their own linkages to local cultures and global phenomena, a breakthrough occurs. This epiphany reveals to students and practitioners a key component of global competency—that knowledge is not a still photo that is based upon *one* perspective from *one* point of view. Rather, disciplines, cultures, and individuals define knowledge and practices differently in various contexts. Similarly, acquiring a self-responsiveness to one's own, often multiple, identities, transforms students into scholars who are civically and internationally engaged. The ability to look at one's self is extremely critical. This intuitive reflexivity and ability to implicate one's self in the production of knowledge demonstrates how subjectivity is involved in the interpretation of cultural and academic experiences. Recognition and application of subjectivity is essential to becoming culturally insightful and globally competent. It is also a broader academic method that can be applied to the interpretation and application of various bodies of knowledge, methods, and skills across the disciplines and which rejects the superiority that can accompany certainty and objectivity. Vérité merges subjectivities and cultural complexities into tangible images upon which our eyes can gaze and in which we can see our own reflections.

Decolonizing methods (Tuhiwai Smith, 1999) incorporate locals, students, and communities as agents who are seeing and seen, hearing and heard, and fully integrated into the research agenda and protocols. Community research is ultimately dependent on multiple definitions and values, and decolonizing methods are thus developed with communities, not away from them. ISL research is not only about seeking and seeing knowledge, but is equally about exploring the ways to improve programs, enhancing student learning, problematizing basic concepts, and always about involving, not just benefiting, the multiplicity of people within communities.

Researchers, directors, and faculty have a responsibility to employ methods and paradigms that integrate various viewpoints into applicable and effective service and learning (Kiely & Hartman, chapter 13). This is vital for all phases, activities, and constituents of ISL. Transparency situates locals who are informed, heard, and fully incorporated into programming and research. Insight requires that faculty, directors, staff, and programs embrace local definitions, needs, and practice and embody respect, equality, and adaptability. Students too must also have the ability to see all of this theorizing and their own interconnectedness amongst themselves, their careers, and the invisible cultural systems in which we live, practice our professions, and think. Genuine *vérité* does decolonize worldviews and dissolve distinctions between objects and subjects, selves and others, and insiders and outsiders. Collaborative vérité encourages students and their guides to jump off verandas and to see and be seen. It breaks down barriers, reaches deep into a community's core, and internationally educates. It makes visible the invisible connections between students, service, culture, and the way we learn . . . deeply, globally, and always with challenging complexities. It shares authority and looks at phenomena from within and from beyond and through multiple and often divergent lenses of insight. Research that contributes to our understanding of ISL must, similarly, respect and reflect the potential for vérité.

References

Anderson, L. W., & Krathwohl, D. R. (Eds.). (2000). *A taxonomy for learning, teaching, and assessing: A revision of Bloom's Taxonomy of Educational Objectives.* Boston, MA: Allyn & Bacon.

Barnouw, E. (1993). *Documentary: A history of the non-fiction film.* New York, NY & Oxford, UK: Oxford University.

Colligan, S. (2001). Building a "multi-sited imaginary": Case studies in service learning from the Berkshires and beyond. *Anthropology of Work Review, 22*(2), 14–18.

Fox, D. (2002). Service learning and self-reflexivity in rural Jamaica. *Practicing Anthropology, 24*(2), 1–7.

Gillespie, A. (2006). Tourist photography and the reverse gaze. *Ethos, 34,* 343–366.

Ginsburg, F. (1995). Production values: Indigenous media and the rhetoric of self-determination. In D. Battaglia (Ed.), *Rhetorics of self-making* (pp. 121–138). Berkeley, CA: University of California.

Grimshaw, A. (2001). *The ethnographer's eye: Ways of seeing in anthropology*. Cambridge, UK: Cambridge University.

Hathaway, W., & Kuzin, J. (2007). Engaging ethnography: Student engagement as a means for creating change. *NAPA Bulletin, 27*, 40–63.

Henley, P. (1998). Film-making and ethnographic research. In J. Prosser (Ed.), *Image-based research: A sourcebook for qualitative researchers* (pp. 42–59). London, UK: Falmer.

Kiely, R. (2005). Transformative international service-learning. *Academic Exchange Quarterly, 9*(1), 275–281.

Kintz, E. R. (1999). Buying explosives and feeding the elders: Student, anthropologist, and the local perspectives on community development. *Anthropology of Work Review, 19*(4), 29–32.

Lutz, C. (2006). Empire is in the details. *American Ethnologist, 33*, 593–611.

MacDougall, D. (1998). *Transcultural cinema*. Princeton, NJ: Princeton University.

Ogden, A. C. (2007). The view from the veranda: Understanding today's colonial student. *Frontiers, 15*, 35–56.

Paragg, R. R. (1980). Canadian aid in the commonwealth Caribbean: Neo-colonialism or development? *Canadian Public Policy, 6*, 628–641.

Ruby, J. (2000). *Picturing culture: Explorations of film & anthropology*. Chicago, IL: University of Chicago.

Spanos, W. V. (2000). *America's shadow: An anatomy of empire*. Minneapolis, MN & London, UK: University of Minnesota.

Tuhiwai Smith, L. (1999). *Decolonizing methodologies: Research and indigenous peoples*. London, UK & New York, NY: Zed Books Ltd.

Wickett, E. (2007). Video as critique, praxis and process. *Visual Anthropology Review, 23*(1), 69–75.

7

SERVICE LEARNING AS LOCAL LEARNING

The Importance of Context

Susan Buck Sutton

This chapter revolves around three propositions: (a) international service learning (ISL) programs must be framed by a deep understanding of the local context; (b) the methods of service learning, in and of themselves, constitute a valid and valuable platform for some of the research necessary to build this understanding; and (c) such ground-level research can (and should) also serve as a foundational element of broader ISL research programs. All three propositions are anthropological in nature; they also assert a connection between the design and implementation of ISL and the methods of anthropological or qualitative field research (something also noted by Kahn, chapter 6; Keene & Colligan, 2004). The implications of this connection, however, go beyond either this specific discipline or the process of course design. This connection also reveals the complexity of deploying any concept outside the cultural setting in which it was developed, a cautionary tale not only for the practice of ISL but for research about it as well.

ISL spreads what has been largely a Western concept beyond its areas of origin. In this process, the general field of service learning sometimes enters contexts where its terminology is foreign, its concepts at right angles to local frames of reference, and its understandings of engagement culture-bound. The idea that a Western concept must be reworked and adapted in non-Western contexts is not new (Erasmus, chapter 15), as the history of such diverse enterprises as international development, global marketing, and even pop music readily attest. What is so interesting about the move of domestic service learning into ISL is that the ground-level, collaborative methods of service learning can provide the very means by which this reworking and adaptation might occur. To phrase this slightly differently, ISL research requires the same processes of discovery and theoretical reformulation we ask of students in our classes, and this, in turn, means that ISL courses have a role to play on the front lines of a comprehensive program of ISL research.

The pedagogies subsumed by the term "service learning" have, of course, arisen in Western academic contexts (Stanton, Giles, & Cruz, 1999). ISL is thus faced with the issues of fit, ethnocentrism, and imperialism that inevitably arise when translating from one part of the world to another, issues exacerbated by global inequalities and colonial histories (Kahn, chapter 6). In this light, ISL must be something more than simply repeating the same procedures used in the United States or the United Kingdom in new locations. Invoking a romanticized, hence well-meaning but nevertheless stereotypical, version of "local culture" as all the context one needs to know, assuming service means the same thing regardless of location, and restricting service placements to the kinds of organizations and issues relevant back home misunderstands situations, devalues communities as coeducators, and creates a flimsy scaffold for ISL courses and research alike.

More specifically, this chapter argues that both the practice of ISL and research about ISL require close, thoughtful attention to local context and a clear understanding of the forces shaping that context. Courses should not be transplanted unchanged from one setting to another; neither should theoretical frameworks and research programs. ISL research and ISL courses must invoke the principles of international learning, no matter what the subject matter of the course, no matter what the nature of the service activity. And this means they must connect to local contexts. Planting trees without knowing why an area is deforested, without knowing what trees are locally valued, without knowing who controls the land on which the trees are planted is naïve, dangerous, and misses the research and learning opportunities inherent in this activity.

This chapter further argues that, when crossing national borders, gaining an understanding of the local context requires validation of dialogue, experience, and inductive discovery as authentic tools of research. There is much value in working from the ground up when attempting to understand a new context. This is the level at which the goodness of fit of preexisting concepts is tested, at which one comes to understand how life is lived from the perspective of those living it. In this light, students and the organizations with which they do their service become active research agents who expand the horizons not only of specific courses but also ISL research more broadly, and course-by-course, locally based research becomes the bedrock for the global understandings that must frame all ISL research, even that of a comparative, multisite kind.

In framing this analysis, I must make clear at the outset that I use the term *local* where many might use *cultural*. This is deliberate. As a cultural anthropologist, I recognize the importance of culture (see Ortner, 2006; Ulin, 2001, for contemporary anthropological understandings of this concept so central to the discipline), but I also know that not all differences are cultural, despite the common practice of using the term as a gloss for a complex array of cultural, economic, demographic, and political factors (Fox & King, 2002). Using the term *local* dodges such oversimplifications, but even here, we must be careful (Clifford, 1997). As will become clear later in this chapter, *local* does not mean isolated. It does not mean unchanging. Furthermore, local systems are not always geographically based, and even when they are, they refer to all who inhabit an area, not just those who have been there a long time.

Building from the Ground Up

These arguments are supported through a case study, drawn from my own experience—a strategy consistent with the belief that ground-level engagement and dialogue as well as personal experience and reflection are important, even essential, research methodologies for cross-cultural work. Well-contextualized case studies are not mere illustrations; they are the building blocks of cross-cultural theory and essential for the conceptual reformulations that must accompany thinking about service learning outside the context where it arose. It is my hope that this particular case is useful both as a model for the kind of exploration that can inform other ISL programs and as a demonstration of the kind of multilayered, locally based understandings required to frame ISL research.

Certain assumptions guide this analysis: Every community presents its own distinctive constellation of global, national, and local forces; ISL faculty (and researchers) must understand the particular constellations in which they operate; and painting the local landscape with overly broad strokes does a disservice to local complexities. There are many points of entry into understanding local contexts. The one presented in this chapter as a whole, and the case study in particular, reflects my own background as an anthropologist. Anthropological methods and theory are well suited to the task, but there is no presumption that this is the only way to develop such knowledge. More essential are openness to the idea that civic engagement might be conceived in different ways in different places and a methodology for exploring what these ways might be in any particular instance (as presented repeatedly in Tonkin, 2004).

The trademark methods of anthropology complement those of broad-based questionnaire surveys (not that anthropologists do not sometimes use surveys, and not that more quantitative researchers do not sometimes engage in participant-observation). Anthropological research is driven by its goals of uncovering how others construe the world, comparing action with belief, and developing a multilayered understanding of the forces that shape and impel life in particular communities (whether these are rural villages, urban neighborhoods, or non-geographically based networks and organizations). As a result, anthropologists focus attention on inductive, experiential, participatory, and dialogical modes of research within small groups or networks—which gives their research methods a distinct resonance with what students in ISL programs are doing (Kahn, chapter 6; Keene & Colligan, 2004; Kiely & Hartman, chapter 13). Also as a result, anthropologists often find themselves rethinking their original theoretical premises and increasingly writing their accounts with some measure of collaboration with those whom they have studied (Clifford & Marcus, 1986; Lassiter, 2005).

The case I use to substantiate these points concerns the research that surrounded course redesign to include service learning in my existing study abroad course on modern Greece. What began as the seemingly simple addition of a new component to a fairly standard short-term (3-week) course on the anthropology of contemporary Greece, taught for students from the United States by an instructor from that country, ended up as transformational for both the course and the instructor's own understanding of Greek civic engagement. My thirty-some years of research on migration, settlement, and the construction of community in Greece (e.g., Sutton, 1978, 1988, 2000) became intimately intertwined with—and advanced by—these course revisions. The lines between teaching, service, and research faded significantly, and I became deeply aware of the new understandings of community that the service learning component was generating. The course did not simply expand; it was transformed. In this process, I came to understand the kind of contextual research needed to develop meaningful service projects, and also the power of service learning to be an instrument of this research.

Service Learning (and Learning Service) on a Greek Island

The course, originally titled *Modern Greece: Images and Realities*, had the following course description when I began this process:

> This course uses both the disciplinary framework of anthropology and the insights of direct, personal interaction to explore contemporary life in the

nation of Greece. From our base in the port town of Paroikia on the Cycladic Island of Paros, we will attempt to come to grips with modern Greek life on its own terms . . . In so doing, we will very consciously move past reductive stereotypes, affirm that modern Greece is as interesting as ancient, enhance our abilities to comprehend ways of life other than our own, and reflect on our own positions and responsibilities in the globalizing world of the present.

At the broadest level, the course had two overarching learning goals: (a) to understand modern Greek life, and (b) to enhance skills of cross-cultural understanding and interaction. These were threaded into three successive units:

1. Images and Representations of Modern Greece
2. Frameworks of Greek Life: Formative Processes and National Structures
3. Life on the Ground Level: Personal Strategies and Local Communities

Pedagogical strategies included (a) readings, lectures, and class discussions; (b) group experiential learning activities (e.g., field trips); and (c) individual research projects based more on observations than interviews (because most students could not speak modern Greek). I had taught the course for several summers with this format before I turned to service learning. During that time, student responses to the course were quite positive, but we all nevertheless felt something was missing. Course evaluations and my own observations indicated that students did not have much interaction with the local community, despite the research exercises. This was worrisome. Study abroad research has shown that direct engagement with the local population is a key element in deepening student learning (Bolen, 2007; Dwyer, 2004; Hulstrand, 2006; Montrose, 2002), something particularly important for short-term programs, which must accomplish their aims in a compressed period. Furthermore, anthropology has recently been wrenched by 30 years of disciplinary critique exposing the hegemony of many of its practices and pushing its practitioners toward increasing dialogue and collaboration with local communities (Patterson, 2001).

With such thoughts in mind, and with the encouragement and guidance of Robert Bringle, who spent a summer on Paros helping me transition the course, I decided to replace the observational research project with a service learning one. My aim was initially quite simple: to generate more interaction between students and the local community. I did not anticipate that my course material would change as dramatically as it eventually did. I did not anticipate that my conception of civic engagement in Greece would be significantly deepened. And I did not anticipate that the course would both be transformed by this civic engagement and become a player in local social programs. I thought I was just adding one new method to a well-developed course, but the learning engendered by this new element—learning that required me to investigate the local context in much greater detail than I had previously done—took us down unforeseen paths. A new arena of research opened, which was collaborative, dialogical, and focused on very basic understandings of community, civic engagement, service, and social responsibility.

My recognition of what is revealed by ISL has deepened with each successive offering of the course (there have now been five). Key themes emerged, however, even that first summer, one of which I now describe in some detail to demonstrate the research potential inherent in ISL. This theme first emerged as we struggled with the choice of organizations with which students would conduct their service, a task that we came to see required understanding of local modes of civic engagement, local political and economic relations, and local concepts of what constitutes community in the first place. Such locally based understandings opened up a different range of service placements than anticipated; mitigated against the dangers of privilege, ethnocentrism, and paternalism about which the literature on ISL properly warns (e.g., Grusky 2000; Kiely 2004); and ultimately, I believe, provided relevant material for comparative ISL researchers in sorting apples from oranges and rethinking basic concepts.

This is what happened. Service placements on Paros needed to be identified for individual students or small groups of students. As historically conceived, service learning is designed to build habits of social responsibility, awareness of social interconnectedness, and commitment to tackling social problems (e.g., Harkavy, 2004). Most service placements in the United States have been with the wide range of nonprofit organizations and some government agencies that exist to deal with social problems, citizen concerns, mutual interests, and underserved or disrupted communities. Service sites have not typically been profit-making businesses and only sometimes government agencies. When taken overseas, the goal has been to identify a set of agencies carrying out similar service activities, something often connected to theories of civil society (Chisholm, 2003; Keane, 1998).

Such practices translated very imperfectly to Greece, however. Although the numbers have been growing over the last few years, there are relatively few formally recognized nonprofit or nongovernmental organizations in Greece, and those that exist are heavily concentrated in Athens, and often designed and administered by non-Greeks (Phocas, 2008). On Paros, they have been very few and far between. A spate of recent handbooks on doing business in Greece (as well as articles in the business sections of non-Greek newspapers) have translated such statistics into the assertion that Greece lacks the basic structures of civic engagement altogether. As one such book puts it, "the public sector has never been for the average Greek an area which could seriously claim his loyalty or with which he could identify. Corporate loyalty outside the family has been rare" (Buhayer, 2005, pp. 105–106).

Such interpretations of low civic engagement in Greece suffer from the classic ethnocentric fallacy of declaring the absence of one's own institutions for dealing with a certain dimension of social life to be the absence of any institutions for dealing with this dimension at all. The lack of known forms becomes the lack of any. In identifying service placements for the course, however, we took a contrasting approach that quickly overturned such assertions: investigating what constitutes civic engagement and social responsibility within the Parian context, with an openness to whatever turned up.

This investigation began as the entire class visited the Mayor of Paros, Yannis Ragoussis, early during that first service learning summer. The primary purpose of this visit was to ask what he (and the municipality) felt were the pressing issues of the island, something intended to help us frame our service activities. Neither side quite knew what the other was about at this point, but we and Mayor Ragoussis sensed there were connections to be made, if we could just find them. A group of eager, unpaid university students volunteering for action was a novelty indeed. It did not fit what we came to understand were the patterns of civic action more common on Paros, and—besides this—we were socially an unknown quantity. Still our intentions registered as genuine, and over the next few years, and even as Mayor Ragoussis was succeeded by Mayor Christos Vlachoyiannis, the class gradually became integrated into evolving Parian patterns of community engagement, which, in turn, expanded to embrace the concept of foreign volunteerism.

In answer to our question that first summer, Mayor Ragoussis did not miss a beat; however, the most pressing issue was how to manage the tourism that now dominated the island's economy. More specifically, the mayor was striving to understand how to keep tourism from overwhelming life on Paros, from turning Paros into just one more touristically commodified Greek island, interchangeable with any other, with high-rise hotels blocking the beaches from local inhabitants. The Mayor was not talking about preserving Paros as a museum piece. Tourism has been a godsend for the island's economy. He was talking about managing the changes engendered by tourism so that they were to the benefit of the island. Already the municipality was drafting regulations limiting the height of hotels and establishing zones of historic preservation. Above all, Mayor Ragoussis felt Paros needed to identify itself as a center of cultural and ecotourism, thereby protecting much that was valuable about the island.

The Mayor's goals were not uncontested; developers and families who wanted to sell their lands to the highest bidder were among those who disliked the idea of restricting growth for tourism. As we talked about these issues with other Parians, however, we came to see that the Mayor's view was, nevertheless, widely shared across many different levels of Parian society. By using these goals as our starting point, the class was able to explore how the community was pursing them, a process that revealed multiple forms of civic engagement and opened up interesting service placements. There were in fact some nongovernmental organizations involved in this effort: Alkioni Wildlife Rescue Hospital, Paros Animal Welfare Society (which dealt with the boom in stray cats and dogs engendered by tourism), and the Folkdance Group of Naoussa. Equally involved, however, were the municipal Tourism Office, the state-run archaeological museum, the library, and the public health clinic (which was packed with non-Greek speaking patients in the summer). So, too, were the for-profit diving business that conducted free educational programs on marine ecology for Parian school children, the winery that developed a small museum on the island's viticulture, and the private art galleries that had begun to appear in the main town, all of which were going far beyond what they needed to do to turn a profit.

Small groups of students worked with each of these organizations and agencies over the next few summers, and each experience deepened our understanding of the systems of civic engagement, service, and community operating on Paros. As this happened, greater space opened up for us to work within these systems. The course in the summer of 2009 demonstrates the progression. During winter of 2008, the municipality identified a new tourism-shaping project: clearing, restoring, and publicizing the network of old, in some cases, even ancient, stone footpaths that crisscross Paros, recycling them for use as hiking trails of distinctive cultural and historical interest. Through e-discussions prior to the summer, the municipality invited the class to kick-off the project by clearing the rockfalls and overgrowth that now obscured the paths and also by painting signs to guide hikers. A call went out, and a coalition of local groups formed to assist us in the effort, including the Tourism, Environmental, and Sanitation Offices of the municipality, the public library, the local art teacher, the Merchant's Association (which provided water and snacks), the major English website for Paros, several local newspapers, a private tour company (which provided bus transportation), and the newly formed nongovernmental Parian Society for the Development of Alternate Forms of Tourism. Tools were provided, and local volunteers served as daily guides and coworkers. In very short order, a dense and vibrant social network came together, and by the end of the summer, one path was cleared in its entirety.

At this point, the course is substantially different from its preservice learning days. It has a new title, *Encountering Modern Greece: Service Learning and Anthropology on a Greek Island*. It has some added learning objectives, including "developing expanded concepts of community, service, and citizenship"; and "connecting with Paros and its residents in a direct, personal, and meaningful manner." Readings on tourism, community life, and civic engagement in Greece have displaced some previous texts. Above all, I have come to see that the service component generates new knowledge every summer, and the current course description contains this new sentence:

> Collaboration and dialogue with the local community are the means through which we will come to understand contemporary Greece on its own terms . . .

Civic Engagement in Greece

In point of fact, the service learning component of the course revealed aspects of civic engagement in Greece that went far beyond what I knew, despite over 30 years of research on various issues of Greek social life. The conversations and observations captured in student journals and reports, the negotiations involved in arranging service placements and organizing community-based activities, and the evolution of both of these over time were deeply informative. They enabled the class to revisit old studies with new questions, and they pointed the way to more general information we needed to make sense of our experiences.

Probing what constitutes community, nation, social connectedness, and social responsibility in Greece led us to connect the dots among a range of issues. The great historical mobility of Greek families, the relatively recent foundation or growth of many settlements, and historically shifting structures of municipal organization connected to very fluid systems of social organization on the ground level (Sutton, 1988, 2000). The low economic standing of Greece—which no longer receives the kind of foreign aid that generates nongovernmental organizations in the global South but still vies for the title of poorest country in the European Union—became connected to the idea that investing in nongovernmental organizations and eschewing profit are not good options for most Greeks, who already work multiple jobs to support their families. The demeaning assumptions of Balkanism (a variant of Orientalism) in which Greece and its neighbors are deemed to lack the political culture to run their nations responsibly and the direct interference of foreign nations in Greek affairs for the last 800 years (e.g., Jusdanis, 2001; Leontis, 1995) connected to long-standing Greek attitudes of antiauthoritarianism, skepticism, and political savvy, as well as a wariness about both national initiatives and international nongovernmental agencies (Herzfeld, 1988; Phocas, 2008; Triandis, 1972). The rapid and recent spread of mass tourism across Greece connected to the even more recent, varied, and generally disconnected set of responses to it (e.g., Galani-Moutafi, 1993a, 1993b; Herzfeld, 1991). And all of this connected to student reflections on their own actions as travelers and on U.S. involvement in Greece.

What the service learning made clear was the ways in which many Parians, nevertheless, organized themselves to advance their community, conclusions that amplified the relatively scant literature on this topic. Civic engagement is neither rare nor weak in Greece, but it takes different forms than it does in the United States. In this light, the act of creating new villages and neighborhoods can be seen as an act of civic collaboration (something demonstrated to the students by several new hamlets emerging before our eyes). So, too, can the animated participation in the political process that students witnessed in several town hall meetings on Paros. The Paros Agricultural Cooperative that counts 1,300 families among its members was another obvious example, as is the widespread spontaneous giving of fresh produce and labor to neighbors, a pattern of mutual aid known as *allilovoithia* (literally "helping others") (Koster, 2000). Even my long-forgotten dissertation came back into play as we realized that the social clubs in Athens that gathered money for the villages from which their members had come were yet another demonstration of the civic engagement that occurs in a country said to have little (Sutton, 1978).

Above all, however, the students and I came to understand that an underlying principle of all these forms of engagement, and of Parian efforts to manage tourism were the building and maintenance of dense social networks (Koster, 2000) or as Phocas (2008) puts it, "loose networks of people, informal gatherings and various manifestations of civic activism" (p. 63). The anthropology of modern Greece is replete with discussions of cultural practices for establishing social relationships outside the family, an activity that consumes (and complicates) everything from business transactions to recreation (e.g., Hart, 1992; Herzfeld, 1988; Papataxiarchis, 1991). Much has been written on the social fault lines that sometimes emerge as blocs form, and the wariness that accompanies dealings with those outside one's networks. What the Paros service projects have revealed, however, is that these dense social networks also create a flexible matrix for moments of social cohesion and community advancement. These networks can be assembled, reassembled, activated, and intensified at various moments, as happened in 2000 when Parians by the hundreds responded to the tragic sinking of the passenger ferry Samina off their coast, and as also happened with the path-clearing project in 2009. What is doubly interesting about the latter is that the civic engagement that resulted was a very organic combination of governmental, business, and nonprofit entities, occasioned by social networks that threaded across all these arenas. And, of course, by that time the class was part of these networks, too.

Broader Implications

As stated earlier, three propositions have guided this chapter, and I now return to each of these in turn.

(a) *ISL programs must be framed by a deep understanding of the local context.* The Paros course was explicitly directed toward cross-cultural learning, but even ISL courses that are not focused in that direction require such contextualization. All ISL courses and programs contain an implicit imperative that faculty conduct the research necessary to understand the community in which they are working—no matter what the discipline. It is hubris indeed to think that undergraduates and their instructors can conceive the solution to significant problems outside their own countries, in advance and on their own. It is mistaken to think that the forms of civic engagement are universal (Erasmus, chapter 15; Tonkin, chapter 9). Some of this background research will occur as the course is being designed, but—as detailed in (b) below—it should also continue as an integral part of course implementation.

Such contextual research may be easier for anthropologists, political scientists, geographers, and their like, than those from other disciplines, but it is not out of reach for any. There are multiple points of entry, one of which is examination of how whatever discipline is being taught is carried out in the particular national context under consideration. Such examinations and analyses inherently raise cross-cultural issues, such as the factors shaping the discipline in this nation, as well as the problems and questions local practitioners pursue (e.g., Currier, Lucas, & Saint Arnault, 2009, for nursing; Cushner, 2009, for teacher education), which often stand in some contrast to those in the home country of the ISL class. These issues, in turn, make clear the kind of local learning that must be done and how that can be related to the disciplinary issues animating the ISL course or program. This approach may thus well be a good starting point for disciplines not accustomed to international analysis.

Another critical element in the research necessary to conduct ISL programs and another possible entry point for this work concerns local modes of community engagement, problem solving, and decision making, as well as local understandings of social responsibility and even what constitutes community (Kahn, chapter 6). The learning necessary to develop fully the service component of the Paros course gives testimony in this regard. It also underscores that such knowledge may not be well-developed in the existing literature on a particular country, and that this may well be an arena where ongoing research during an ISL program will be most productive. While the case presented in this chapter demonstrates considerable local convergence around certain goals, other cases (including the pursuit of other issues on Paros) may not. It is therefore important to include the modalities of conflict, conflict resolution, and structural change in this examination.

The research needed to develop ISL programs also requires us to move beyond what I sometimes think of as "platitudes about attitudes." There is much in the growing literature on intercultural awareness that would reduce all social difference to cultural values, and thus limit our learning to what are presented as uniform and unchanging ways of thinking in a particular nation or community, sometimes focusing simply on such matters as personal space, forms of politeness, and conversational styles (Dolby, 2007; Drews, Meyer, & Peregrine, 1996; Farrell & Suvedi, 2003; Gray, Murdock, & Stebbins, 2002; Jenkins & Skelly, 2004, for other analyses of the inadequacy of such texts). Saying that a group behaves a certain way because it is "their culture," begs many of the most interesting questions about human difference, denies the changeability and constructedness of culture, and masks critical forces (Baumann, 1999; Fox & King, 2002). As anthropologists understand it (Brumann, 1999; Ortner, 2006; Ulin, 2001), culture refers to shared ways of thinking ("webs of significance" in Geertz's famous formulation [1973]), but it is not the only force at work in shaping human thought and behavior. ISL research should flow from a theoretical framework that recognizes the intersection of politics, economics, environment, identity, and culture; sees change as constant; thinks in terms of contested and sometimes disjointed cultural systems rather than uniform cultures; and understands that the local is shaped by external relations as much as internal dynamics.

The synopsis of contemporary cultural theory just given flies in the face of many commonly held (but overly simple) assumptions about culture and about difference (Baumann, 1999, for a good discussion of this point). Moving beyond these assumptions requires ISL practitioners to read widely and think flexibly about the mix of forces shaping the situations in which they conduct their programs. Much of this learning will occur as programs are implemented. Whether done as background or on-the-ground research, this process requires inquiry into the social groupings and divisions that are present; the environmental, political, demographic, and economic forces shaping (and reshaping) lives and communities; the current issues that focus public debate; the playing out of global forces in this particular local arena; and the various threads of cultural thinking that weave through all this. The process also requires reflection on one's own positioning and that of one's nation, including the imagery and assumptions one holds about the host country.

(b) *The methods of service learning, in and of themselves, constitute a valid and valuable platform for some of the research necessary to build such contextual understanding.* There is a strong resonance between service learning and various modes of qualitative, community-based research, including anthropological fieldwork, especially its collaborative and participatory forms (Lassiter, 2005; McCabe, 2004; Schensul, Berg, & Brase, 2002). Not only will some of the research necessary to build good ISL courses and programs occur after these courses or programs are under way, it should. On Paros, service projects did more than illustrate the subject matter of the course; they brought new material, insights, and voices into it. In many ways, the course has functioned as an ongoing research project in which faculty, students, and community participated, with new insights emerging in each successive year (Whitney & Clayton, chapter 8).

As already established, the contextual understandings necessary for effective ISL may not be fully represented in existing literature. Given this fact, there is much faculty can do to make the research function of the service activities explicit and focused. This begins with establishing the philosophical position that the local knowledge discovered and constructed through service learning is valid, useful, and transformative. Qualitative methods are more than techniques. They reflect an epistemological stance, and they are deployed within a theoretical framework. They are purposefully immersive, collaborative, reflective, and inductive. They treat experience as a research strategy. And they are especially appropriate when moving into new social worlds, where there are concepts to be reformulated and new modes of civic engagement to be discovered.

Ground-level research reveals what might be missed by a survey written from afar (Kahn, chapter 6), although it might be the prelude to a survey written from within. This research also reveals the complex ways in which abstract forces intertwine to produce specific situations. By validating dialogue and experience as modes of research and learning, ground-level research also gives students tools they can use time and again in many other situations.

Once students are alerted to the potential research value of their service, they can be guided in putting this into action. Service learning already employs many of the basic methods of qualitative fieldwork: participating in local activities, conversing with members of the community on a regular and repeated basis, and keeping a record of what happens and how one feels about it. Turning these activities toward social research asks faculty to do several things: establish a framework of research topics that students will pursue in systematic fashion; guide students in the basics of note taking for scholarly purposes, and how this differs from personal reflective journals (students may well end up keeping both a journal and a set of field notes); and guide students in the basics of participant/observation, interviewing, particularly open-ended, conversational interviewing, and note taking (Angrosino, 2002; Kahn, chapter 6; Kiely & Hartman, chapter 13; Kutsche, 1998; Lassiter, 2005). With such guidance and structure, student service interactions can serve research purposes as well as personal growth (and benefit to the organization).

The class can identify topics for research and candidates for interviews and such activities can become part of work of the course. If students are asked to keep field notes, this information can be compiled and analyzed by the class to reach broader understandings. Part of the individual and group reflection that accompanies service learning can be an analysis of what is being learned about the local context, and what new research topics might be productive. As Whitney and Clayton (chapter 8) illustrate, reflection need not be limited to personal growth; it can also be used to advance local understanding. The fact that this information gathering and analysis is ongoing during the course reflects additional strengths of qualitative field research: the local community can be involved in the research design, ideas and information can be checked and rechecked, and felicitous encounters can spontaneously turn into major interviews (Lassiter, 2005). Above all, the ideas driving the research arise from and are informed by local issues, structures, and conceptual frames. Whitney and Clayton (chapter 8) provide questions that can be a basis for students exploring these issues, as well as provide guidelines for involving community constituencies in reflection activities.

(c) *Such ground-level research can (and should) serve as a foundational element of broader ISL research programs.* As stated at the outset of this paper, any program of general research on the learning outcomes, effectiveness, and impact of ISL must be framed by cross-culturally valid concepts of service, community, social responsibility, and civic engagement. As the Paros course demonstrates, the deconstruction and reconstruction involved in developing these concepts can be sparked by the processes of dialogue and discovery, comparison and reflection that accompany locally based service learning programs. Any program of ISL research must also be framed by a deep understanding of the intertwining of global, national, and regional forces as they interact and shape our lives and communities. As the Paros course also demonstrates, this requires moving beyond sweeping generalizations and a reliance on overly simple concepts of culture—something that also becomes clear as faculty and students wrestle with the complexities of local contexts in ISL programs.

In short, ISL programs can operate on the front lines of ISL research and theoretical reformulation, and they can do so in a collaborative way. What was learned about Parian modes of civic engagement is also being learned in other ISL programs. If such learning were conceived as research and if these research results were collected into a comprehensive set of data and conceptualizations, a strong foundation for more general understandings could result. It is time to think about building such a repository, establishing a list of topics (such as those on local forms of civic engagement discussed in this chapter) to which ISL programs could contribute information based on their specific experiences.

Much service learning research focuses on the kinds of student learning that result from service learning programs (Eyler, chapter 10; Whitney & Clayton, chapter 8). The points made in this chapter support adding another item to the list: the level of contextualization achieved by students in ISL programs. No matter what the subject matter of the course, there should be assessment of the depth of student learning concerning the local community. In this light, there is much wisdom in examining the general literature on student learning outcomes in study abroad programs (Kiely, chapter 11), which place much emphasis on learning the contextual specifics of the communities and countries in which the students are studying (see Lewin, 2009, for a broad overview of study abroad research).

Scholarship on the learning outcomes of study abroad has become increasingly sophisticated over the last 30 years and numerous instruments for measuring intercultural learning have been developed (Bolen, 2007; Carlson, Burn, Useem, & Yachimowicz, 1990; Deardorff, 2006; Vande Berg, Balkcum, Scheid, & Whalen, 2004).

As those of us overseeing study abroad and overseeing service learning at IUPUI have found, there is considerable resonance and overlap between the learning objectives standardly defined for each (see also Parker & Dautoff, 2007), especially in the areas of enhanced learning of subject matter, personal growth and self-understanding, intercultural respect, tolerance for ambiguity, and career focus and definition. Service learning brings new dimensions to more conventional forms of study abroad, however, and being embedded in a study abroad program adds something to service learning that goes beyond what happens in domestic settings. In regard to the latter, the following list encompasses some of the elements of student learning that reflect differences between domestic service learning and ISL, as we have come to see this at IUPUI (e.g., Leslie, Hatcher, & Sutton, 2005). It also identifies specific learning outcomes that should be part of ISL research programs and that reflect the contextual learning that ISL requires.

- Development of a global perspective on the student's discipline/profession
- Reflection on how the discipline/profession is carried out in the home country by virtue of contrasting practices between home and host country
- Enhanced knowledge concerning the economic, political, ecological, health, demographic, and cultural systems of the host country
- Appreciation for assets of the host country, the integrity of its way of life, and the manner in which it approaches its problems
- At least some foreign language acquisition
- Reflection upon home country and how others see it
- Intensified awareness of relationships between home and host country
- Reflection upon issues of power, wealth, ethnicity, and class in both host and home country
- Stronger grasp of basic theories, principles, and concepts for understanding a particular way of life
- Stronger grasp of the economic, political, ecological, and cultural dynamics now shaping the whole world
- Growing sense of the global dimensions of citizenship
- Complex understanding of the formation of values and judgments in a multicultural world
- Rethinking concepts of community, service, and civic engagement by virtue of contrast between home and host country

The final point I wish to make about how ISL courses can function as an arm of ISL research concerns the issue of collaboration. A global understanding of ISL cannot be written by one group; it must be written by many, working together. It must be multi-perspectival. It must include the voices of scholars and practitioners from around the world. It should also include those of local communities, something that the course-based research presented in this chapter can contribute. In a closely related vein, course-based research can also serve as the entry point for research on the extent to which local communities understand ISL, what strategies work to expand this understanding over time, and how local participation and collaboration often change ISL courses. And this, in turn, could shed light on what is one of the most important issues for ISL: the role that ISL plays (or not) in creating collaborative, international networks of civic engagement.

References

Angrosino, M. V. (2002). *Doing cultural anthropology: Projects for ethnographic data collection.* Prospect Heights, IL: Waveland Press.

Baumann, G. (1999). *The multicultural riddle: Rethinking national, ethnic, and religious identities.* New York, NY: Routledge.

Bolen, M. C. (Ed.). (2007). *A guide to outcomes assessment in education abroad.* Carlisle, PA: Forum on Education Abroad.

Brumann, C. (1999). Writing for culture. *Current Anthropology, 40,* 1–27.

Buhayer, C. (2005). *Greece: A quick guide to customs and etiquette.* Portland, OR: Graphic Arts Center.

Carlson, J. S., Burn, B. B., Useem, J., & Yachimowicz, D. (1990). *Study abroad: The experience of American undergraduates.* Westport, CN: Greenwood Press.

Chisholm, L. A. (2003). *Partnerships for international service-learning.* In B. Jacoby (Ed.), *Building partnerships for service-learning* (pp. 259–288). San Francisco, CA: Jossey-Bass.

Clifford, J. (1997). *Routes: Travel and translation in the late twentieth century.* Cambridge, MA: Harvard University.

Clifford, J., & Marcus G. E. (Eds.). (1986). *Writing culture: The poetics and politics of ethnography.* Berkeley, CA: University of California.

Currier, C., Lucas, J., Arnault, D. S. (2009). Study abroad and nursing: From cultural to global competence. In R. Lewin (Ed.), *Study abroad and the making of global citizens: Higher education and the quest for global citizenship.* New York, NY: Routledge.

Cushner, K. (2009). The role of study abroad in the preparation of globally responsible teachers. In R. Lewin (Ed.), *Study abroad and the making of global citizens: Higher education and the quest for global citizenship* (pp. 151–169). New York, NY: Routledge.

Deardorff, D. K. (2006). Identification and assessment of intercultural competence as a student outcome of internationalization. *Journal of Studies in International Education, 10,* 241–266.

Dolby, N. (2007). Reflections on nation: American undergraduates and education abroad. *Journal of Studies in International Education, 11*, 141–156.

Drews, D. R., Meyer, L. L., & Peregrine, P. N. (1996). Effects of study abroad on conceptualizations of national groups. *College Student Journal, 30*, 452–462.

Dwyer, M. M. (2004). Charting the impact of studying abroad. *International Educator, 13*(1), 14–20.

Farrell, P., & Suvedi, M. (2003). Studying abroad in Nepal: Assessing impact. *Frontiers, 9*, 175–188.

Fox, R. G., & King B. J. (Eds.). (2002). *Anthropology beyond culture*. New York, NY: Berg.

Galani-Moutafi, V. (1993a). From agriculture to tourism: Property, labor, gender, and kinship in a Greek island village. *Journal of Modern Greek Studies, 11*, 241–279.

Galani-Moutafi, V. (1993b). From agriculture to tourism: Property, labor, gender, and kinship in a Greek island village. *Journal of Modern Greek Studies, 12*, 113–131.

Geertz, C. (1973). *The interpretation of culture*. New York, NY: Basic Books.

Gray, K. S., Murdock, G. K., & Stebbins, C. D. (2002). Assessing study abroad's effect on an international mission. *Change, 34*(3), 45–51.

Grusky, S. (2000). International service learning: A critical guide from an impassioned advocate. *American Behavioral Scientist, 43*, 858–867.

Harkavy, I. (2004). Service-learning and the development of democratic universities, democratic schools, and democratic good societies in the 21st century. In M. Welch & S. H. Billig (Eds.), *New perspectives on service-learning: Research to advance the field* (pp. 3–22). Greenwich, CT: Information Age Publishing.

Hart, L. K. (1992). *Time, religion, and social experience in rural Greece*. Lanham, MD: Rowman & Littlefield.

Herzfeld, M. (1988). *The poetics of manhood: Contest and identity in a Cretan mountain village*. Princeton, NJ: Princeton University.

Herzfeld, M. (1991). *A place in history: Social and monumental time in a Cretan town*. Princeton, NJ: Princeton University.

Hulstrand, J. (2006). Education abroad on the fast track. *International Educator, 15*(3), 46–55.

Jenkins, K., & Skelly, J. (2004). Education abroad is not enough. *International Educator, 13*(1), 7–12.

Jusdanis, G. (2001). *The necessary nation*. Princeton, NJ: Princeton University.

Keane, J. (1998). *Civil society: Old images, new visions*. Stanford, CA: Stanford University.

Keene, A. S., & Colligan S. (2004). Service-learning and anthropology. *Michigan Journal of Community Service Learning, 10*(3), 5–15.

Kiely, R. (2004). A chameleon with a complex: Searching for transformation in international service-learning. *Michigan Journal of Community Service Learning, 10*(2), 5–20.

Koster, H. A. (2000). Neighbors and pastures: Reciprocity and access to pasture. In S. B. Sutton (Ed.), *Contingent countryside: Settlement, economy, and land use in the southern Argolid since 1700* (pp. 241–260). Stanford, CA: Stanford University.

Kutsche, P. (1998). *Field ethnography: A manual for doing cultural anthropology*. Upper Saddle River, NJ: Prentice Hall.

Lassiter, L. E. (2005). *The Chicago guide to collaborative ethnography*. Chicago, IL: University of Chicago.

Leontis, A. (1995). *Topographies of Hellenism: Mapping the homeland*. Ithaca, NY: Cornell University.

Leslie, S., Hatcher, J. A., & Sutton, S. B. (2005, November). *Transforming learning objectives by combining service learning and study abroad*. Paper presented at Council on International Education and Exchange Annual Conference, Miami, FL.

Lewin, R. (Ed.). (2009). *Study abroad and the making of global citizens: Higher education and the quest for global citizenship*. New York, NY: Routledge.

McCabe, M. (2004). Strengthening pedagogy and praxis in cultural anthropology and service learning: Insights from postcolonialism. *Michigan Journal of Community Service Learning, 10*(3), 16–30.

Montrose, L. (2002). International study and experiential learning: The academic context. *Frontiers, 8*, 1–15.

Ortner, S. B. (2006). *Anthropology and social theory: Culture, power, and the acting subject*. Durham, NC: Duke University.

Papataxiarchis, E. (1991). Friends of the heart: Male commensal solidarity, gender and kinship in Aegean Greece. In P. Loizos & E. Papataxiarchis (Eds.), *Contested identities: Gender and kinship in modern Greece* (pp. 156–179). Princeton, NJ: Princeton University.

Parker, B., & Dautoff, D. A. (2007). Service-learning and study abroad: Synergistic learning opportunities. *Michigan Journal of Community Service Learning, 13*(2), 40–53.

Patterson, T. C. (2001). *A social history of anthropology in the United States*. New York, NY: Berg.

Phocas, E. (2008, January/February). The art of giving. *Odyssey*, 62–65.

Schensul, J., Berg, M. J., & Brase, M. (2002). Theories guiding outcomes for action research for service-learning. In A. Furco and S. H. Billig (Eds.), *Service-learning: The essence of the pedagogy* (pp. 125–142). Greenwich, CT: Information Age Publishing.

Stanton, T., Giles, D., & Cruz, N. (1999). *Service-learning: A movement's pioneer reflects on its origins, practice, and future*. San Francisco, CA: Jossey-Bass.

Sutton, S. B. (1978). *Migrant voluntary associations: An Athenian example and its implications*. (Doctoral Dissertation), University of North Carolina, Chapel Hill.

Sutton, S. B. (1988). What is a 'village' in a nation of migrants? *Journal of Modern Greek Studies, 6*, 187–215.

Sutton, S. B. (2000). Introduction: Past and present in rural Greece. In S. B. Sutton (Ed.), *Contingent countryside: Settlement, economy, and land use in the southern Argolid since 1700* (pp. 1–24). Stanford, CA: Stanford University.

Tonkin, H. (Ed.). (2004). *Service-learning across cultures: Promise and achievement.* New York, NY: International Partnership for Service-Learning and Leadership.

Triandis, H. (1972). *The analysis of subjective culture: An approach to cross-cultural social psychology.* New York, NY: Wiley-Interscience.

Ulin, R. C. (2001). *Understanding cultures: Perspectives in anthropology and social theory* (2nd ed.). Oxford, UK: Blackwell.

Vande Berg, M. J., Balkcum, A., Scheid, M., & Whalen, B. J. (2004). The Georgetown University consortium project: A report at the halfway mark. *Frontiers, 10,* 101–116.

8

RESEARCH ON AND THROUGH REFLECTION IN INTERNATIONAL SERVICE LEARNING

Brandon C. Whitney and Patti H. Clayton

Vignette 1: During a week-long Alternative Spring Break (ASB) service learning trip a group of 20 undergraduates and a faculty/staff mentor live and work in a community in Ecuador, building a house with Habitat for Humanity and members of the community. Some have traveled abroad previously, but for many this is the first experience outside the United States. Few have prior experience with domestic or international service learning (ISL). The group members met regularly before departing campus, completed a few readings on the history and culture of Ecuador, and reflected on their objectives for the trip and on their expectations and assumptions going into it. While in-country, they reflect on their community experiences every other night through a one-hour group discussion facilitated by the student trip leaders, and at the end of each reflection session the participants are invited to capture their thoughts by writing in an individual journal. Several of them post descriptions of their activities and explorations of the challenges they are encountering to a blog once a day. Upon returning to campus, students submit a journal on their experience in Ecuador, including consideration of whether their initial assumptions and expectations proved true, the extent to which they met their objectives, their experiences moving between their own and another culture, and the trip's implications for their studies and for their interactions with local communities around their university.

Vignette 2: A semester-long program takes 30 students from a variety of majors in their sophomore and junior year to study and serve in the Ecuadorian capital city, Quito. The program partners with one of the major private universities in the city to offer a course tailored for visiting students on the history and culture of Ecuador as well as courses in Spanish; students choose two additional elective courses in political economy, conservation biology, or regional economic development. All students are placed in homestays with local families scattered throughout the city and are required to serve at least 15 hours a week at one of a number of local organizations; they might work with the homeless, immigrants, or adoption agencies; teach English to primary school students or the elderly; or assist human rights or environmental nonprofits. Students are required to keep an ongoing guided journal, with prompts designed to help them connect their service experiences to their coursework; and they meet with program leaders as a group weekly for two hours for a reflection session that includes a mix of focused and open-ended discussions of experiences across the various community settings. Through the weekly submission of a formal reflective essay in one of their elective courses (on which they receive written feedback prior to final submission for grading) the students demonstrate how the integration of their academic perspective and the perspective gained through their service placement has enhanced their understanding of Ecuadorian society, their own society, and themselves.

Vignette 3: A student who has traveled and studied abroad extensively designs a capstone community-engaged research project to be undertaken in Ecuador during the summer before his senior year. He works closely with two faculty mentors for the six months prior to his departure, designing a curriculum and accompanying reflection framework to support his examination of his project from academic, civic, and personal perspectives. In Ecuador, he works with residents and community leaders in a small village to catalogue indigenous knowledge of local plants while reading extensively on sustainable community development and environmental ethics. He makes notes throughout each day in a small notebook, develops those notes into key ideas for further thought most evenings, and several times a week writes in response to the prompts in his pre-determined reflection framework. He sends reflective essays home to his faculty mentors as his schedule and access to the Internet allow, and they provide feedback while reflecting themselves on their role in his project and on the new perspective it is bringing to their own work. Upon his return to campus, he produces a critical evaluation of the project, mentors another student in designing a similar capstone project, and presents on the design of capstone projects at a variety of national conferences.

As these vignettes (derived from actual experiences) and other chapters in this volume (particularly Jones & Steinberg, chapter 5) make clear, ISL can be undertaken in a variety of ways. One of the key variables is the design of the reflection component: Is reflection written or oral or both? Is it individual or collaborative or both? Who is involved in it? When, where, and how often does it occur? How is it facilitated? What outcomes does it support students and other participants in achieving? What products does it yield? When and how are these products evaluated? The flexibility of the reflection component allows the ISL experience to be customized in light of the particular participants, settings, objectives, and constraints; and it provides a rich environment for assessing student learning, evaluating ISL programs, and collecting data for research on ISL courses and programs.

Reflection can serve as an independent variable in the design of research and can therefore be studied in terms of its role in producing outcomes; it can also be a source of data, which can be mined to investigate many questions that include but transcend student learning outcomes. Consider some examples of the types of questions suggested by the opening vignettes that could be investigated about reflection and through examination of reflection products.

- *Vignette 1:* What difference might the nature of the trip leader's training in facilitating reflection make on learning or service outcomes achieved by participants and by trip leaders themselves? In what ways does the experience of the participants in peer-led reflection sessions conform to and differ from the norms of peer-assisted learning as described in the literature and from faculty-led reflection (Eyler, chapter 10)? What patterns in the changes in students' assumptions and expectations occur over the course of the week, and are they in any way correlated with student gender or nationality? What influence does previous experience with international travel or service learning have on the extent and nature of a student's difficulties with entry into and exit from the international community (Kiely, chapter 11), as these difficulties are examined in their post-trip journals?

- *Vignette 2:* How does faculty participation in the group reflection sessions influence their teaching and their professional and civic development? How does students' understanding of the local community change over the course of the semester, and what are the primary forces contributing to these changes? In what ways does the freedom to choose the courses and the corresponding service placement affect the range of learning outcomes students demonstrate?
- *Vignette 3:* How does feedback from faculty mentors shape the evolution of the project over the course of the summer? In what ways does their feedback change over the course of the project, and what does their own reflection suggest about the reasons for these changes? How do patterns in the student's use of daily notes inform his weekly essays? In what specific ways is the student's understanding of the ethics of sustainable development enhanced through reflection on his community experiences? Does the student demonstrate enhanced critical thinking abilities over the course of the project?

As these questions begin to suggest, reflection is a key ingredient in the design of effective service learning, whether domestic or international; and designing it effectively, in turn, is key to harnessing the capacity of ISL to generate significant learning and service outcomes. The reflection process is important in ISL because it is the primary mechanism that generates meaningful and powerful learning. Especially important in the international arena, reflection serves as a needed safeguard against some of the problematic potential outcomes associated with students being directly involved in communities with which they are unfamiliar, including misinterpretations of the motives and behaviors of others, reinforcement of entrenched stereotypes, and the tendency to make insufficiently informed judgments across cultural differences. Although these unintended yet dangerous outcomes are all important issues in domestic service learning, they may be of heightened concern in international settings both for educational reasons and in terms of cross-cultural relations in an increasingly interconnected world. A research agenda conducted on and through reflection in ISL, then, should not only be focused on measuring and improving learning outcomes but should also enhance the ability of practitioners to confront and address these concerns more explicitly through the use of reflection.

Both the process and the products of reflection provide rich grounds for investigating the relationship between the nature of the ISL experience and the outcomes achieved and for examining the ISL experience in-depth so as to understand better its dynamics. Many practitioners find the reflection component of service learning challenging to implement, however, and the difficulties may well be enhanced when service learning is undertaken in an international context. Conducting meaningful research on and through reflection in ISL requires thoughtful, intentional design, so we first establish some of the best practices associated with reflection and then explore possibilities for related inquiry. This chapter will discuss the meaning and role of critical reflection in service learning, explore issues of effective design, and consider the implications of an international context. With this foundation, the chapter provides recommendations for constructing research to study both outcomes and the role of reflection in reaching them.

As intimated in the sample questions above, examining an ISL experience, or any service learning experience for that matter, in terms of the role of reflection naturally allows for consideration of issues well beyond student learning outcomes—issues related to faculty learning and to perceptions of community impact, for example. These are nontrivial questions—vital ones, perhaps, given the context of cultural differences and the partnerships at stake. Further, it is a foundational principle of service learning that all participants in the process teach, learn, serve, and are served, and it is the conviction of the authors that reflection is key to the shared learning promised by the pedagogy. The discussion in this chapter focuses first on the design of reflection for enhanced student learning; we then turn to consideration of questions related to process and outcomes as they apply to faculty and community members in the penultimate section.

The Meaning and Role of Critical Reflection in Service Learning

An important source of difficulty many practitioners have in designing and implementing effective reflection is the widespread misunderstanding of it (Ash & Clayton, 2004; Ash & Clayton, 2009a; Ash & Clayton, 2009b; Clayton & Moses, 2006; Clayton, Moses, & Hayden, 2008; Zlotkowski & Clayton, 2005). All too often the word *reflection* conjures images of stream-of-consciousness writing, keeping a diary, or navel-gazing. It can easily be associated with touchy-feely introspection, too subjective to evaluate in a meaningful way and lacking in the rigor required for substantive academic work. Designing reflection effectively so as to make service learning (or any other form of experiential learning) an educationally meaningful experience for everyone involved and so that it can contribute to an ever-deeper understanding of the pedagogy requires that we "reclaim" the meaning of reflection as an integrative, analytical, capacity building process (Ash & Clayton, 2009b; Clayton & Moses, 2006; Clayton et al., 2008; Zlotkowski & Clayton, 2005).

Dewey (1910) provides a strong foundation for re-conceptualizing reflection, defining it as "active, persistent and careful consideration of any belief or supposed form of knowledge in the light of the grounds that support it and the further conclusions to which it tends" (p. 6). In a concept analysis of reflection as used since Dewey, Rogers (2001) posits that one of the central understandings of reflection is as a process that allows the learner to "integrate the understanding gained into one's experience, in order to enable better choices or actions in the future as well as enhance one's overall effectiveness" (p. 41). Schön (1983) echoes the link to action; he defines reflection as "a continual interweaving of thinking and doing" and suggests that the reflective practitioner is one who "reflects on the understandings which have been implicit in [one's] action, which [one] surfaces, criticizes, restructures, and embodies in further action" (p. 281). Reflection, then, is best understood as "critical reflection": as a process of metacognition that functions to improve the quality of thought and of action and the relationship between them.

Despite the oft-cited maxim that "experience is the best teacher," we know that experience alone is, in fact, an incomplete and problematic teacher; service learning, implemented without well-designed critical reflection, all too easily leads to reinforced stereotypes, simplistic solutions to complex problems, and inaccurate generalization from limited data (Ash & Clayton, 2004; Conrad & Hedin, 1990; Dewey, 1910; Hondagneu-Sotelo & Raskoff, 1994; Stanton, 1990; Strand, 1999). As noted by Stanton (1990), when reflection on service is weak, students' learning may be "haphazard, accidental, and superficial" (p. 185); learning outcomes are likely to be described vaguely with phrases such as, "I learned a lot," or "I got so much out of my experience" (Ash & Clayton, 2004), which are useful neither in assessing learning, evaluating programs, nor conducting research. Without strong critical reflection, even given the short nature of the spring break trip in Vignette 1, for example, students might tend to believe that they have seen, and thus understand, the country and community they have visited. Or, in Vignette 2, students might miss the connections between their coursework and their work with community organizations and thereby both lose rich opportunities to deepen their theoretical understanding and fail to improve their service during the course of the semester through critical integration of academic and community perspectives. Thus, if we are to maximize the outcomes of ISL, practitioners need to understand reflection as Dewey did—as critical reflection—and use it as Dewey's definition implies—as a means of examining thinking.

FIGURE 8.1
Critical reflection as the component of service learning that advances learning.

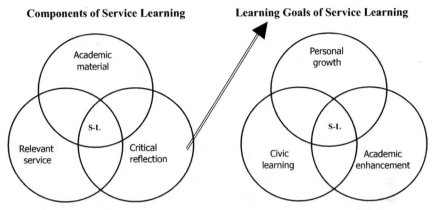

As Figure 8.1 makes explicit, critical reflection is the component of service learning that helps learners make connections between their experiences in communities and bodies of thought (content) that are related to those experiences (Ash & Clayton, 2009a; Ash & Clayton, 2009b; Clayton et al., 2005). Critical reflection helps service learning students achieve a deeper understanding of academic material—including how to think from the perspective of their discipline—of civic agency and citizenship, and of themselves as authors of their own growth. Through the multifaceted approach to critical reflection in his capstone experience, for example, the student in Vignette 3 brought competing theories of sustainable development and of ethical deliberation into conversation not only with one another but also with the lived experience of community members and thereby began to develop his own working theories and his sense of the questions that need to be investigated in the field; he considered questions of voice in international development and in local community development activities and thereby came to understand the role of power and hegemony as constraints on civic agency; and he critically examined his own personal and professional interests in issues related to environmental fieldwork and as a result modified his plan for graduate work to include a heavy focus on environmental social sciences.

Eyler, Giles, and Schmiede (1996) echo this understanding of the essential role of reflection in service learning: "It is critical reflection . . . that provides the transformative link between the action of *serving* and the ideas and understanding of *learning*" (p. 14). When understood in this light and designed accordingly, critical reflection *generates* learning (articulating questions, confronting bias, examining causality, contrasting theory with practice, and pointing to systemic issues), *deepens* learning (challenging simplistic conclusions, inviting alternative perspectives, and asking "why" iteratively), and *documents* learning (producing tangible expressions of new understandings for evaluation) (Ash & Clayton, 2009a; Ash & Clayton, 2009b; Clayton & Moses, 2006; Clayton et al., 2008).

Eyler and Giles (1999) found that the more rigorous the reflection in service learning, the better the learning outcomes. In extensive interviews with students taking service learning enhanced classes across the country, they found that quantity and quality of reflection were modest but significant predictors of many outcomes. In particular, they were associated with academic learning outcomes, including deeper understanding and better application of subject matter and increased complexity of problem and solution analysis. They were also predictors of openness to new ideas, problem solving, and critical thinking skills. Overall, their research showed that challenging reflection activities helped to push students to think in new ways and develop alternative explanations for experiences and observations.

Critical reflection, if well understood and effectively designed, then, can improve the quality of learning and thinking. It can also help improve the quality of students' involvement with the community (Ash & Clayton, 2009b; Clayton & Moses, 2006; Clayton et al., 2008). Critical reflection can be structured to build students' capacity to work in teams, through critical examination of difficulties in making decisions, allocating responsibility, or holding one another accountable. It can serve as a vehicle for monitoring progress toward objectives and, through consideration of the factors that help and hinder progress, for determining appropriate changes in their approaches. Critical reflection can surface misunderstandings of objectives or lack of shared understanding, it can call attention to the importance of clarity regarding objectives and strategies, and it can provide a space for all voices to be heard as objectives and approaches are reconsidered. In Vignette 2, critical reflection could help students better understand how they are being perceived by others in their group and by members of the community; this could support them in making appropriate changes in their behavior as the semester proceeds. In Vignette 3, critical reflection on the effectiveness of his interview protocol could help the student revise unhelpful questions or questions that are being misinterpreted; this could enable him to respect better the time of community members and to produce a more accurate and meaningful inventory.

In summary, as Plater, Jones, Bringle, and Clayton (2009) conclude, "Meaning making before, during, and after the ISL experience is the function of reflection (Ash & Clayton, 2004; Ash, Clayton & Atkinson, 2005; Bringle & Hatcher, 1999; Eyler & Giles, 1999; Eyler et al., 1996; Hatcher & Bringle, 1997);

and any well-designed ISL course or program will include effective reflection" (p. 493). Beyond its role in generating, deepening, and documenting learning, however, in both process and product, critical reflection provides a means of investigating outcomes. The central task, then, is not only to design reflection to generate desired outcomes but also to investigate carefully both those outcomes and the means by which they are generated.

Designing Critical Reflection

The sort of reflection process that generates, deepens, and documents the learning in service learning, and that lends itself to rigorous investigation, does not occur automatically—rather, it must be carefully and intentionally designed. Calling for intentional design of reflection, Eyler et al. (1996) note that it "need not be a difficult process, but it does need to be a purposeful and strategic process" (p. 16). Plater et al. (2009) apply this call specifically to ISL, noting that "maximizing the role of reflection in ISL . . . hinges on its intentional design toward desired learning and service outcomes" (p. 495). Consider the design of critical reflection in the opening vignettes: the preparation of the students on the Alternative Spring Break trip, the timing and form of their guided reflection sessions, and the production of a final product were intentionally designed to maximize the role of reflection during the limited amount of in-country time and to imbed a short (though intense) episode of service in a longer framework of reflection. So too the student in the capstone experience in Vignette 3 carefully created the curriculum, reflection framework, and schedule for communicating with his faculty mentors around his own specific interests and around the particular challenges associated with working alone and without regular faculty contact.

Designing critical reflection in domestic service learning or ISL (or any other form of experiential learning) requires, as does intentional design of any other instructional component or process, beginning with the end in mind (Covey, 1989; Wiggins & McTighe, 1998). Instructional design in service learning is a multistep process (Clayton & Moses, 2006; Clayton et al., 2008). It begins with the identification of learning goals or outcomes, proceeds with the expression of these goals in terms of assessable learning objectives, and continues to the design and implementation of teaching and learning strategies aligned with those objectives and of assessment strategies that are well-matched with the teaching and learning strategies and well suited to contribute to and document attainment of the objectives. Running throughout this process is the use of assessment data to revise the design for enhanced effectiveness in achieving the desired outcomes (and sometimes to revisit the outcomes themselves).

Effectively designing critical reflection involves making a series of choices that are informed by the nature of the learning objectives, the opportunities and constraints that come with the teaching strategy in its context, and the abilities of the participants (Clayton & Moses, 2006; Clayton et al., 2008). These choices produce an overall reflection *strategy* that involves such issues as the following: When, where, and how often will reflection occur? Who will participate in it? Will feedback be provided and if so when and by whom? Which reflection products will be graded, by whom, and when during the semester? How will multiple reflection activities build on one another cumulatively? The reflection strategy includes one or more specific reflection activities or *mechanisms*, the development of which requires the designer to determine such issues as: Toward what specific learning objectives will reflection be structured in a particular activity? What prompts will be used to guide it? What products will demonstrate the learning it generates? What criteria will be used to assess the learning so demonstrated in light of the learning objectives?

Various reflection mechanisms may thus be woven into the overall reflection strategy, both tailored around particular objectives and specific circumstances; the result is a customized plan that integrates critical reflection into the core of ISL experiences. As an example, the student in Vignette 3 designed a tiered reflection strategy that consisted of three primary reflection mechanisms: taking notes throughout each day, developing his notes each evening, and drawing on these notes as he wrote per the prompts in his pre-designed reflection framework several times each week, all of this over the course of eight months; his strategy also included feedback from his faculty mentors and a pre-, mid-, and post-trip progress assessment (per an additional set of predetermined reflection prompts). Some of his reflection mechanisms were individual and some (the subset that engaged with feedback from his mentors on previous products) were collaborative, and all were written so as to keep a record of the development of his thinking over time. The different tiers of mechanisms nested into a single strategy still allowed great flexibility for dealing with unexpected circumstances and the nuances of his cultural setting.

The choice points suggested by this example are at the heart of the task of designing critical reflection, and a body of principles of best practice has emerged to support the course designer in making these choices. Bringle and Hatcher (1999) suggest the following criteria for well-designed reflection: It links experience to learning, is guided, occurs regularly, involves feedback to the learner to enhance the learning, and helps clarify values. Zlotkowski and Clayton (2005) add that it is oriented toward specific learning objectives, is integrative, is assessed in terms of critical thinking, includes goal setting, and generates change in the learner's life. Eyler et al. (1996) posit the "4 C s" of quality reflection: it is continuous (ongoing), connected (with assignments and activities related to and building on one another and including explicit integration with learning goals and academic material), challenging (including in terms of the expectation that students take responsibility for their own learning), and contextualized (to the community setting and broader public issues and to the students' own particular roles). Clayton (2004) offers 10 tips for designing critical reflection, which include the following useful reminders:

- Everything is reflection-worthy: few if any details are too small or insignificant to have meaning.
- Reflection can be written or oral or both, and it can be individual or collaborative or both; perhaps the strongest reflection combines all four possibilities.
- Critical reflection can generate learning outcomes that include knowledge, skills, attitudes/values, and behaviors. If it is to generate assessable learning, critical reflection should be guided in accordance with the desired learning outcomes.
- Critical reflection can be designed iteratively and therefore builds on itself cumulatively. Relatedly, it is helpful to use a pre-, mid-, and post-experience structure that focuses the learner's attention on changes in thinking and on progress toward fulfilling objectives.
- It is useful to begin designing a reflection strategy or mechanism by asking a series of questions:
  ○ Who are the participants (what experience, skills, attitudes, and presumptions do they bring and not bring)?
  ○ Who is the facilitator, if there is one (what experience, skills, attitudes, and assumptions does the facilitator bring and not bring)?
  ○ What are the objectives?
  ○ What are the constraints?
- Reflection requires a safe yet critical space, meaning that the risks associated with meaning making need to be acknowledged and managed while adhering to high standards of rigor in reasoning; learning through critical reflection is often an unfamiliar (therefore risky) process, which requires intentional capacity building.

Several models for designing reflection mechanisms in accordance with such standards have been developed by practitioner-scholars. Perhaps the most widely known model was created by the Campus Opportunities Outreach League; it invites students to consider "What?" they are doing in the community, to ask "So what?" or to explore the significance of their service, and to conclude by asking "Now what?" or to examine implications for the future. Welch's (1999) ABC model suggests guiding reflection so as to include *A*ffective, *B*ehavioral, and *C*ognitive dimensions of learning. More precisely structured than either of these, the DEAL Model for Critical Reflection (Ash & Clayton, 2004; Ash & Clayton, 2009a; Ash & Clayton, 2009b; Clayton & Moses, 2006; Clayton et al., 2008; Jameson, Clayton, & Bringle, 2008) posits three important, sequential steps in critical reflection: *D*escription of experiences in an objective and detailed manner, *E*xamination of those experiences in light of specific learning objectives (in the case of service learning, at least in the categories of academic enhancement, civic learning, and personal growth), and *A*rticulation of *L*earning. The DEAL model requires the development of specific prompting questions in each of the three steps, as shown in Table 8.1.

The DEAL model includes associated tools and rubrics grounded in Paul and Elder's (2005, 2006) standards of critical thinking and in Bloom's (1956) Taxonomy, which are used for both formative and summative assessment of learning. Students are challenged to support their claims with evidence, to clarify the meaning of the terms they use, to consider alternative perspectives, to reason logically, and to represent others' ideas with fairness. And they are supported in such critical thinking to developmentally appropriate levels of reasoning—from identification, explanation, and application to analysis, synthesis, and evaluation—within each category of learning goal (e.g., academic enhancement, civic learning, personal growth). Applying the DEAL rubrics (or adaptations thereof) to Articulated Learnings and other reflection products produces quantitative documentation of student learning outcomes (Ash et al., 2005; Jameson et al., 2008; McGuire et al., 2007).

Intentionally designing critical reflection thus allows for the investigation of a range of questions, especially about student learning outcomes and the processes that generate them. Hatcher, Bringle, and Muthiah (2004) suggest that research into the relationship between reflection mechanisms and student learning can help put into practice the guidelines for the design and implementation of effective reflection. Ash, Clayton, Day, and David (2004) and Ash et al. (2005) point out the limitations associated with the common practice of using as evidence of learning data from student surveys with statements such as "The service experience helped me to understand better course material"; students who say they agree with that statement have not indicated what they learned or provided any evidence in support of their claim to understand better the material (Steinke & Buresh, 2002). Eyler (2000) suggests that such an assessment strategy often confuses student satisfaction

TABLE 8.1
Sample Prompting Questions from the *DEAL* Model for Critical Reflection

Describe	➤ When did this experience take place?
	➤ Where did it take place?
	➤ Who else was there? Who wasn't there?
	➤ What did I do? What did others do? What actions did I/we take?
	➤ What did I/we say or otherwise communicate?
	➤ Who didn't speak or act?
	➤ Did I/others laugh, cry, make a face, etc.?
	➤ What did I/we hear? See? Smell? Taste? Touch?
	➤ Why, as a matter of objective fact, did the situation occur?
Examine *Academic* *Enhancement*	➤ What specific elements of academic material relate to this experience?
	➤ How was I able to apply a skill, perspective, or concept related to the academic material?
	➤ What similarities and differences are there between the perspective on the situation offered by the academic material and the situation as it in fact unfolded?
	➤ Does this experience challenge or reinforce my prior understanding of the academic material?
	➤ Based on analysis of the experience in light of the academic material, is the material (or my prior understanding of it) adequate? What reasons might there be for any differences or inadequacies? What questions should I ask to put myself in a better position to judge the adequacy of the material?
	➤ How can I best express my new understanding of the material?
Civic *Learning*	➤ What was I/someone else trying to accomplish? In taking the actions I/they did, was the focus on symptoms or underlying causes? Was the focus (symptom or cause) appropriate to the situation? How might I/they focus more on underlying causes in the future?
	➤ What roles did each person/group/organization involved in the situation play and why? What alternative roles could each have played? Did I/other individuals act unilaterally or collaboratively and why? Should I/they have worked with others in a different way?
	➤ In what ways did differentials in power and privilege emerge in this experience? What are the sources of power and privilege in this situation, and who benefits and is harmed? How might any inappropriate dependencies be eliminated?
	➤ How did leadership emerge in this situation, on my/others part?
	➤ What is in the interest of the common good in this situation? In what ways is the individual good (mine/others) linked to and/or contrary to the common good? What trade-offs between them are involved? In what way did any other trade-offs (long-term/short-term; justice/efficiency; etc.) emerge in this situation? Who made the trade-offs? Were the trade-offs made appropriate or inappropriate and why?

TABLE 8.1
(*Continued*)

Civic Learning (cont.)	➤ How does this experience help me to understand better my partner organization's vision, mission, and goals? What does it reveal about the relationship between the organization and those it serves? What does it suggest about how this relationship might be improved?
Personal Growth	➤ What assumptions or expectations did I bring to the situation? How did they affect what I did or did not think, feel, decide, or do? To what extent did they prove true? If they did not prove true, why was there a discrepancy?
	➤ How did this experience make me feel (positively and/or negatively)? How did I handle my emotional reactions (e.g., what did I do as a result of my feelings)? Should I have felt differently? Why or why not?
	➤ How did I interpret the thoughts, feelings, decisions, and/or behaviors of others [e.g., How do I think others felt? What assumptions and expectations do I think others brought to the situation (including their assumptions about me)]? What evidence do I have that my interpretations were or were not accurate?
	➤ In what ways did I experience difficulties (e.g., interacting with others, accomplishing tasks) and what personal characteristics contributed to the difficulties (e.g., skills, abilities, perspectives, attitudes, tendencies, knowledge)? In what ways did I succeed or do well in this situation (e.g., interacting with others, accomplishing tasks, handling difficulties) and what personal characteristics helped me to be successful (e.g., skills, abilities, perspectives, attitudes, tendencies, knowledge)?
	➤ How did this situation challenge or reinforce my values, beliefs, convictions (e.g., my sense of right and wrong, my priorities, my judgments)? My sense of personal identity (e.g., how I think of myself in terms of gender, sexual orientation, socioeconomic status, age, education level, ethnicity, nationality, mental/physical health)?
Articulate Learning	➤ What did I learn? ➤ How did I learn it? ➤ Why does it matter? ➤ What will I do in light of it?

with student learning, and she therefore calls for the development of mechanisms that support students in demonstrating concrete learning outcomes. The DEAL model is an explicit response to this call, and its careful integration of reflection with assessment is one example of how intentional design in light of learning objectives can produce not only learning but a sound context for investigating learning.

What sort of questions, then, does a critical reflection process so designed allow researchers to investigate and through what sort of process? Ash et al. (2005) examined changes in students' critical thinking and higher order reasoning abilities across drafts of a single reflection product and over the course of a semester. They also examined variation in critical thinking and higher order reasoning across the learning goal categories of academic enhancement, civic learning, and personal growth. They collected first, second, and final drafts of student reflection products throughout the semester and scored them (blind to author, draft, and date) using the two rubrics associated with the DEAL model. Scores of written products for both the learning objective and critical thinking rubrics demonstrated improvement over the course of the semester; students showed more improvement on the latter and struggled more in the academic enhancement category than in the categories of personal growth or civic learning. Building on this work, Jameson et al. (2008) modified the DEAL reflection prompts and rubrics for application in a nonprofit studies minor in which sequentially designed service learning runs across multiple courses to help the students achieve ever-higher levels of reasoning within the learning goals of five leadership challenges facing the nonprofit sector (aligning mission, methods, and resources; balancing individual interests and the common good; earning the public trust; moving beyond charity to systemic change; and capitalizing on opportunities associated with diversity). They gathered student reflection products from the minor's introductory course, a mid-level course, and the capstone course and scored them using an adaptation of the Bloom-based rubrics in order to examine three questions: Do the reflection and assessment tools facilitate student learning to the level of reasoning desired within each course? Do the reflection and assessment tools facilitate student learning to the level of reasoning desired across the courses in the minor? Is there greater evidence of higher-level reasoning in some leadership challenges than in others? As a third example, McGuire et al. (2007) examined critical thinking demonstrated in reflection products produced by students whose grades on prior assignments were used to identify them as either high, medium, or low competence; they gathered two Articulated Learning products from each of six students in three classes, one produced near the beginning of the semester and one produced near the end, after receiving feedback on interim assignments using the standards of critical thinking as packaged in the DEAL model. The investigators found greater improvement by the students with highest and lowest competence.

In summary, a structured reflection process yielding products that demonstrate learning that is well integrated with an assessment strategy (e.g., through the design of reflection prompts and feedback tools that align with assessment criteria) allows for systematic assessment of student learning. Such an approach can also be used for program evaluation, as when reflection products are similarly produced, gathered, and scored across multiple courses or other program sites, with an eye to the impact of variables across the courses or sites. And this approach supports research related to teaching and learning as well. Theory regarding learning styles, cognitive development, moral reasoning, collaborative learning, learning communities, and peer-facilitated learning, for example, can be applied, tested, and further developed by close examination of student reflection products and through implementing intentional variations in the reflection process as independent variables. We will return to the question of the role of reflection in such investigations after a brief exploration of the implications of the international context for reflection in ISL.

Taking Critical Reflection International

Most of the discussion of critical reflection, here and elsewhere, has considered service learning generically, without regard to its domestic or international implementation. There are, however, significant implications to take into account when designing critical reflection as a component of ISL. Besides merely being an international experience, ISL also appears to both the instructional designer and the participants as interestingly different—though not entirely distinct—from domestic service learning experiences (see chapters in Part One in this volume). No doubt, these differences are part of the reason universities have witnessed recent growth in interest in international experiences generally and ISL more specifically (Plater et al., 2009). But what exactly is packaged in that "international" modifier and the elements of practical experience it captures, and, particularly for the purposes of this discussion, what are the implications of such differences for reflection?

One assumption of many practitioners is that ISL has a unique—or at least significantly different—set of intended learning outcomes in comparison with domestic service learning. Unpacking this international element is important for scholars and practitioners when creating programs or courses tailored to ISL-specific learning objectives, assessing learning, evaluating the influence of ISL programs on communities and on partnerships, and understanding the role of ISL in nurturing students as global citizens. We posit that critical reflection is particularly useful in examining the differences as scholars and practitioners consider the possibilities for and means of conducting assessment, evaluation, and research on ISL. This requires, however, that the critical reflection processes in ISL experiences be carefully designed in accordance with desired learning and service outcomes for international contexts per se and also in anticipation of the unique challenges (and opportunities) that ISL presents.

Unique Learning Outcomes of ISL

As others have addressed in this volume (Eyler, chapter 10; Plater, chapter 2; Tonkin, chapter 9), understanding how to approach research on learning outcomes of ISL begins with consideration of the desired outcomes and how they differ from those of domestic service learning, international education, or traditional study abroad. In addition to program- or course-specific objectives, the designers of most ISL experiences might agree upon, at the very least, the general "intentional goal of developing in students a set of knowledge, skills, and dispositions that are focused on global citizenship," which might include more specifically: "increasing global awareness and knowledge, deepening cross-cultural understanding and an appreciation of diversity, and of experiencing (some other part of) the world first hand" (Plater et al., 2009, p. 485).

How might these goals look when expressed as specific learning objectives that can be assessed through reflection and what sort of unique reflection prompts might be used to help generate such learning? Returning to the categories of academic enhancement, civic learning, and personal growth that are detailed in the DEAL model: What interestingly different types of learning might be produced within these categories of learning goals in ISL? A non-exhaustive list of potential reflection prompts of particular relevance in ISL is presented in Table 8.2.

Well-designed critical reflection is essential in order to support students asking and exploring answers to the sort of questions shown in Table 8.2. However, the ISL situations that provide valuable experiences for reflection in accordance with the questions in Table 8.2 often present significant challenges, leading the course designer to think even more carefully about crafting reflection strategies and mechanisms. Our goal for the remainder of this chapter is to consider the practice of reflection in ISL contexts and the role that reflection and its products might play in assessment, evaluation, and research related specifically to ISL. In doing so, we consider how critical reflection may be complicated by and designed in response to the particular, sometimes challenging, characteristics of the international context.

TABLE 8.2
Sample Prompting Questions for Critical Reflection in ISL

Academic Enhancement	➢ What are the influences of this culture on the applicability of a particular theory or other academic material to a situation encountered in the host community?
	➢ What elements of a given theory might have to be changed to apply to this culture meaningfully?
	➢ What might the role be of ethnicity/national history/culture in the development of theory in the discipline?
	➢ In what ways might the discipline differ in the international context from my experience with it in the context of my home university?
	➢ How would the central metaphors of the discipline be different if they developed in this culture?
Civic Learning	➢ What connections do I see between local (my home community? my host community?) and global communities?
	➢ What are the points of tension between my responsibilities to each of these local communities and to global communities?
	➢ What are the trade-offs I experience between my responsibility to my home community and to this community? How might these trade-offs influence the choices made at home and vice versa?
	➢ What is the interest of the common good from the perspective of the national or political culture of my host country? From the perspective of the global community?
	➢ To what extent and in what ways am I a citizen of my host country while I am there?
	➢ In what ways should I/do I have voice in this community?
	➢ How do members of this community define concepts such as community, leadership, and power? What are the similarities and differences between their definitions and my own?
	➢ What roles do nationality, ethnicity, culture, and history play in these differences? How do these perspectives influence attitudes about social change and the role of politics and public policy in everyday life?
Personal Growth	➢ How has my experience moving in and out of cultures affected me (in terms of my emotional life, my sense of self, and my confidence level)?
	➢ What assumptions have I realized I held about different people/cultures to which I have had little or no previous exposure?
	➢ What skills in communicating across language and cultural barriers have I realized I possess, lack, or need to develop?
	➢ How willing am I to modify my behaviors in accordance with local norms? When and why do these modifications happen (if they do)? What trade-offs am I making (or not making) when doing so (or not doing so)?
	➢ What (if anything) do I compromise in terms of my own values and beliefs in the name of social interactions, access to others/situations, gaining approval, or learning in a different culture that I would otherwise not be willing to compromise? In what ways do my interactions here shed new light on or lead me to rethink my values and beliefs?

Challenges for Reflection in ISL

Given an understanding of how reflection is both an important process that must be carefully designed and a source of products, there are hosts of ways in which the international context can sometimes challenge designing and facilitating reflection in ISL courses or programs. These challenges vary greatly depending on the type of program and on the myriad circumstances involved in students studying in foreign contexts, as detailed throughout this volume, and include, but are certainly not limited to, those variables detailed in Table 8.3.

This list is certainly not exhaustive, nor is it meant to be an account of the ways that ISL differs from domestic versions of service learning; indeed, many of these challenges are present in domestic service learning as well. We are merely attempting to spell out here some of the particular ways that the international context of ISL influences one element of these courses and programs: reflection. We also do not mean to suggest that these challenges are to be seen negatively, as problems or obstacles. On the contrary, many of these challenges should be viewed in a positive light, as components of important life experiences in a globalizing world. Furthermore, in the sense that everything is worthy of reflection, even the more seemingly negative elements of this list provide valuable learning experiences. Service learning is a counter-normative way for most students to learn (Howard, 1998), and in many ways it is its unfamiliar nature that both gives rise to learning challenges and, in turn, gives the pedagogy transformational potential, which is important to fully tap (Clayton & Ash, 2004). If the international dimension of ISL heightens the challenges, then there may be even more value in intentionally engaging the students with the difficulties they are facing, positioning them as the keys to maximized learning, and, even more fundamentally, accomplishing the paradigm shifts at the heart of becoming both self-directed learners and global citizens.

ISL, then, often includes situations that are substantively unique from domestic service learning experiences in terms of designing and implementing critical reflection. Since these variables rarely occur singly, the interactions between them needs to be considered. We offer a few examples of such interacting variables in Table 8.4, which makes explicit from each of the opening vignettes one example of the many challenging situations common to ISL and highlights the elements of the critical reflection design created in response.

The examples in Table 8.4 represent just a few of the ways in which the designers of these specific instances of ISL confronted challenging circumstances with intentionally designed reflection strategies and mechanisms, but

TABLE 8.3
Challenging Variables for Reflection in ISL

Variable	Impacts on Reflection
Distance	• Students may not have regular contact with faculty mentor(s) (e.g., if abroad without faculty presence) to receive feedback or guidance on reflection. • The absence of a group of peers (e.g., during extended periods of time alone) may leave students without the benefit of shared experience on which to reflect or without the benefit of group discussion to generate ideas or to pose alternative perspectives.
Proximity	• The converse of the above, students and faculty members may live shared experiences abroad, making the benefit of outside "objectivity" during reflection harder to achieve. • Students may be so immersed in peer group settings or in their work with community partners that they feel mentally exhausted and/or deprived of private time to think on their own, resulting in lower quality thinking (e.g., a student saying, "I'm not sure *what* I think").
Intensity	• The experiences on which students are to reflect may not be short and episodic interactions with the community partners (e.g., two hours, twice a week, as is sometimes the case for domestic service learning), but rather the entire lived experience of a student, sometimes for months. • Students may have such a wealth of opportunities available in their host communities that they find it difficult to stop and take time to engage in reflection.
Structure	• The daily program schedule may be much less rigid than regular classroom meetings on campus, meaning both the scheduling and process of reflection need to be similarly flexible. • Conversely, days may be so tightly scheduled that quality reflection time is shunted aside in favor of seemingly more immediately necessary activities (e.g., seeing the country, having fun, exploring the city, or even catching up on rest).
Culture	• Cultural issues become a filter (e.g., a set of assumptions, partial understanding, stereotypes) through which students attempt to reflect on their experiences, but this filter must itself constantly be reexamined during reflection. • Students' sense of how well they understand the world around them may be challenged by exposure to a very different way of life, resulting in a lack of confidence in their own ability to grasp experiences on which they are trying to reflect.
Comfort Zone	• Students often have very different comfort levels in foreign contexts (e.g., travel experience, different diet, changes in climate, communication difficulties), which can sometimes make group reflection challenging as certain individuals may have strong reactions to particular circumstances when others do not.

TABLE 8.3
(*Continued*)

Variable	Impacts on Reflection
Technology	• Low technology contexts may limit the possible mechanisms for reflection (e.g., students without access to the Internet or computers). • Relatedly, students may not have the ability to transmit reflection products quickly to their faculty mentor, and the faculty mentor may not be able to return feedback to students easily. • Students may be challenged by a return to pen and paper in capturing their thinking or transmitting their reflection products.
Language	• International contexts may not always involve language barriers, but even when they do not, cultural norms of communication may create confusion for students either during reflection sessions or during daily experiences on which they reflect. • When language is a factor, myriad issues with translation and the level of command of the language can challenge students trying to learn from community members, communicate with community partner staff, or participate in reflection with them.
Entry and Exit	• By design, ISL courses and programs are finite experiences, often viewed as trips or journeys, but (due to intensity, structure, and any of the variables above) they often require preparation before leaving and debriefing after returning home; this may be at odds with the academic calendar. • Much of the actual culture shock occurs in the first few days or weeks, but it can often be most significant upon return to the home culture (i.e., reverse culture shock); learning is very important in these moments, but finding time for reflection activities and support can be a challenge. • Sometimes the transformational impacts of the experience can occur weeks, months, or even years after the end of the program; capturing and capitalizing on these impacts through reflection is thus temporally challenging.

they also illustrate issues that participants might face in the context of ISL and the ways reflection can help program leaders and participants confront them. Importantly, as the examples show, circumstances that present challenges to the design of critical reflection vary greatly with the type of program and its particular characteristics. A common orientation toward these situations does, however, emerge. Although appropriate planning in anticipation of the unique aspects of any program is necessary, part of the design process should also include room for flexibility. Seizing unforeseen learning opportunities, such as impromptu side trips, visiting lectures by host-country experts, cultural performances, or serendipitous moments from everyday life such as seeing an important detail previously unnoticed while walking a routine path

TABLE 8.4

Overcoming Challenging Circumstances Through the Design of Reflection

Challenging Situations for Reflection in ISL	Variables Interacting	Designing Reflection in Response to Challenges
Vignette 1: For the students of the week-long spring break ISL program, actual experience in the international context is both brief and intense; time for assimilation of a new culture and a new place is thus quite short, but reflection while in-country is essential so as to not miss the opportunity to rethink their surroundings while in the moment or to see with new eyes the same experience they saw the day before (after reflecting on their initial observations). Yet, reflection aimed at understanding the cultural, social, and economic contexts of an entirely new place must be a focus before more analytical reflection on the implications of these contexts—where some of the richest learning can occur—is possible. Further, due to the short nature of the program, students may perceive the opportunity cost of time spent in collaborative reflection to be quite high, given that there are numerous activities they might wish to squeeze into the short duration of the trip.	Intensity Comfort Zone Proximity Culture Entry & Exit	This example draws into sharp focus the importance of using early-middle-late strategies to keep students focused on reexamining what they thought they had previously understood or learned—during the trip, but also before and after. Since this trip is not in the context of a course and therefore it is more difficult to do the capacity building needed for effective reflection ahead of time, significant reflection was used before departure to help prime the students to see issues when they arrived. Guided reflection every other day provides a rigorous but not overwhelming routine; faculty are also available on an as-needed basis for students to schedule informal conversations as they feel the need for additional guidance in their thinking. Understanding their objectives and expectations before the trip and reexamining these back on campus in light of their time spent in-country provides a strategy to capture learning. The final product, a form of post return reflection, which guides students to begin to consider the personal implications of their learning from the trip, is a step toward integration of the experience into future growth.

TABLE 8.4
(*Continued*)

Challenging Situations for Reflection in ISL	Variables Interacting	Designing Reflection in Response to Challenges
Vignette 2: As students in the semester-long ISL program become more comfortable in their new surroundings, they must learn not to distinguish between time spent with community partners and the rest of their experiences during the other—though equally new and different—parts of their days (e.g., navigating a new city, wandering through markets, living with a host family, learning a language); as the exotic becomes more routine, it is harder to maintain an outlook in which everything is reflection worthy. Students may become acclimated to serving in their community partner placements to the point that the newness of the experience slips into routine.	Culture Structure Intensity Comfort Zone	In this particular context, the students' guided daily journal includes prompts that push them to not forget their more routine daily matters and interactions. In addition to looking over their journal before the elaboration of their formal reflective essays, students also have the opportunity to be reminded in reflection sessions of other students' experiences with community partners, homestays, and making their way around. Guided discussion in these sessions also focuses on keeping the critical perspective alive. Feedback from instructors on formal essays and the chance to rewrite provides yet another opportunity to remain open to new possibilities.
Vignette 3: The student undertaking his capstone experience is not accompanied by anyone else from the university, as are the students in Vignettes 1 and 2 and, although the design of the reflection strategy calls for continuous written feedback from faculty mentors, the student is often an entire day's journey from Internet access. Further, sometimes long periods of immersion without time for processing are necessary, either for cultural reasons (e.g., during meetings or assemblies, when it may not be appropriate to write in a notebook) or for logistical reasons (e.g., when significant travel means time away from his laptop, such as hikes deep into the forest).	Distance Technology Culture Intensity	The detailed reflection framework developed by the student with his mentors guides the regular integration of old ideas with new ones. Even when there is a communication lag between feedback and new reflection, the frameworks allow for the integration of feedback on previous learning with new insights. The use of multiple notebooks for daily and evening reflection, along with reflection prompts and reflective essays allows for flexibility in both the documentation of ideas and experiences and the ability to keep these elements alive for future use. When not able to type during reflection (i.e., no laptop) or send products to his mentors (i.e., no Internet access), the student becomes accustomed to carrying forward important ideas as well as feedback.

through town (just a few possible examples), is a critically important aspect of ISL experiences, and reflection strategies (and those who implement them) should have the flexibility to respond to these opportunities.

Moreover, even after the greatest attention to detail and the best efforts to anticipate both challenging variables and learning opportunities, coordinating an ISL experience invariably involves unanticipated challenges. Critical reflection should be understood as capable of helping to make meaning of these situations as well. For example, the student in Vignette 3 had planned to involve the community leaders in some instances of his reflection on environmental ethics for his capstone project, but early conversations suggested that some of the community leaders felt uncomfortable with academic philosophy. The student instead found ways to surface some of their opinions through informal conversations not overtly focused on philosophy. He also spent time in reflection with his mentors exploring the possible reasons behind the community leaders' aversion to his academic conversations, his initial assumptions and how they failed to consider the connotations of expert knowledge, and the implications of his discovery on the question of the direct applicability of theory in the particular case of his service.

Addressing challenges such as these necessitates that reflection processes and products be creatively managed in program design so that both rigor and flexibility become institutionalized, mutually reinforcing ways of doing reflection—an important goal of such efforts being that students are shown in explicit ways what it is like to be reflective-in-action and to live as reflective practitioners (Schön, 1983). The ability to engage in such creative design and the confidence that one's designs are generating desired results are enhanced through evidence-based best practices and through continuous scholarly experimentation and inquiry. The following section explores approaches to assessment, program evaluation, and research related to critical reflection in the ISL context, including possibilities for investigations that might yield insight into effective design.

Opportunities for Inquiry on and through Critical Reflection in ISL

ISL confronts the practitioner and the scholar with a rich mix of similarities to and differences from domestic service learning and, for that matter, other forms of international education as well. We now turn our attention to the investigation of ISL, largely in terms of the aspects that lend it unique or at least interestingly different characteristics; note, along these lines, that although the questions derived from each of the vignettes in the opening discussion are rather generic and could apply for the most part to domestic as well as ISL, the discussion in subsequent sections has pointed to additional dimensions of critical reflection as related to ISL per se that warrant further investigation. In the discussion that follows, we will revisit the three vignettes to surface potential questions that focus primarily on the international dimension of ISL, as it manifests in issues related to assessment of learning, program evaluation, and research.

Reflection is both process and a source of products and, thus, can be seen from the perspective of the researcher as both an object of inquiry and a vehicle for inquiry (suggested by the title of this chapter: research *on* reflection and research *through* reflection). As the description of scholarship related to the DEAL model implicitly suggests, however, much investigation related to reflection takes "on" and "through" forms simultaneously: the investigators in each of the three studies described above (Ash et al, 2005; Jameson et al., 2008; McGuire et al., 2007) inquired into the dynamics of the reflection process (the use of instructor feedback, for example)—an *on* reflection lens—by using reflection products as the data source—a *through* reflection lens.

Assessment of Student Learning

In terms of assessing student learning outcomes via investigations on and through reflection, with an eye toward the specific dimensions of learning associated with the international component of ISL, what does the context provided by each of the vignettes suggest in terms of an agenda? In other words, how might intentionally designed critical reflection lend itself to the investigation of learning associated with global citizenship, cross-cultural understanding, and other related outcomes?

- *Vignette 1:*
  - Written products from the students' pre-departure reflection on their assumptions and expectations about the people of Ecuador and the nature of their interactions might be compared to their final journal for evidence of changes in their understanding of their own stereotypes about other cultures, poverty, and privilege (*through* reflection); analysis of the evidence or lack thereof could be used to strengthen the reflection prompts used in both of these assignments and in the group reflection sessions in-country, in order to improve the extent and nature of students' self-awareness (*on* reflection).
  - The students' informal journaling after the evening group reflection sessions and/or the discussion of challenges in their blog posts could be reviewed for indications of the challenges they faced in adapting

to different cultural norms or for examples of the ways in which their understanding of themselves as citizens within multiple communities changed during the week (*through* reflection); comparison could be made between the depth of learning demonstrated in the final journal by the students who chose to engage in this informal journaling and blog-posting and those who did not, in order to understand better the role of writing as a supplement to the oral reflection sessions in-country (*on* reflection).

- ○ A rubric could be applied to the discussion in the students' final journals of the trip's implications for their studies and for their interactions with local communities around their university in order to determine the quality of their ability to apply lessons learned in one culture to behaviors in another (*through* reflection) and the efficacy of the prompts guiding the journal (*on* reflection)

- • *Vignette 2:*
  - ○ The learning expressed in the students' guided journals might be examined from the perspective of the different courses and disciplinary material they bring into their reflection in order to find examples of students integrating different theories or building interdisciplinary approaches (*through* reflection). These results could be used to understand the kinds of prompting mechanisms that best guide students in transcending a particular disciplinary focus and in applying cross-disciplinary academic content to their lived experiences (*on* reflection), toward the goal of helping students become more interdisciplinary in their approach to understanding their cultural context.
  - ○ Notes could be taken during the collaborative reflection sessions (*through* reflection) and examined for examples of student learning that were generated in the collaborative context in order to understand the role of this type of reflection mechanism in helping students process their own experiences in light of experiences and views shared by their peers and mentors (*on* reflection); notes from these sessions could capture the students' identification of the cross-cultural communication skills they both have and need to develop as well as the evolution throughout the semester of their ability to understand and handle misunderstandings and conflicts that arise as a result of differences in communication (*through* reflection).
  - ○ The students' formal essays could be analyzed for specific learning generated both from their own thinking during their required journaling time and from the collaborative reflection sessions (*through*

reflection). The results could be compared to determine the overall efficacy of each of these mechanisms (and the relationships between them) in helping students to process the tremendous amount of material presented throughout the program, particularly if certain kinds of learning are more easily or often generated in the international context through certain types of reflection mechanisms (*on* reflection).

- *Vignette 3:*
  - The written products of student's multi-tier reflection process could be analyzed in order to understand the sort of information each mechanism routinely recorded over the course of the capstone project; this information could be compared with the learning demonstrated in his formal reflection in order to understand the suitability of the different mechanisms to capture important ideas correlated to different kinds of learning (*on* and *through* reflection).
  - The student's written engagement with faculty feedback could be reviewed for instances in which the student demonstrates learning connected to the predetermined learning goals (*through* reflection) in order to analyze the role of remote faculty feedback in the student's reasoning process (*on* reflection).
  - The critical evaluation of the project submitted by the student at the conclusion of the capstone could be analyzed with a critical thinking rubric for evidence of critical thinking skills (*through* reflection).

These examples illustrate how reflection in the ISL experiences described in the vignettes might contribute to assessing learning outcomes. It is also useful to consider how the design of these experiences (specifically, the role of reflection in them) might be enhanced for greater rigor in producing and assessing learning. Any of these experiences could, for example, include before-and-after application of a quantitative scale on cross-cultural competencies and communication skills, or before-and-after completion of a problem-solving narrative related to working with people in the host country; these instruments would then produce additional data on changes in the students' perspectives to triangulate with analysis of their predeparture writing and their final products. Further, any of these experiences could be designed so as to make visible to the students—if not involve them in creating—the criteria for assessing their own learning. The explicit use of rubrics upfront could also include referring to them intentionally in the design of reflection mechanisms and strategies as well as in any processes of peer or instructor feedback on reflection products. Such integration of reflection and assessment promotes stronger design and deeper learning (Ash et al., 2005; Clayton & Moses, 2006; Clayton et al., 2008; Jameson et al., 2008).

Program Evaluation

Among the many variables involved in ISL program design are "the nature of the student population, the language skills of students, the history of prior contacts in the host country, the specific learning outcomes of the course or program, [and] the capacity of the higher education partners to provide desired services" (Plater et al., 2009). In addition, the nature of the service opportunities for students, the form and delivery of the academic content, and, particularly with respect to reflection, the integration of the reflection strategy and its specific component mechanisms into other elements of the program are also important variables. Given this complexity of variables, program architecture and design, or some categorization thereof (see, e.g., Eyler, chapter 10; Jones & Steinberg, chapter 5; Plater et al., 2009; Tonkin, chapter 9), emerges as another important level of investigation on and through reflection. How might the extent to which any particular program design is effective in generating its intended student learning outcomes be investigated? How might different approaches to critical reflection in different program designs (mapping each to its desired student learning outcomes) be studied? How might reflection products be used to examine choice points in program design beyond reflection, particularly as related to student outcomes?

Assessing student learning, as mentioned above, can provide an important basis for program evaluation—at least insofar as the effectiveness of program design in generating desired learning outcomes is of interest in such evaluation. Of course, the number of variables contributing to the learning demonstrated in any of the reflection mechanisms confounds causal analysis and limits the interpretation of results primarily to claims of correlation. Nevertheless, examining each of the vignette's reflection strategy and component mechanisms against its intended and achieved student learning outcomes can aid in both the identification of improvements within each program and the critical comparison of program designs.

- *Vignette 1:*
  - If the students do not demonstrate significant positive change in their assumptions about the people of Ecuador between their predeparture writing and their final journal, for example (*through* reflection), then a next step is to investigate the structure of the reflection sessions in-country, the training of the facilitators of these sessions, and the predeparture orientation of the students in order to focus attention

on the influence of reflection mechanisms on students' previous assumptions while in-country (*on* reflection).

- o Given the increasing use of this Alternative Spring Break model in higher education and the fact that many campuses support several versions of such experiences, variations in program design could be investigated both inter- and intra-institutionally through the use of common reflection mechanisms and products. Students on various trips could all be required to submit final narratives upon their return home, holding the guiding framework constant, so as to evaluate the impact of other pre-identified variables, such as number of reflection sessions in-country and the training of peer facilitators (*on* and *through* reflection).

- o To explore the influence of the public nature of the blogging reflection mechanism compared with the more private nature of journaling or group discussions, program leaders might compare the assessment of student learning across the groups of students who kept a blog and those who did not (*through* reflection). Questions might be posed as to whether students demonstrate their critical thinking and learning through the blog and, if so, how this might lead to a more nuanced approach on the part of the students in how they relate their experiences in a new culture to those back home who cannot share directly in their experience. Examining the content of the students' blogs in relation to the learning assessments, looking particularly at what students chose to share on their blogs in chronological relation to what learning they express in their other reflection mechanisms, might help program leaders better integrate the task of blogging into the reflection strategy through the use of guiding questions to focus students' efforts to share their learning with those reading about their trip from a distance (*on* reflection). This evaluation might also be useful in helping program leaders develop mechanisms to prepare students for the challenges of reentry, as those students who posted to a blog presumably have a starting point from which to share their experience with peers and family members.

- *Vignette 2:*
  - o If program leaders wish to investigate the influence of weekly collaborative reflection sessions (*on* reflection) on the students' assimilation of peer experiences (in or out of their service placement) into their own learning (and thus possibly the effect of individualized service opportunities in a group setting), then they might control for the influence of each instance of the reflection session by examining the

student's guided journal entries (*through* reflection) over the prior week and comparing them to those after the reflection session in order to understand the factors that shape students' learning from each other's varied experiences. The results of such inquiry could be used to develop more effective ways to help students learn from the experience of their peers through, perhaps, prompts that require them to compare and contrast their own experiences with others or activities that build their listening skills and their ability to evaluate critically and apply others' reasoning. Improvements in reflection mechanisms might also be applied to other ISL courses or programs. In a model such as the Alternative Spring Break program, which includes regular collaborative reflection sessions, program leaders could use such prompts to focus students on the comparative aspect of their discussions about their differing experiences while in-country.

- ○ The assessment of the students' formal essays could be examined with respect to the role of instructor feedback on their thinking, perhaps tracing the evolution of student thinking before and after feedback from the faculty member (*through* reflection). By examining the chronological expression of student ideas before and after instructor feedback, for example through examination of their guided journal entries, program leaders might gain insight on the nature and form of feedback that is most useful to students—as well as the role of the guided journal in the students' efforts to process feedback beyond the submission of formal essays (*on* reflection).

- • *Vignette 3:*
  - ○ The student's explicit articulation of learning objectives and his design of a closely matched curriculum and reflection prompts could be examined in light of an assessment of learning for each of the stated objectives (*through* reflection), so as to understand the influence of the self-designed nature of the process on learning outcomes (*on* reflection). Insight from this student's experience could be applied in other program designs in order to focus attention at the individual student level on the desired learning objectives (rather than general prompts for all students).
  - ○ An evaluation of the ways in which the student used the feedback given by his mentors might be conducted in order to understand the role of instructor presence from a distance, particularly through feedback on reflection. Using the multiple notebooks, journals, guided reflection responses, and the final reflective essays, the evolution of the student's ideas and his engagement with faculty feedback could

be traced across his experience (*through* reflection), including the use of feedback in his future reflection, how incorporating feedback influenced the learning demonstrated, and how his self-designed prompts helped to make this an intentional process, even when the flow of reflection and feedback was challenged by distance or logistical issues (*on* reflection). Because feedback is a regular component of program design, such as that in Vignette 2, insights from this evaluation could be applied to the instructor feedback process used there.

○ The critical evaluation of the project submitted by the student at the conclusion of the capstone could be analyzed for evidence of connections between various design choices, the variables associated with its international component (as noted in Table 8.3), and his entire reflection strategy so as to improve understanding of the relationship between self-designed programs and well-adapted rigorous reflection and to aid in both the replication and the scalability of this type of experience (*on* reflection).

As these examples illustrate, program leaders can look at reflection products to compare and contrast the reflection components of various program designs, make recommendations for better designs of reflection in particular programs given the desired outcomes, and build their capacity to adapt and create reflection strategies in light of the unique challenges of ISL. In addition, program evaluation on and through reflection might be used to examine choice points beyond reflection itself, as intimated in a few of the examples above. Reflection products often shed a great deal more light on the nature of ISL courses or programs than the discussion of learning objectives has thus far suggested. Examining reflection products and the processes that produce them might provide insight on non-reflection-related aspects of program design such as: the most appropriate country context; whether and in what ways faculty mentors need to be present; how intense the service experience should be; the length and complexity of the partnership with host communities; how many and what type of opportunities to shadow people vs. work with people vs. interview people in the host country are most appropriate; how much preparation is needed for students to be able to successfully take part in the ISL course or program; and what sorts of trade-offs should be made between strict program structure and student freedom to design particular elements of their experience. All of these considerations also influence student learning and are essential choices in designing successful ISL courses and programs; although these issues transcend the design of particular reflection strategies and mechanisms, student ideas as expressed through reflection as well as the evaluation of reflection as a program element are incredibly rich resources to draw upon when making these design choices.

Research

The discussion thus far has considered the ways reflection in the ISL context is influenced by a number of variables, many of which are unique in the international settings of ISL programs. Investigating reflection accordingly holds the potential to shed light on the nature of ISL; the results of such inquiry could include a better understanding of how to implement effective ISL and a clearer conceptualization of the value of ISL, including its frequently noted transformational effects. Fruitful avenues for research related to reflection in ISL might entail questions similar to those sketched in the sample research agenda here for each of our vignettes:

- *Vignette 1:*
  ○ In what ways does prior experience abroad influence the pace of students' cross-cultural adaptation and with what consequences (e.g., ability to learn in new cultural settings), as demonstrated by the application of rubrics to their reflection products? Are these outcomes moderated by prior service learning experience, and, if so, are they significantly moderated by the extent and nature of the critical reflection component of that prior experience?
  ○ Are the gender dynamics of collaborative learning moderated by the gender-related norms of the host country and, if so, how does this dynamic operate differently in the home country? Does this impact vary with the presence or absence of community members in the reflection sessions? Does it vary with the gender distribution of the student group or with the gender of the reflection facilitator?
  ○ Are students' comfort level and confidence upon entry into a short-term ISL experience predictors of their comfort level and confidence upon exit? What is the relationship between this predictive power in an ISL experience and in a domestic experience?
  ○ How does a reflection strategy integrated into the students' experience before and after the trip moderate the effects of culture shock upon arrival and of reentry shock upon return (Kiely, chapter 11)? What relationship exists between the intensity level of reflection and the degree to which students report a smoother, less challenging experience with their entry and exit?

○ How might the experience of the ISL spring break trip compare with a domestic service learning version of the same program model in terms of transformational impact on students beyond the end of the trip, particularly as captured by reflection?

- *Vignette 2:*
  ○ In what ways is the impact of guided practice in learning through reflection sensitive to students' prior experience in international learning environments? To what extent does this relationship apply to instances of domestic service learning with populations from cultures significantly different from the students' own?
  ○ What is the most effective mix of individual and collaborative reflection in supporting students' cross-cultural adaptation in a long-term immersion? What student variables have the greatest impact in determining the most effective combination (e.g., age, maturity level, prior international experience, prior service learning experience, prior experience with collaborative learning) and why?
  ○ In what ways do homestay environments that include similar-age family members affect the rate at which students begin to question the primacy of their own culture's understandings of such concepts as community, power, and voice? How are these effects moderated by prior experience abroad and by the presence or absence of other peer-learning relationships in the students' lives?
  ○ How does the reflection strategy of the program help students capture and learn from all aspects of their experience in the international context (i.e., not only time spent in service with the community partner)? How does this compare to the extent of learning connected to non-service-related experiences in a domestic service learning course or other forms of international education?
  ○ To what degree does the element of self-designed experience present in the semester-long program (i.e., students being able to select their own combination of courses, choose their service placements, and direct their own learning between multiple categories of academic content and their service experience) contribute to a stronger sense of self-authorship and ownership of their own learning? By way of comparison, how might this same variable be measured during a regular semester on their home campus and what influence does the international context have on any differences?
- *Vignette 3:*
  ○ What is the role of the self-authorship of the reflective learning process in building students' confidence in their ability to manage a

potentially overwhelming international capstone (one that presents them with multiple, interconnected new experiences and contexts)? Does this role vary along with the emotional and/or cognitive maturity level of the student? Does it vary with the extent of the student's prior international experience?

○ Do particular learning styles lend themselves more readily to students making effective use of remote instructor feedback in the reflection process?

○ How do the student's expressed motivations for designing the capstone, compared with the learning and critical evaluation of the project, give insight into the role of the self-designed context in creating circumstances for juniors and seniors to further their academic enhancement, civic learning, and personal growth? Of these insights, which are due to the self-designed nature of the program and which are due especially to the international context in which the program was carried out? Of these insights, which are most applicable to the design of domestic service learning capstone projects?

○ How does engagement with faculty members as mentors at a distance alter the student's understanding of faculty/student relationships? How might the "expert" status conferred by his lived international experience, which is not being shared by the faculty members, contribute to this understanding?

Inquiry Beyond Student Outcomes

One of the major limitations associated with investigations on and through reflection in ISL is that student reflection provides primary access only to students' thinking and learning, whereas the goals of ISL can be broader than that—including mutual growth of students, faculty, and community partners; enhanced partnership building between institutions; and cross-cultural sharing, among others, as several other authors in this volume have described (Kiely, chapter 11; Plater, chapter 2; Sutton, chapter 7; Tonkin, chapter 9). Student reflection can provide access to outcomes for faculty, residents, or staff at partnering institutions and nongovernmental organizations, but these insights may contain biases inherent in any attempt to represent others' thoughts.

However, reflection need not be—and, given our understanding of pedagogy, perhaps should not be—an activity that involves only students. As reflection is the aspect of ISL that generates, deepens, and documents learning outcomes, insofar as scholars and practitioners are interested in outcomes of ISL beyond students, reflection should by extension be useful in doing assessment, program evaluation, and research related to outcomes for the full range of participants.

Considering how this might best be done takes us back to one of the fundamental elements for effective design of critical reflection: beginning "with the end in mind." Hence, for reflection strategies and mechanisms to be appropriately designed to include the full range of participants, the objectives or intended outcomes for a particular ISL course or program as they relate to other constituencies would first need to be determined. In so doing, in accordance with the spirit of engagement, instructors or faculty might not want to decide upon these objectives (or go about designing reflection) alone. All potential participants in the reflection process could be involved in its design and could draw on their understanding of its intended outcomes (Kahn, chapter 6).

It follows then that particular strategies for reflection, as well as methods of assessment, evaluation, and/or research, could also be mutually designed and agreed upon. Given the concern about the impacts of ISL on the local community noted elsewhere in this volume (e.g., Kiely & Hartman, chapter 13; Sutton, chapter 7; Tonkin, chapter 9), researchers might not want to investigate the question "What impact does the ISL program have on the local community?" through community participation in reflection until the question "What should we be trying to achieve together?" has been asked and the implications of the answer have been worked into the overall design of the program (Kahn, chapter 6). Communities and, to the greatest extent possible, students as well, might be positioned alongside faculty in outlining objectives and designing reflection strategies best suited to meet them rather than faculty or researchers retrofitting broad participation in reflection on existing program structures.

The important questions raised about community outcomes, partnerships, and faculty development—to which institutional change might also be added—should be areas for research on ISL and through ISL (see Kiely & Hartman, chapter 13, for a discussion on community-based research). However, designing critical reflection for these partners needs careful groundwork in order to be maximally beneficial and effective. Explorations of community impact, partnerships, and non-U.S. perspectives on international programs (e.g., Erasmus, chapter 15) seem highly relevant to thinking about the groundwork for mutually constructed learning objectives and the reflection processes that might help achieve them. This is a significant future direction for domestic service learning and ISL, not only for research but for practice as well. In that spirit, the remainder of this section considers the potential of such an expanded approach.

Given that ISL also generates outcomes and produces impacts at scales larger than the individual partners, scholars and practitioners might also be interested in broader levels of analysis, such as from the perspective of various *institutions* involved (primarily, colleges and universities, and the organizations providing the service opportunities, including public, private, and nongovernmental organizations) or the outcomes generated specifically from within the *partnership* created between all involved in the enterprise of ISL. Table 8.5 polishes the lens of a broader use of reflection in ISL programs and explores examples of the types of questions researchers might ask in investigations *on* and *through* reflection related to the other partners in service learning and at these levels beyond the individual partners.

These questions begin to explore the potential of critical reflection as a process not designed only for students, but rather as an inclusive activity involving each of the partners in ISL and each of their respective relationships (Bringle, Clayton, & Price, 2009). In order for reflection to provide answers to many of these questions, data would need to be gathered that many ISL courses and programs (including those types illustrated in the vignettes) are not necessarily ready to produce or acquire. This does not, however, mean that reflection could not or should not provide such information, but rather that collecting such data would necessitate rethinking the ISL program and course design, operations, and assessment. Nevertheless, considering the potential types of information that these additional processes might yield would be important in monitoring, evaluating, and studying ISL programs and courses.

There are challenges and trade-offs associated with such multi-partner reflection. Although it has the potential benefit of creating a more inclusive space for shared learning, it also risks making the reflection space—whether physical or virtual—less authentic through the silencing of voices associated with reluctance to examine critically issues in which others are involved when those others are present. Not unique to ISL, this would necessitate the investment of time and capacity building into making the reflection space safe for this type of multi-partner reflection while also keeping it critical—in turn heightening the significance of ISL in producing outcomes associated with deliberative democracy and with multicultural exchanges. In instances of multi-partner reflection where students, faculty, and community members are involved in individual reflection activities, there is the issue of added time involved in also engaging in collaborative reflection. Additionally, there is the very practical point that greater investments of time would likely be needed on the part of faculty members and community partners in order to take part in a program that uses reflection strategies focused on all partners rather just on students. Acknowledging that many situations in which the aspirations of

TABLE 8.5
Sample Questions Across All Partners in ISL for Inquiry *on* Reflection and *Through* Reflection

Across All Partners	• What are the current learning outcomes for each partner in ISL programs? What elements of the ISL experience are the most significant influences on that learning? • Why does each of the partners choose to participate in particular ISL programs (e.g., motivations, expectations, assumptions)? • What types of common understandings are necessary in order to design an effective and appropriate multi-partner reflection process? • What partner-specific forms of reflection might be most effective in producing the desired program outcomes? How might these be integrated into a common reflection strategy in which all partners participate?
Faculty	• What types of faculty development activities best prepare faculty members to both facilitate and be participants in collaborative reflection aimed at making meaning of shared experience? • Through increased participation of faculty mentors in student reflection, what relationship might exist between faculty learning and improved service outcomes?
Community Partners	• How might the outcomes of an ISL course or program for community partners be understood better through reflection? What challenges do community partners face while participating in reflection activities and how do they influence such documentation activities? • How might critical reflection produce better service outcomes for communities? In what ways might this effect be enhanced and/or diminished through the participation of community partners in reflection? • How might various cultural understandings of reflection (or of knowledge, the appropriate role of students, the meaning of service, or the dynamics of citizenship) influence the participation, roles, or effectiveness of community partners in the reflection process?
Institution	• In what ways does ISL advance institutional goals, and how might the way the institution conceptualizes ISL be changed to deepen that impact? How might reflection products better help institutions measure the impact ISL programs have on faculty development? On student development? On community voice? On partnership processes? • How could an institution learn to build capacity for the practice of reflection in domestic service learning and non-service learning campus courses (e.g., practica, internships) through information gathered from studies on reflection in ISL (e.g., mission, learning outcomes across curricular components, program review, accreditation)? • Where, at the level of the university as an institution, are students being adequately prepared for international competency objectives of ISL through the curriculum?

TABLE 8.5
(Continued)

Institution *(cont.)*	• How does the integration of international education, study abroad, and service learning through ISL suggest or provide examples of institutional infrastructure and/or instructional design that support the desired outcomes of ISL? • How can ISL courses and programs provide narrative and information that can be used in campus web pages, articles in alumni publications, communications and marketing, and institutional assessment?
Partnership	• Which particular reflection mechanisms might lead to enhanced or diminished levels of communication between community partners and faculty, program leaders, or partnering institutions? • How might a strategy for reflection involving students, faculty mentors, and community residents and leaders help to arrive at an understanding of the most appropriate form of partnership fostered between the university and the community? • How might reflection be used in understanding the meaning and importance of sustainability in particular ISL partnerships? • What variables determine the extent to which partnership relationships are transactional? Transformational? Growing or withering?

the spirit of an engaged pedagogy like service learning (such as multi-partner reflection and learning) must be balanced against time and other constraints, the underlying point is that all partners need to be interested in learning through reflection from the ISL experience (including learning how to make the partnership and the collaborative arrangements more effective) and need to have the opportunity to build their capacity to do so in order to take full advantage of the opportunity provided by reflection.

The discussion of multi-partner reflection is based on the conviction that, to be aligned with the spirit of engagement upon which the service learning pedagogy is founded, ISL programs should consider designing critical reflection so as to include all partners—despite the impracticalities or logistical challenges such activities would present. Although the primary motivation would be to enact more inclusively the principle that all learn and all are served, an important potential result—at least for our purposes here—would be the elaboration of data rich with potential insights for scholars and practitioners. To further press the point of an inclusive endeavor, an even more appropriate orientation—again, despite the challenges it would seem to present—would be to have all partners involved in the shared articulation of the agenda for monitoring, assessment, evaluation, or research (see Kiely & Hartman, chapter 13, for a discussion on community-based participatory research). Just as the presumed starting point for creating optimal multi-partner reflection strategies would be multi-partner collaborative design of ISL programs themselves (including discussion of shared outcomes), the ideal starting place for the design of a related inquiry process is the creation of a shared set of research questions and an appropriate, collaborative methodology to pursue them.

Conclusion

As an inherent part of any form of service learning and thus a requisite element of ISL, critical reflection can best be understood as the component of the pedagogy that generates, deepens, and documents learning and that, consequently, can function to improve the quality of the service learning activities and their educational and community benefits. These are strengths that service learning adds to both study abroad and international education (Bringle & Hatcher, chapter 1). For it to fulfill this potential, it must be carefully designed with circumstance-specific reflection mechanisms carefully woven into an overall reflection strategy—one that contributes in integral ways to the broader course and program design. ISL presents particular challenges to the reflection process, which can be met through intentional design that is both rigorous in terms of critical perspective and flexible in its orientation to unique and evolving circumstances.

Connecting what we know about research on service learning (Eyler, chapter 10) and on study abroad and international learning (Kiely, chapter 11; Lewin, 2009) and the goals of proposed frameworks for research on ISL throughout this volume with our discussion of the vital role of critical reflection in the ISL context, it is clear that reflection is an important component of any framework for investigating ISL. Inquiry into the reflection process (inquiry *on* reflection) and inquiry via reflection products (inquiry *through* reflection) are potential simultaneous avenues for better understanding both outcomes in ISL and the role of critical reflection in achieving them.

Although reflection is both a process and a product, the focus here has been primarily on its instrumental use in analytic inquiry. Critical reflection is ultimately a strategy to generate and deepen learning and, in the educational enterprise, reflection has immense value in and of itself. Our goal has been to capitalize on the synergistic potential of the reflective process, via its intentional design, to also produce extremely useful forms of data for conducting both quantitative and qualitative research on ISL courses and programs. The vignettes suggest sample questions and surface relevant issues that might facilitate assessment of student learning, evaluation of programs, and research into the unique nature of the ISL experience (particularly as contrasted with domestic service learning, domestic international education, or traditional study abroad).

Underlying much of the discussion about how reflection can improve the understanding and practice of ISL is the suggestion that investigations of ISL can improve service learning more broadly. Despite their interesting differences, a research agenda conducted on and through reflection in ISL, then, should not only be focused on measuring and improving outcomes for all involved in ISL (and on the related task of enhancing the ability of the partners to more explicitly design ISL courses and programs toward shared outcomes) but should also shed light on the understanding and practice of the pedagogy of service learning more generally and, in fact, of teaching and learning more broadly. Good research and practice in ISL can and should drive good research and practice in domestic service learning and vice versa. As they are grounded in shared fundamental commitments that arguably neither yet fully enacts, developments in ISL can thus help compel and enable service learning in all its forms to better fulfill its potential, and inquiry on and through reflection perhaps has a key role to play in helping them evolve together in a way that is true to their common ideals.

Acknowledgments

We would like to thank Julie Reed for helpful insights and clarifications, particularly a constant eye toward broadening the discussion of ISL to encompass community partners and instructors. We thank Richard Kiely for review of an early draft and insight on the challenges of reflection. And we are grateful to Robert Bringle and Julie Hatcher for organizing the author roundtables, which provided many useful spaces for collaboratively exploring our thinking.

References

Ash, S. L., & Clayton, P. H. (2004). The articulated learning: An approach to reflection and assessment. *Innovative Higher Education, 29,* 137–154.

Ash, S. L., Clayton, P. H., & Atkinson, M. P. (2005). Integrating reflection and assessment to improve and capture student learning. *Michigan Journal of Community Service learning, 11*(2), 49–59.

Ash, S. L., & Clayton, P. H. (2009a). Generating, deepening, and documenting learning: The power of critical reflection for applied learning. *Journal of Applied Learning in Higher Education, 1*(1).

Ash, S. L., & Clayton, P. H. (2009b). *Teaching and learning through critical reflection: A tutorial for service-learning students (Instructor Version)*. Raleigh, NC: Ash & Clayton.

Ash, S. L., Clayton, P. H., Day, M. G., & David, J. S. (2004). *When what you say isn't what they do: The development of formative and summative assessment strategies to help guide teaching and learning*. Invited pre-conference workshop presented at AAHE's Assessment Conference, Denver, CO.

Bloom, B. S. (1956). *Taxonomy of educational objectives, handbook I: Cognitive domain*. New York, NY: David McKay Company.

Bringle, R. G., Clayton, P., & Price, M. (2009). Partnerships in service learning and civic engagement. *Partnerships: A Journal of Service-Learning and Civic Engagement*. Elon, NC: North Carolina Campus Compact.

Bringle, R. G., & Hatcher, J. A. (1999, Summer). Reflection in service learning: Making meaning of experience. *Educational Horizons, 77,* 179–185.

Clayton, P. H. (2004). *10 tips for designing reflection activities*. NC State service-learning program. NC State University.

Clayton, P. H., & Ash, S. L. (2004). Shifts in perspective: Capitalizing on the counternormative nature of service-learning. *Michigan Journal of Community Service Learning, 11,* 59–70.

Clayton, P. H., Ash, S. L., Bullard, L. G., Bullock, B. P., Moses, M. G., Moore, A. C., O'Steen, W. L., Stallings, S. P., & Usry, R. H. (2005, Spring). Adapting a core service-learning model for wide-ranging implementation: An institutional case study. *Creative College Teaching, 2,* 10–26.

Clayton, P. H., & Moses, M. G. (2006). *Integrating service-learning: A resource guide*. Boston, MA: Jumpstart.

Clayton, P. H., Moses, M. G., & Hayden, E. (2008). *Project SHINE faculty resource guide: Strategies for incorporating SHINE service-learning into academic courses*. Philadelphia, PA: Project SHINE, Temple University.

Conrad, D., & Hedin, D. (1990). Learning from service: Experience is the best teacher—or is it? In J. Kendall and Associates (Eds.), *Combining service and learning* (pp. 87–98). Raleigh, NC: National Society for Internships and Experiential Education.

Covey, S. R. (1989). *The seven habits of highly successful people*. New York, NY: Simon & Schuster.

Dewey, J. (1910). *How we think*. Boston, MA: D.C. Heath and Company.

Eyler, J. (2000, Fall Special Issue). What do we most need to know about the impact of service-learning on student learning? *Michigan Journal of Community Service Learning*, 11–17.

Eyler, J., & Giles, D. E. (1999). *Where's the learning in service-learning?* San Francisco, CA: Jossey-Bass.

Eyler, J., Giles, D. E., & Schmiede, A. (1996). *A practitioner's guide to reflection in service learning*. Nashville, TN: Vanderbilt University.

Hatcher, J. A., & Bringle, R. G. (1997). Reflection: Bridging the gap between service and learning. *College Teaching, 45*(4), 153–158.

Hatcher, J. A., Bringle, R. G., & Muthiah, R. (2004). Designing effective reflection: What matters to service learning? *Michigan Journal of Community Service Learning, 11,* 38–46.

Hondagneu-Sotelo, P., & Raskoff, S. (1994). Community service-learning: Promises and problems. *Teaching Sociology, 22,* 248–254.

Howard, J. (1998). Academic service learning: A counter normative pedagogy. *New Directions in Teaching and Learning, 73,* 21–29.

Jameson, J. K., Clayton, P. H., & Bringle, R. G. (2008). Investigating student learning within and across linked service learning courses. In M. A. Bowdon, S. H. Billig, & B. A. Holland (Eds.), *Advances in service learning research: Scholarship for sustaining service-learning and civic engagement* (pp. 3–27). Greenwich, CN: Information Age.

Lewin, R. (2009). Introduction: The quest for global citizenship through study abroad. In R. Lewin (Ed.), *The handbook of practice and research in study abroad: Higher education and the quest for global citizenship* (pp. xii–xxii). New York, NY: Routledge.

McGuire, L., Ardemagni, E., Wittberg, P., Strong, D., Lay, K., & Clayton, P. H. (2007). *Faculty learning, student learning, and the relationship between them: A collaborative scholarship of teaching and learning project*. Indianapolis, IN: Assessment Institute.

Paul, R., & Elder, L. (2005). *The miniature guide to critical thinking; Concepts and tools. The Foundation for Critical Thinking*. Dillon Beach, CA: The Foundation for Critical Thinking.

Paul, R., & Elder, L. (2006). *Critical thinking: Tools for taking charge of your learning and your life* (2nd ed.) Saddle River, NJ: Prentice Hall.

Plater, W. M., Jones, S. G., Bringle, R. G., & Clayton, P. H. (2009). Educating globally competent citizens through international service learning. In R. Lewin (Ed.), *The handbook of practice and research in study abroad: Higher education and the quest for global citizenship* (pp. 485–505). New York, NY: Routledge.

Rogers, R. (2001). Reflection in higher education: A concept analysis. *Innovative Higher Education, 26,* 37–57.

Schön, D. (1983). *The reflective practitioner: How professionals think in action*. New York, NY: Basic Books.

Stanton, T. K. (1990). Liberal arts, experiential learning and public service: Necessary ingredients for socially responsible undergraduate education. In J. Kendall and Associates (Eds.), *Combining service and learning* (pp. 175–189). Raleigh, NC: National Society for Internships and Experiential Education.

Steinke, P., & Buresh, S. (2002). Cognitive outcomes of service-learning: Reviewing the past and glimpsing the future. *Michigan Journal of Community Service Learning, 8*(2), 5–14.

Strand, K. J. (1999). Sociology and service-learning: A critical look. In J. Ostrow, G. Hesser, & S. Enos (Eds.), *Cultivating the sociological imagination* (pp. 29–37). New York, NY: American Association for Higher Education.

Welch, M. (1999). The ABCs of reflection: A template for students and instructors to implement written reflection in service learning. *NSEE Quarterly*, 25, 22–25.

Wiggins, G., & McTighe, J. (1998). *Understanding by design*. Alexandria, VA: Association for Supervision & Curriculum Development.

Zlotkowski, E., & Clayton, P. (2005). *Reclaiming reflection*. Presentation at the Gulf South Summit on Service-Learning and Civic Engagement, Cocoa Beach, FL.

PART THREE

CONDUCTING RESEARCH
ON INTERNATIONAL
SERVICE LEARNING

9

A RESEARCH AGENDA
FOR INTERNATIONAL
SERVICE LEARNING

Humphrey Tonkin

A considerable amount of research literature on domestic service learning has accumulated over the past several years, including a number
of attempts at developing a comprehensive research agenda (Boyte &
Hollander, 1999; Giles & Eyler, 1998; Ramaley, 2000; see Bringle & Tonkin,
2004, p. 369, for additional references), and there is also an extensive and
growing literature on education abroad (see the online bibliographies of Chao,
n.d.; Weaver, 1989; the two extensive updates by Comp, 2003, n.d.; and also
Bachner, 1994),[1] but the literature on international service learning (ISL) is
less extensive and no comprehensive research agenda appears to exist, beyond
the preliminary work by Bringle and Tonkin (2004). The present chapter
is intended to build on this earlier work and to serve as a guide for those
interested in conducting research into this growing field.

Our first problem is one of definition: What constitutes ISL? Is it simply
a way of packaging learning or is it a pedagogical philosophy? Are its North
American roots in community service or in study abroad? The concept was
born 50 or more years ago in two parallel developments: the founding in
Britain of Voluntary Service Overseas (VSO; initially as a gap-year program
for men), in the late 1950s,[2] and the growth of national service programs in
developing countries—self-help efforts aimed at advancing development, particularly in the newly independent countries of Africa. Both of these efforts
were directed not so much at the participants as at the people they served,
though VSO (and its later descendant, the U.S. Peace Corps) was intended

to harness the energy of young people around service that would give them a different perspective and engage them in civil society (Adams, 1968; Bird, 1998; Dickson, 1976; Dickson, 2004; National Student Volunteer Program, 1977). The national service programs, modeled on nation-building activities in Israel and elsewhere, did not involve an international component, nor were they necessarily integrated into university programs of study (they were sometimes intended to alleviate manpower shortages and in other cases to deal with their opposite: youth unemployment), but many of these programs were intended to address issues of commitment to the public good, were conceived in the context of capacity building in higher education, and were established through international cooperation under the auspices of the United Nations and United Nations Educational, Scientific and Cultural Organization (UNESCO). Since the early days, forms of in-country community service, often with a curricular component, have been introduced in national settings, sometimes by government fiat. The Philippines and Mexico are examples (Innovations in Civic Participation, n.d; Metz, Alessi, Stroud, Riquelme, & Smith, 2008; Perry & Thompson, 2004; Tonkin, 2004, pp. 259, 309). Other examples from the past include the voluntary youth summer work-camp programs that were organized in the years following World War II to assist in postwar construction. Many were loosely connected with UNESCO.[3] Today, there is a vast range of service and service learning activities all across the world, described comprehensively, though in very preliminary fashion, by Berry and Chisholm (1999)—in a survey that needs updating.

We should recognize at the outset the rather obvious point that North American views on the nature of service and service learning are not common to all cultures, and that not all ISL has an American educational underpinning (Erasmus, chapter 15). The foundation of such organizations as VSO, and the debate in UNESCO on community service at that time, were conceived primarily (though not exclusively) in terms of the benefits to the communities served rather than in terms of their effects on the participating volunteers.

Missing from such early examples (and we should note in passing the need for good historical studies of these early days: we are constantly in danger of reinventing the wheel, or the flat tire) was much consideration of the pedagogy of service learning—particularly the relationship of action and reflection that is so central to North American models. However, this is not the *only* consideration in ISL: the planner, educator, or researcher approaching the field should recognize that ISL involves a multiplicity of actors. Fundamentally, the process serves, or should serve, two groups: the service learners themselves and the population with which, to a greater or lesser degree, they interact. Behind the learners stretch the vast perspectives of educational theory and practice, institutional structures, and the like; behind the population served stretches the equally vast panorama of historical antecedents, cultural influences, public policy, concepts of service, and social structures.

In what follows, I will focus above all on North American practice, but not to the exclusion of the larger scene. The researcher coming to the ISL field must sort these varied practices out, and recognize that the American experience is determined in large part by American higher-education structures, American ideologies of service and of international engagement, and American concepts of experiential education.[4] One of the biggest challenges facing the researcher in this field is overcoming this parochial bias.

American models of ISL stress impact on students rather than on the community—sometimes to an unsettling degree, as Erasmus points out in her contribution in chapter 15. One reason for the relative neglect of community impact is the fact that, historically, ISL emerged as an expansion of study abroad in the direction of community service, rather than an expansion of community service in the direction of study abroad. This perception is reinforced by the painfully widespread view in many study abroad circles that the study abroad enterprise exists to serve an American purpose, namely, the liberal education of the student passing through it (e.g., Hovland, McTighe Musil, Skilton-Sylvester, & Jamison, 2009). It is but one step from this belief to the damaging notion that the larger world exists as a kind of classroom where the American student can learn values or skills that can be transferred to the United States and that student's adult life. To see the world in this way is to lose all sense of reciprocity, an issue central to service learning and explored by Longo and Saltmarsh (chapter 4). At best, study abroad programs are expected to do no harm to the communities in which they are located: rarely is the question raised as to how they can actually do good.[5]

Given the foregoing, we can define three fundamental elements in ISL and in service learning generally:

1. *Students*, participating in . . .
2. A *service learning process* that engages . . .
3. The *community served* . . .

We are often so preoccupied with the feedback from number two that we ignore the impact on number three. If we cannot demonstrate that that impact is benign and useful, it is ethically questionable whether we should be engaged in it at all. Our goal must be to do good with regard to all three components of the definition.

Whereas most students enrolled in domestic service learning remain at home and engage in service learning as one of many activities, ISL takes students to a different country where they generally devote the bulk of their time to service learning activities and related experiences. In the domestic setting, service learning is but one part of a more diverse set of parallel curricular activities; in the international setting, it may consume most of the students' time. Thus, the overseas experience tends to be more intense, more demanding, and ultimately perhaps more transformative (Cluett, 2002; Kiely, 2004, 2005) than the domestic experience. We should, of course, ask ourselves whether intensity and self-transformation are or should be part of our goal— and we should note in passing that the concept of youthful transformation may itself have roots in American, or Christian, ideologies (and American preoccupation with subjectivity), and may be a concept superimposed on American ideas of higher education that are more cultural than educational (e.g., ideas of study abroad as travel to the "frontier" [Grünzweig, 2002] or as Odyssey [Chisholm, 2000; Smelser, 2009], and indeed of education itself as transformative).[6] Because of the nature of the experience and of the learning expectations placed on students, most ISL takes place at the college level, or at the level of advanced degrees, whereas much of domestic service and service learning comes about as a result of high school requirements as well as college-level activities.

At the other end of the process, the communities served may be very different, and the impact on these communities may vary. In the overseas context, some ISL courses and programs are project oriented: students build a school, or provide specific kinds of health care. Others are process oriented: students spend time working with agencies that serve communities. Sometimes students will work as teams, and thus may reinforce one another's essentially North American perceptions (albeit challenged by their interaction with the local culture and well-structured reflection, Whitney & Clayton, chapter 8), whereas in others (particularly in the process-oriented courses and programs) they will be immersed to a greater or lesser degree in the host culture (possibly with homestay). Sometimes there will be a translingual element involved: students will be expected to use a foreign language to carry out their service, or they will perform their service in spite of language differences; in others, the local population will speak the same language as the students. Programs will also vary in length—from a few days to a semester or more. Indeed, increasingly ISL programs are conceived as experiences of short duration, wedged into the interstices between other educational commitments, in winter terms, in spring breaks, and the like. In sum, generalization is all but impossible. Although we can argue that some models achieve certain objectives better than others, what matters is that program design be matched to intended objectives and that we not try to do everything with a single model (Eyler, chapter 10; Jones & Steinberg, chapter 5; Whitney & Clayton, chapter 8).

In an earlier discussion (Bringle & Tonkin, 2004) we noted the following design variables:

- The relationship between agency and classroom and the role of reflection in this relationship,
- The nature of the agency work and students' engagement in it, particularly the distinction between process-based and project-based experiences,
- The degree of embeddedness (in some service learning programs students may work with their peers, whereas in others they may work exclusively or almost exclusively with in-country coworkers and separately from their peers),
- The intensity of the service (the number of hours per week, the degree of responsibility put on the student),
- The duration of the service (short-term versus semester-long or year-long experiences),
- The nature of the population served, and
- The setting (e.g., urban environment, rural environment, industrialized country, developing country).

Different designs produce different outcomes, and are accordingly related to program goals, student goals, and pedagogical goals. Thus, when a course or program is in the planning stages, it is crucially important to align course and program design with expected outcomes (including learning outcomes and service outcomes) and, as the program moves forward, to employ formative methods of assessment to be sure that programs are meeting their objectives. Learning outcomes may be narrowly focused on disciplinary achievement, or may include cross-cultural competence or more general notions of global citizenship (a notoriously slippery term, but an important variable; see Lewin, 2009b).

Berry and Chisholm (1999) found a number of interests uppermost in the minds of educators involved in service learning programs around the world: education reform, the development of humane values, leadership, citizenship, cross-cultural communication, the melding of theory and practice, and student interest. Many of them seem quite sharply different from North American views and remind us that transnational cooperation in service learning activities requires particular attention to assumptions about shared values. Berry and Chisholm's investigation reminds us again that ISL may have many purposes, and may achieve its goals to varying degrees. We must also make a clear distinction between actual practice and desired or desirable outcomes: significant in the literature is the ease with which researchers latch on to stated hypotheses rather than examining actual practice.

One fairly comprehensive effort at examining both practice and ideals was a Ford Foundation-sponsored study, *Service-Learning Across Cultures* (Tonkin, 2004), of the programs of the International Partnership for Service-Learning and Leadership (IPSL), conducted in 2001–2002 around three groups of actors: students, host institutions (the colleges and universities where the students were based and under whose auspices they studied and served), and service agencies.

Assessment and Research

We should distinguish among planning (which may or may not include preliminary research), evaluation and assessment (the application of a set of criteria derived from a prior definition of goals), and what might be called pure research (which may include subsequent analysis of data accumulated through the assessment process, but involves a wide range of other considerations). *Service Learning Across Cultures* (Tonkin, 2004) contains a chapter, *Evaluating Partnership Programs*, which lays out criteria that might be used to assess the effectiveness of individual programs. These criteria were based in part on the Model Assessment Practice that IES Abroad uses for its study abroad programs, but were adapted and expanded to fit ISL, particularly the programs of IPSL (IES Aboard, 1999). They grew out of extensive discussion among program directors, board members, students, and others within IPSL (Tonkin, 2006a, 2006b). All too often, planning for ISL is limited, and enthusiasm for execution tends to outrun environmental scans or feasibility studies, except with respect to the bare logistics of getting programs up and running.

The checklist that follows does not attempt to limit the analysis to "pure" research, but includes what might be better called assessment and evaluation as well. Indeed, many of the interesting research questions listed below require that the means of measurement be devised for the previously unmeasured. But obviously research that goes beyond merely descriptive data collection is desirable. Student assessment is commonly divided into three categories of increasing complexity: knowledge, skills, and dispositions (attitudes and beliefs). There is a vast literature on knowledge assessment, a rather more restricted literature on the acquisition of skills, and what can only be described as an ocean of approaches to the measurement of changes in attitudes and beliefs (for a sense of their range, see Bringle, Phillips, & Hudson, 2004; Eyler, chapter 10; Kiely, chapter 11; Long & Saltmarsh, chapter 4). Virtually all of this literature is ancillary to ISL, though efforts have been made to establish connections. On the service side, the impressive work of Perry and Thomson (2004) to make sense of the impact of civic service in the American context will be useful to ISL researchers in the international context.

Efforts to create a research agenda for ISL began in a workshop in Chiang Mai, Thailand, in January 2004, conducted during a conference of primarily American educators. Later we revisited the list, adding observations on the methodology, limitations, and possible outcomes of research on ISL (Bringle & Tonkin, 2004). The present list is a refinement of this earlier work, taking into consideration also the larger context of the field. As we contemplate this list, it is worth reiterating that such related fields as study abroad research, (domestic) service learning research, experiential education research, research on international education, research on the scholarship of teaching and learning, and research on cross-cultural communication and intercultural sensitivity intersect with and need to inform subsequent ISL research.[7]

Broad, Fundamental Issues in ISL Research

Informative assessment, evaluation, and research on ISL will be possible when several broad, fundamental issues are clarified by scholars.

The nature of ISL.   Can we distinguish between ISL as a programmatic practice and ISL as a particular philosophical approach to teaching and learning? With its early association with the experiential learning movement, and with its emphasis on Deweyan definitions of learning, service learning is often conceived as a quite different, collaborative, and experiential approach to learning (Billig & Eyler, 2003; Longo & Saltmarsh, chapter 4; Montrose, 2002; Plater, chapter 2). To what extent does this philosophy of learning, based as it is on action and reflection and on values clarification, manifest itself in ISL, or is ISL simply an extension of more or less conventional teaching practices in a new setting? Is ISL merely an extension of study abroad, and, if so, to what extent can study abroad be defined as involving a different approach to education or different pedagogies? The relationship between study abroad and ISL sheds light on the unique qualities and ideological underpinnings of ISL (Bringle & Hatcher, chapter 1), and serves as an important reminder that ISL, like most other educational practices, is *not* ideologically neutral, but *is* ideologically diverse. We might add that people who have worked in ISL over many years tend to relish the educational value of questioning received assumptions and they see the combination of learning and service as both complementary and oppositional, just as they see this apparently profoundly North American idea of service learning as philosophically challenging when transported into an international setting, as Erasmus discusses in chapter 15.

The concept of ISL, or, as Longo and Saltmarsh (chapter 4) prefer to call it, global service learning, would seem relatively easy to define, but in fact it raises numerous questions. How can service, learning, and service learning (terms associated above all with American approaches to education) be defined or redefined from multiple (non-American) perspectives? And what has the American experience in formal programs of study abroad (with a history dating back to the 1920s and 1930s, see Hoffa, 2007) and in other forms of international engagement (ranging from warfare to development assistance and nongovernmental organization work) brought to these interrelated issues? What has the experience of other countries contributed to the development of ISL? Study of the history of service learning and its various precursors, especially the early concept of study-service, and its manifestation in its near-relative, national service (Hoffa, 2007), will help to define its roots and will contextualize the American experience in a wider setting. Currently, no such comprehensive study exists.

ISL and internationalization. Many colleges and universities seek to open themselves up to the larger world and some aspire to become "global" universities (Kehm & Teichler, 2007; Kelleher, 1996; Mestenhauser, 2002; Tonkin & Edwards, 1981). How does ISL contribute, and how could it contribute, to the internationalization of higher education (Plater, chapter 2; Plater, Jones, Bringle, & Clayton, 2009)? The internationalization of higher education is both a positive force (more knowledge of the world can only be regarded as a benefit) and a negative force: it reinforces a trend toward homogenization in higher education—or, more optimistically called harmonization—that may be constricting as well as liberating, since one way to increase student mobility is by decreasing organizational and curricular diversity (Ninnes & Hellsten, 2005). This trend toward homogenization (Engle & Engle, 2002) may be countered by the cultural immersion of ISL, with its stress on difference and on reciprocal engagement (Altbach & Knight, 2007; Longo & Saltmarsh, chapter 4). At the same time, to embark on ISL is often to come into contact with non elite sections of the population whose worldviews are as different from those of their own in-country elites as they are from those of the elites of America (Berger, 2000). This essentially subversive nature of ISL is particularly worthy of study.

The cultural and philosophical context of ISL. How do theories of development and theories of culture interact with practical experience in ISL settings?

As Kahn suggests in chapter 6 and Erasmus in chapter 15, ISL mediates between a largely Western, often North American, view of education and its purposes (e.g., a view tied to accreditation, definitions of academic quality, awarding academic credit, a particular educational philosophy), and an often non-Western cultural view, in which epistemological assumptions may be quite different, and ideas about the nature of service, or the purpose of the alleviation of poverty, or even of poverty and education themselves, may differ from ours (Chisholm, 2004; Monard, 2002; Monard-Weissman, 2003; Porter & Monard, 2001; Reagan, 2005). The literature of international development and capacity building addresses this complex issue quite frequently (e.g., the UNDP's 2004 Human Development Report, Fukuda-Parr, 2004). Chisholm (2004) considers the ways in which five of the world's great religions look at the concept of service and at the individual's responsibility to society (as already observed, we should not ignore the strong Christian bias in American models of service). In his book on non-Western educational traditions, Reagan (2005) points out that an understanding of how other peoples educate their young "may help us to think more clearly about some of our own assumptions and values" (p. xi). One of these assumptions may be our notions of helping. Are students engaged in ISL to help or to learn, and are notions of helping the less fortunate or the less educated expressive of a certain condescension?

The economic and political context of ISL. How can ISL researchers conceptualize and address the economic and political context of ISL, particularly in a world that is increasingly globalized in ways that inform theories, hypotheses, and the nature of future research? What has brought the phenomenon into being, and what has determined its growth? Braham (1999) examines the relationship between volunteer service abroad and the relative prosperity of a given society. The growth of ISL as an element in higher education would seem to be related not only to theories of education but also to the economic status of institutions and of students and their parents (we need to know more about the demographics of ISL participation). It may also intersect with public policy considerations, such as those examined by Perry and Thomson (2004), with theories of civic engagement and its surrounding social discourse (Ehrlich, 2000; Longo & Saltmarsh, chapter 4; Zemach-Bersin, 2009), and with assumptions about globalization (Grünzweig & Rinehart, 2002).

Reciprocity and mutuality. How can research assess the degree of reciprocity and mutuality between programs and host countries? An assumption fundamental to effective ISL is that it should be beneficial to both sender and host (Sutton, chapter 7). Maintaining that balance is both an ethical and a pedagogical issue, and also an issue related to research (Erasmus, chapter 15). Respect for the customs, culture, and peoples of the host country is essential. What are the assumptions that go into such a balance, and how can it be assessed and studied? Bound up with such assumptions are issues of power and authority in ISL, and the relationship between information and expertise on the one hand and experience on the other hand (contested territory that can easily destabilize ISL relationships). The issue of reciprocity, as we have already noted, is more and more frequently addressed in study abroad circles (on reciprocity as an element in study abroad, see Grünzweig & Rinehart, 2002; Lutterman-Aguilar & Gingerich, 2002). Ogden (2007) points to the possibly growing problem of the "colonial student" abroad—the study abroad student who does not integrate with the host culture and tends, through such aloofness and sense of superiority, to reinforce anti-American stereotypes in the host country. Might ISL inadvertently reinforce such "colonial" attitudes (Grusky, 2000; Kahn, chapter 6; on multicultural education and service learning, see Langseth, 2000)?

Education and teaching. What are the pedagogical and educational assumptions behind ISL? Vande Berg (2007) notes a growing gap in study abroad between the assumptions and desires of administrators and professors on the one hand, and program design and student expectations on the other hand (see also Ogden, 2007; Zemach-Bersin, 2009). Does that apply to ISL? We have already noted the philosophical groundings of ISL in Deweyan theory (both action/reflection and the democratization of education, see Longo & Saltmarsh, chapter 4; Plater, chapter 2), in the experiential education movement in the 1970s and 1980s, and in North American ideas of liberal education, civic engagement, and career preparation. The late Howard Berry has provided some of the most stimulating analyses of the pedagogy of service learning, particularly as it relates to the international dimension; see his essays in Chisholm (2005; see also Bringle, 2003).

Action and reflection. The process of reflection lies at the heart of all service learning, but it is a concept with more resonance in a North American setting than elsewhere—in part because of the faculty member's particular relationship with the student (a culturally and institutionally determined relationship that is not shared, by and large, by other cultures or higher education systems). It is a process not easily mastered even by American professors; if professors from other countries are involved, they must be very carefully incorporated in the course design. Furthermore, the American professor well equipped to deal with reflection in an American cultural context will probably be less comfortable in a cross-cultural setting. Bringle and Hatcher (1999, see also Hatcher, Bringle, & Muthiah, 2004) have rightly called for more investigation of the reflection process; it is a particularly important priority in an international setting, as Whitney and Clayton (chapter 8) explore in detail. We also need research to understand better how to teach this skill to both professors and students in ways that reach intended outcomes, which may require institutional investment in infrastructure to support faculty to develop ISL courses and programs.

Institutional structures and the taxonomy of ISL. ISL programs can take many forms (Barnhill, Gilmore, Sawada, & Brown, 2007; Jones & Steinberg, chapter 5). One way of thinking about ISL programs is in terms of the institutional arrangements for their operations. With a preliminary taxonomy of such courses and programs (Jones & Steinberg, chapter 5) and dimensions on which ISL courses and programs vary (Bringle & Tonkin, 2004), subsequent research can explore issues such as defining how they are related to study abroad offices and community service offices, how they are financed, and to what extent they are institution-based (both at home and in the host country), operated by third parties, or developed at host institutions. Other considerations include the role of faculty and the role of host-country institutions (both academic and civic). Do they aim primarily at cultural immersion or primarily at practical results (or is that a false dichotomy)? Some, of course, grow out of study abroad programs in individual institutions (Sutton, chapter 7; Wessel, 2007) or are appended as additional options. Often, they are conceived by faculty members to achieve a particular curricular goal or because of particular international research interests. Such programs may result in a high level of educational intensity but a low level of continuity, and they may or may not be adequately integrated into local needs and priorities in the host country.

Program design. What are the relative merits of different forms of program design? Achieving clarity on the goals and objectives of ISL programs before they go into effect is crucially important (Whitney & Clayton, chapter 8; Grusky, 2000), and that design should take into account not only learning objectives and outcomes for students (including the extent to which these objectives include values clarification and change, see Jones & Steinberg, chapter 5; Pusch, 2005; Steinberg, 2002; Whitney & Clayton, chapter 8) but also service objectives for the larger community (Erasmus, chapter 15). An examination of the different ways of organizing ISL programs (and their outcomes) will help clarify the differences between, and relative strengths of short-term vs. long-term programs (Dwyer, 2004; Smith-Pariolá, &

Gòkè-Parióla, 2006), project-based vs. process-based activities, and individual vs. cohort-based ISL courses and programs. It may include assessment of the particular constraints on program design (curricular, institutional, financial, cultural, durational), and lead to definition of the role, or potential role, of host-country colleges and universities on the one hand and service agencies on the other hand (or, indeed local authorities, see Riner & Becklenberg, 2001; Sutton, chapter 7). As already noted (Jones & Steinberg, chapter 5), there is no ideal model for ISL, because different models can serve differing purposes and produce differing outcomes (and may have to take local factors into consideration).

Leadership education and ISL. What is the relationship of leadership education to ISL? The field of leadership education has spawned a large literature and an abundance of programs. The concept itself may make ISL practitioners uneasy (can service and leadership ever coincide?), even in its recent mutation, led by Greenleaf (1977, 2002) and others, into what is known as servant-leadership. Brown (chapter 3) explores the role of leadership as a set of educational outcomes and Plater (chapter 2) explores the importance of having leadership in higher education play a role in developing and supporting ISL programs and the broader purposes of internationalizing higher education.

Study abroad and ISL. What, then, is the relationship of study abroad to ISL? Given that study abroad has proved the major design factor in the development of ISL (similar accreditation and validation arrangements, similar assumptions about program design, overlapping assumptions about outcomes), how can we differentiate between the two, not just in terms of design, but also in terms of outcomes (culture learning, global citizenship, language proficiency, all of which are articulated as goals of both)? Bringle and Hatcher (chapter 1) and Plater et al. (2009) provide an analysis of study abroad and ISL that concludes that ISL is more than just study abroad with a community service component added. The implications of this analysis need to be further clarified through research that carefully studies the consequences of these differences. Does ISL reach outcomes more effectively, or less effectively, than study abroad, or are they fundamentally different? Research on study abroad has expanded greatly in recent years; there may be much in its research literature that is applicable to ISL or useful for comparative purposes. Kiely (chapter 11) explores these issues from the point of view of similarities and differences between study abroad and ISL, with particular emphasis on how conceptual models can inform ISL research. He also demonstrates that research on study abroad is quite weak in scale, rigor, and contributions to a cumulative knowledge base, and better research on study abroad and ISL will improve practitioners' capacity to design programs and courses that meet intended educational outcomes and community outcomes.

The ethics of ISL. What are the ethical implications of service learning in an international setting? Organizers of service learning programs have an ethical obligation to balance student development against commitment to service; students have a responsibility to agency clients and to community members; agencies have a responsibility to their volunteers. Recent years have seen advances in defining the complex ethical issues involved (Aquino, 2001; Chapdelaine, Ruiz, Warchal, & Wells, 2005; Langseth, 2000; Rich, 2002; Schaffer, Paris, & Vogel, 2003; Wells, Warchal, Ruiz, & Chapdelaine, chapter 14), but little or no work has been done on framing these considerations as research questions, nor on setting them in an international context, where host-country ethical behavior may also differ from American assumptions. We might add that many ISL courses and programs are designed with relative indifference to these important issues. Whitney and Clayton (chapter 8) explore the use of reflection as a mechanism for enhancing community voice in developing, implementing, and evaluating ISL courses and programs; Kiely and Hartman (chapter 13) suggest that community-based participatory research can be a means for informing practice and empowering communities through the research process; and Sutton (chapter 7) illustrates how the ISL course can be a mechanism for gaining additional information from the community to inform revisions to subsequent offerings of a course. Finally, Wells et al. (chapter 14) present strategies for representing the host country in ethical considerations across the entire research process.

Student Recruitment, Application, and Acceptance

With students at the center of any analysis of ISL, future research needs to address how and why student-based issues are related to outcomes in ISL courses and programs.

Student motives. What motivates students to engage in ISL (or convinces them against it), including religion and other personal convictions, academic priorities (especially language learning), and prior experience with service and service learning? It is at least possible that the principal determining factor in students' engagement in ISL is a prior history of civic engagement or charitable activity, perhaps as a result of the expansion in recent years of K-12 service learning programs or a parental history of volunteering (Eyler, chapter 10).

Perhaps such considerations are crowded out by more immediate concerns, like progress toward a degree, a desire to study abroad in a different setting, peer influence, or alienation from conventional academic study.

Student finances. What can research discover about students' financial resources as a selection factor? More and more institutions, and even state and federal bodies, are trying to address the problem of the equitable financing of study abroad. Nonetheless, many students fail to choose it apparently because of the need to have a job, or to support family members. It may be that certain ethnic or socioeconomic groups are largely excluded from participation because of cost, or because of a confluence of financial and social factors. The problem of financial resources to support student participation in ISL raises many public policy issues that can be explored with research (Martinez, Ranjeet, & Marx, 2009).

Student selection. What criteria and procedures for student selection should be put in place to ensure that students have a successful ISL experience? What student qualities are indicators of success with ISL? The very term *successful ISL experience* raises questions about assumptions on the part of students and their institutions, and hence of stated or assumed student and institutional criteria for success. Defining such success will depend in part on the assumptions and expectations of institutions, professors, and the students themselves (Kim & Goldstein, 2005). To the extent that students do not exhibit such indicators of success, programs may be needed to compensate for shortcomings, or mechanisms put in place to exclude students who may not be able to work effectively in an ISL setting (where the client and the client's needs are as important as the student and the student's needs).

Student readiness and preparedness. What can research determine about the needs of ISL students for orientation and advice prior to departure? Is it different from the needs of other study abroad students? Predeparture orientation is increasingly regarded as an important part of preparation for study abroad. Research can investigate to what extent students are academically prepared to engage in ISL, and to what extent preparation for ISL extends to cross-cultural training, language training, values clarification, and country-specific knowledge. Kiely (chapter 11) provides an extensive summary of models, theories, and past research that can frame how research questions are generated and how they might differentiate between, for example, traditional study abroad and ISL.

The gender gap in ISL. What can research reveal about the extent and nature of the gender gap in ISL? The demographics of ISL show a significant gender gap; Tonkin reports that in IPSL programs some 80% of participating students are women (Tonkin, 2004). This bias may in part reflect biases across fields of study, or merely replicate the female bias in the helping professions, the female bias in such fields as language learning (Kissau, 2007), and the female bias in study abroad in general (Kim & Goldstein, 2005). Perhaps the problem lies in male self-perceptions or an unwillingness to compromise identity, or simply commitments to educational priorities or family. On the other hand, perhaps research on ISL programs can guide in designing recruitment strategies and ISL courses and programs to counteract such biases.

Student Characteristics and Outcomes

ISL promises to have significant and possbily tranformational consequences on students. Future research can explore a host of questions related to the nature of these outcomes.

Assessing student outcomes. Much research on ISL inevitably requires the development of survey instruments to assess student attitudes and beliefs. Bringle et al. (2004) offer valuable advice and survey instruments from the perspective of service learning (Bringle, Hatcher, & Williams, chapter 12). Durrant and Dorius (2007) provide a brief review of survey instruments for study abroad. Volume 10 (2004, Fall) of the journal, *Frontiers*, was dedicated to study abroad assessment and contains numerous helpful contributions, as do Vande Berg, Balkum, Scheid, and Whalen (2004) on study abroad, and Kiely and Hartman (chapter 13), Tonkin (2004), and Tonkin and Quiroga (2004). Each of these resources can contribute to considering what outcomes are expected from ISL (Whitney & Clayton, chapter 8) and how to systematically assess those outcomes in ways that can enhance an understanding of why they are or are not occurring in the student (Bringle et al., chapter 12).

Language competence. What is the role of language acquisition and proficiency in ISL courses and programs? How important is it to know the local language or—in multilingual settings—local languages? How does use of language in ISL contribute to deeper cultural understanding and skills? How can such language proficiency be acquired, and is it aided by placement in service settings? Can programs be designed to minimize the effects of language difference, and at what cost? It is a common American failing to underestimate the importance of engaging with local people at all levels and on their terms. Thus we conclude that, at most, students need to know French to manage in Morocco, or English to do community service work in Ghana. But if they wish really to engage with local populations beyond their immediate circle, they clearly need more. How can they be provided with basic language knowledge quickly, and how can this be supplemented with reasonable communicative competence? And what is the relationship in such settings between linguistic competence and communicative competence? How can research identify strategies for overcoming a language deficit? Related to this question is another, namely, the extent to which students ever receive instruction in their home institutions about how to learn languages in general. Often, the focus is entirely on the acquisition of a particular language with no attention to the basics of language learning. Finally, is the ISL experience likely to be more rewarding in a foreign-language setting than in an English-language setting? The study abroad evidence would seem to suggest so. For example, Norris and Steinberg (2008) provide a brief bibliography of other studies of language proficiency gains in study abroad; these can provide a starting point for research in ISL courses and programs.

Comparative language acquisition.   What are the comparative language proficiency gains among students in differing settings abroad (study abroad, ISL, community service), and how can these gains be maximized in ISL? Recent attention to the assessment and measurement of language gains in study abroad settings (Cohen, Paige, Shively, Emert, & Hoff, 2005; Freed, 1995; Norris & Steinberg, 2008; Vande Berg, Balkum, Scheid, & Whalen, 2004) has produced some surprising results (particularly the lack of linearity in registering language gains). Little has been done to examine such issues in ISL settings. First impressions would suggest that active engagement with the population of the host country through community service and the need for efficient task-oriented communication in agency settings should lead to more rapid and more permanent gains in proficiency, when compared to typical instruction and study abroad, but no research has evaluated this hypothesis.

Attitudinal changes: political beliefs and behavior.   What can research tell us about changes in students' political, social, cultural, and personal views on international issues (e.g., foreign aid, peace initiatives, monetary policies), attitudes toward them (optimism, cynicism) and changes in behavior (e.g., voting, public service, volunteer service, career choices), as a result of ISL, both short term and long term? In study abroad research there is a growing literature on such changes (Dwyer & Peters, 2004) as there is in the service learning literature (Eyler, chapter 10), but we know relatively little about these outcomes for ISL (see Kiely, chapter 11 for some preliminary results). If we recognize that the intensity of the ISL experience is likely to produce change, how can research increase the understanding of how and why these changes occur, their effects over time, years after the event (an important variable in this context)—and what is the relationship between changed beliefs and changed behavior (Kiely, 2004; Peterson 2002; Pusch, 2004; Tonkin, 2004; Tonkin & Quiroga, 2004)?

Attitudinal changes: global perspectives. How can research inform us about changes, as a result of ISL, in students' knowledge, values, and behavior that encompass a global perspective on civic concerns—a defining issue of ISL (Bringle & Hatcher, chapter 1; Longo & Saltmarsh, chapter 4)? Does ISL cause the development of such a perspective more effectively than domestic service learning, study abroad, or domestic international education? There are almost as many definitions of a global perspective as there are people working in the field (Lewin, 2009 a; Longo & Saltmarsh, chapter 4). In many respects Hanvey's description of an attainable global perspective (Hanvey, 1976) has never been bettered (but see also Lambert, 1994a, particularly the essays by Lambert himself [Lambert, 1994b] and Wilson, 1994; see also Bennett, 1993). Developing instruments to measure such changes is extremely difficult (Torney-Purta, 1994) but is a necessary step in developing research that attends to these key questions. Gillespie, Braskamp, and Dwyer (2009) present a comprehensive model for viewing these issues from a holistic perspective and provide direct and indirect measures for assessing some outcomes.

Attitudinal changes: cultural and emotional integration. Many critics of study abroad have noted that young Americans, particularly, have difficulty in integrating fully with the local population (Citron, 2002; Engel & Engel, 2002), perhaps because of particularly American traits that militate against integration, perhaps because of the American cohort-based approach to study abroad design, or perhaps because of linguistic limitations. If such integration is a goal—and it is more likely to be a goal in long-term ISL courses and programs—does ISL offer a better model for such integration than traditional study abroad or various other forms of international educational experiences? Might ISL also offer opportunities for reflection and experience that could lead to a higher level of what Goleman (1995), echoing Salovey, calls "emotional intelligence"—defined as the ability, for example, "to motivate oneself and persist in the face of frustration; to control impulse and delay gratification; to regulate one's moods and keep distress from swamping the ability to think; to empathize and to hope" (Goleman, 1995, p. 34; see also Salovey & Mayer, 1990, and, for the application of these findings to study abroad, Harrison & Voelker, 2008)?

Students' academic preparedness, knowledge, and persistence. To what extent does ISL increase students' academic preparedness, knowledge, and persistence—goals that extend beyond the course level of analysis? Many colleges and universities actively encourage study abroad, or, at the least, some form of international educational experience, as a part of an undergraduate's education; but the relationship between these experiences and the educational process at home (e.g., graduation, seeking postgraduate degrees) remains unclear. Outcomes assessment is crucially important if study abroad and international experiences are to find a firm foothold in the curriculum and if curricular designers are to make wise decisions that earn the support of the executive leadership of the campus. Research needs to determine how ISL contributes to a student's readiness and preparedness to learn after returning to the home campus. Does ISL affect the ways in which students study? Does it increase self-reliance and self-efficacy, as domestic service learning does (Eyler, chapter 10)?

The psychological challenge of ISL.   What are the psychological challenges confronting ISL students? One of the many issues facing ISL administrators and instructors is the problem of students who find adaptation difficult. Students may have adjustment problems at home, and these problems are often exacerbated by foreign study; they may be even more acute for a student in ISL. What can be done to anticipate and manage such challenges and problems, and how can their effect on other students be minimized or contained? Kiely (chapter 11) provides an overview of theories and research on these questions from the study abroad literature; future ISL research can further inform the international education field about the nature and limits of these issues for ISL students.

ISL and other international experiences.   Research comparing ISL with other forms of international experience and international education is much needed. Advocates of ISL (e.g., Berry & Chisholm, 1992; Plater et al., 2009; Tonkin, 2004) often maintain that it offers unique opportunities for engagement with the host-country culture—opportunities of a quite different kind from that offered by conventional study abroad, domestic international education, cocurricular international community service, or cocurricular international travel. Research on ISL needs to develop the capacity to compare and contrast these different experiences, realizing that the variability within each category may be greater than the differences between them (Eyler, chapter 10).

Reentry and reverse culture shock.   Given the intensity of ISL experiences in many settings, will research demonstrate that returning ISL students undergo greater problems of adjustment than returning study abroad students, and what are the adjustment challenges and problems likely to be? The phenomenon of culture shock (Ward, Bochner, & Furnham, 2001) and its definition are hotly contested by study abroad specialists (see a review by Kiely, chapter 11). The work of Siegel (2004), Whiteley (2004), Quiroga (2004), and Pusch (2004) suggests that reentry is particularly problematic for ISL returnees, indeed that the depth of immersion abroad during ISL may be directly proportional to the intensity of adjustment following return. How can subsequent research clarify this? And how does this process of adaptation lead to values accommodation that may produce an integrated view of the larger world in relation to American society, or does it lead to cynicism or alienation? In short, in what ways does the adjustment process have positive or negative outcomes? All of these questions are, of course, ideologically fraught and the models of adaptation that are presented by Kiely (chapter 11) need to be evaluated more thoroughly for students in ISL.

Effects of ISL on career choice. What can we learn about the influence of the ISL experience on students' career choices? Akande and Slawson (2000) report that 95% of study abroad alumni stated that study abroad affected their worldview and their career paths; does ISL have a comparable effect? Sullivan (1988, 2004, 2005) has renewed the call of John Dewey, Jane Addams, and others for universities to educate students toward civic professionalism (Longo & Saltmarsh, chapter 4; Plater, chapter 2). In Sullivan's view, the civic-minded professional embarks on a career with a public-service orientation in mind, rather than a purely technical or economic/profit orientation to the career of choice. One of the clearest ways in which students can manifest these attributes is by choosing a career in the nonprofit service sector, or by developing civic dimensions to a career in any field. In making these choices, students are clearly demonstrating that they value civic engagement. There seems to be some evidence that ISL affects career choice (Tonkin, 2004), but it may be that the students who participate are already predisposed to the careers they eventually enter. Subsequent research can clarify the nature of these effects and determine the extent to which ISL manifests its transformational nature on subsequent career decisions and pathways, particularly in ways that reflect a civic orientation.

Faculty Practices, Attitudes, and Beliefs

Faculty are the instructional designers of ISL experiences and are key individuals in providing high quality experiences for students and host communities. However, even when faculty are motivated to embark on designing ISL courses or programs, there can be serious gaps in their knowledge and skills to do so. Future research can clarify how faculty development programs can be designed and improved to produce rewarding outcomes for all.

Faculty assumptions. Although the preparation of students for study abroad and ISL receives extensive attention, the preparation of faculty to be global educators (Schattle, 2009, p. 6) cannot and should not be taken for granted. Just because a faculty member has been a Peace Corps volunteer, traveled extensively in a country, or collaborated with international scholars does not necessarily provide the requisite knowledge to design an ISL course or program; but what is that knowledge and how can it be provided? What does it take to assist faculty to design effective ISL courses and programs? What assumptions do faculty members bring to ISL and how do these assumptions change across ISL experiences? Does involvement in or awareness of ISL change faculty attitudes on international issues, global awareness, and pedagogy? Research can address these questions with several different groups: the faculty members who sit on curriculum committees and approve the programs, the American faculty members who travel with students to the host country, and host-country faculty members who collaborate on American ISL (Erasmus, chapter 15). We know relatively little about faculty attitudes on such matters, and even less about how to influence them. However, there is evidence that international education and study abroad are viewed as marginal by the rest of the academy and that this skepticism will also apply to ISL (Gore, 2009; Nolan, 2009). The decision makers on ISL may be relatively inexperienced in the subject (Plater, chapter 2); faculty committees and senior administrators make decisions on ISL programs with perhaps very little understanding of the nature of experiential education, the value of the action/reflection approach to education, or any of the many other philosophical and pedagogical concepts associated with ISL. What can be done both to assess attitudes and to change them in faculty and administrators (Stohl, 2007)? Service learning itself, and particularly ISL, carries its own pedagogical beliefs and assumptions. Might a better understanding of these beliefs and assumptions, or practical experience with ISL, make a difference to a faculty member's approach to teaching in general? Recent work on the marginalization of study abroad in the academy (Gore, 2005, 2009; Nolan, 2009) and of service learning (Butin, 2009) taken together, raises questions about faculty perceptions of teaching and learning that constitute major impediments to change.

Policies on ISL and their effects. How do institutional policies affect faculty members' willingness to get involved in ISL? We know that all forms of service learning tend to be very demanding on faculty members' time (Abes, Jackson, & Jones, 2002). Some institutions are more ready than others to recognize this fact and to adjust for it as part of faculty roles and rewards, despite the financial factors involved (particularly in the form of release time). We know little about how ISL fits into this picture.

Faculty development. How can ISL research inform how to design effective faculty development for American faculty who accompany students on ISL programs and for host-country faculty who teach American students? Berry and Chisholm (1992) have pointed out that educational practices vary from country to country. A common assumption among North American academics is that educational practice abroad ought to be more like such practice at home, but other systems value other skills and other levels of independence. More research can be done to assess American faculty members' experience abroad in order to anticipate difficulties and modify their preparation. The same holds for the interaction of host-country faculty in their dealings with their American students and peers.

Service Abroad in ISL

ISL engages a host of players in the implementation of the educational experiences and the consequences of their involvement provides opportunities for expanding the research domain beyond the students and faculty.

The impact of community service. What is the impact of ISL on nongovernmental organization agencies, their constituencies or clients, and communities? What is the role of students and others in responding to and shaping community issues? Many smaller agencies depend heavily on volunteer help of the kind provided by American students in process-based programs, and obviously the populations served by project-based programs benefit directly (or should do so). It is, however, quite unusual to ask those served how they respond to the service. Longo and Saltmarsh (chapter 4), Kiely and Hartman (chapter 13), and Whitney and Clayton (chapter 8) discuss the importance of community voice as an integral element of reciprocity and the ISL educational experience, including research on ISL. Research is needed to investigate the ways in which such reciprocity contributes to students' educational outcomes of students (Eyler, chapter 10) and to outcomes for nongovernmental organizations and the communities they serve. Such study might help to define the factors involved in maximizing the students' usefulness and assist in identifying effective practices for subsequent ISL course and program design. It may be that the very cultural difference of the visitors from abroad will prove beneficial, or such difference may create barriers, at least because of different assumptions about collaborative work, productivity, and modes of questioning received assumptions (Erasmus, chapter 15).

Agency placements. Are there ways in which the suitability of particular students for particular tasks can be better assessed, both by their mentors and by the agencies? Given the range of agencies involved (a range determined in part by the diversity of programmatic activities in ISL) and the variety of cultural settings, it may be very difficult to arrive at a clear sense of what works and what does not work, but a better awareness of the factors involved would allow better selection and preparation of students and better service outcomes. Eyler (chapter 10) discusses the importance of different dimensions of the placement and nature of the community service activities (e.g., direct interaction with clients of a nongovernmental organization agency) in domestic service learning; parallel analyses need to be conducted for ISL (see Sutton, chapter 7, for some specific examples).

Agency placement and student learning.   To what extent can agency leaders or community residents help in the education of the students, and how appropriate is it to include them in feedback or assessment? Research by Sandy and Holland (2006) demonstrates that one of the most valued roles of community supporters of domestic service learning is that of coeducator of students. We should surely see agencies and communities as places to learn as well as serve. How can that learning process be maximized, and how can skills and knowledge acquired through service be integrated with skills and knowledge acquired through conventional study? ISL research should also study the processes through which students develop an appreciation of and respect for indigenous ways of knowing in an international setting (Erasmus, chapter 15).

Views of agency leaders.   Deeley (2004) made the solicitation and interrogation of agency views on service learning central to her study of student impact on agencies. It is an important question, both because merely asking it helps to engage agency leaders in the common enterprise, and also (and more importantly) because it can provide valuable feedback on program design and on student placement (Sutton, chapter 7).

Faculty and student attitudes toward agencies and their clients.   Students are often asked to be both respectful of the agencies in which they serve and also constructively critical. This is a hard balance to maintain, especially in an unfamiliar culture, and particularly by those with little experience. Hence, research on how students (and also faculty members, who are engaged in the reflection process and in helping students make use of their experience in the field) feel about their agencies and their clients may be very important. Whitney and Clayton (chapter 8) demonstrate how this critical assessment can be built into structured reflection during an ISL experience and also provide evidence that can be used in research on these issues.

The Practice of ISL

Although researchers have a tendency to focus on the micro level of analysis (e.g., a particular student outcome), there is an opportunity for future research to inform the broader practice of ISL, international partnerships, international learning, student abroad, institutional approaches, policy issues, and teaching and learning in general.

Structuring effective ISL preparation. As suggested earlier, a key question in ISL research is, how does ISL intersect with institutional strategic planning? Careful planning is essential when launching a new program like ISL, and ongoing assessment is important if ISL program design is to be modified to address changing needs. Not all programs will have the same goals, and accordingly the preparation of their participants (e.g., students, professors, agency leaders, support services) for the experience will require different approaches.

Technology and connectivity. As study abroad specialists often lament, the days of isolation in the host culture are over, students are in constant contact with their friends and families at home, and as a result the individual international experience is changing (Grünzweig & Rinehart, 2002, pp. 13–15), in tune with the changes in the management of knowledge itself (Erasmus, 2007; Holzmüller, Stöttinger, & Wittkop, 2002). Is this increase in connectivity evident in ISL and are there strategies for turning it to good account by encouraging students to consult with home-campus experts even as they are working in an international location (see Whitney & Clayton, chapter 8, for an example)? Alternatively, does ISL encourage students to cut their ties with home by forcing them to engage with the host culture?

Curriculum development. Students abroad have obligations at home— among them the need to complete their degrees. Accordingly, the academic work that they do abroad must fit with their work at home. At the same time, designing academic work that supports the service experience is also important, as is the exploitation of the uniqueness of the experience in the host country. Reconciling these potentially conflicting needs requires careful consideration of likely outcomes, which should, in turn, be based on a clear understanding of attitudes and expectations. ISL research should explore the role of students as sources of curricular development of ISL courses and programs (see Whitney & Clayton, chapter 8, for an example of student-designed reflection). Student voice and sense of ownership have been found to be important predictors of civic engagement (Morgan & Streb, 2003) and these effects warrant exploration in ISL. Research can also explore the role of technology in influencing curricular design (Plater, chapter 2; Whitney & Clayton, chapter 8).

Narratives of service learning and approaches to reflection. A feature of most ISL courses and programs is a focus on personal development. Students are encouraged or required to keep journals, and to assess their own progress in relation to certain targets or categories (on journal writing in study abroad, see Brandt & Manley, 2002; Chen, 2002; Taylor, 1991; Wagner & Magistrale, 1995; Whitney & Clayton, chapter 8). Electronic portfolios, allowing for the assembly of a variety of materials, are also now becoming more common. To what extent do these narratives and journals follow preconceived generic lines (Tonkin & Quiroga, 2004)? Is there, in other words, a genre of self-discovery narratives that dominates student writing, and to what extent does this writing follow the expectations of teachers and peers (Chisholm, 2000, in providing helpful models for ISL narratives by reference to other journeys of self-discovery, indirectly invites such comparisons; see also Smelser, whose fourth chapter deals specifically with study abroad)? To what extent does such journal writing encourage self-absorption or to what extent does it overcome it? Can close textual analysis of such journals provide evidence about students' assumptions and beliefs? Whitney and Clayton (chapter 8) detail ways in which reflective journals can be structured as a means for developing student growth across personal, civic, and academic domains, and they provide specific prompts to which ISL students can respond that encourage personal growth. They also present details on using reflective journals as a source of information for research on ISL, including rubrics based on Bloom's taxonomy for evaluating reflection narratives (Ash & Clayton, 2004; Ash, Clayton, & Atkinson, 2005).

Conducting ISL Research

What special issues are associated with conducting research on ISL? Such considerations might include distant sites, opportunities for collaboration with academics and others in the host country, the availability of technology, language issues, framing community impact around local issues, and appropriate comparison groups. Bringle et al. (chapter 12) and Kiely and Hartman (chapter 13) detail quantitative and qualitative approaches to conducting ISL research. In both cases, the authors identify criteria for rigorous research—a characteristic often lacking in research on ISL. Particularly important is the question of community impact; work by outside researchers can be quite unsettling for communities, raising ethical issues familiar to anthropologists and ethnographers but perhaps less familiar to some ISL researchers (Kahn, chapter 6; Sutton, chapter 7). Subsequent ISL researchers have an opportunity to show sensitivity to these issues. As in other areas of educational and social research, the presumptions and hypotheses of ISL researchers may go unchallenged. It is important not only to strike out in new research directions, but also to attempt to replicate or interrogate the findings of other researchers.

Conclusion

If ISL is to find a secure place in the curriculum of North American institutions of higher education, as it should, and if it is to bring about an engagement with the world that is truly reciprocal, the basic facts about the field and the data to support them must be assembled. There is therefore a political and philosophical reason for studying ISL with high-quality research. But, academic politics aside, more needs to be known about whether present ISL practices are achieving their objectives, or indeed achieving any objectives at all. Not only are ISL practitioners and researchers accountable to funders, institutions, and students, they are also accountable to their hosts and the public good. Thus, research is more than an academic exercise: it is an ethical imperative.

Notes

1. The Forum on Education Abroad maintains a research database on study abroad on its website http://www.forumea.org/research-READ.htm.

2. Both VSO and the Peace Corps have moved away from notions of mobilizing youthful idealism to a concentration on the delivery of skilled services, though one such organization, the Norwegian Fredskorpset (Peace Corps), founded in 1963, has moved in the opposite direction, becoming an exchange program for college students. Perhaps the VSO and Peace Corps experience should remind us that mere youthful idealism may not be enough, indeed may be counter-productive if not tempered by cold realism of a kind not always displayed either by professors or by students. At the same time, harnessing this idealism is important and may be fundamental to the development of effective ISL programs.

3. For an example of a 1951 announcement, see United Nations Educational, Scientific, and Cultural Organization, 1951.

4. See the brief compilation of model programs by Barnhill, Gilmore, Sawada, and Brown (2007). The field still lacks a more comprehensive examination of the kind provided by Kelleher (1996) for study abroad.

5. For an informal survey of some of the ways of "doing good" in study abroad, see Branan (2008).

6. See also Peterson (2002) for an interesting approach to "transformation" through social justice in study abroad.

7. On experiential learning, see Kolb (1984); on intercultural communication, see Bennett (1998); on intercultural sensitivity see Paige (1993) and Pusch (2005). Berry (1985) is an early attempt to link experiential education and the international dimension. And see Eyler (chapter 10), Kiely and Hartman (chapter 13).

References

Abes, E. S., Jackson, G., & Jones, S. R. (2002). Factors that motivate and deter faculty use of service-learning. *Michigan Journal of Community Service Learning, 9*(1), 5–17.

Adams, M. (1968). *Voluntary service overseas: The story of the first ten years*. London, UK: Faber.

Akande, Y., & Slawson, C. (2000). A case study of 50 years of study abroad alumni. *International Educator, 9*(3), 12–16.

Altbach, P. G., & Knight, J. (2007). The internationalization of higher education: Motivations and realities. *Studies in International Education, 11*, 290–305.

Aquino, D. R. (2001). Ethics and values in civil society: The service learning paradigm. *Anthropos* (Trinity College of Quezon City), *1*(2), 109–117.

Ash, S. L., & Clayton, P. H. (2004). The articulated learning: An approach to reflection and assessment. *Innovative Higher Education, 29*, 137–154.

Ash, S. L., Clayton, P. H., & Atkinson, M. P. (2005). Integrating reflection and assessment to capture and improve student learning. *Michigan Journal of Community Service Learning, 11*(2), 49–60.

Bachner, D. (1994). Global competence and international student exchange: Attitudinal preparation for effective overseas learning. In R. D. Lambert (Ed.), *Educational exchange and global competence* (pp. 189–197). New York, NY: Council on International Educational Exchange.

Barnhill, J. H., Gilmore, K., Sawada, M., & Brown, W. N.-E. (2007). *Promising practices of international service and service learning*. Elon, NC: North Carolina Campus Compact.

Bennett, M. J. (1993). Toward ethnorelativisim: A developmental model of intercultural sensitivity. In R. M. Paige (Ed.), *Education for the intercultural experience* (pp. 21–71). Yarmouth, ME: Intercultural Press.

Bennett, M. J. (1998). *Basic concepts of intercultural communication*. Yarmouth, ME: Intercultural Press.

Berger, P. L. (2000). Four faces of global culture. In O. Patrick, D. M. Howard, & K. Matthew (Eds.), *Globalization and the challenges of a new century* (pp. 419–427). Bloomington & Indianapolis, IN: Indiana University Press.

Berry, H. A. (1985, Spring-Summer). Experiential education: The neglected dimension of international/intercultural studies. *International Programs Quarterly, 1*(3–4), 23–27.

Berry, H. A., & Chisholm L. A. (1992). *How to serve and learn abroad effectively: Students tell students.* New York, NY: Partnership for Service-Learning.

Berry, H. A., & Chisholm, L. A. (1999). *Service-learning in higher education around the world: An initial look.* New York, NY: The International Partnership for Service-Learning.

Billig, S. H., & Eyler, J. (2003). *Deconstructing service-learning: Research exploring context, participation, and impacts.* Greenwich, CT: Information Age Publishing.

Bird, D. (1998). *Never the same again: A history of VSO.* London, UK: Lutterworth.

Boyte, H., & Hollander, E. (1999). *Wingspread declaration on the civic responsibility of research universities.* Providence, RI: Campus Compact.

Braham, M. (1999). *Volunteers for development: A test of the post-materialist hypothesis in Britain, c. 1965–1987.* Discussion papers in economic and social history 30. Oxford, UK: Oxford University. Retrieved July 2, 2009, from http://www.nuff.ox.ac.uk/economics/history/paper30/30braham.pdf

Branan, N. (2008, January–February). Lending a helping hand. *International Educator*, 34–41.

Brandt, C., & Manley T. (2002). The practice of the fieldbook: Facilitating and evaluating field-based learning. *Frontiers, 8,* 113–142.

Bringle, R. G. (2003). Enhancing theory-based research on service-learning. In S. H. Billig & J. Eyler (Eds.), *Deconstructing service-learning: Research exploring context, participation, and impacts* (pp. 3–21). Greenwich, CN: Information Age Publishing.

Bringle, R. G., & Hatcher J. A. (1999). Reflection in service learning: Making meaning of experience. *Educational Horizons, 77,* 179–185.

Bringle, R. G., Phillips, M. A., & Hudson, M. (2004). *The measure of service learning: Research scales to assess student experiences.* Washington DC: American Psychological Association.

Bringle, R. G., & Tonkin, H. (2004). International service-learning: A research agenda. In H. Tonkin (Ed.), *Service-learning across cultures: Promise and achievement* (pp. 365–374). New York, NY: International Partnership for Service-Learning and Leadership.

Butin, D. W. (2009). *Rethinking service learning: Embracing the scholarship of engagement within higher education.* Sterling, VA: Stylus.

Chao, M. (n.d.). *Research on US students abroad, an update 1988–2000: An annotated bibliography.* Retrieved July 2, 2009, from http://www.globaled.us/ro/book_research_chao.htm

Chapdelaine, A., Ruiz, A., Warchal, J., & Wells, C. (2005). *Service-learning code of ethics.* Boston, MA: Anker.

Chen, L. (2002). Writing to host nationals as cross-cultural collaborative learning in study abroad. *Frontiers: The Interdisciplinary Journal of Study Abroad, 8,* 143–164.

Chisholm, L. A. (2000). *Charting a hero's journey.* New York, NY: International Partnership for Service-Learning.

Chisholm, L. A. (Ed). (2004). *Visions of service.* New York, NY: International Partnership for Service-Learning.

Chisholm, L. A. (Ed.). (2005). *Knowing and doing: The theory and practice of service-learning.* New York, NY: International Partnership for Service-Learning.

Citron, J. L. (2002). U.S. students abroad: Host culture integration or third culture formation? In W. Grünzweig & N. Rinehart (Eds.), *Rockin' in red square: Critical approaches to international education in the age of cyberculture* (pp. 41–56). Münster, Germany: Lit Verlag.

Cluett, R. (2002). From Cicero to Mohammed Atta: People, politics, and study abroad. *Frontiers: The Interdisciplinary Journal of Study Abroad*, *8*, 17–39.

Cohen, A. D., Paige, M. R., Shively, R. L., Emert, H. A., & Hoff, J. G. (2005). *Maximizing study abroad through language and culture strategies: Research on students, study abroad program professionals, and language instructors.* Minneapolis, MN: Center for Advanced Research on Language Acquisition, University of Minnesota. Retrieve July 2, 2009, from http://www.carla.umn.edu/maxsa/documents/MAXSAResearchReport.pdf

Comp, D. J. (2003). *Research on US students abroad, additional resources: A bibliography with abstracts 1988–2000.* Retrieved July 2, 2009, from http://www.globaled.us/ro/book_research_chao_add.htm

Comp, D. J. (n.d.). *Research on US students study abroad: An update, volume III, 2001–2003, with updates to the 1989 and volume II editions: An annotated bibliography.* Retrieved July 2, 2009, from http://www.globaled.us/ro/book_research_comp.html

Deeley, S. J. (2004). The impact of experience: A comparative study of the effects of International Partnership for Service-Learning students within welfare agencies in Scotland and Jamaica. In H. Tonkin (Ed.), *Service-learning across cultures: Promise and achievement* (pp. 197–232). New York, NY: International Partnership for Service-Learning.

Dickson, A. (1976). *A chance to serve.* London, UK: Dennis Dobson.

Dickson, M. (2004). *Portrait of a partnership.* New York, NY: International Partnership for Service-Learning.

Durrant, M. B., & Dorius, C. R. (2007). Study abroad survey instruments: A comparison of survey types and experiences. *Journal of Studies in International Education* *11*(1), 33–53.

Dwyer, M. M. (2004). More is better: The impact of study abroad program duration. *Frontiers: The Interdisciplinary Journal of Study Abroad*, *10*, 151–163.

Dwyer, M. M., & Peters, C. K. (2004, March–April). The benefits of study abroad. *Transitions abroad.* Retrieved July 1, 2009, from http://www.transitionsabroad.com /publications/magazine/0403/benefits_study_abroad.shtml

Ehrlich, T. (2000). *Civic responsibility and higher education.* Phoenix, AZ: Oryx.

Engle, J., & Engle, L. (2002). Neither international nor educative: Study abroad in the time of globalization. In W. Grünzweig & N. Rinehart (Eds.), *Rockin' in red square: Critical approaches to international education in the age of cyberculture* (pp. 25–39). Münster, Germany: Lit Verlag.

Erasmus, M. A. (2007). Service learning: Preparing for a new generation of scientists for a mode 2 society. *Journal for New Generation Sciences* 5(2), 26–40.

Freed, B. (Ed.) (1995). *Second language acquisition in a study abroad context.* Amsterdam, Netherlands: Benjamins.

Fukuda-Parr, S. (Ed.) (2004). *Human development report 2004: Cultural liberty in today's world.* New York, NY: United Nations Development Program.

Giles, D. E., Jr., & Eyler, J. (1998). A service learning research agenda for the next five years. In R. Rhoads & J. Howard (Eds.), *Academic service-learning: A pedagogy of action and reflection* (pp. 65–72). San Francisco, CA: Jossey-Bass.

Gillespie, J., Braskamp, L., & Dwyer, M. (2009). Holistic student learning and development abroad: The IES 3-D Program Model. In R. Lewin (Ed.), *The handbook of practice and research in study abroad: Higher education and the quest for global citizenship* (pp. 445–465). New York, NY: Routledge.

Goleman, D. (1995). *Emotional intelligence.* New York, NY: Bantam.

Gore, J. E. (2005). *Dominant beliefs and alternative voices: Discourse, belief and gender in American study abroad.* New York, NY: Routledge.

Gore J. E. (2009). Faculty beliefs and institutional values: Identifying and overcoming these obstacles to education abroad growth. In R. Lewin (Ed.), *The handbook of practice and research in study abroad: Higher education and the quest for global citizenship* (pp. 282–302). New York, NY: Routledge.

Greenleaf, R. K. (1977). *Servant leadership: A journey into the nature of legitimate power and greatness.* Mahwah, NJ: Paulist Press.

Greenleaf, R. K. (2002). *Servant leadership: A journey into the nature of legitimate power and greatness.* New York, NY: Paulist Press.

Grünzweig, W. (2002). The rockies in Poland: International education as frontier experience. In W. Grünzweig & N. Rinehart (Eds.), *Rockin' in red square: Critical approaches to international education in the age of cyberculture* (pp. 105–116). Münster, Germany: Lit Verlag.

Grünzweig, W., & Rinehart, N. (Ed.) (2002). *Rockin' in Red Square: Critical approaches to international education in the age of cyberculture.* Piscataway, NJ: Transaction.

Grusky, S. (2000). International service learning: A critical guide from an impassioned advocate. *American Behavioral Scientist*, *43*, 858–867.

Hanvey, R. G. (1976). *An attainable global perspective.* New York, NY: American Forum for Global Education.

Harrison, J. K., & Voelker, E. (2008). Two personality variables and the cross-cultural adjustment of study abroad students. *Frontiers: The Interdisciplinary Journal of Study Abroad*, *17*, 69–87.

Hatcher, J. A., Bringle, R G., & Muthiah, R. (2004). Designing effective reflection: What matters to service-learning? *Michigan Journal of Community Service Learning*, *11*(1), 38–46.

Hoffa, W. W. (2007). *A history of U.S. study abroad: Beginnings to 1965.* Carlisle, PA: Frontiers & Forum on Education Abroad.

Holzmüller, H. H., Stöttinger, B., & Wittkop, T. (2002). Information and communication technologies in internationalized business education: Technical opportunities and interpersonal threats. In W. Grünzweig & N. Rinehart (Eds.), *Rockin' in red square: Critical approaches to international education in the age of cyberculture* (pp. 127–146). Münster, Germany: Lit Verlag.

Hovland, K., McTighe Musil, C., Skilton-Sylvester, E., & Jamison, A. (2009). It takes a curriculum: Bringing global mindedness home. In R. Lewin (Ed.), *The handbook of practice and research in study abroad: Higher education and the quest for global citizenship* (pp. 466–484). New York, NY: Routledge.

IES Abroad. (1999). *IES Abroad MAP*. Retrieved July 7, 2009, from https://www.iesabroad.org/IES/Advisors_and_Faculty/iesMap.html

Innovations in Civic Participation. (n.d.). *Innovations in Civic Participation*. Retrieved July 7, 2009, from http://www.icicp.org/index.php

Kehm, B. M., & Teichler, U. (2007). Research on internationalisation in higher education. *Studies in International Education, 11*, 260–273.

Kelleher, A. (1996). *Learning from success: Campus case studies in international program development*. New York, NY: Peter Lang.

Kiely, R. (2004). A chameleon with a complex: Searching for transformation in International service learning. *Michigan Journal of Community Service Learning, 10*(2), 5–20.

Kiely, R. (2005). Transformative international service-learning. *Academic Exchange Quarterly, 9*(1), 275–281.

Kim, R. I., & Goldstein, S. B. (2005). Intercultural attitudes predict favorable study abroad expectations of U.S. college students. *Journal of Studies in International Education, 9*, 265–278.

Kissau, S. (2007). Is what's good for the goose good for the gander? The case of male and female encouragement to study French. *Foreign Language Annals, 40*, 419–432.

Kolb, D. A. (1984). *Experiential learning*. Englewood Cliffs, NJ: Prentice Hall.

Lambert, R. D. (Ed.). (1994a). *Educational exchange and global competence*. New York, NY: Council on International Educational Exchange.

Lambert, R. D. (1994b). Parsing the concept of global competence. In R. D. Lambert (Ed.) *Educational exchange and global competence* (pp. 11–24). New York, NY: Council on International Educational Exchange.

Langseth, M. (2000). Maximizing impact, minimizing harm: Why service-learning must more fully integrate multicultural education. In C. R. O'Grady (Ed.), *Integrating service learning and multicultural education in colleges and universities* (pp. 247–262). Mahwah, NJ: Erlbaum.

Lewin, R. (Ed.). (2009a). *The handbook of practice and research in study abroad: Higher education and the quest for global* citizenship. New York: Routledge.

Lewin, R. (2009b). Introduction: The quest for global citizenship through study abroad. In R. Lewin (Ed.), *The handbook of practice and research in study abroad: Higher education and the quest for global citizenship* (pp. xiii–xxii). New York, NY: Routledge.

Lutterman-Aguilar, A., & Gingerich, O. (2002). Experiential pedagogy for study abroad: Educating for global citizenship. *Frontiers: The Interdisciplinary Journal of Study Abroad*, *8*, 41–82.

Martinez M. D., Ranjeet, B., & Marx, H. A. (2009). Creating study abroad opportunities for first-generation college students. In R. Lewin (Ed.), *The handbook of practice and research in study abroad: Higher education and the quest for global citizenship* (pp. 527–542). New York, NY: Routledge.

Mestenhauser, J. A. (2002). In search of a comprehensive approach to international education: A systems perspective. In W. Grünzweig & N. Rinehart (Eds.), *Rockin' in red square: Critical approaches to international education in the age of cyberculture* (pp. 165–213). Münster, Germany: Lit Verlag.

Metz, E., Alessi, B., Stroud, S., Riquelme, D. A., & Smith D. (2008). Policy scan: An exploratory study of national youth service policy in 19 countries in Latin America and the Caribbean. In H. Perold & M. N. Tapia (Eds.), *Civil service and volunteering in Latin America and the Caribbean* (pp. 67–86). Buenos Aires, Argentina: Centro Latinoamericano de Aprendizaje y Servicio Solidario; St. Louis, MO, Washington University Center for Social Development.

Monard, K. (2002). *Nurturing senses of care, justice and reciprocity through international service-learning.* (Doctoral dissertation, University of Pittsburgh, 2002).

Monard-Weissman, K. (2003). Enhancing caring capacities: A case study of an international service-learning program. *Journal of Higher Education Outreach and Engagement*, *8*(2), 41–53.

Montrose, L. (2002). International study and experiential learning: The academic context. *Frontiers: The Interdisciplinary Journal of Study Abroad*, *8*, 1–15, 35–55.

Morgan, W., & Streb, M. J. (2003). First, do no harm: Student ownership and service-learning. *Metropolitan Universities Journal*, *14*(3), 36–52.

National Student Volunteer Program. (1977, Spring). *Study-service: An international force for change.* Special issue of *Synergist.* Washington, DC: [US] National Student Volunteer Program.

Ninnes, P., & Hellsten, M. (Eds.). (2005). *Internationalizing higher education: Critical explorations of pedagogy and policy.* Hong Kong, China: Springer.

Nolan, R. W. (2009). Turning our back on the world: Study abroad and the purpose of U.S. higher education. In R. Lewin (Ed.), *The handbook of practice and research in study abroad: Higher education and the quest for global citizenship* (pp. 266–281). New York, NY: Routledge.

Norris, E. M., & Steinberg, M. (2008). Does language matter? The impact of language of instruction on study abroad outcomes. *Frontiers: The Interdisciplinary Journal of Study Abroad*, *17*, 107–131.

Ogden, A. C. (2007). The view from the veranda: Understanding today's colonial student. *Frontiers: The Interdisciplinary Journal of Study Abroad*, *15*, 35–55.

Paige, R. M. (Ed.). (1993). *Education for the intercultural experience.* Yarmouth, ME: Intercultural Press.

Perry, J. L., & Thomson, A. M. (2004). *Civic service: What difference does it make?* Armonk, NY: M.E. Sharpe.

Peterson, C. F. (2002). Preparing engaged citizens: Three models of experiential education for social justice. *Frontiers: The Interdisciplinary Journal of Study Abroad, 8,* 165–206.

Plater, W. M., Jones, S. G., Bringle, R. G., & Clayton, P. H. (2009). Educating globally competent citizens through international service learning. In R. Lewin (Ed.), *The handbook of practice and research in study abroad: Higher education and the quest for global citizenship* (pp. 485–505). New York, NY: Routledge.

Porter, M., & Monard, K. (2001). *Ayni* in the global village: Building relationships of reciprocity through international service-learning. *Michigan Journal of Community Service Learning, 8*(1), 5–17.

Pusch, M. D. (2004). A cross-cultural perspective. In H. Tonkin (Ed.) *Service-learning across cultures: Promise and achievement* (pp. 103–130). New York, NY: International Partnership for Service-Learning.

Pusch, M. D. (2005). Teaching intercultural skills and developing the global soul. In L. Chisholm (Ed.) *Knowing and doing: The theory and practice of service-learning* (pp. 145–162). New York, NY: International Partnership for Service-Learning.

Quiroga, D. (2004). Beyond the comfort zone. In H. Tonkin (Ed.), *Service-learning across cultures: Promise and achievement* (pp. 131–146). New York, NY: International Partnership for Service-Learning and Leadership.

Ramaley, J. A. (2000, Fall). Strategic directions for service-learning research: A presidential perspective. *Michigan Journal of Community Service-Learning,* 91–97.

Reagan, T. (2005). *Non-western educational traditions* (3rd ed.). Mahwah, NJ: Erlbaum.

Rich, B. L. (2002, October). *Ethical issues and questions for service learning practitioners and researchers.* Paper presented at the Second Annual Conference on Service-Learning Research, Nashville, TN.

Riner, M. E., & Becklenberg, A. (2001). Partnering with a sister city organization for an international service-learning experience. *Journal of Transcultural Nursing, 12,* 234–240.

Salovey, P., & Mayer J. D. (1990). Emotional intelligence. *Imagination, Cognition, and Personality, 9,* 185–211.

Sandy, M., & Holland, B. (2006). Different worlds and common ground: Community partner perspectives on campus–community partnerships. *Michigan Journal of Community Service-Learning, 13*(1), 30–43.

Schaffer, M. A., Paris, J. W., & Vogel, K. (2003). Ethical relationships in service-learning partnerships. In S. H. Billig, J. Eyler (Eds.), *Advances in service-learning research* (pp. 147–168). Greenwich, CT: Information Age Publishing.

Schattle, H. (2009). Global citizenship in theory and practice. In R. Lewin (Ed.), *The handbook of practice and research in study abroad: Higher education and the quest for global citizenship* (pp. 3–20). New York: Routledge.

Siegel, M. J. (2004). Making the strange familiar: Dealing with ambiguity. In H. Tonkin (Ed.), *Service-learning across cultures: Promise and achievement* (pp. 147–162). New York, NY: International Partnership for Service-Learning and Leadership.

Smelser, Neil J. (2009). *The odyssey experience: Physical, social, psychological, and spiritual journeys.* Berkeley & Los Angeles, CA: University of California.

Smith-Pariolá, J., & Gòkè-Parióla, A. (2006). Expanding the parameters of service learning: A case study. *Journal of Studies in Higher Education, 10*(1), 71–86.

Steinberg, M. (2002). Involve me and I will understand: Academic quality in experiential programs abroad. *Frontiers, 8,* 207–229.

Stohl, M. (2007). We have met the enemy and he is us: The role of the faculty in the internationalization of higher education in the coming decade. *Studies in International Education, 11*(3–4), 359–372.

Sullivan, W. M. (1988). Calling or career: The tensions of modern professional life. In A. Flores (Ed.), *Professional ideals* (pp. 40–46). Belmont, CA: Wadsworth Publishing Company.

Sullivan, W. M. (2004). Can professionalism still be a viable ethic? *The Good Society, 13*(1), 15–20.

Sullivan, W. M. (2005). *Work and integrity. The crisis and promise of professionalism in America.* San Francisco, CA: Jossey-Bass.

Taylor, N. (1991). *The travel journal: An assessment tool for overseas study.* New York, NY: Council on International Educational Exchange.

Tonkin, H. (2004). *Service-learning across cultures: Promise and achievement.* New York, NY: International Partnership for Service-Learning.

Tonkin, H. (2006a, March). *Assessing and evaluating international service-learning.* Paper presented at International Service-Learning Workshop, Indianapolis, IN.

Tonkin, H. (2006b, March). *The intersection of institutional strategic planning and international service-learning.* Paper presented at International Service-Learning Workshop, Indianapolis, IN.

Tonkin, H., & Edwards, J. (1981). *The world in the curriculum: Curricular strategies for the 21st century.* New Rochelle, NY: Change Magazine Press.

Tonkin, H., & Quiroga, D. (2004, Fall). A qualitative approach to the assessment of international service-learning. *Frontiers, 10,* 163–182.

Torney-Purta, J. (1994). Assessment and measurement of global competence: A psychologist's view of alternative approaches. In R. D. Lambert (Ed.), *Educational exchange and global competence* (pp. 257–268). New York, NY: Council on International Educational Exchange.

United Nations Educational, Scientific, and Cultural Organization. (1951). *International voluntary work camps.* Retrieved July 7, 2009, from http://unesdoc .unesco.org/images /0017/001787/178739eb.pdf

Vande Berg, M. (2007). Intervening in the learning of US students abroad. *Journal of Studies in International Education, 11,* 392–399.

Vande Berg, M., Balkum, A., Scheid, M., & Whalen, B. J. (2004, Fall). The George-town University consortium project: A report from the halfway mark. *Frontiers*, *10*, 101–116.

Wagner, K., & Magistrale, T. (1995). *Writing across culture: An introduction to study abroad and the writing process.* New York, NY: Peter Lang.

Ward, C., Bochner, S., & Furnham, A. (2001). *The psychology of culture shock.* (2nd ed.). Philadelphia, PA: Taylor & Francis.

Weaver, H. D. (Ed.). (1989). *Research on US students abroad: A bibliography with abstracts.* Retrieved July 2, 2009, from http://www.globaled.us/ro/book_research_weaver.htm

Wessel, N. (2007). Integrating service learning into the study abroad program: US sociology students in Mexico. *Journal of Studies in International Education, 11*(1), 73–89.

Whiteley, J. (2004). The partnership vision. In H. Tonkin (Ed.), *Service-learning across cultures: Promise and achievement* (pp. 167–178). New York, NY: International Partnership for Service-Learning.

Wilson, A. H. (1994). The attributes and tasks of global competence. In R. D. Lambert (Ed.), *Educational exchange and global competence* (pp. 37–50). New York, NY: Council on International Educational Exchange.

Zemach-Bersin, T. (2009). Selling the world: Study abroad marketing and the priva-tization of global citizenship. In R. Lewin (Ed.), *The handbook of practice and research in study abroad: Higher education and the quest for global citizenship* (pp. 303–320). New York: Routledge.

10

WHAT INTERNATIONAL SERVICE LEARNING RESEARCH CAN LEARN FROM RESEARCH ON SERVICE LEARNING

Janet Eyler

T he quality and quantity of research on service learning for both K-12 and higher education in the United States has increased dramatically over the past 20 years. A good deal is now known about the impact of service learning on students' outcomes and on the particular characteristics of service learning that affect specific types of results. A field once made up of small-scale evaluation studies with poorly specified independent and dependent variables now includes some well-designed quasi-experimental studies and greater attention to measurement. This work can be a foundation for both further research activities including research focused on college programs that incorporate service learning into study abroad semesters or other international programs, including international service learning (ISL).

What We Know About the Impact of Service Learning on Students

The cumulative body of research and evaluation studies over the past decades has yielded a fairly consistent pattern of small but significant impact of service learning on adolescents' and college students' personal, academic, and social outcomes; and there is growing evidence of an impact on behavior and civic engagement. These findings have been noted in reviews of numerous small studies of K-12 service learning programs (Billig, 2000) and of college and university programs (Eyler, Giles, Stenson, & Gray, 2001). Although many of the studies reviewed were one-shot, preexperimental designs, findings have held up in large-scale studies using stronger designs, more extensive samples, and more sophisticated analysis of the data. A review of community service programs (Perry & Thomson, 2004) that addresses the impact of civic service found similar personal and social effects from activities that engage students in service to community without necessarily connecting it to academic programs.

Personal Outcomes

Studies of college students have found that participation in service learning contributes to the development of life skills (Gray et al., 1998) as well as personal efficacy, reduced stereotypes and increased tolerance, sense of personal responsibility, and moral and spiritual development (Boss, 1994; Eyler et al., 2001). Similar findings have been found for middle school and high school students who reported higher levels of self-confidence, personal efficacy, personal responsibility, tolerance, acceptance of cultural diversity, and trust and reliability when they participated in service learning; they were also less likely to show behavior problems, be referred for school discipline, and participate in some risky behaviors (Billig, 2000).

Academic and Intellectual Development Outcomes

Most reported impact of service learning on academic outcomes uses student self-report measures. Where grades have been used in higher education studies, the designs of the study rarely allowed for a clear comparison with identical assessment measures (Eyler, 2002). There is some evidence linking service learning to school engagement and subsequently to improved test scores and performance (Billig, 2000). One challenge to assessing academic outcomes has been conceptualizing the expected impact (Denson, Vogelgesang, & Saenz, 2005). Eyler and Giles (1999) argued that factual knowledge and traditional classroom measures might not tap the unique contribution that service learning makes to academic growth, but that researchers should look to the impact of challenging service learning on intellectual development. Their research used intensive problem-solving interviews to examine the changes in the students' capacity to reason over the course of a semester and showed that both problem-solving complexity and reflective judgment increased with involvement in high-quality service learning. Batchelder and Root (1994) analyzed student essays embedded in both a traditional classroom and a classroom with a service learning component, and also found an impact on higher order thinking skills and pro-social reasoning. Other researchers have begun to build tools of measurement based on problem analysis that can be used in assessment and research and are finding similar outcomes (Ash, Clayton, & Atkinson, 2005; Steinke, Fitch, Johnson, & Waldstein, 2002).

Social and Community Engagement Outcomes

There has been increased interest in social competence and engagement outcomes partly because one of the pedagogical strengths of service learning is that it increases students' interest and engagement in the classroom. This then leads to civic engagement as well as personal and academic development (Billig, Root, & Jesse, 2005). Other larger studies that compared students who participated in service learning with those who did not, found that service learning contributed to political interest and efficacy, a sense of connectedness to community, social responsibility, and future intent to participate in community life and life skills (Eyler & Giles, 1999; Gray et al., 1998; Melchior, 1998). Denson et al. (2005) used Cooperative Institutional Research Program (CIRP) longitudinal data to track the relationship of service learning and the climate for engagement in college to community participation years after graduation. They found some evidence that volunteering during college and perhaps service learning inclined students to later participation.

Characteristics of Service Learning That Lead to Particular Desired Outcomes

Early in the development of service learning as a pedagogy, best practices were identified by practitioners in the field (Honnet & Poulsen, 1989) and those practices have been tested by researchers. There is now considerable evidence to link particular practices with outcomes. Most of these studies have used student descriptions of their particular program experiences using items developed by Conrad and Hedin (1980) who found that, although program type was not predictive of outcomes, differences in practice identified by students were. They found that, within a program type (e.g., internships, service learning, community service projects), students' experiences (e.g., time they spent on site, their interaction with community members, participation in teacher-led discussion, keeping journals) varied dramatically within programs of similar type and among students in the same program and these qualities were predictive of outcomes. The Conrad and Hedin measures have been adapted or emulated in many subsequent studies in higher education that attempt to determine the effects of varying elements of service learning on outcomes (Astin, Vogelgesang, Ikeda, & Yee, 2000; Eyler & Giles, 1999; Gray et al., 1998). These studies have generally found a relationship between the students' reports of interesting and valuable service, applicability of the service to the learning goals, intensity and duration of the service, student voice, and structured reflection on their personal, social, and academic outcomes.

Probably the most consistent predictor of outcomes is reflection; although studies often measure experiences with both discussion and written reflection, generally, faculty-led discussion of the experience has been the best predictor (Denson et al., 2005; Eyler & Giles, 1999; Gray et al., 1998). Although reflection is often included in the descriptions of service learning in studies and products of reflection such as journals are also used to as a data source, there have been relatively few studies that have examined variations in quantity or quality of reflection. Studies that have looked at this have found a connection between frequency and thoroughness of reflection and outcomes (Eyler & Giles, 1999; Hatcher, Bringle, & Muthiah, 2004; & Giles, 1999; Mabry, 1998).

Another critical characteristic has been the quality of the service experience itself. A quality placement provides adequate support for students and gives them important responsibilities that they can see are meaningful to the community partner. Having interesting, important, and challenging service activities was consistently associated with positive personal and social outcomes. Doing work that is perceived as important engages students and leads to positive connections to school, faculty, and peers (Astin et al., 2000; Billig et al., 2005; Eyler & Giles, 1999; Gray et al., 1998).

Working with high school students in Indiana, Morgan and Streb (2003) found that student voice and sense of ownership were important predictors of civic engagement. Other characteristics associated with student outcomes included quality of preparation for service; application of the service to what was being learned in the classroom and vice versa; the time spent in performing service; whether the service involved direct service to people in the community (vs. indirect service); opportunities to work with diverse others; and community voice in planning the projects (Morgan & Streb, 2003).

In the higher education literature, the chance to work closely with faculty has been associated with positive outcomes (Pascarella, 2005; Pascarella & Terenzini 1991). Eyler and Giles (1999) chose closeness to faculty as an alternative hypothesis to service learning and found that both were independent predictors of increased tolerance, personal efficacy, community efficacy, and leadership skills, although each had some independent impact on particular outcomes. For example, closeness to faculty was linked to improved communication skills, whereas service learning was more closely linked to values outcomes and commitment to service. They also found that students in high-quality programs were more likely to feel a close connection to faculty at the end of their service learning experience, compared to those in less engaging programs.

Filling Gaps in Knowledge

Research on international education and study abroad can add to the understanding of service learning by building on strong studies and strengthening the quality of the research design, by filling gaps in the literature, and by identifying and pursuing questions that are unique to the potential value that can be added through combining service with study abroad and international education (Tonkin, chapter 9).

Improving Research Design

Service learning research has been criticized for its methodological weaknesses. These have included failing to carefully define the experience of service learning, failing to design effective measures of the outcome variables, relying on student self-reports of learning outcomes, failing to create designs with adequate control groups, failing to conduct longitudinal research, and for lacking theoretical rigor (Bringle & Steinberg, in press; Eyler, 2002; Jones & Steinberg, chapter 5). Many of the studies cited in this chapter have begun to take steps to remedy these problems, but much work remains to be done. As research on ISL courses and programs is mounted, attention should be given to building on the stronger studies completed in the United States and improving the research on ISL (Jones & Steinberg, chapter 5; Bringle, Hatcher, & Williams, chapter 12; Kiely & Hartman, chapter 13).

A first challenge in designing such studies is carefully specifying the learning experiences students are having and then evaluating their impact; this would build a literature that could guide practice (Tonkin, chapter 9). Even where attempts have been made to select high-quality service learning programs in research in the United States, enormous variability has been found (Melchior, 1998). Study abroad experiences vary in the degree to which participants are immersed in local culture and work with local community partners in planning service and in the types of preparation and follow-up that occur (Bringle & Hatcher, chapter 1; Jones & Steinberg, chapter 5; Kiely, chapter 11). Practitioners could benefit from exploring the effects of different strategies for engaging students with local communities (Kahn, chapter 6; Sutton, chapter 7), processes for reflecting on this experience (Whitney &

Clayton, chapter 8), and methods for preparation and follow-up (Kiely, chapter 11; Tonkin, 2004). More studies that are vaguely defined in assessing the impact of service learning will not be useful. Studies that carefully identify and vary qualities of service learning, including ISL, and test them in carefully controlled settings (e.g., in rigorous experimental or quasi-experimental designs) will provide more important contributions to a curriculum knowledge base (Bringle et al., chapter 12).

There has been little experimental research in service learning; it is difficult to use random assignment in natural educational settings (see Bringle et al., chapter 12, for alternative approaches) and so most of the stronger studies have used quasi-experimental designs with control groups of students in classes that do not employ service learning. Even with statistical controls, the difference in students who choose and do not choose service learning undercuts the conclusions to be drawn; these differences can often be clearly documented in the pretest portion of the study (Eyler & Giles, 1999). The closest approach to an experimental design in higher education service learning research is a small, oft-cited study of political science classes that compared learning outcomes among sections of a course at one university (Markus, Howard, & King, 1993). Although individual students were not randomly assigned, two of eight class sections were randomly assigned to service learning and students were not allowed to change sections; the experimental groups did show greater learning on common semester tests, perhaps explained through their better attendance. A more recent study of service learning and civic engagement in high schools used a quasi-experimental design that matched classes to controls, thus providing some confidence about equivalence of the groups and the findings (Billig et al., 2005). A series of studies in which students could be randomly assigned to sections of courses allowing various service learning pedagogies to be compared would advance understanding of effective practice. Ideally, teachers would be recruited who use service learning approaches and would agree to alternate teaching with alternative approaches. And specific forms of reflection for example, or types of service experience could be contrasted.

International study programs, including ISL, may offer a particularly good opportunity to deal with the selectivity problem. The most powerful motive for choosing an international study program that includes service may be the opportunity to study abroad; thus, other study abroad programs within an institution may provide control groups that include students equally eager for international experiences. Any studies on the impact of an ISL program should include other study abroad programs that draw from the same student body. In a large quasi-experiment on ISL, it should also be possible to contrast various service learning practices (e.g., direct versus indirect service, different forms of reflection) as well as service versus non-service-oriented international courses or programs. This would allow an evaluation of the value added of including service in an international experience as well as in exploring the most effective ways to implement ISL programs. If an institution does not have large enough study abroad programs to allow for random assignments to service learning projects, an institutional cycle design might be employed to allow variations in program implementation from year to year.

Comparing alternative forms of service learning would provide useful information, but these studies should be designed to provide the field with a better understanding of the reasons that the service learning had a particular impact. Very little research on service learning has attempted to test theory or even alternative hypotheses. The Eyler and Giles (1999) study that found that service learning had an independent effect on student outcomes when compared with student relationships with faculty is a rare exception. Conrad and Hedin (1980) attempted to contrast different types of experiential education programs, but there was a lack of clear distinctions among the programs that may account for the lack of differential impact. Since some recent research now demonstrates that different experiences may lead to different outcomes, research on ISL courses or programs should present clear goals for particular students and programs components and match these practices to outcomes as the research questions are formulated. In ISL programs, it is possible to test alternative theories about why such programs differentially affect outcomes. Theories that account for reduced stereotyping, for example, could be put to the test through ISL courses or programs that compare having students work with peers in the host country and contrasting that with programs that provide direct service to disadvantaged residents (Fitch, 2005). The effects of language facility, previous cultural study, preparation and follow-up, reflection practices, the involvement of students with community members in designing the service could be studied as independent variables, mediating variables, or moderator variables (Bringle & Hatcher, 2000). Investigations framed by these types of issues would provide valuable information for practitioners designing ISL programs.

Another area of weakness in the extant service learning research literature is clear articulation of expected outcomes and powerful measurement of those outcomes. Measurement has come a long way since the first self-report measures in this field. Several resources of measurement tools have been compiled (see Compendium of Assessment on Research Tools, n.d.) including Bringle's collection of well-tested instruments (Bringle, Phillips, & Hudson, 2004). There are also instruments that are particularly apt for assessing international programs such as those that address modern racism and international attitudes used by Myers-Lipton in his studies of an intensive service learning program in Colorado (Myers-Lipton, 1996a; Myers-Lipton, 1996b) and the Global Perspective Inventory that assesses cognitive, intrapersonal, and interpersonal development using self-reports (Braskamp, Braskamp, & Merrill, 2009).

Clear conceptualization of the dependent variable and developing a rationale for the basis of a particular intervention to a particular outcome are challenges in ISL research. What exactly is the unique value added to academic learning by ISL and how can it be measured are questions that will have varying answers depending on the goals of the ISL course, context, and implementation. There have been several studies that attempt to measure complex intellectual outcomes of service learning (Ash et al., 2005; Batchelder & Root, 1994; Eyler & Giles, 1999; Steinke et al., 2002), but much work remains to be done here. Civic engagement outcomes are also a challenge; there is not clear agreement about what good citizenship or civic engagement means in the United States (Battistoni, 2002; Kahne & Westheimer, 2003) and it is likely to be that much more complex in an international context (Lewin, 2009; Whitney & Clayton, chapter 8). Some international comparative work has been done on civic engagement that may be a useful place to start (Lewin, 2009; Torney-Purta & Barber, 2005).

Before adequate research on ISL can commence, those designing ISL experiences need to clearly articulate the expected outcomes, many of which are likely to fall largely into the personal development category. Study abroad programs are touted as a means to better global understanding. Does adding a service component to study abroad enhance such outcomes? One might expect engagement with communities abroad to affect cultural understanding, build empathy, reduce stereotyping, and increase tolerance as well as a sense of personal efficacy. Evidence for these relationships as well as linking particular features of ISL programs to such outcomes would be useful information for program design and a precursor for good research.

Understanding the Process of Service Learning

Even well-designed research studies of ISL programs will be of limited value if they primarily replicate the growing body of literature linking service learning and particular service learning course characteristics to specific outcomes at only a descriptive level. There are many surveys that show small but marginally significant impacts of service learning on students; but there is little in these program evaluation studies that increases understanding of precisely how students' experience and process the challenges they face in their work with community partners. These are some gaps that ISL programs might be particularly well equipped to explore.

There is an assumption in the study abroad movement that experience with another culture helps increase tolerance, understanding, and reasoning abilities but there is not clear understanding of what that process might look like or even if the experiences advocates hope will occur do occur for individual students (Deardorff, 2009). A promising approach is the holistic model that examines how experiences are related to cognitive, intrapersonal, and interpersonal development using both direct and indirect measures (Gillespie, Braskamp, & Dwyer, 2009). Understanding the process by which ISL experiences shape participants' developing views of other cultures, their own citizenship roles, and perhaps their increased abilities to think critically about international issues would strengthen a very limited body of qualitative work in the field (Kiely, chapter 11; Kiely & Hartman, chapter 13). This could lead to generating questions of utility to practitioners. Do international experiences challenge basic assumptions about self and other cultures? Does this dissonance lead to growth and to reduced stereotyping? If the answer to both questions is yes, then is there an optimal level of challenge, or are other mechanisms at work? And this work might also lead to the development of alternative hypotheses that test theory. There have been studies of intercultural understanding (Fitch, 2005) in which theories are invoked, but the theories have not been used to create testable hypotheses.

There have been a few small studies in which researchers explored changes in how students described the community members with whom they worked over time. For example, Eyler and Giles (1994) used descriptions of expectations written before service and observations after service to trace such changes. Ostrow (1995) used student journals to trace the arc of students' conceptions of self and others during the course of service. Using similar approaches, including a series of written analyses by ISL students over time, or repeated interviews, would allow researchers to observe and describe changing perceptions of cultures, individuals in other groups, and the role of service and citizenship during ISL experiences. Comparing the changing perceptions of students with different types of international educational experiences (i.e., study abroad, ISL, international education in the United States) would help identify program characteristics associated with transformation of student perspectives. Because students are involved in an intensive ISL program or course, it would be easier to rule out confounding contextual variables of the home campus. It might also be easier to engage students' enthusiasm in the activities necessary to gather this type of qualitative data when they are immersed in emotionally powerful experiences like community-based service

activities in a different culture. Students who are engaged in intensive ISL activities with community members might be more inclined to write about their
observations of self and others at length while students in more traditional
classrooms have difficulty engaging in such writing assignments. Certainly,
attempts to include open-ended essays as part of survey research data collection have often failed to produce adequate material for analysis (Conrad &
Hedin, 1980; Eyler & Giles, 1999).

One of the arguments for the power of service learning to affect intellectual
outcomes is based in cognitive theory; students confronted with challenges to
their view of the world will be forced to evaluate alternative perspectives and
perhaps develop more complex capacities for judgment. Batchelder and Root
(1994) and Eyler and Giles (1999) have used pre- and postservice, open-ended
problem-solving measures to show changes in thinking related to service
learning experiences; the former using essays and the latter hour-long interviews. Students in intensive ISL programs may be more likely to experience
such challenges, therefore resulting in more detailed process measures of their
changing conceptions. Models of the development of critical thinking could
be tested by tracing the thought processes exhibited in structured journal
entries or other written assignments (Ash & Clayton, 2004; Ash et al., 2005).
Understanding the processes by which students construct meaning as they
interpret their experiences could help practitioners structure and mediate experiences in unfamiliar cultures and provide evidence for research (Whitney
& Clayton, chapter 8).

Theories of identity development could also be explored through analysis
of intensive writing by students and by interviewing students about their sense
of themselves in the community and world over time. The role of experiential
learning in identity development has a long history in the literature and several
service learning researchers have addressed the relationship of service in the
construction of identity, including civic identity (Torney-Purta & Barber,
2005; Youniss, McLellan, & Yates, 1997).

Just as domestic service learning results in vastly different experiences
for different students, so too does international study abroad. Some students
are intimately involved with members of the culture they visit, speak the
language, and are immersed in the culture, but others may spend most of
the trip carousing with other American students in a movable party. Moore
(1981) conducted ethnographic studies of students in school-to-work programs
and found that the goals of such programs, though lofty and placing much
emphasis on the connection of learning with real-world practice, often did
not match the actual job site activities of students. Students' experiences
were often fragmented and isolated from any understanding of the work
of the organization. Further study that has built on these observations has

resulted in recommendations for more effective practice (Bailey, Hughes, & Moore, 2003). The gap between the experiences imagined by educators when they design programs and students' actual experience in the field so vividly documented by Moore and others supports the importance of doing some careful observations of what students in ISL programs actually see and do (see Zemach-Bersin, 2009, for one example).

ISL programs are likely to be small and intense and lend themselves to systematic observations of what the students do, how much contact they have with community members in other cultures, the nature of their communication, the tasks they complete, the level of agency they are afforded in the projects with which they work, and how these experiences are connected to learning goals through reflective opportunities (Kiely & Hartman, chapter 13; Tonkin, chapter 9). Multiple data sources and close observation can be used to paint a complex picture of the experience of being a student in a particular ISL course or program (Tonkin, 2004). Similar observations of other study abroad courses or programs would provide helpful insights for curricular design and help identify the important and unique elements for growth afforded by ISL compared to other types of study abroad programs. It may be that the inclusion of service leads to qualitatively different interactions with local community members, for example, and it is this level of engagement that challenges students' previous assumptions or commitment to values articulated by the program (Sutton, chapter 7). But these relationships cannot be understood without careful systematic observation (Kiely & Hartman, chapter 13).

Well-developed qualitative research will help develop a more complete understanding of the experiences that students have in ISL courses and programs, but also contribute to an understanding of the nature of the transformation of student identity, understanding, and capacity for critical judgment over time (Kiely & Hartman, chapter 13; Whitney & Clayton, chapter 8). Such studies also generate questions for more systematic quantitative study (Bringle et al., chapter 12).

Longitudinal Research

Service learning goals include preparing students for lives as engaged citizens, but most research focuses on single courses or programs stretching over a semester or less. Research documents that service learning has a short-term impact on personal, intellectual, and social development outcomes, but less is known about what kinds of experiences influence lifelong behavior. This is made even more urgent by the decline in political interest and civic engagement among young people; while youth participation in voluntary community service has increased, political involvement has declined (Sax, 2000).

Participation in community-based classroom programs and cocurricular activities during high school has long been a good predictor of active engagement in the community in later years (Lindsay, 1984). In the early political socialization literature there was a clear link established between attitudes and experiences of community or school engagement and later voting behavior (Almond & Verba, 1963; Beck & Jennings, 1991). Researchers who have focused on service learning and identity development have also summarized several decades of work linking adolescent engagement in school and community activity with development of civic identity and adult engagement in community activities (Eyler, 2002; Youniss et al., 1997).

More recently, there have been attempts to track the impact of community service and service learning in college on civic participation after graduation. One study focused on alumni of a small Catholic college who had graduated over a 41-year period to determine if community service or service learning would be associated with career choices and community participation. The college experience of the alumni as well as their current community involvement and career choice were measured with a retrospective survey; although the return rate was low, service learning was found to be a predictor of both career choice and community involvement (Warchal & Ruiz, 2004).

Researchers at the Higher Education Research Institute (HERI) have built a longitudinal study onto the CIRP database of freshman and senior data from over 200 institutions; they did a follow-up six years after college graduation, which allowed them to look at the relationship of college community service and service learning to later civic participation. Both community service and service learning during college, especially when mediated by faculty-led reflection, were associated with later interest in public policy issues and community involvement (Astin et al., 2006).

International programs are designed to create citizens who understand cultural diversity and who have a sustained interest in international issues. Many of these goals are reflected in observable or reportable behaviors. Retrospective studies of alumni of study abroad and ISL courses or programs would allow researchers to see if participants in such programs demonstrate enhanced knowledge of international issues, interest in such matters, have continued with international travel, maintained connections with people they met abroad, and held positive attitudes compared to alumni who did not have these experiences. Of course, a genuine longitudinal study in which careful data about the ISL experiences were gathered and the cohort then tracked over time would be more powerful.

Conclusion

Research on domestic service learning programs provides a solid base for future ISL research. There is no need to repeat survey studies that contrast service learning with non-service learning courses or programs; there is a large and consistent body of literature that shows modest relationships between service learning and personal, social, and academic development. Research on ISL courses and programs is particularly well positioned to advance the field in several ways. First, the intensity and high interest for students in international programs suggests that the problem of selectivity that may account for service learning effects is less likely to be an issue in research design. The attraction of study abroad may well mitigate the attraction of service learning and allow different models of international study (e.g., study abroad, ISL, domestic international education) to be compared; the chance to study abroad rather than the chance to do service alone is likely to have brought students into the programs and thus create enthusiastically engaged participants in different programs.

Second, students are immersed in these programs and isolated from many of the other college influences that might affect student outcomes. This allows for control group designs in which critical elements of ISL can be varied and tested. ISL courses or programs with participants drawn from the same student body can vary models of reflection, type of service, and other program elements to sharpen understanding of the characteristics that make a difference.

The isolation and intensity of ISL courses or programs also may make it easier to conduct qualitative research in which the activities and experiences of students can be observed over time. This may strengthen mixed method studies using control groups or simply provide complex descriptive information that can lead to further research. Students may also be more amenable to reflective journal writing or repeated interviews to trace how their sense of self, their critical thinking capacity, and their conceptions of other cultures change and develop during and after the experience. Research on ISL provides a context in which to advance an overall understanding of how students develop and an understanding of the program characteristics that are most conducive to personal, social, and academic development.

References

Almond, G. A., & Verba, S. (1963). *The civic culture*. Princeton, NJ: Princeton University Press.

Ash, S. L., & Clayton, P. H. (2004). The articulated learning: An approach to guided reflection and assessment. *Innovative Higher Education, 29*(2), 137–154.

Ash, S. L., Clayton, P. H., & Atkinson, M. P. (2005). Integrating reflection and assessment to capture and improve student learning. *Michigan Journal of Community Service Learning*, *11*(2), 49–60.

Astin, A. H., Vogelgesang, L., Ikeda, E. K., & Yee, J. (2000). *How service-learning affects students*. Los Angeles: Higher Education Research Institute, UCLA.

Astin, A., Vogelgesang, L., Misa, K., Anderson, J., Denson, N., Jayakumar, U., et al. (2006). *Understanding the effects of service-learning: A study of students and faculty*. Los Angeles: Higher Education Research Institute, UCLA.

Bailey, T. R., Hughes, K. L., & Moore, D. T. (2003). *Working knowledge: Learning and education reform*. New York: Routledge Falmer.

Batchelder, T. H., & Root, S. (1994). Effects of an undergraduate program to integrate academic learning and service: Cognitive, prosocial cognitive and identity outcomes. *Journal of Adolescence*, *17*, 341–356.

Battistoni, R. M. (2002). *Civic engagement across the curriculum: A resource book for service-learning faculty in all disciplines*. Providence, RI: Campus Compact.

Beck, P. A., & Jennings, M. K. (1991). Family traditions, political periods and the development of partisan orientation. *Journal of Politics*, *53*(2), 742–763.

Billig, S. H. (2000). Research on K-12 school-based service-learning: The evidence builds. *Phi Delta Kappan*, *81*(9), 658–664.

Billig, S. H., Root, S., & Jesse, D. (2005, May). *The impact of participation in service-learning on high school students' civic engagement*. (Circle Working Paper 23). Denver, CO: RMC Research Corporation.

Boss, J. A. (1994). The effect of community service work on the moral development of college ethics students. *Journal of Moral Education*, *23*, 183–198.

Braskamp, L. A., Braskamp, D. C., & Merrill, K. C. (2009). *Global Perspective Inventory*. Retrieved August 3, 2009, from https://gpi.central.edu/index.cfm

Bringle, R. G., & Hatcher, J. A. (2000, Fall). Meaningful measurement of theory-based service-learning outcomes: Making the case with quantitative research. *Michigan Journal of Community Service Learning*, 68–75.

Bringle, R. G., Phillips, M., & Hudson, M. (2004). *The measure of service learning: Research scales to assess student experiences*. Washington, DC: American Psychological Association.

Bringle, R. G., & Steinberg, K. (in press). Educating for informed community involvement. *American Journal of Community Psychology*.

Compendium of Assessment on Research Tools (CART). (n.d.). *Compendium of Assessment of Research Tools Home Page*. Retrieved October 19, 2009, from http://cart.rmcdenver.com/index.cgi?autoid=72601

Conrad, D., & Hedin, D. (1980). *Executive summary of the final report of the experiential education evaluation project*. Minneapolis, MN: Center for Youth Development and Research, University of Minnesota.

Deardorff, D. K. (2009). Understanding the challenges of assessing global citizenship. In R. Lewin (Ed.), *The handbook of practice and research in study abroad: Higher education and the quest for global citizenship* (pp. 61–77). New York: Routledge.

Denson, N., Vogelgesang, L., & Saenz, V. (2005, April). *Can service-learning and a college climate of service lead to increased political engagement after college?* Paper presented at the Annual Meeting of the American Educational Research Association, Montréal, Canada.

Eyler, J. (2002). Stretching to meet the challenge: Improving the quality of research to improve the quality of service-learning. In S. H. Billig & A. Furco (Eds.), *The name assigned to the document by the author. This field may also contain sub-titles, series names, and report numbers. Service-learning: Through a multidisciplinary Lens. Advances in service-learning research series* (pp. 3–14). Greenwich, CT: Information Age.

Eyler, J., & Giles, D. E., Jr. (1994). The impact of a college community service laboratory on students' personal, social and cognitive outcomes. *Journal of Adolescence, 17*(4), 327–339.

Eyler, J., & Giles, D. E., Jr. (1999). *Where's the learning in service-learning?* San Francisco: Jossey-Bass.

Eyler, J., Giles, D. E., Jr., Stenson, C. M., & Gray, C. J. (2001). *At a glance: What we know about the effects of service-learning on college students, faculty, institutions and communities, 1993–2000: (3rd ed.).* Nashville, TN: Vanderbilt University.

Fitch, P. (2005). In their own voices: A mixed-methods approach to studying outcomes of intercultural service-learning with college students. In S. Root, J. Callahan, & S. Billig (Eds.), *Improving service-learning practice: Research on models to enhance impacts* (pp. 187–211). Greenwich, CT: Information Age.

Gillespie, J., Braskamp, L., & Dwyer, M. (2009). Holistic student learning and development abroad: The IES 3-D Program Model. In R. Lewin (Ed.), *The handbook of practice and research in study abroad: Higher education and the quest for global citizenship* (pp. 445–465). New York: Routledge.

Gray, M. J., Ondaatje, E. H., Fricker, R., Feschwind, S., Goldman, C. A., Kaganoff, T., et al. (1998). *Coupling service and learning in higher education: The final report of the Evaluation of Learn and Serve America, Higher Education Program.* Washington, DC: Corporation for National Service.

Hatcher, J. A., Bringle, R. G., & Muthiah, R. (2004). Designing effective reflection: What matters to service-learning? *Michigan Journal of Community Service Learning, 11*(1), 38–46.

Honnet, E. P., & Poulsen, S. (1989). *Principles of good practice in combining service and learning.* Racine, WI: Johnson Foundation.

Kahne, J., & Westheimer, J. (2003). Teaching democracy: What schools need to do. *Phi Delta Kappan, 85*(1), 34.

Lewin, R. (Ed.). (2009). *The handbook of practice and research in study abroad: Higher education and the quest for global* citizenship. New York: Routledge.

Lindsay, P. (1984). High school size, participation in activities, and young adult social participation. *Educational Evaluation and Policy Analysis, 6*(1), 73–83.

Mabry, J. B. (1998). Pedagogical variations in service-learning and student outcomes: How time, contact and reflection matter. *Michigan Journal of Community Service Learning, 5*, 32–47.

Markus, G. B., Howard, J., & King, D. (1993). Integrating community service and classroom instruction enhances learning: Results from an experiment. *Educational Evaluation and Policy Analysis, 15*(4), 410–419.

Melchior, A. (1998). *National evaluation of Learn and Serve America School and Community-Based Programs, final report.* Washington, DC: Corporation for National Service.

Moore, D. T. (1981). Discovering the pedagogy of experience. *Harvard Educational Review, 51*(2), 286–300.

Morgan, W., & Streb, M. J. (2003). First, do no harm: Student ownership and service-learning. *Metropolitan Universities Journal, 14*(3), 36–52.

Myers-Lipton, S. J. (1996a). Effect of service-learning on college students' attitudes toward international understanding. *Journal of College Student Development, 37*(6), 659–68.

Myers-Lipton, S. J. (1996b). Effect of a comprehensive service-learning program on college students' level of modern racism. *Michigan Journal of Community Service Learning, 3,* 44–54.

Ostrow, J. (1995). Self-consciousness and social position: On college students changing their minds about the homeless. *Qualitative Sociology, 18*(3), 357–375.

Pascarella, E. T. (2005). *How college affects students: A third decade of research.* San Francisco: Jossey-Bass.

Pascarella, E. T., & Terenzini, P. T. (1991). *How college affects students: Findings and insights from twenty years of research.* San Francisco: Jossey-Bass.

Perry, J. L., & Thomson, A. M. (2004). *Civic service: What difference does it make?* New York: M.E. Sharpe.

Sax, L. J. (2000). Citizenship development and the American college student. In T. Ehrlich (Ed.), *Civic responsibility and higher education* (pp. 3–18). Phoenix, AZ: Oryx.

Steinke, P., Fitch, P., Johnson, C., & Waldstein, F. (2002). An interdisciplinary study of service-learning predictors and outcomes among college students. In S. H. Billig & A. Furco (Eds.), *The name assigned to the document by the author. This field may also contain sub-titles, series names, and report numbers. Service-learning: Through a multidisciplinary Lens. Advances in service-learning research series* (pp. 73–102). Greenwich, CT: Information Age.

Tonkin, H. (Ed.). (2004). *Service-learning across cultures: Promise and achievement.* New York: International Partnership for Service-Learning and Leadership.

Torney-Purta, J., & Barber, C. (2005). Democratic school engagement and civic participation among European adolescents: Analysis of data from the IEA Civic Education Study. *Journal for Social Science Education. Special Edition: European Year of Citizenship through Education.* Retrieved October 8, 2008, from http://www.jsse.org/2005-se/torney_purta_barber_iea_analysis.htm

Warchal, J., & Ruiz, A. (2004). The long term effects of undergraduate service-learning programs on postgraduate employment choices, community engagement and civic leadership. In M. Welch & S. Billig (Eds.), *New perspectives in service-learning: Research to advance the field* (pp. 87–106). Greenwich, CT: Information Age.

Youniss, J., McLellan, J., & Yates, M. (1997). What we know about engendering civic identity. *American Behavioral Scientist, 40*(5), 620–631.

Zemach-Bersin, T. (2009). Selling the world: Study abroad marketing and the privatization of global citizenship. In R. Lewin Ed.), *The handbook of practice and research in study abroad: Higher education and the quest for global citizenship* (pp. 303–320). New York: Routledge.

11

WHAT INTERNATIONAL SERVICE LEARNING RESEARCH CAN LEARN FROM RESEARCH ON INTERNATIONAL LEARNING

Richard Kiely

O ver the past two decades, service learning programs have grown significantly in institutions of higher education in the United States and across the globe (Campus Compact, 2007). Not surprisingly, two- and four-year college administrators and faculty who are familiar with service learning literature, and who have experienced firsthand the benefits of this innovative experiential pedagogy, are increasingly searching for ways to incorporate service learning more broadly into their study abroad programs and courses (H. Berry, 1990; Crabtree, 2008; Grusky, 2000; Kiely & Kiely, 2005; Parker & Dautoff, 2007; Plater, Jones, Bringle, & Clayton, 2009). By focusing on ways to increase students' understanding of what it means to be active and socially responsible global citizens (Hartman, 2008; Lewin, 2009), international educators have begun to view the infusion of service learning into overseas study as an effective way to complement and expand on existing study abroad course objectives that are meant to enhance students' language skills, knowledge of the host country, intercultural sensitivity, and global competence (Crabtree, 2008; Parker & Dautoff, 2007; Pusch & Merrill, 2008; Tonkin, 2004). By providing opportunities to conduct collaborative, community-based work and research with international community partners to address issues in the host country, service learning pedagogy makes an important intellectual and social contribution to study overseas and general international education, and international service learning (ISL) offers a variety of benefits to students, faculty, institutions, and communities (Bringle & Hatcher, chapter 1; Crabtree, 2008; Kiely & Nielsen, 2002; Kraft & Dwyer, 2000; Tonkin, 2004).

Parallel to the rise of service learning in international education, a fledgling scholarly discourse describing purposes, program models, course components, concepts, theories, goals and outcomes that distinguish ISL from study abroad has begun to emerge in practitioner and scholarly literature (Berry & Chisholm, 1999; Bringle & Tonkin, 2004; Crabtree, 1998, 2008; Kiely, 2002; Kraft, 2002; Parker & Dautoff, 2007; Porter & Monard, 2001; Plater et al., 2009). However, most of the writing to date is descriptive and tends to focus on programmatic issues, guiding principles, and instructional strategies; very few articles draw substantially from previous empirical research and/or theory in ISL (Kiely, 2005; Kraft, 2002; Parker & Dautoff, 2007). This chapter provides a comparative review and analysis of concepts, purposes, theories, and approaches in intercultural learning, international education, and study abroad and explains how this analysis might inform ISL research. In particular, this chapter will discuss central organizing concepts driving research in study abroad (i.e., culture shock, adaptation, acculturation, reverse culture shock or reentry); developmental theories and frameworks for study abroad, (i.e., U- and W-curves; developmental models of intercultural sensitivity, intercultural transformation, and transformational learning theory); and purposes, goals, and outcomes of study abroad (i.e., language learning, intercultural awareness, sensitivity, and competence) and their relevance and connection to learning and research in ISL.

Historical Context

In order to understand the linkages between international education, culture learning, study abroad, and ISL, a historical understanding of the rationales underpinning the internationalization of higher education and the rise of study abroad and ISL that can inform program design and research questions will be reviewed (De Wit, 2002; Goodwin & Nacht, 1991; Grunzweig & Rinehart, 1998; McCabe, 2001; Tonkin, chapter 9). De Wit (2002) notes that international programs in higher education were enhanced in the United States after World War II (WWII) as a way to support foreign policy objectives, national security, and greater cooperation (economic integration) among national governments recovering from extensive physical damage, and socioeconomic, cultural, and political upheaval caused by WWII.

For many international relations scholars and political scientists, the end of WWII brought new hope for greater integration (Deutsch, 1953, 1968; Haas, 1958, 1961, 1964; Mitrany, 1948, 1966, 1975) among nation-states through various forms of cultural, intellectual, and economic exchange as well as technical and financial assistance (De Wit, 2002). The post-WWII period opened up numerous opportunities for greater cross-cultural understanding and more peaceful integration through the exchange of ideas, people, technology, and consumer goods among nation-states (Kim, 2001; Ward, Bochner, & Furnham, 2001). With the rise of the Cold War and United States and Soviet Union as competing superpowers, along with the establishment of military bases, trade agreements, and foreign aid, international education and exchange offered an opportunity for the governments of the two superpowers to expand their spheres of influence (De Wit, 2002).

From WWII through the Cold War to September 11, 2001, and to the present day, the movement to internationalize higher education has been very much a matter of satisfying national interests in order to compete more effectively with other nation-states in an increasingly interdependent, and sometimes contentious, world (De Wit, 2002; Falk & Kanach, 2000; Grunzweig & Rinehart, 1998; McCabe, 2001). International education policies and activities in the United States and the rhetoric of intercultural competence in study abroad, have therefore evolved within the larger context of cultural, social, political, economic, and educational dimensions of national priorities; in the United States, and this seemingly immutable pattern is particularly salient post-September 11, 2001 (De Wit, 2002, p. 100). Indeed, reviewing the mission statements of some of the largest universities with extensive study abroad programs, the theme of preparing students to compete in an increasingly globalized and interdependent economy would surely be the most dominant rationale, with intercultural competence (i.e., skilled global worker) a close second, with its requisite personal skills, attitudes, and behaviors (Deardorff, 2006; Hunter, 2004; Woolf, 2004).

What is clear, and perhaps ironic, is that much of what constitutes international education exchange and study abroad in higher education has always been defined by activities that support national political, economic, and security interests (Commission on the Abraham Lincoln Study Abroad Fellowship Program, 2005; Hunter, 2004; McCabe, 2001; Mestenhauser, 2003).[1] Thus, any comparison of the purposes, theories, and approaches to culture learning, study abroad and ISL, and the role of higher education in fostering international education, needs to be framed within competing views of the socioeconomic and political context of globalization and its asymmetrical effect on different regions of the world (Cornwell & Stoddard, 1999;

De Wit, 2002; Falk & Kanach, 2000; Grunzweig & Rinehart, 1998; Johnson & Mulholland, 2006; McCabe, 2001; Schattle, 2009). These asymmetrical relations of power that frame international exchange are rarely measured or considered part of research and documentation of study abroad and international education exchange (see Institute of International Education, 2008; and also more recently, Savicki, 2008).

Literature Review: Intercultural Learning and Study Abroad

After WWII, the increase in different types of international exchanges led scholars to initiate a substantial research agenda to assess the quality, level, type, and impact of cross-cultural contact and in particular, the experience of the cross-cultural sojourner[2] (Ward et al., 2001). Scholars focused much of their attention on how university, corporate, and military personnel sent overseas adjusted and coped with issues and problems associated with living, studying, and working in a new and unfamiliar culture (Kim, 2001; Ward et al., 2001). The U.S. government exchange programs, such as the U.S. Fulbright Scholarly Exchange Program and the U.S. Peace Corps, also led to an increase on studies that looked at the cognitive, affective, and behavioral dimensions of sojourner adaptation to new and unfamiliar cross-cultural environments (Kim, 2001; Ward et al., 2001). This included studies on personality traits of successful sojourners, factors that result in stress, skills, and competencies; and the stress appraisal, coping, and learning strategies sojourners use to adjust to foreign cultures and contexts (Kim, 2001; Savicki, 2008; Ward et al., 2001). By examining factors and variables related to successful (and unsuccessful) intercultural experiences researchers endeavored to control better for, and predict more effectively, cross-cultural adaptation (Ward et al., 2001). The next section will describe major concepts and theories that emerged from a review of scholarly literature in the field of study abroad and intercultural learning.[3]

Central Organizing Concepts in Study Abroad and Intercultural Learning

ISL presents instructional designers and students with heightened concerns associated with their capacity for integrating students into typically unfamiliar settings. The next section analyzes past work on preparing students for the immersion of ISL and their return to the U.S. as well as the potential for them to develop cross-cultural knowledge and skills as a result of making those transitions.

Culture Shock

An important organizing concept driving research on sojourner adaptation in intercultural learning and study abroad is *culture shock* (Ward et al., 2001).[4] According to Kim (2001), there are two major strands of research pertaining to sojourner adjustment with culture shock as a variable, "the problem approach and the learning/growth approaches" (Kim, 2001, p. 17). Research from a problem approach tends to view "culture shock" as the most important variable or construct driving cross-cultural adaptation (Kim, 2001). Problem-oriented or "recuperation" models assume that culture shock is a temporary condition the cure of which depends on sojourners' personality and skill set (Anderson, 1994, p. 293). Problem approaches tend to focus on identifying the causes and symptoms of culture shock in order to develop effective interventions (i.e., pre-orientation training) to "inoculate" (Paige, 1993, p. 4) individual sojourners (Kim, 2001; Ward et al., 2001).

Research that focuses on culture learning, personal growth, and development views culture shock as a part of intercultural learning (Kim, 2001; Ward et al., 2001). The shift from cultural adaptation as a problem to a process has led to more systematic empirical study on specific situational and personal factors that influence sojourner adjustment, more sophisticated theory and model building, and targeted training to learn appropriate knowledge, skills, and behaviors for adapting to a new culture (Ward et al., 2001). This line of research examines the appraisal, coping, and learning strategies that sojourners use to respond more actively and effectively to culture shock (Savicki, Cooley, & Donnelly, 2008).

Although much of the early literature focused on the clinical and problematic symptoms of culture shock, some scholars (Lysgaard, 1955; Oberg, 1960) theorized the process of sojourner's culture shock as a chronological and linear pattern of adjustment in the shape of a "U-curve" (Kim, 2001, Ward et al., 2001). For example, Oberg's (1960) U-curve model describes the process of culture shock as four linear stages that sojourners experience as they adapt to a foreign setting: (a) the initial "honeymoon phase" is a positive upward experience where the sojourner feels excitement upon arrival in the new culture; (b) during the subsequent "disillusionment phase," the sojourner descends into feelings of anxiety and frustration in attempting to adjust to the stressors (i.e., culture, language, religion, food, relationships) associated with living in an unfamiliar cultural environment; (c) the "coping and recovery stage" depicts a period in which sojourners practice new ways of thinking, acting, and communicating to address intercultural stressors; and (d) the "final stage" is a more functional and balanced adjustment to culture shock (Ward et al., 2001, p. 80).

Reverse Culture Shock or Reentry[5]

Gullahorn and Gullahorn (1963) described an expanded version of the U-curve model into a "W-curve" or "double U-curve" to explain more fully the sojourner experience during and after the sojourn. The "W-curve" incorporates the linear U-shaped process of culture shock during the sojourn, but then also includes an additional U-curve to describe sojourner adjustment upon reentry into the home culture (Austin, 1983, 1986; Martin, 1984, 1993). Scholars have theorized that reverse culture shock might be a more difficult adjustment in the home country than culture shock in the host country (Austin, 1986; Martin, 1993; Pusch, 2004; Ward et al., 2001). A number of studies have identified challenges sojourners experience during reentry including: personal, (e.g., psychological, lifestyle changes, eating habits, career, consumption, increased self-efficacy), political (e.g., critical of political policies, nationalism), social (e.g., boredom, alienation, loneliness, isolation), cultural (e.g., more informed and/or critical view of one's home country, ambivalence about cultural norms and values), physical (e.g., adjustments to diet, climate, time zones), and interpersonal (e.g., difficulties with relationships, friends, and family) (Gaw, 2000; Martin, 1984, 1986; Raschio, 1987; Uehara, 1986; Ward et al., 2001).

Although the U-curve and W-curve models are still widely used in the field of study abroad and by intercultural educators, the generalizability of these models has been inconsistent (Savicki, Adams, & Binder, 2008; Ward et al., 2001). More recent longitudinal research that examined the U-curve pattern of sojourner adjustment found that unlike Oberg's description of a honeymoon phase upon entry, study participants levels of stress, depression, anxiety, and difficulty were most severe during the first few months of their sojourn (Ward et al., 2001). On the basis of their review of studies examining the value of the U-curve for explaining sojourner adjustment, Ward et al. (2001) conclude that in spite of its intuitive appeal, the "U-curve hypothesis appears to be largely atheoretical, deriving from a combination of post hoc explanation and armchair speculation" (p. 80). They further contend that the U-curve model continues to be popular among intercultural educators due to its simplicity and because researchers have not developed a robust and parsimonious theoretical model for sojourner adjustment to replace it (Ward et al., 2001).

Partly to address this theory gap, researchers have attempted to integrate diverse culture shock models, as well as to incorporate pertinent theoretical lenses developed in the fields of intercultural communication and social psychology (Kim, 2001; Savicki, 2008; Ward et al., 2001). More recent research suggests that sojourner adjustment entails both psychological and sociocultural processes that lead to a variety of affective, cognitive, and behavioral outcomes depending on structural and institutional factors, contact stressors, duration of stay, program activities, cultural context, and personal experience (Kim, 2001; Savicki, 2008, Ward et al., 2001).

Ward et al. (2001) developed an empirically derived theoretical framework that integrates and expands on previous models of culture shock. To get out of the "culture shock" box, Ward et al. (2001) use the concept of acculturation to explain the sojourn experience by examining and explaining sojourners' affective, cognitive, and behavioral responses to contact with another culture. They claim that during the process of acculturation sojourners typically experience both "psychological adjustment" and "sociocultural adaptation" (pp. 42–44). Psychological adjustment has to do with affective reactions whereby sojourners draw on personal and interpersonal resources and support to actively cope with the stress related to adjusting to a new culture (Ward et al., 2001, p. 42). Sociocultural adaptation entails learning appropriate behaviors and social skills to communicate, interact, and function more effectively with the host culture (Ward et al., 2001, p. 42). Ward et al.'s (2001) acculturation model integrates and expands on previous approaches to cross-cultural adaptation by describing both the psychological and sociocultural processes and outcomes of intercultural contact, by identifying individual and societal level variables, and by drawing from multiple theoretical lenses (i.e., stress and coping, culture learning, attribution and social identification theories) (Ward et al., 2001, p. 44).

Intercultural Competence

Another important organizing concept that bridges research on intercultural learning and study abroad is intercultural competence (Deardorff, 2006, 2008, 2009; Lambert, 1994; Savicki, 2008). Study abroad scholars place tremendous value on the development of intercultural and global competence as both a precursor to and outcome of effective cross-cultural adjustment, interaction, and communication (J. Bennett, 2008; Deardorff & Hunter, 2006; Kim, 2001; Savicki, 2008). Much of the research and training in study abroad literature emphasizes the development of different types of intercultural competencies (Deardorff, 2004, 2006, 2009; Dinges & Baldwin, 1996; Gillespie, Braskamp, & Dwyer, 2009; Kim, 2001; Lustig & Koester, 2003; Ward et al., 2001) and global competencies (Hunter, 2004; Lambert, 1994; Olsen & Kroeger, 2001) as the key to successful cross-cultural adaptation.[6]

Although there is a lack of consensus on what constitutes competence in terms of adapting to another culture, based on a Delphi study conducted with 23 intercultural scholars, Deardorff (2004, 2006, 2009) has not only provided the study abroad field with greater consensus on a definition for intercultural competence, she has also constructed a process model of intercultural competence to assist educators in designing programs that align with specific intercultural competencies. Deardorff (2004, 2008, 2009) generated a list of elements that comprise intercultural competence on which there was 80–100% agreement among scholars and then developed a model that indicates broader categories for understanding and assessing the knowledge, skills, and attitudes (KSAs) represented in intercultural competence. Deardorff's (2008) framework connects the requisite KSAs with internal affective outcomes (i.e., tolerance for ambiguity, flexibility) and more observable external behavioral outcomes (i.e., effective communication, culturally appropriate responses) (see pp. 36–39). Deardorff (2008) highlights a number of useful strategies for fostering intercultural competence (e.g., preparation, skill development, reflection, meaningful intercultural interactions, assessment) as well as tools for enhancing intercultural skills and methods for evaluating intercultural competence. However, there is a need for further empirical study to assess transfer of learning from predeparture training to onsite sojourner adjustment and competence and, as Deardorff's (2008) study implies, greater clarity of what intercultural competence means from the sojourner, programmatic, or host culture perspective.

Research on Study Abroad

An analysis of research in study abroad over the past four decades (see Center for Global Education, 1998-2002; Vande Berg, 2001) tends to confirm more recent reviews (Deardorff, 2009; Parker & Dautoff, 2007; Gillespie et al., 2009; Hoff, 2008; Savicki, 2008) of study abroad research that found that the majority of empirical studies in study abroad are impact studies assessing student outcomes related to content learning (e.g., disciplinary learning, language proficiency, competencies), affective learning (e.g., personal growth, self-efficacy, competencies), and to a lesser extent on learning processes (Hoff, 2008) or what Parker and Dautoff (2007) deem connective learning (i.e., relationships, connection with others), and emotional learning (Savicki, 2008). Empirical studies in study abroad outcomes have also focused on the knowledge, skills, attitudes, and personality traits reflective of intercultural competence (Deardorff, 2004) and global competence (Hunter, 2004; Olsen & Kroeger, 2001; see also ACE-FIPSE International Learning Assessment Project www.acenet.edu/programs/international/FIPSE, for results of study on knowledge, skills, and attitudes of globally competent students). Lastly, studies have examined the variables that affect intercultural adjustment including socioeconomic and political context, previous intercultural training, language proficiency, duration of program, housing, social support, previous travel experience, personality characteristics, type of program and coursework, expectations, and culture distance, and the various knowledge, skills, and coping and learning strategies students use to adapt to international cultures including emotional regulation, openness, flexibility, language proficiency, knowledge acquisition, content mastery, critical thinking, observation, reflection, conceptual understanding, empathy, and personal and interpersonal skills (Hoff, 2008; Savicki, Binder, & Heller, 2008; Savicki, Cooley, & Donnelly, 2008; Ward et al., 2001).

More recently, there is a line of study abroad research (Savicki, Binder, & Heller, 2008) that has used Matsumoto et al's. (2001) Intercultural Adjustment Potential Scale (ICAPS) to explore the relationship between students' actual and potential for intercultural adjustment (Matsumoto et al., 2001; Savicki, Binder, & Heller, 2008). Although a more complete summary of the studies and instruments above is not possible in this chapter, that empirical research on study abroad has become more methodologically diverse, theory based, and systematic over the past decade and provides a number of good examples for ISL researchers to draw from.

Theories of Intercultural Learning and Transformation

There is general agreement in the study abroad field that outcome assessment is important for accountability and credibility and that intercultural competence is a key predictor for and outcome of successful intercultural adaptation (Parker & Dautoff, 2007; Savicki, 2001; Ward et al., 2001). A number of scholars have also conducted research to document the learning process that results from intercultural contact (Kim, 2001, 2005; Taylor, 1994a; Savicki, 2008; Ward et al., 2001). There is also an emerging recognition that sometimes the struggles with culture shock and reentry lead to powerful forms of learning that are transformational (Kiely, 2002, 2004, 2005; Kim, 2001; Savicki, 2008; Taylor, 1994a). The section below will briefly describe some of the more prominent theoretical models that focus on the cognitive developmental process and transformational learning sojourners experience through intercultural contact.

Adler (1975) developed one of the earliest theoretical models to describe the process of sojourners' cognitive development that results from intercultural adaptation. Adler's (1975, 1987) model describes cross-cultural adaptation as a set of developmental transitions leading to greater personal and cultural awareness: contact, disintegration, reintegration, autonomy, and independence (Adler, 1975). Adler (1977) contends that multiculturalism (a condition of independence) is the highest stage of a sojourners' identity development.

Adler's (1977, 1987) model envisioned the development of a multicultural person who would think, act, and behave in a culturally sensitive manner and who could benefit society by effectively navigating and negotiating different cultures (Shames, 1997). However, heightened sense of self and ability to adapt might also create a vulnerability to self-disintegration (Shames, 1997). In spite of the developmental tensions caused by the process of cultural adaptation, Adler's (1987) developmental model highlights the benefits of individual self-awareness and transformation that result from the process of intercultural adjustment.

J. Bennett's research (1993) on "cultural marginality" lends insight to Adler's developmental model and the concept of the multicultural person. J. Bennett (1993) contends that multicultural and bicultural individuals, who do not maintain a single cultural frame of reference, (i.e., set of values and/or belief system), often live on the margins of each culture. J. Bennett introduces the concept of "encapsulated marginality" to describe multicultural persons who are entrenched in "conflicting cultural loyalties and unable to construct a unified identity" (J. Bennett, 1993, p. 113). She uses the concept of "constructive marginals," to describe multicultural persons who, in spite of their epistemological and cultural relativism, function more effectively because they "tend to avoid getting lost in every new cultural frame of reference that presents itself. While being able to understand the other frame, constructives do not re-invent their frames on a weekly basis" (J. Bennett, 1993, p. 130). For Shames (1997), "the encapsulated marginal is one who is never at home in the world, while the constructive marginal is never *not* at home. Having transcended culture shock, the homeless mind becomes the global mind" (p. 140). The models developed by Adler (1975) and J. Bennett (1993) offer study abroad and ISL researchers with developmental frameworks for assessing the level and frequency of different stages and dimensions of intercultural adaptation that study abroad and ISL sojourners experience in different international courses, programs, and contexts.

One of the more prominent conceptual models used in study abroad, is M. Bennett's (1986, 1993) Developmental Model of Intercultural Sensitivity (DMIS) (J. Bennett, 2008; Lou & Bosley, 2008). M. Bennett's (1986) DMIS model suggests that culture learning can transform ethnocentric individuals into becoming more developmentally sensitive to cultural differences. M. Bennett's model describes intercultural learning as a developmental process along six stages from ethnocentrism, (i.e., denial, defense, minimization are the three lowest levels of intercultural sensitivity), to ethnorelativism, (i.e., acceptance, adaptation, and integration are the three highest stages of intercultural sensitivity). Ethnorelativism constitutes a major cognitive shift in the way individuals experience and interpret their cultural identity and cultural difference (M. Bennett, 1993). In ethnorelativistic stages, individuals embrace rather than eschew cultural differences (M. Bennett, 1993, p. 46). Similar to Adler's independence stage, M. Bennett's (1993) model represents integration as the highest stage of intercultural development. According to M. Bennett (1993), integration indicates that sojourners have become pluralistic, multicultural individuals who have "discarded" their "primary cultural affiliation" as a result of an extended stay in another culture (p. 60). Similar to J. Bennett's (1993) analysis above, sojourners who have reached the integration stage of intercultural sensitivity often exist as cultural marginals,

> outside all cultural frames of reference by virtue of their ability to consciously raise any assumption to a meta-level . . . there is no natural cultural identity for the marginal person . . . And it is certainly true that many marginal people experience great discomfort and dysfunction as a result of their status. (M. Bennett, 1993, p. 63)

M. Bennett (1993) contends that educators can help sojourners move from "encapsulated" to constructive marginal status and adds that it "may be as simple as labeling the stage as both marginal and constructive" (M. Bennett, 1993, pp. 64–65) so that people can become more explicitly conscious of their identity. M. Bennett (1993) claims that "being conscious of this dynamic process, people can function in relationship to cultures while staying outside the constraints of any particular one" (M. Bennett, 1993, p. 60). Bennett and Bennett (2004) designed the Intercultural Development Inventory (IDI) to assess sojourners' experience with different stages represented in the DMIS model (see Lou & Bosley, 2008, for a discussion on the value of the IDI to assess study abroad students' experience with DMIS stages).

Although these cognitive developmental models above offer potentially useful conceptual lenses for explaining how sojourners experience the process of intercultural adaptation, there are questions about the generalizability of stages to diverse programs, people, and places. For example, based on research with 20 students from diverse backgrounds participating in a course on cultural identity, Sparrow's (2000) study highlights and critiques the constructivist set of assumptions implicit in the models above (Adler, 1977; J. Bennett, 1993; M. Bennett, 1993) and offers an alternative social constructionist perspective on multicultural identity development. Sparrow (2000) argues that constructivist models of intercultural adaptation neglect to consider the social, cultural, economic, political, and historical factors that influence the development of intercultural identity. Based upon her analysis of study participants' interviews and papers, her findings suggest that members of oppressed or minority groups have difficulty navigating multiple cultural frames of reference assumed in "multicultural man" (Sparrow, 2000).

Kim's (2001) integrative theory of communication and cross-cultural adaptation conceptualizes the sojourner experience as an ongoing "cyclical process of stress, adaptation and growth" (p. 57). Kim (2001) claims that sojourners' "adaptive journey follows a pattern that juxtaposes novelty and confirmation, attachment and detachment, progression and regression, integration and disintegration, construction and destruction. The process is continuous as long as there are new environmental challenges" (2001, p. 57). There are four dimensions to Kim's (2001) model: personal and social communication competence; host environmental conformity and receptivity; the sojourner's adaptive predisposition; and intercultural transformation (pp. 71–94). Intercultural transformation characterizes sojourners effective intercultural adaptation through the integration of the other three dimensions. Intercultural transformation entails three adaptive processes; "*functional fitness* in carrying out daily transactions, improved *psychological health* in dealing with the environment, and a movement from the original cultural identity to a broader, *intercultural identity*" (Kim, 2001, p. 61). How well sojourners integrate the four dimensions determines whether they will experience what Kim refers to as "intercultural personhood" (p. 194) or what she refers to as the "highest degree of internal harmony" and "psychic evolution" (p. 195).

Studies on Intercultural and Transformational Learning

Empirical research in study abroad and intercultural education has increasingly recognized the transformative impact that results from contact with, adaptation to, and learning in new and unfamiliar cultures (Hunter, 2008; Kiely, 2002; Kim, 2001; Savicki, 2008). Mezirow's (1978, 1991) groundbreaking research led to the development of an 11-stage transformational learning model that documents how people experience perspective transformation. Mezirow's original model along with more recent work with colleagues (Mezirow & Associates, 1990, 2000) and numerous empirical studies on different aspects of Mezirow's theory (see Taylor, 2000, 2007, for reviews of transformational learning research) provides a robust conceptual framework for study abroad and ISL researchers to assess the transformative learning processes and outcomes that sojourners experience as a result of their participation in international programs, including ISL. A variety of studies in study abroad and ISL have begun to study different dimensions of Mezirow's transformational learning theory to better understand sojourners' experience with intercultural adjustment (Harper, 1994; Holt, 1994; Kennedy, 1994; Kiely, 2002; Lee, 1997; Lyon, 2001; Taylor, 1993; Temple, 1999; Whalley, 1995).

Prior to research on transformational learning theory in study abroad and ISL, there were anecdotal claims and conceptual models that described the life-changing aspects of sojourner experiences. Earlier research did not draw from learning theory and there was very little theoretically based empirical evidence to explain sojourner transformations (Taylor, 1994a). Based on a review of the intercultural learning literature, Taylor (1993, 1994a, 1994b) identified a strong link between Mezirow's (1991) transformational learning theory and intercultural learning models. Taylor (1994a) theorized "that intercultural competency is a transformative process whereby the stranger develops an adaptive capacity, altering his or her perspective to effectively understand and accommodate the demands of the host culture" (p. 156). Taylor (1993) also found that cognitive and developmental intercultural learning models do not adequately explain the processes of intercultural learning.

Taylor (1993, 1994a, 1994b) argued that Mezirow's transformational learning theory offered a more valid conceptual framework for describing and explaining how sojourners experience the process of intercultural learning and adaptation. He suggested that Mezirow's model mirrored the process of cross-cultural adaptation and the development of intercultural competence in three ways: "1) the precondition for change; 2) the learning process; and 3) the outcome" (Taylor, 1994b, p. 395). The precondition for change in intercultural learning is culture shock that parallels Mezirow's notion of the "disorienting dilemma" or cognitive dissonance that sojourners experience in a new and unfamiliar culture (Taylor, 1994b). Culture shock and disorienting dilemmas trigger processes that may lead to greater intercultural learning and competence (Taylor, 1994b).

The processes in both intercultural and transformative learning models are developmental whereby sojourners become progressively more adaptive and competent (Taylor, 1993, p. 159). Lastly, Taylor theorized that the outcome of intercultural adaptation as intercultural competence reflects Mezirow's concept of perspective transformation as a shift in perspective that is a "more inclusive, differentiated, permeable and integrated world view" (Taylor, 1993, p. 159).

Taylor (1993) conducted research to examine the link between the learning processes in Mezirow's transformational learning theory, with dimensions of cross-cultural adaptation and intercultural competence. Based on an analysis of the interviews with 12 North Americans (four women, eight men, three African Americans) who had lived overseas in countries in Western Europe, Africa, South America, and Asia for over two years, Taylor (1993) found that participants experienced a transformational process of becoming interculturally competent entailing five components "setting the stage, cultural disequilibrium, cognitive orientations (non-reflective and reflective orientations), behavioral learning strategies, and evolving intercultural identity" (Taylor, 1993, p. 129). Taylor's (1993) research adds important insight into the process of learning in cross-cultural settings including the role of preconditions for change, emotions, nonreflective and reflective learning strategies, and personal context in intercultural learning.

Lyon (2002) provides an excellent review of eight empirical studies (Harper, 1994; Holt, 1994; Kennedy, 1994; Lee, 1997; Lyon, 2001; Taylor, 1993; Temple, 1999; Whalley, 1995) that draw on Mezirow's theory to understand how sojourners experience intercultural adaptation. Lyon (2002) found a number of common patterns across each of the studies including: the identification of disorienting dilemmas or culture shock as catalysts for transformational and intercultural learning, reflective and nonreflective learning processes, diverse outcomes for perspective transformation, and the importance of relationships for facilitating transformative learning. Lyon (2002, p. 239) also found that most of the studies were based on participants' self-reports in interviews with one case study (Harper, 1994) and one study that analyzed student journals (Whalley, 1995). None of the studies examined reentry, nor did they study how structural and contextual factors shape the transformational learning process.

Implications for ISL Research

The foregoing examination of study abroad literature highlights important organizing concepts, theoretical frameworks, models, and outcomes that might inform ISL theory and research. This review demonstrates that research in study abroad has grown significantly over the past four decades (Savicki & Selby, 2008). As a result, the quality of research approaches, the level of knowledge accumulation and transfer, as well as what constitutes quality learning, theory, programming, and research on study abroad has become more cohesive, comprehensive, consistent, and useful. Although there are different ways of organizing how knowledge produced from research in study abroad and intercultural learning might inform ISL research (Kiely & Kiely, 2005; Parker & Dautoff, 2007; Pusch & Merrill, 2008), this analysis has identified some relevant concepts, theories, models, instruments, and strategies for ISL researchers to consider, including the concept of culture shock and models of sojourner adjustment, developmental models for intercultural learning and adaptation, and learning outcomes, such as intercultural competence and transformation. The following section will synthesize the above areas and will discuss limitations, issues, and challenges associated with conducting research on learning in study abroad and ISL.

First, an analysis of scholarly literature and research in study abroad and intercultural learning found that the concept of culture shock continues to drive discourses on intercultural education. Given personal, professional, and academic dilemmas caused by culture shock, researchers have generated substantial knowledge on sojourner adjustment factors, variables, and strategies and have developed a number of instruments to measure sojourner adjustment that might guide research on student adjustment in ISL programs and settings.

In terms of future directions for ISL research, findings from this review indicate that although culture shock was considered a temporary symptom of the challenges of cross-cultural contact, newer and more comprehensive acculturation models such as those developed by Kim (2001) and Ward et al. (2001) offer theoretical frameworks that describe and explain more adequately the micro and macro factors and variables that influence sojourners' psychological well-being and sociocultural adjustment (Ward et al., 2001). Empirical studies have tested and confirmed the influence of these stressors and other specific personal and situational factors that influence sojourners' experience with and response to culture shock and cross-cultural adjustment (Savicki, Cooley, & Donnelly, 2008; Ward et al., 2001). Therefore, it behooves ISL researchers to focus on factors and variables associated with both psychological and sociocultural adjustment. This could include determining the degree to which the community service component plays a role in accelerating or ameliorating the phases of adjustment.

ISL researchers might also test Paige's (1993) hypotheses on cross-cultural stressors and risk factors and/or identify the unique types of stressors and risk factors that contribute to the intensity of the ISL experience (Pusch, 2004; Pusch & Merrill, 2008; Tonkin, chapter 9). Paige (1993) hypothesized that the intensity of an intercultural experience is largely dependent on the interaction of situational and personal factors. He identified and described how 10 "intensity factors" (i.e., cultural differences, ethnocentrism, language, cultural immersion, cultural isolation, prior intercultural experience, expectations, visibility and invisibility, status, power and control) might affect the "psychological intensity of the sojourner's intercultural experience" (p. 2). He also describes six risk factors (i.e., risk of personal disclosure, failure, embarrassment, threat to one's cultural identity, becoming culturally marginal, and self-awareness) that intercultural educators should take into consideration when determining the type and sequence of intercultural learning activities.

More recently, there is a line of study abroad research (Matsumoto et al., 2001) that focuses on identifying and enhancing students' intercultural adjustment potential and abilities to increase the likelihood that they will experience "positive outcomes" while overseas (Savicki, Binder, & Heller, 2008, p. 111). Again, ISL researchers have an excellent opportunity to extend this research.

There is limited research in ISL (see Kiely, 2002) that has examined similar constructs to stressors and culture shock. For example, Kiely's (2002) study identified specific types of dissonance (e.g., environmental, physical, social, economic, cultural, political, linguistic) that occur in ISL. His study also found that dissonance occurs at different levels of intensities (i.e., high and low) and that the type and intensity of the dissonance affects how participants learn in ISL contexts over time. Kiely's (2002) research highlighted how specific types of high-level dissonance can lead participants to experience different types of transformational learning and importantly, how such powerful shifts in worldview can cause their adjustment onsite and upon return to be highly problematic over time. Because this research conflicted with study abroad research that held that sojourners adjustment to culture shock and stressors diminishes over time, research that furthers the understanding of how ISL participants experience adjustment over time would be highly beneficial to the study abroad field.

This line of research would provide knowledge not only on the type, level, and intensity of dissonance that participants experience in diverse ISL contexts, but also how different types and intensities of dissonance foster and/or hinder ISL participants' learning over time. In addition, research that focuses on dissonance and stressors would provide useful information for developing ISL training programs and activities to help sojourners prepare for and learn from specific types of stressors and dissonance that result from intercultural contact. There are numerous publications devoted to intercultural training (Brislin & Yoshida, 1994; Landis & Bhagat, 1996; see also Ward et al., 2001, pp. 248–269 for a review) that support study abroad and intercultural adjustment; however, initial ISL research (Kiely, 2002) on adjustment suggests that ISL participants may need different types of training that prepares them before, during, and after their ISL experience. Based on what is known about the psychological and sociocultural factors influencing sojourner adjustment in the studies summarized above, ISL researchers should consider how participants prepare for, respond to, cope with, and learn from stressors and dissonance in diverse ISL programs and settings.

Second, research and theory in intercultural learning and study abroad have also described and explain the *process of culture shock or sojourner adaptation*. Early researchers (Gullahorn & Gullahorn, 1963; Lysgaard, 1955;

Oberg, 1960) identified U-curve and W-curve patterns that suggest that so-journers experience culture shock as an ongoing process of adjustment and adaptation before, during, and after the sojourn. In addition, the conceptual models described by Adler (1975, 1977, 1987), J. Bennett (1993), M. Bennett (1993), Bennett and Bennett (2001), and Kim (2001) imply that sojourner's experiences adapting to another culture is progressively developmental. These descriptive theoretical models combined with empirical research on intercul-tural learning and adaptation above are useful for ISL researchers in that they describe different ways in which sojourners can potentially learn and grow to become more self-aware and culturally sensitive as a result of their ISL experience (Adler, 1975; J. Bennett, 2008; M. Bennett, 1993; Kim, 2001).

Although there is some skepticism with regard to the generalizability and accuracy of early culture shock (e.g., U- and W-curve) models (Ward et al., 2001), the shift from seeing culture shock as an adjustment problem to a patterned process of adaptation has a number of implications for ISL research. More substantial developmental models in intercultural learning (Adler, 1975; M. Bennett, 1986; Kim, 2001) offer theories on different stages of identity de-velopment that might reflect the kind of developmental shifts in identity and self-awareness that students experience adapting to ISL settings (Eyler, chap-ter 10). There may be patterns in how students adapt to issues and challenges that are unique to ISL because of the community service and reflection that are integral parts of the ISL experience and not part of traditional study abroad. By identifying and examining patterns of the ways in which students adjust in both short- and long-term ISL programs, researchers can provide important insight to faculty, practitioners, host-country partners, and agency personnel on how to assist ISL students at different stages before, during, and after their sojourn. Because ISL and study abroad programs have experienced an increase in students participating in short-term programs, researchers might examine how applicable developmental models are in light of different program factors (e.g., duration, content, activities, immersion, structure, format).

Drawing from more comprehensive developmental, intercultural learn-ing, and acculturation models (see M. Bennett, 1993; Kim, 2001; Savicki, 2008; Ward et al., 2001), combined with research on factors that hinder and/or en-hance adjustment, researchers could expand on or develop new models that more adequately describe and explain specific micro and macro adjustment factors, stressors, and the process of student adaptation in ISL contexts. In ad-dition, developmental process models that identify culture shock and reverse culture shock as important stages of cross-cultural adaptation have implica-tions for students' preparation, learning, and experiences before, during, and after participating in ISL programs.

In terms of limitations, developmental models for intercultural learning and adaptation (Adler, 1975, 1987; M. Bennett, 1993; Kim, 2001; Oberg, 1960) provide scant empirical documentation to support their claims and the models do not explain how contextual factors and learning processes (some of which might be uniquely present in ISL) influence sojourners' transformations and/or intercultural competence (Jacobson, 1996; Taylor, 1993, 1994a). More recently, study abroad scholars do allude to the need for reflection and other forms of learning (J. Bennett, 2008; Deardorff, 2008; Hunter, 2008; Savicki, 2008), but these learning processes that support learning have neither been studied nor explained in detail in study abroad research. Empirical studies (Lyon, 2001; Taylor, 1993) that have linked transformational learning to intercultural learning explain how reflective and nonreflective transformational learning processes assist sojourners in the process of cross-cultural adaptation (Lyon, 2001, 2002). However, these studies have not shed light on how contextual factors and asymmetrical relations of power that are experienced in cross-cultural interactions (and particularly in ISL contexts), influence learning and transformation (Kiely, 2002, 2005). Developmental models and empirical studies above assume that intercultural transformation and competence are largely the result of an individual's cognitive processing of the cross-cultural experience. However, the manner in which contextual, institutional, and structural factors affect learning remains largely unexamined (Kiely, 2002, 2004, 2005). ISL involves quantitatively and qualitatively different interpersonal interactions with members of the host country, and these interpersonal processes are unexplored as variables that can contribute to change over time. Models of intercultural development and sensitivity also describe the transformative nature of intercultural learning but assume that the end point of transformation equals successful integration, adaptation, and intercultural competence (i.e., "constructive marginality," "multicultural person," and "intercultural personhood") (see Adler, 1977, 1987; J. Bennett, 1993; M. Bennett, 1993; Kim, 2001). Kiely's (2002) longitudinal research suggests that ISL participants experience substantial difficulty integrating and transferring their ISL experience upon reentry and over time. This relates to Sparrow's (2000) critique of the constructivist epistemology underpinning cognitive developmental theories in intercultural learning that do not adequately consider how structural factors affect intercultural learning and identity development of individuals from underrepresented groups (Sparrow, 2000). Hence, the research and models above have not adequately explained how sojourners who live in another country and return home (i.e., study abroad and ISL students) critique and resist adaptation to existing local and global social, cultural, economic, political, and institutional arrangements before, during, and after the intercultural learning process (Kiely, 2002). This has particularly interesting implications for research that would focus on the effects of ISL experience in the "Sandwich" structures of ISL courses and for professionally oriented ISL courses (see Jones & Steinberg, chapter 5).

Research on student learning and transformation in study abroad empirical studies (Lyon, 2001, 2002; Savicki, 2008; Taylor, 1993) has not investigated learning processes after reentry through longitudinal studies. The role of learning processes after reentry might have an effect on sojourners' intercultural competence and transformational learning and subsequent decisions made during postgraduate life course. Because there have been relatively few longitudinal studies looking at the process of transformation in service learning and intercultural learning (see Kiely, 2002, as well as Tonkin, 2004, for exceptions), there is very little empirical evidence to support the critical assumption that cognitive transformation leads to subsequent personal and/or social behavioral change and/or action. Although the study of transformational learning processes have increased over the past decade, the learning processes entailed in intercultural learning and study abroad, and the phenomenon of transformation over time need greater attention. Research on both individual and social transformation will assist the ISL field in understanding the long-term and possible harmful effects of intercultural learning programs and experiences over time (Kiely, 2002, 2004, 2005).

Third, this review has implications for ISL research on student learning outcomes. In terms of focusing ISL research on outcomes, the central organizing concepts of intercultural and global competence might provide a useful point of departure. Study abroad studies (Deardorff, 2004, 2006, 2008, 2009; Hunter, 2004) have identified constructs and developed models that advance a long-standing tradition in study abroad to support intercultural competence as the primary learning objective in all study abroad programs. By identifying the individual and social knowledge, skills, attitudes, and behavioral outcomes that make up intercultural and global competence, each of these models provides a fairly cohesive and consistent set of indicators for ISL researchers to measure the impact of ISL on students' intercultural and global competence (Gillespie et al., 2009; Hovland, McTighe Musil, Skilton-Sylester, & Jamison, 2009). Although intercultural competence is a core learning objective in both study abroad and ISL program curricula, research on ISL outcomes tends to cite global citizenship and global consciousness as important transformative outcomes (Annette, 2002; Hartman, 2008; Kiely, 2002, 2004; Kiely & Hartman, 2004; Longo & Saltmarsh, chapter 4; Plater et al., 2009). Future outcome-oriented research in ISL should explore the meaning and value of these constructs to students, faculty, institutions, and community partners in ISL program contexts.

Connected to research on outcomes in study abroad, there are also a few studies that have identified how contextual factors (e.g., program, curricula, language, demographics, host country factors) affect learning outcomes in study abroad (Engle & Engle, 2003; Laubscher, 1994; Medina-Lopez-Portillo, 2004; Paige, Cohen, Kappler, Chi, & Lassegard, 2002; Ward et al., 2001). Although there are studies that have identified how context shapes the quality and type of learning in ISL (Kiely, 2002; Tonkin, 2004), participant observation would contribute significantly to understanding and corroborating more substantially the relationships among the context, outcomes, and the process of learning in ISL (Kiely & Hartman, chapter 13; Whitney & Clayton, chapter 8). For example, diverse programmatic foci (e.g., community service and community-based research) may lead to different types of learning (e.g., the experience of a student studying language and art in Spain may experience intercultural competence and transformational learning very differently than the experience of an ISL student conducting a health clinic in Nicaragua).

Fourth, research on study abroad and intercultural learning places a strong emphasis on bridging research, theory, and practice in order to assist sojourners with adjustment and adaptation. Therefore, this review also highlights the need for ISL educators to connect research with curriculum development in order to more effectively assist students in preparing for and learning from their ISL experience. From a practical standpoint, the ISL field has much to learn from research on programming in study abroad and intercultural learning. There is abundant research and literature on intercultural education that focuses on developing training curricula aimed at controlling and predicting personal and sociocultural adjustment factors that have been empirically documented to assist sojourners with intercultural adaptation (Brislin & Yoshida, 1994; Landis & Bhagat, 1996; Ward et al., 2001). According to Ward et al. (2001), common intercultural training techniques include preorientation information about the host culture, cultural sensitization, simulations, role playing, critical incidents, culture assimilators, and experiential learning (see pp. 256–265). More recent research indicates that preorientation training programs that increase sojourners' knowledge, skills, abilities, and attitudes (KSAAs) prior to departure may have some success assisting sojourners with culture shock and adjustment (Ward et al., 2001). However, factors such as trainer expertise and transfer of learning of sojourners' KSAAs in distinct cultural contexts and programs needs further study, particularly for ISL (Ward et al., 2001). Given the importance of reciprocity, problem solving, research, community development and partnership building with diverse communities in ISL programs, training in ISL will also need to incorporate curricula that go beyond traditional study abroad orientations that tend to limit their focus on enhancing sojourners' KSAAs.

Research in study abroad provides important insights on factors that influence students' intercultural adjustment and on how study abroad influences students' cognitive, affective, and behavioral learning; however, what is missing from most of this research are studies that examine more accurately (and perhaps inductively) what and how contextual factors and learning processes (e.g., cognitive, affective, visceral, somatic, emotional) relate to adjustment, behavior, and performance in study abroad and ISL (Kiely, 2002, 2005; Parker & Dautoff, 2007; Savicki, 2008). These studies suggest that sojourners' intercultural experience can lead to diverse forms of transformation and that there are specific patterns and dimensions of learning that influence sojourner transformation and cross-cultural adaptation. However, there is very little theoretical guidance and empirical documentation of not only how individuals are transformed by study abroad and, also, how study abroad affects social transformation. The linkage between learning context, learning processes, and outcomes as well as the connections between individual and social transformation are missing pieces in study abroad and ISL research. For example, Savicki's (2008) recent work indicates that the field of study abroad has identified the outcome of transformation, in particular, Mezirow's (1991) notion of perspective transformation, as a major learning goal for study abroad along with intercultural competence. However, much of their discussion on how students are transformed through study abroad is without strong empirical documentation. Although that review of current study abroad theory and research did not include much of the empirical work on ISL cited above (see also Taylor, 2000) that links intercultural learning with transformational learning, their incorporation of a chapter (see Hunter, 2008) describing Mezirow's transformational learning theory as well as other chapters that highlight the need to examine other learning processes (i.e., reflective, emotional, and affective learning) influence how students learn in study abroad, provides both study abroad and ISL researchers with new avenues for researching how students learn from intercultural experiences. Kiely's (2002, 2004, 2005) longitudinal research does provide an expanded conceptualization of service learning, intercultural learning, and transformational learning by incorporating and exploring the relationship among context, dissonance (similar to culture shock), critical reflection, other nonreflective forms of knowing (i.e., affect, connection, emotion, spirituality) and the learning link between individual perspective transformation and social action (reentry issues). Empirical study based on an expanded conceptualization of transformational learning above, would also contribute significantly to advancing understanding of the forms and processes of transformational learning and other forms of learning in ISL. Study abroad provides both study abroad and ISL researchers new avenues for researching how students learn from intercultural experiences.

Conclusion

Although this review has highlighted how research and theory in study abroad and intercultural learning might inform and assist ISL researchers, it is important to keep in mind the competing rationales that underpin the design of study abroad and ISL curricula and programs. Against the backdrop of September 11, 2001, and the subsequent intensification of the "war on terror" and emerging political, economic, cultural, and technological dimensions of contemporary globalization at the national level, the primary rationale for promoting international education in the United States and Europe has been to ensure that "borders are secured before doors are opened" to international exchange and partnerships (Johnson & Mulholland, 2006). Even when doors are opened further and support for international education increases, the post-September 11, 2001, rationale for study abroad and ISL is that each nation's citizenry can function and compete more effectively in the global economy (De Wit, 2002; Johnson & Mulholland, 2006). ISL, with a focus on problem solving through community engagement and social responsibility, has emerged as an alternative approach to traditional study abroad programs that continue to support that dominant discourse of intercultural competence as competitive global worker (Plater et al., 2009).

Globalization will continue to have an influence in shaping how study abroad and ISL are understood and practiced (Grunzweig & Rinehart, 1998; McCabe, 2001). Any comparative analysis of the rationale, goals, and outcomes of study abroad and ISL must take into consideration the unequal socioeconomic and political impact of globalization on different regions of the world. The rhetoric of intercultural competence (i.e., language proficiency, tolerance, openness, empathy, intercultural sensitivity) (Deardorff & Hunter, 2006), and more recently, transformation (Savicki, 2008) in study abroad promotes very little dialogue regarding the role of study abroad in fostering socially responsible action to address global injustice and inequality, which is more reflective of the dominant discourse in ISL. Creating a dialogue to bridge, and if possible, reconcile these two discourses, as this chapter attempts to do, is central to an analysis of the relationship between study abroad and ISL and any future research agenda (Kiely, 2002).

Notes

1. One need look no further than the U.S. Department of Homeland Security and new regulatory guidelines for international education as perhaps the most powerful example of the connection between international education exchange and national interests and the enforcement of a more explicit link between them.

2. Consistent with previous work (Kiely, 2002; Kim, 2001; Ward et al., 2001), the term "sojourner" refers to a person who lives temporarily in another country but at some point returns to the country of origin. Sojourners include but are not limited to tourists, businessmen, missionaries, military personnel, exchange students/scholars, and Peace Corps volunteers.

3. Given space limitations, this review is meant to describe important concepts and dimensions rather than provide a substantial account of existing empirical and theoretical studies in these areas. For a more detailed review of study abroad research, the author will highlight useful sources throughout the chapter.

4. As numerous scholars have pointed out (Church, 1982; Savicki, Binder, & Heller, 2008; Ward & Kennedy, 1994; Ward et al., 2001), the concept of adjustment has been used in a variety of ways including accommodation, acculturation, and adaptation (see J. Berry 1990, 2005; Furnham & Bochner, 1986; Kim, 2001; Savicki, Cooley, & Donnelly 2008; Ward et al., 2001; Ward & Kennedy, 1994). I will use the terms adjustment and adaptation interchangeably and consistent with more recent reviews (Kim, 2001; Ward et al., 2001; Savicki, 2008) both terms encompass psychological and sociocultural dimensions of the sojourners' experience.

5. I use reverse culture shock and reentry to describe the process of culture shock upon return from a sojourn to the home country.

6. See also Deardorff (2004, 2006, 2008) for research identifying the elements of intercultural competence as well as a discussion of the Pyramid and Process Models of Intercultural Competence; and Hunter (2004) for greater detail on the Global Competence Model.

References

Adler, P. (1975). The transitional experience: An alternative view of culture shock. *Journal of Humanistic Psychology, 15*(4), 13–23.

Adler, P. (1977). Beyond cultural identity: Reflections on cultural and multicultural man. In R. W. Brislin (Ed.), *Culture learning: Concepts, application and research* (pp. 24–41). Honolulu, HI: University of Hawaii Press.

Adler, P. (1987). Culture shock and the cross-cultural learning experience. In L. Luce & E. Smith (Eds.), *Readings in cross-cultural communication: Toward internationalism* (pp. 24–35). Cambridge, MA: Newbury House.

Anderson, L. E. (1994). A new look at an old construct: Cross-cultural adaptation. *International Journal of Intercultural Relations, 18*(3), 293–328.

Annette, J. (2002). Service learning in an international context. *Frontiers: The Interdisciplinary Journal of Study Abroad, 8*(1), 83–94.

Austin, C. (1983). *Cross-cultural reentry: An annotated bibliography.* Abilene, TX: ACU Press.

Austin, C. (1986). *Cross-cultural reentry: A book of readings.* Abilene, TX: ACU Press.

Bennett, J. (1993). Cultural marginality: Identity issues in intercultural training. In R. M. Paige (Ed.), *Education for the intercultural experience* (pp. 109–136). Yarmouth, ME: Intercultural Press.

Bennett, J. (2008). On becoming a global soul: A path to engagement during study abroad. In V. Savicki (Ed.), *Developing intercultural competence and transformation: Theory, research, and application in international education* (pp. 13–31). Sterling, VA: Stylus.

Bennett, M. (1986). Modes of cross-cultural training: Conceptualizing cross-cultural training as education. *International Journal of Intercultural Relations, 10,* 179–196.

Bennett, M. (1993). Towards ethnorelativism: A developmental model of intercultural sensitivity. In R.M. Paige (Ed.), *Education for the intercultural experience.* Yarmouth, ME: Intercultural Press.

Bennett, M., & Bennett, J. (2001). *The Intercultural Development Inventory (IDI) manual.* Portland, OR: Intercultural Communication Institute.

Bennett, J., & Bennett, M. (2004). Developing intercultural sensitivity: An integrative approach to global and domestic diversity. In D. Landis, J. M. Bennett, & M. J. Bennett (Eds.), *Handbook of intercultural training* (3rd ed., pp. 147–165). Thousand Oaks, CA: Sage.

Berry, H. A. (1990). Service learning in international and intercultural settings. In J. C. Kendall, & Associates (Eds.), *Combining service and learning: A resource book for community and public service, 1* (pp. 311–313). Raleigh, NC: National Society for Internships and Experiential Education.

Berry, J. W. (1990). Psychology of acculturation: Understanding individuals moving between cultures. In R. W. Brislin (Ed.), *Applied cross-cultural psychology* (pp. 232–253). Newbury Park, CA: Sage.

Berry, J. W. (2005). Acculturation. In W. Firedlmeier, P. Chakkarath, & B. Schwarz (Eds.), *Culture and human development* (pp. 291–302). New York: Psychology Press.

Berry, H. A., & Chisholm, L. A. (1999). *Service-learning in higher education around the world: An initial look.* New York, NY: The International Partnership for Service-Learning.

Bringle, R. G., & Tonkin, H. (2004). International service learning: A research agenda. In H. Tonkin (Ed.), *Service-learning across cultures: Promise and achievement* (pp. 365–374). New York, NY: International Partnership for Service-Learning and Leadership.

Brislin, R., & Yoshida, T. (1994). *Intercultural communication training*. Thousand Oaks, CA: Sage.

Campus Compact. (2007). *2006 Service statistics: Highlights and trends of Campus Compact's annual membership survey*. Providence, RI: Campus Compact.

Center for Global Education. (1998–2002). *Study Abroad Research On-Line*. Retrieved August 25, 2009, from http://www.globaled.us/ro/index.html

Church, A. (1982). Sojourner adjustment. *Psychological Bulletin, 91,* 540–572.

Commission on the Abraham Lincoln Study Abroad Fellowship Program. (2005). *Global competence and national needs. One million Americans studying abroad*. Retrieved August 30th, 2009, from http://www.nafsa.org/resourcelibrary/Default .aspx?id=16035

Cornwell, G., & Stoddard, E. (1999). *Globalizing knowledge: Connecting international and intercultural studies*. Washington, DC: Association of American Colleges & Universities.

Crabtree, R. D. (1998, May). Mutual empowerment in cross-cultural participatory development and service learning: Lessons in communication and social justice from projects in El Salvador and Nicaragua. *Journal of Applied Communication Research, 26,* 182–209.

Crabtree, R. D. (2008).Theoretical foundations for international service learning. *Michigan Journal of Community Service Learning, 15*(1), 18–36.

Deardorff, D. (2004). Internationalization: In search of intercultural competence. *International Educator, 13*(2), 13–15.

Deardorff, D. (2006). Identification and assessment of intercultural competence as a student outcome of internationalization. *Journal of Studies in International Education, 10*(3) 241–266.

Deardorff, D. (2008). Intercultural competence: A definition, model, and implications for study abroad. In V. Savicki (Ed.), *Developing intercultural competence and transformation: Theory, research, and application in international education* (pp. 297–321). Sterling, VA: Stylus.

Deardorff, D. K. (2009). Understanding the challenges of assessing global citizenship. In R. Lewin (Ed.), *The handbook of practice and research in study abroad: Higher education and the quest for global citizenship* (pp. 61–77). New York: Routledge.

Deardorff, D., & Hunter, W. (2006). Educating global-ready graduates. *International Educator, 15*(3), 72–83.

De Wit, H. (2002). *Internationalization of higher education in the United States of America and Europe: A historical, comparative, and conceptual analysis*. Westport, CT: Greenwood Press.

Deutsch, K. W. (1953). *Nationalism and social communication: An inquiry into the foundations of nationality*. New York, NY: John Wiley & Sons.

Deutsch, K. W. (1968). *The analysis of international relations*. Englewood Cliffs, NJ: Prentice Hall.

Dinges, N., & Baldwin, K. (1996). Intercultural competence. In D. Landis & R. Bhagat (Eds.), *Handbook of intercultural training* (pp. 106–123). Thousand Oaks, CA: Sage.

Engle, L., & Engle, J. (2003, Fall). Study abroad levels: Toward a classification of program types. *Frontiers: International Journal of Study Abroad*, *9*, 1–20.

Falk, R., & Kanach, N. (2000). Globalization and study abroad: An illusion of paradox. *Frontiers: The Interdisciplinary Journal of Study Abroad*, *4*, 155–168.

Furnham, A., & Bochner, B. (1986). *Culture shock: Psychological reactions to unfamiliar environments.* London, UK: Methuen.

Gaw, K. F. (2000). Reverse culture shock in students returning from overseas. *International Journal of Intercultural Relations*, *24*(1), 83–104.

Gillespie, J., Braskamp, L., & Dwyer, M. (2009). Holistic student learning and development abroad: The IES 3-D Program Model. In R. Lewin (Ed.), *The handbook of practice and research in study abroad: Higher education and the quest for global citizenship* (pp. 445–465). New York: Routledge.

Goodwin, C., & Nacht, M. (1991). *Missing the boat: The failure to internationalize American higher education.* New York, NY: Cambridge University Press.

Grunzweig, W., & Rinehart, N. (1998). International understanding and global interdependence. *International Educator*, *7*(4), 41–48.

Grusky, S. (2000). International service learning. *The American Behavioral Scientist*, *43*(5), 858–867.

Gullahorn, J., & Gullahorn, J. (1963). An extension of the U-curve hypothesis. *Journal of Social Issues*, *14*, 33–47.

Haas, E. B. (1958). *The uniting of Europe: Political, social and economic forces.* Stanford, CA: Stanford University Press.

Haas, E. B. (1961). International integration: The European and the universal process. *International Organization*, *15*, 366–392.

Haas, E. B. (1964). *Beyond the nation state.* Stanford, CA: Stanford University Press.

Harper, L. A. (1994). *Seeing things from different corners; A story of learning and culture* (Unpublished Master's Thesis, University of British Columbia, 1994).

Hartman, E. M. (2008). Educating for global citizenship through service-learning: A theoretical account and curricular evaluation (Doctoral dissertation, University of Pittsburgh, 2008) *Dissertations & Theses: A&I* (Publication No. AAT 3349185).

Hoff, J. (2008). Growth and transformation outcomes in international education. In V. Savicki (Ed.), *Developing intercultural competence and transformation: Theory, research, and application in international education* (pp. 53–73). Sterling, VA: Stylus.

Holt, M. (1994). *Retesting a learning theory to test intercultural competency.* Paper presented at the European International Business Association, Warsaw, Poland.

Hovland, K., McTighe Musil, C., Skilton-Sylvester, E., & Jamison, A. (2009). It takes a curriculum: Bringing global mindedness home. In R. Lewin (Ed.), *The handbook of practice and research in study abroad: Higher education and the quest for global citizenship* (pp. 466–484). New York: Routledge.

Hunter, W. (2004). Knowledge, skills, attitudes and experiences necessary to become globally competent (Unpublished doctoral dissertation, Lehigh University, 2004).

Hunter, W. (2008, October). *Knowledge, skills, attitudes, and experiences necessary to become globally competent*. Paper presented at the Pennsylvania Council for International Education, State College, PA.

Institute of International Education. (2008). *Open doors: Report on international student exchange*. New York, NY: Institute of International Education.

Jacobson, W. (1996). Learning, culture, and learning culture. *Adult Education Quarterly, 47*(1), 15–28.

Johnson, V. C., & Mulholland, J. (2006, May–June). Open doors, secure boarders: Advantage of education abroad for public policy. *International Educator*, 4–7.

Kennedy, J. (1994). *The individual's transformational learning experience as a cross-cultural sojourner: Descriptive models* (Unpublished doctoral dissertation, The Fielding Institute).

Kiely, A., & Kiely, R. (2005). Study abroad with a conscience. *Abroad View: The Global Education Magazine for Students, 8*(1), 40.

Kiely, R. (2002). Toward an expanded conceptualization of transformational learning: A case study of international service-learning in Nicaragua (Doctoral dissertation, Cornell University, 2002). *Dissertation Abstracts International, 63*(09A), 3083.

Kiely, R. (2004). A chameleon with a complex: Searching for transformation in international service-learning, *Michigan Journal of Community Service Learning, 10*(2), 5–20.

Kiely, R. (2005). A transformative learning model for service-learning: A longitudinal case study. *Michigan Journal of Community Service Learning, 12*(1), 5–22.

Kiely, R., & Hartman, E. (2004, October). Developing a framework for assessing learning for global citizenship: A comparative case study analysis of three international service-learning programs. *Proceedings of the 4th Annual International Service-learning Research Conference*. Greenville, SC: Clemson University.

Kiely, R., & Nielson, D. (2002, Fall). International service learning: The importance of partnerships. *Community College Journal*, 39–41.

Kim, Y. Y. (2001). *Becoming intercultural: An integrative theory of communication and cross-cultural adaptation*. Thousand Oaks, CA: Sage.

Kim, Y. Y. (2005). Adapting to a new culture: An integrative communication theory. In W. B. Gudykunst (Ed.), *Theorizing about intercultural communication* (pp. 375–400). Thousand Oaks, CA: Sage.

Kraft, R. J. (2002). International service learning, University of Colorado, Boulder. In M. E. Kenny, K. Kiley-Brabeck, & R. M. Lerner (Eds.), *Learning to serve: Promoting civil society through service learning* (pp. 297–314). Norwells, MA: Kluwer Academic Publishers.

Kraft, R. J., & Dwyer, J. F. (2000). Service and outreach: A multicultural and international dimension. *Journal of Higher Education Outreach and Engagement, 6*(1), 41–47.

Lambert, R. D. (1994). Parsing the concept of global competence. In R. D. Lambert (Ed.) *Educational exchange and global competence* (pp. 11–24). New York, NY: Council on International Educational Exchange.

Landis, D., & Bhagat, R. (Eds.). (1996). *Handbook of intercultural training.* Thousand Oaks, CA: Sage.

Laubscher, M. R. (1994). *Encounters with difference: Student perceptions of the role of out-of-class experiences in education abroad.* Westport, CT: Greenwood.

Lee, L. (1997, February). *Civic literacy, service learning, and community renewal.* Retrieved July 14, 2009, from http://www.eric.ed.gov/ERICDocs/data/ericdocs2sql/content_storage_01/0000019b/80/16/6b/32.pdf

Lewin, R. (Ed.). (2009). *The handbook of practice and research in study abroad: Higher education and the quest for global citizenship.* New York: Routledge.

Lou, K., & Bosley, G. (2008). Dynamics of cultural contexts: Meta-level intervention in the study abroad experience. In V. Savicki (Ed.), *Developing intercultural competence and transformation: Theory, research, and application in international education* (pp. 276–296). Sterling, VA: Stylus.

Lustig, M., & Koester, J. (2003). Intercultural competence: Interpersonal communication across cultures. Boston, MA: Allyn & Bacon.

Lyon, C. R. (2001). *Cultural mentors: Exploring the role of relationships in the adaptation and transformation of women educators who go overseas to work.* Chicago, IL: National-Louis University (DAI, 61, no 12A, 2001).

Lyon, C. R. (2002). Trigger event meets culture shock: Linking the literature of transformatonal learning theory and cross-cultural adaptation. *In Proceedings of the 43rd Annual Adult Education Research Conference* (237–242). Raleigh, NC: North Carolina University.

Lysgaard, S. (1955). Adjustment in a foreign society: Norwegian Fulbright grantees visiting the United States. *International Social Science Bulletin, 7,* 45–51.

Martin, J. N. (1984). Communication in the intercultural reentry: Student sojourners' perceptions of change in reentry relationships. *International Journal of Intercultural Relations, 8,* 115–134.

Martin, J. N. (1986). Communication in the intercultural reentry: Student sojourners' perspectives of change in reentry relationships. *International Journal of Intercultural Relations, 10,* 1–22.

Martin, J. N. (1993). The intercultural reentry of student sojourners: Recent contributions to theory, research and training. In R.M. Paige (Ed.), *Education for the intercultural experience* (301–328). Yarmouth, ME: Intercultural Press.

Matsumoto, D., LeRoux, J. A., Ratzlaff, C., Tatani, H., Uchida, H., Kim C., et al. (2001). Development and validation of a measure of intercultural adjustment potential in Japanese sojourners: The Intercultural Adjustment Potential Scale (ICAPS). *International Journal of Intercultural Relations, 25,* 483–510.

McCabe, L. (2001). Globalization and internationalization: The impact on education abroad programs. *Journal of Studies in International Education, 5*(2), 138–145.

Medina-Lopez-Portillo, A. (2004). Intercultural learning assessment: The link between program duration and the development of intercultural sensitivity. *Frontiers: The Interdisciplinary Journal of Study Abroad, 10,* 179–199.

Mestenhauser, J. (2003). Building bridges. *International Educator, 12*(3), 6–11.

Mezirow, J. (1978). Perspective transformation. *Adult Education, 28,* 100–110.

Mezirow, J. (1991). *Transformative dimensions of adult learning.* San Francisco: Jossey-Bass.

Mezirow, J., & Associates. (1990). *Fostering critical reflection in adulthood: A guide to transformational learning.* San Francisco: Jossey-Bass.

Mezirow, J., & Associates (2000). *Learning as transformation: Critical perspectives on a theory in progress.* San Francisco: Jossey-Bass.

Mitrany, D. (1948, July). The functional approach to world organization. *International Affairs, 24*(3), 350–363.

Mitrany, D. (1966). *A working peace system.* Chicago, IL: Quadrangle.

Mitrany, D. (1975). *The functional theory of politics.* New York: St. Martin's Press.

Oberg, K. (1960). Culture shock: Adjustment to new cultural environments. *Practical Anthropology, 7,* 177–182.

Olsen, C., & Kroeger, K. (2001). Global competency and intercultural sensitivity. *Journal of Studies in International Education, 5*(2), 116–137.

Paige, M. (1993). On the nature of intercultural experiences and intercultural education. In M. Paige (Ed.), *Education for the intercultural experience* (pp. 1–20). Yarmouth, ME: Intercultural Press.

Paige, R. M., Cohen, A. D., Kappler, B., Chi, J. C., & Lassegard, J. P. (2002). *Maximizing study abroad: A student's guide to strategies for language and culture learning and use.* Minneapolis, MN: University of Minnesota, Center for Advanced Research on Language Acquisition.

Parker, B., & Dautoff, D. A. (2007). Service-learning and study abroad: Synergistic learning opportunities. *Michigan Journal of Community Service Learning, 13*(2), 40–53.

Plater, W. M., Jones, S. G., Bringle, R. G., & Clayton, P. H. (2009). Educating globally competent citizens through international service learning. In R. Lewin (Ed.), *The handbook of practice and research in study abroad: Higher education and the quest for global citizenship* (pp. 485–505). New York: Routledge.

Porter, M., & Monard, K. (2001). *Ayni* in the global village: Building relationships of reciprocity through international service-learning. *Michigan Journal of Community Service Learning, 8*(1), 5–17.

Pusch, M. (2004). A cross-cultural perspective. In H. Tonkin (Ed.), *Service-learning across cultures: Promise and achievement* (pp. 103–129). New York, NY: International Partnership for Service-Learning and Leadership.

Pusch, M., & Merrill, M. (2008). Reflection, reciprocity, responsibility, and committed relativism: Intercultural development through international service-learning. In V. Savicki (Ed.), *Developing intercultural competence and transformation:*

Theory, research, and application in international education (pp. 297–321). Sterling, VA: Stylus.

Raschio, R. A. (1987, March). College student's perceptions of reverse culture shock and reentry adjustments. *Journal of College Student Personnel*, *28*(2), 156–162.

Savicki, V. (2008). (Ed.). *Developing intercultural competence and transformation: Theory, research, and application in international education.* Sterling, VA: Stylus.

Savicki, V., Adams, I., & Binder, F. (2008). Intercultural development: Topics and sequences. In V. Savicki (Ed.), *Developing intercultural competence and transformation: Theory, research, and application in international education* (pp. 154–172). Sterling, VA: Stylus.

Savicki, V., Binder, F., & Heller, L. (2008). Contrasts and changes in potential and actual psychological intercultural adjustment. In V. Savicki (Ed.), *Developing intercultural competence and transformation: Theory, research, and application in international education* (pp. 111–127). Sterling, VA: Stylus.

Savicki, V., Cooley, E., & Donnelly, R. (2008). Acculturative stress, appraisal, coping, and intercultural adjustment. In V. Savicki (Ed.), *Developing intercultural competence and transformation: Theory, research, and application in international education* (pp. 173–192). Sterling, VA: Stylus.

Savicki, V., & Selby, R. (2008). Synthesis & conclusions. In V. Savicki (Ed.), *Developing intercultural competence and transformation: Theory, research, and application in international education* (pp. 342–352). Sterling, VA: Stylus.

Schattle, H. (2009). Global citizenship in theory and practice. In R. Lewin (Ed.), *The handbook of practice and research in study abroad: Higher education and the quest for global citizenship* (pp. 3–20). New York: Routledge.

Shames, G. (1997) *Transcultural odysseys: The evolving global consciousness.* Yarmouth, ME: Intercultural Press.

Sparrow, L. M. (2000). Beyond multicultural man: Complexities of identity. *International Journal of Intercultural Relations*, *24*(2), 173–201.

Taylor, E. (1993). *A learning model of becoming interculturally competent: A transformative process* (Unpublished doctoral dissertation, University of Georgia, 1993).

Taylor, E. W. (1994a). Intercultural competency: A transformative learning process. *Adult Education Quarterly*, *44*(3), 154–174.

Taylor, E. W. (1994b). A learning model for becoming interculturally competent. *International Journal of Intercultural Relations*, *18*(3), 389–408.

Taylor, E. W. (2000). Analyzing research on transformative learning theory. In J. Mezirow & Associates (Eds.), *Learning as transformation* (pp. 285–328). San Francisco, CA: Jossey-Bass.

Taylor, E. W. (2007). An update of transformative learning theory: A critical review of the empirical research (1999–2005). *International Journal of Lifelong Education*, *26*(2), 173–191.

Temple, W. (1999). *Perspective transformation among mainland Chinese intellectuals reporting Christian conversion while in the United States* (Unpublished doctoral dissertation, Trinity Evangelical Divinity School, Deerfield, IL, 1999).

Tonkin, H. (Ed.). (2004). *Service-learning across cultures: Promise and achievement. A report to the Ford Foundation.* New York: International Partnership for Service-Learning and Leadership.

Uehara, A. (1986). The nature of American student re-entry adjustment and the perceptions of the sojourn experience. *International Journal of Intercultural Relations, 10,* 415–438.

Vande Berg, M. (2001, Spring). SECUSSA/IIE electronic sampling results: Survey #2: The assessment of learning outcomes in study abroad. *International Educator, 10*(2), 31. Retrieved July 8, 2009, from http://www.secussa.nafsa.org/samplingresults2.html

Ward, C., Bochner, S., & Furnam, A. (2001). *The psychology of culture shock.* Philadelphia, PA: Routledge.

Ward, C., & Kennedy, A. (1994). Acculturation strategies, psychological adjustment, and sociocultural competence during cross-cultural transitions. *International Journal of Intercultural Relations, 18*(3), 329–343.

Whalley, T. R. (1995). *Toward a theory of culture learning: A study based on journals written by Japanese and Canadian young adults in exchange programs* (Unpublished doctoral dissertation, Simon Fraser University, 1995).

Woolf, M. (2004). International education and the question of quality. *International Educator, 13*(2), 26–32.

12

QUANTITATIVE APPROACHES TO RESEARCH ON INTERNATIONAL SERVICE LEARNING

Design, Measurement, and Theory

Robert G. Bringle, Julie A. Hatcher, and Matthew J. Williams

I nternational service learning (ISL) is a complex endeavor. Engaging
college students in service experiences as an integrated aspect of study
abroad and international education is challenging. As other chapters in
this volume attest, such an educational strategy requires deliberate design of
the pedagogical strategies for specific educational outcomes, strong collaboration between faculty and international partners, adequate preparation for
students, a respect for cultural context and difference, and an understanding
of a wide range of ethical issues related to service and community-based research in another country. Each of these factors contributes to a great deal
of variety in terms of ISL course design (Jones & Steinberg, chapter 5). This
complexity and variety brings challenges to the research process; however, the
study of and research on ISL warrants the same conscientious rigor as all areas
of scholarship of teaching and learning.

By what set of aspirations can rigor guide the development of the empirical analysis of ISL and by what standards can rigor be evaluated? There
is extensive discussion of rigor that ranges from epistemology and paradigms
to operationalizations and statistics. Disciplinary paradigms shape the types
of questions asked and the methods that are appropriate to employ. We posit
that a quantitative approach to research on ISL will yield fruitful results

that can guide program design, improve practice, test theory, contribute to a knowledge base, and provide a basis for funding and support for program expansion, both at the campus level and among foundations and government agencies. Quantitative research has the capacity to influence decision makers, and yet the rigor of the research is dependent upon the research design, the measurement strategy, and the degree to which the findings are generalizable and contribute to theoretical understanding of why particular outcomes are obtained for students who participate in ISL.

The current dominant form of research on ISL is qualitative in nature (Kiely & Hartman, chapter 13; Jones & Steinberg, chapter 5), with most analyses being descriptive case studies of particular courses and programs. Like much of past research on service learning (Eyler, chapter 10), these analyses represent little more than program evaluations of outcomes from ISL courses or programs, rarely beyond being descriptive in nature. In contrast, the quantitative approach that we summarize for ISL differs from program evaluation in the ways that Patton describes:

> Research, especially fundamental or basic research, differs from evaluation in that its primary purpose is to generate or test theory and contribute to knowledge for the sake of knowledge. Such knowledge, and the theories that undergird knowledge, may subsequently inform action and evaluation, but action is not the primary purpose of fundamental research. (Patton, 2002, pp. 10–11)

Unfortunately, advocating for a quantitative approach to studying ISL is too frequently stigmatized as being aligned with a positivistic approach, which emphasizes the scientific method as the primary way to gather knowledge of the world. The positivistic approach is often discredited because it is viewed as detached, deterministic, and rigid. We will present a view of quantitative research methods that is consistent with a post-positivistic perspective that views knowledge as a description that is probabilistic, entailing error, and resulting in tentative but verifiable assertions based on empirical information (Trochim & Donnelly, 2007). In doing so, we will present a discussion of the role of three interrelated, but distinct areas that contribute to a rigorous quantitative approach to the study of ISL: (a) research design, (b) measurement, and (c) theory.

Research Design

Good research needs to go beyond mere description of the outcomes that are evident at the end of an ISL experience. As important as these descriptions are, they tell us little about why these outcomes occurred and how to ensure that the design of subsequent ISL experiences result in similar outcomes in the future. As Gueron (2000) points out,

> Any evaluation must differentiate between the test program's *outcomes* (for example, the number of people who get a job or graduate from school) and its *net impact* (the number who get a job or graduate who would not have done so without the program). The measure of net impact is the difference between what would have occurred anyway and what actually happened because of the program. (p. 3)

Designing research using quantitative designs can contribute to understanding both why particular outcomes occurred and the net impact of the program intervention.

One research design that adds information to mere description is to use a design that compares one group to another. Comparisons can be made between any number of factors that shape the ISL experience (e.g., length of time in the foreign country, amount of service, type of service experience, frequency of structured reflection activities, type of community organization, role of faculty member before and after the ISL experience, level of involvement of staff in terms of planning and supervision; see Eyler, chapter 10; Tonkin, chapter 9). For example, to understand student learning outcomes, one could compare the outcomes for students who participated in ISL to those who (a) participated in a more traditional study abroad program, (b) stayed on campus and studied international issues, (c) did international volunteer work, or (d) worked with immigrant groups in a domestic location. Preexisting differences in the students (e.g., language proficiency, degree of prior travel, volunteer participation, prior enrollment in service learning courses) would need to be measured and, using statistical methods to control for preexisting differences (e.g., analysis of covariance, multiple regression), inference can be made about the differences among groups due to the variables in program design. The fewer the differences that exist between the experiences being compared, the more confidence there will be in identifying key elements that contributed to different outcomes. For example, if traditional study abroad for a semester in a country during which students have a set curriculum can be compared to an equivalent experience with service added to one or more of the courses, then more confident inferences can be made about the reasons for the differences. As Jones and Steinberg (chapter 5) note, very few past studies on ISL have any type of comparison group against which to compare the ISL experience.

A superior way to gain information about what is producing the *net impact* for a particular group is to ensure that the groups are equivalent prior to the intervention(s). In addition to statistically controlling for preexisting differences, some of the strategies that can be used to help ensure equivalence include: (a) random assignment of participants to different types of interventions; (b) blind selection of participants to programs (e.g., Markus, Howard, & King, 1993; Osborne, Hammerich, & Hensley, 1998); (c) when there are more students than capacity, random assignment of students to enrollment into the ISL program at Time 1, with the remaining students delayed in enrollment in the program until Time 2 being the comparison group; or (d) using the same group for comparison (e.g., pre-, posttest) across time. Random assignment to a treatment and a control/comparison condition is the most powerful way to arrange data collection so that causal inferences can be made about the phenomenon under study (i.e., ISL) and what causes the differences that occur. Unfortunately, it may not be practical to assign students randomly to, for example, ISL versus study abroad programs for a true experimental research design. However, it may be possible to assign ISL students to different types of program characteristics (e.g., hours of service, types of reflection, types of service experiences). For example, in the same ISL program, students could be randomly assigned to community service activities that either (a) involve direct contact with residents or (b) work with organizational staff and do not have direct contact with residents. Randomly assigning students to current participation and delayed participation may also be possible when an ISL program has limited capacity and some students are put on a wait list. Although the design of the research (e.g., random assignment versus nonexperimental designs) is the main determinant of the researcher's capacity to make causal inferences, some statistical approaches can help when random assignment is not possible. However, the use of those statistical procedures (e.g., analysis of covariance, multiple regression) does not ensure equivalence on unmeasured differences and, too often, the nature of the statistical analysis to control for self-selection clouds shortcomings in the design. Statistical analyses that control for preexisting differences are also dependent on a sufficient sample size, which is traditionally small in studies of ISL (Jones & Steinberg, chapter 5). The rigor of the design is the most important factor to consider when evaluating the quality of the information that is used to make recommendations about ISL practice and these design attributes are largely absent from past research on study abroad (Deardorff, 2009), service learning (Bringle & Steinberg, in press; Eyler, chapter 10), and ISL (Jones & Steinberg, chapter 5).

Hierarchical multiple regression is one example of how statistics can improve an experimental design. In part, these methods can control for preexisting differences, group variables into meaningful categories (i.e., latent variables), evaluate measurement error (see next section), analyze nested models (e.g., programs within countries; courses within programs), evaluate the relative importance of program attributes, and evaluate longitudinal effects for their causal importance. The use of these methods, however, requires appropriately large numbers of students, which is typically not the case for ISL programs. This suggests the value of structuring ISL research across programs and campuses and designing multicampus ISL research studies that can increase the number of students, faculty, community organizations, and locations, thus lending strength to any of the statistical approaches used when comparing programs (but also increasing heterogeneity within groupings).

Measurement Issues

Design and measurement are often confounded in discussions of quantitative research. The above discussion about experimental design assumes good measurement; however, the best measurement does not ensure the capacity to make good assertions about what the *net impact* is of ISL. Those assertions are dependent on the quality of the design. Similarly, the best design is of questionable value if the outcomes are measured in a manner that lack integrity (i.e., inconsistent, not meaningful).

Detailing the nature of the intervention (i.e., the independent variable) is not often viewed as a measurement issue, but it is a critical one to understanding the net impact of ISL. As Gueron (2000) notes,

> This "Compared to what?" issue may sound simple, but we have found it to be the most profound. The tendency in program evaluations is to focus on the treatment being assessed: make sure it is well implemented so that it gets a fair test. While this is critical, our experience suggests that it is as important to define the treatment for the control group, because it is the difference in experience that you are assessing. (p. 5)

Clarity about the nature of ISL (e.g., a clear definition; fidelity between the definition and program implementation), conceptualizing its component parts and how it differs from the comparison experience (e.g., study abroad, domestic study of international issues) warrants careful attention as a measurement issue (Eyler, chapter 10; Jones & Steinberg, chapter 5; Kiely, chapter 11; Tonkin, chapter 9; Bringle & Tonkin, 2004). Shumer (2000) contends that the educational experiences of students (service learning or otherwise) are idiosyncratic and varied to the extent that quantification is not possible. We disagree and believe that both ISL program attributes (e.g., learning objectives, how program activities are structured, nature of the service activity, structured reflection activities, role of faculty, role of community site supervisor) and student experiences (e.g., use of foreign language, degree of contact with host country's populations, time involved at community site, types of reflection activities, interaction with faculty and peers) can be described and measured in ways that are appropriate to the research question that is being studied and permit summaries of these qualities in a systematic way. Bringle and Tonkin (2004) identified the following design variables that could be considered when describing differences in existing ISL courses or designing research to evaluate the relative importance of different courses elements:

- the relationship between agency and classroom and the role of reflection in this relationship,
- the nature of the agency work and students' engagement in it, particularly the distinction between process-based (e.g., research, advocacy) and project-based (e.g., health clinic, tutoring) experiences,
- the degree of embeddedness (in some ISL programs students may work with their peers, whereas in others they may work exclusively or almost exclusively with in-country coworkers and separately from their peers),
- the intensity of the service (e.g., the number of hours per week, the degree of responsibility put on the student),
- the duration of the service (e.g., short-term versus semester-long or year-long experiences),
- the nature of the population served,
- the setting (e.g., urban environment, rural environment, industrialized country, developing country).

Tonkin provides an elaboration of this list as he develops a research agenda for ISL (chapter 9).

Measurement is also relevant to the assessment of ISL outcomes. Quantitative approaches to measurement focus on the consistency (i.e., reliability) and meaningfulness (i.e., validity) as attributes that can be assessed (Bringle & Hatcher, 2000; Bringle, Phillips, & Hudson, 2004). In general, measurement procedures that incorporate multiple indicators can strengthen both of these attributes of good measurement. This is the case whether one is assessing behavioral indices (e.g., cultural sensitivity, interest in foreign policy, career decisions), written communications (e.g., journal entries, formal papers), testimony by others (e.g., from community partners, from other students), or self-reported beliefs, attitudes, and values (e.g., scales, inventories; see Bringle et al., 2004). Aggregation can occur across occasions in the same situation (e.g., multiple observations of students in the same service site), across situations (e.g., observing students' intercultural communication skills in homestays, at the service sites, on field trips), across modalities (e.g., cross-cultural sensitivity in verbal expression, in written expression, in nonverbal expression), and across domains of a construct (e.g., global civic activities in the political domain, social domain, interpersonal domain). In all cases, aggregation can improve the quality of the measure, presuming that the individual components that are being aggregated are coherent. For this reason, we recommend that ISL researchers consider collecting multiple samples and forms of evidence from students (e.g., log of activities completed at the service site, multiple items for each construct on a self-report satisfaction survey, final self-reflective narrative, focus group, evaluations from site supervisors, log of activities upon return to campus). These multiple measures can be aggregated as appropriate to create a composite indicator of an outcome. Gillespie, Braskamp, and Dwyer (2009) provide a systematic way for conceptualizing outcomes and collecting direct and indirect evidence about intrapersonal, interpersonal, and cognitive aspects of international educational experiences (see also Braskamp, Braskamp, & Merrill, 2008).

Self-Report Scales in ISL Research

Self-report scales are a good example of a measurement procedure that uses multiple indicators (i.e., items). Appropriate scales can be a practical and meaningful way of collecting evidence in ISL research. There are very few published articles of ISL courses or programs using quantitative research methods, including self-report scales (Jones & Steinberg, chapter 5; Kiely, chapter 11). Most research articles on ISL to date focus exclusively on qualitative research methods (e.g., case studies, interviews, reflection activities), and too frequently they do so without systematically comparing the effectiveness of one ISL program versus another. In order to provide a starting point for quantitative research on ISL, there are self-report scales from other areas of educational research that may be potentially used by ISL researchers as measures of moderator variables, mediating variables, and outcome variables (see Bringle et al., 2004).

Some scales that have been used in study abroad research may be useful to ISL researchers. For example, Matsumoto et al. (2001) used an Intercultural Adjustment Potential Scale to explore students' intercultural adjustment (Matsumoto, LeRoux, Ratzlaff, Tatani, Uchida, Kim, & Araki, 2001; Savicki, Binder, & Heller, 2008). Scales have also been developed to measure professional intercultural competencies in the health sciences (Transcultural C.A.R.E. Associates, 2009), as well as multicultural competencies (Sodowsky, Taffe, Gutkin, & Wise, 1994) and intercultural competencies for counseling (Pedersen, Draguns, Lonner, & Trimble, 2007). Braskamp et al. (2008) developed the Global Perspective Inventory that is a self-report measure of cognitive, intrapersonal, and interpersonal development domains. Each domain has two scales that are based on (a) cultural development, and (b) intercultural communication theory.

Hartman and Heinisch (2003) used multivariate regression analyses to compare civic values of two groups of students, those involved in ISL through the Amizade program, and those enrolled in a traditional English course. Several self-report scales were combined to create a 39-item civic values index, and that included items from the Civic Values Scale (Myers-Lipton, 1998), the Community Service Self-Efficacy Scale (CSSES; Reeb, Katsuyama, Sammon, & Yoder, 1998), and the Social Responsibility Inventory (SRI; Markus et al., 1993). The original measures' scoring systems were altered to adhere to a five-point response scale (A = *Strongly Agree*, B = *Agree*, C = *Neutral*, D = *Disagree*, E = *Strongly Disagree*). The scoring system for the response scale was coded so that A = 4, B = 3, C = 2, D = 1, and E = 0; responses were summed across the three scales to create an index. Internal consistency was not reported for the composite *Index of Civic Values*. The index score, along with a score that represented previous service involvement and a score that represented current socioeconomic status, were summed together to produce a Global Civic Values score. The results from this study indicate "that there were few statistically significant shifts in students' attitudes before and after global service learning participation, and that where there were shifts they were actually negative" (Hartman, 2008, p. 141). According to Hartman and Heinisch (2003),

> students who were exposed to ISL had slight decreases in their sense of global civic virtue over the time period in question, which ranged from a minimum of four weeks for a summer ISL course to a maximum of slightly over one semester for an ISL course that merged a spring semester course with a summer independent study. (pp. 28–29)

We believe that future quantitative scales for ISL research should be developed and incorporate items such as those found in the *Index of Civic Values* (Hartman & Heinisch, 2003), while still maintaining "characteristics of good standardized scales" (e.g., providing reliability and validity evidence; see Bringle et al., 2004, pp. 17–22).

Theory

Conceptual frameworks or theories provide important scholarly context to both the research question that is being investigated through a research project, whether quantitative or qualitative methods are used, and to the measurements that comprise the evaluation of the research question. Theory is a critical element in conducting good quantitative (and qualitative, see Kiely, chapter 11; Kiely & Hartman, chapter 13) research on ISL, and it is as necessary to the enterprise for contributing to a body of knowledge as are good research design and good measurement, a point emphasized by Eyler (chapter 10). Two examples from psychology will illustrate the role that theory can play to enhancing the meaningfulness of data collected.

Case I

What sense might it make to raise infant monkeys in isolation with two dummy mothers to study maternal bonding? On the one hand, nothing could be more artificial and further from natural conditions than studying infant monkeys under such conditions in the laboratory. These are circumstances that monkeys never face in natural environments. On the other hand, there are certain types of questions that may be best analyzed under what appear to be contrived but controlled conditions. The value of this approach is linked to the theoretical question that Harlow (1958) investigated because of the debate, at that time, concerning the basis for the maternal bond. A common assumption was that maternal bonding (i.e., love) was best explained as a result of the mother being associated with need satisfaction (e.g., reduced hunger and thirst). Harlow thought that a different mechanism was the basis of maternal attachment. Harlow's experiment presented infant monkeys with artificial mother surrogates that were wrapped in terry cloth or sandpaper and he varied the site of the nursing bottle, both decidedly unnatural circumstances. The research and its results only make sense when they are understood within the theoretical context of attempting to differentiate two causes for the maternal bond: tactile stimulation versus satisfaction of hunger. What Harlow was able to do with this artificial setting and his experimental approach was to provide useful information for determining which process (i.e., tactile stimulation rather than nourishment) was responsible for the maternal bond and which factors associated with tactile stimulation influenced its development.

This example illustrates that, when testing theoretical propositions, investigations that control for extraneous explanations may produce powerful information about causal factors, even if they are dramatically artificial. This research example also highlights the irrelevance of random sampling and realism of the experimental circumstances to research questions that are testing theory (Mook, 1983). That is, random sampling and realism were not relevant to this research because the question that was being investigated was a theoretical question and the results of the research were relevant in evaluating the veracity of one theoretical proposition over another. The lack of experimental research on issues related to ISL, study abroad, service learning, and international education reflects the lack of attention that theory has played in guiding, informing, and shaping research. When theory becomes more salient in this research, experimental studies in laboratories will be considered along with other approaches as a viable means for answering theory-based questions that have implications for ISL program design.

Case II

What sense does it make to observe whether or not someone salts food before or after tasting it? Snyder made this observation in restaurants after interviewing patrons with a series of questions that assessed their inclination to monitor social environments (high self-monitors) or not (low self-monitors). Learning that high self-monitors were more likely to taste first was consistent with the theoretical prediction that those who pay attention to the cues in the social environment and adjust their behavior accordingly would be more likely to taste their food in order to determine if they would salt or not. Thus, what is normally a trite observation is made much more meaningful by its interpretation within the context of Snyder's theory (Snyder, 1974). This case illustrates the importance of the theoretical context to the meaningfulness of the observation (or any other measurement); that is, simply making the observation about the salting behavior is not meaningful in and of itself, without the theory. Furthermore, the relevance of a measure or observation is linked to what it is intending to measure and the meaning that it has within a theoretical context. Asking if a scale is good or if a measurement has value ignores the importance to theoretical context and broad research issues when designing good research.

When theory is integrated with design and with measurement in research, it provides the most powerful method for analyzing the nature of ISL. Theories can come from multiple sources, including developing new theories specifically for ISL and study abroad (Kiely, chapter 11) or from cognate disciplines (Bringle, 2003, 2005; Bringle & Hatcher, 2000; Gillespie et al., 2009). Theories from education, cognitive sciences, psychology, sociology, anthropology, and communications studies can provide a basis for contributing to the development and interpretation of ISL research. But the theory is not independent of the strategies that are used for designing the data collection and measuring the outcomes.

Mixed Methods

ISL research will benefit for greater utilization of quantitative methods; quantitative methods may also be paired with qualitative methods (Kiely & Hartman, chapter 13). Creswell (2009) presents a typology of methods that mix quantitative and qualitative methods: (a) *triangulation designs* where quantitative and qualitative data are collected concurrently; (b) *exploratory* and (c) *explanatory* designs where data is conducted in two sequential phases; and (d) *embedded* designs where one form of data is embedded in the other (Creswell, 2009). Mixed methods are frequently presented as a better alternative to either only quantitative or only qualitative approaches; however, as Yanchar, Gantt, and Clay (2005) note,

> Clearly, a methodological position that prizes [flexibility,] multiple methods, and a question-driven (rather than method-driven) approach . . . assuming that one's research options are limited to either a qualitative perspective, a quantitative perspective, or some hybrid combination of the two, merely serves to reintroduce the potential for methodological rigidity. (pp. 28, 33)

Bryman (2008) reported research in which he had analyzed the use of mixed methods in published papers and interviewed a number of researchers. In a significant number of cases (27%), research papers failed to explain why mixed methods had been used. In addition, Bryman (2006) conducted a content analysis of 232 journal articles between 1994 and 2003 that employed a mixed-method approach, and found that only 18% of these articles fully combined both qualitative and quantitative findings. Generally, researchers used mixed methods in a pragmatic way without much reflection or concern. Researchers often derived a wider range of outcomes from combining methods than they expected. Some participants felt that researchers who use mixed methods often report findings based on one method only (Bryman, 2006).

Conclusions

There is consensus (Bringle, 2003; Bringle et al., 2004; Deardorff, 2009; Gelmon, Furco, Holland, & Bringle, 2005; Eyler, chapter 10; Gillespie et al. 2009; Kiely, chapter 11; Kiely & Hartman, chapter 13) that good research on service learning, and therefore ISL, should:

- *Be guided by theory.* All research, whether quantitative or qualitative in nature, should be guided by a theoretical framework and be based on and contribute to the existing knowledge base in the field.

- *Involve clearly defined constructs.* Many studies do not clearly outline the experiences being defined as service learning (Billig & Eyler, 2003). The definition provided of ISL (Bringle & Hatcher, chapter 1) is important for this reason. In addition to defining the independent and dependent variables, researchers also need to identify and explore the role of important moderator variables (such as type of community organization, size and type of college) and mediating variables (e.g., self-efficacy, civic-mindedness) (Bringle, 2003).
- *Control for, or account for, differences among groups.* Researchers should use scientific research design (e.g., experimental method, analysis of covariance to control for preexisting differences) to control for extraneous explanations and allow causal inferences (see Bringle & Hatcher, 2000). Self-selection of participants into ISL courses creates the problem of nonrandom assignment of students to an ISL group versus a non-ISL group.
- *Use psychometrically defensible measures that have multiple indicators.* ISL research measurement procedures should possess demonstrable reliability and validity (Bringle et al., 2004). Because constructs such as civic-mindedness and global responsibility are "socially desirable" attributes, researchers need to counteract socially desirable response bias in measures by including neutral or negatively worded items in survey or interview protocols or writing items in ways that control for the bias. Most service learning research that involves student measures utilizes tools that are based on student testimony or self-report, which presents a number of problems (Bringle et al., 2004; Steinke & Buresh, 2002). ISL researchers should consider using other measurement procedures, such as behavioral ratings by an external observer and independent coding of student products (Ash, Clayton, & Atkinson, 2005; Whitney & Clayton, chapter 8).
- *Use multiple methods if possible, and establish converging results across different methods.* Incorporating multiple measures and multiple methods allows triangulation of converging results to increase understanding, confidence, and generalizability about ISL research findings.
- *Use designs that result in confidence in the conclusions that are reached.* Many ISL studies do not include adequate control or comparison groups that contrast the intervention with other interventions in ways that would permit appropriate conclusions. ISL research is plagued by small sample size or limited data, such as basing the research on a single course experience measured only at the end of a semester (Jones & Steinberg, chapter 5).

- *Have implications for teaching and learning in general.* Limitations of generalizability can apply to many aspects of the research (e.g., sampling, nature of the intervention, context-specific elements, measurement procedures). However, ISL as an engaging and active pedagogy may have implications for all teaching and learning (e.g., cognitive processes, student-centered instruction, collaborative learning). As assessment of instruction becomes more outcome oriented and based on theory, there will be opportunities to assess how different pedagogical approaches, including ISL, contribute to achieving many desired learning outcomes.

ISL is an educational strategy that holds great promise for preparing college students to gain skills of active citizenship in the ever-diverse global context of the 21st century (Lewin, 2009; Plater, Jones, Bringle, & Clayton, 2009). Crossing cultural boundaries, navigating differences, and finding common voice to address complex social issues, around the world and at home, requires that college graduates are equipped with skills unlike those needed a generation ago. Identifying ISL program characteristics that yield these results is an important goal for educators, and can be accomplished through systematic research. Very few studies currently exist that employ quantitative social research methods to contribute to the best practices in designing, implementing, and assessing ISL courses and programs. Responsible and reflective ISL practitioners need to rectify this deficiency in a way that can inform practice and enhance the knowledge base for why ISL is such powerful pedagogy. This will best be done when ISL research, whether quantitative or qualitative, is framed by strong design, good measurement, and relevant theory. Kiely and Hartman (chapter 13) summarize criteria for evaluating the rigor of qualitative approaches and ways in which they parallel similar criteria associated with quantitative approaches. However, regardless of paradigm and approach, past research on ISL has lacked the integration and coherence that Bringle et al. (2004) referred to:

> Researchers must use good judgment and creativity to determine which tools are appropriate (e.g., scales, observations, archival measures, interviews, qualitative methods), which procedures are best suited to investigate a particular question, what inferences should be drawn from their research, and what are the best ways to communicate the results to multiple audiences. (p. 30)

This chapter, along with others in the book, is designed to provide researchers with a stronger skill set and knowledge base to advance understanding of ISL through systematic research.

References

Ash, S. L., Clayton, P. H., & Atkinson, M. P. (2005). Integrating reflection and assessment to capture and improve student learning. *Michigan Journal of Community Service Learning, 11*(2), 49–60.

Billig, S. H., & Eyler, J. (Eds.) (2003). *Deconstructing service-learning: Research exploring context, participation, and impacts.* Greenwich, CT: Information Age.

Braskamp, L. A., Braskamp, D. C. & Merrill, K. C. (2008). *Assessing progress in global learning and development of students during their education abroad experiences.* Chicago: Global Perspective Institute. www.gpinv.org.

Bringle, R. G. (2003). Enhancing theory-based research on service-learning. In S. H. Billig & J. Eyler (Eds.), *Deconstructing service-learning: Research exploring context, participation, and impacts* (pp. 3–21). Greenwich, CT: Information Age.

Bringle, R. G. (2005). Designing interventions to promote civic engagement. In A. Omoto (Eds.), *Processes of community change and social action* (pp. 167–187). Mahwah, NJ: Erlbaum.

Bringle, R. G., & Hatcher, J. A. (2000). Meaningful measurement of theory-based service-learning outcomes: Making the case with quantitative research. *Michigan Journal of Community Service Learning* [Special issue], 68–75.

Bringle, R. G., Phillips, M., & Hudson, M. (2004). *The measure of service-learning: Research scales to assess student experiences.* Washington, DC: American Psychological Association.

Bringle, R. G., & Tonkin, H. (2004). International service learning: A research agenda. In H. Tonkin (Ed.), *Service-learning across cultures: Promise and achievement* (pp. 365–374). New York, NY: International Partnership for Service-Learning and Leadership.

Bryman, A. (2006). Integrating quantitative and qualitative research: How is it done? *Qualitative Research, 6*, 97–113.

Bryman, A. (2008, April). *Mixed methods research—Implications of recent research.* Paper presentation at the Symposium on Mixed Methods Research, BPS Dublin Conference, Dublin, Ireland.

Creswell, J. (2009). Editorial: Mapping the field of mixed methods research. *Journal of Mixed Methods Research, 3*(2), 95–108.

Deardorff, D. K. (2009). Understanding the challenges of assessing global citizenship. In R. Lewin (Ed.), *The handbook of practice and research in study abroad: Higher education and the quest for global citizenship* (pp. 61–77). New York: Routledge.

Gelmon, S., Furco, A., Holland, B., & Bringle, R. G. (2005, November). *Beyond anecdote: Challenges in bringing rigor to service-learning research.* Paper presented at the 5th Annual International K-H Service-Learning Research Conference, East Lansing, MI.

Gillespie, J., Braskamp, L., & Dwyer, M. (2009). Holistic student learning and development abroad: The IES 3-D Program Model. In R. Lewin (Ed.), *The handbook of practice and research in study abroad: Higher education and the quest for global citizenship* (pp. 445–465). New York, NY: Routledge.

Gueron, J. M. (2000, January). *The politics of random assignment: Implementing studies and impacting policy.* Retrieved August 22, 2008, from http://www.mdrc.org/publications/45/workpaper.pdf

Harlow, H. (1958). The nature of love. *American Psychologist, 13,* 673–685.

Hartman, E. M. (2008). *Educating for global citizenship through service-learning: A theoretical account and curricular evaluation* (Doctoral dissertation, University of Pittsburgh, 2008) *Dissertations & Theses: A&I* (Publication No. AAT 3349185).

Hartman, E., & Heinisch, R. (2003, August). *Fostering civic attitudes and an appreciation for diversity through international service-learning: A qualitative and quantitative analysis.* Paper presented at the American Political Science Association Annual Conference, Philadelphia, PA.

Lewin, R. (2009). *The handbook of practice and research in study abroad: Higher education and the quest for global citizenship.* New York, NY: Routledge.

Markus, G. B., Howard, J., & King, D. (1993). Integrating community service and classroom instruction enhances learning: Results from an experiment. *Educational Evaluation and Policy Analysis, 15*(4), 410–419.

Matsumoto, D., LeRoux, J., Ratzlaff, C., Tatani, H., Uchida, H., Kim, C., & Araki, S. (2001). Development and validation of a measure of intercultural adjustment potential in Japanese sojourners: The Intercultural Adjustment Potential Scale (ICAPS). *International Journal of Intercultural Relations, 25,* 483–510.

McMurtrie, B. (2007, March 2). The global campus: American colleges connect with the broader world. *Chronicle of Higher Education, 53*(26), A37.

Mook, D. (1983). In defense of external invalidity. *American Psychologist, 38,* 379–387.

Myers-Lipton, S. J. (1998). Effects of a comprehensive service-learning program on college students' civic responsibility. *Teaching Sociology, 26,* 243–258.

Osborne, R. E., Hammerich, S., & Hensley, C. (1998). Student effects of service-learning: Tracking change across a semester. *Michigan Journal of Community Service Learning, 5,* 5–13.

Patton, M. Q. (2002). *Qualitative research & evaluation methods, 3rd Edition.* Thousand Oaks, CA: Sage Publications.

Plater, W. M., Jones, S. G., Bringle, R. G., & Clayton, P. H. (2009). Educating globally competent citizens through international service learning. In R. Lewin (Ed.), *Study abroad and the making of global citizens: Higher education and the quest for global citizenship* (pp. 485–505). New York, NY: Routledge.

Pedersen, P. B., Draguns, J. G., Lonner, W. J., & Trimble, J. E. (Eds.). (2007). *Counseling across cultures* (6th ed.). Los Angeles: Sage.

Reeb, R. N., Katsuyama, R. M., Sammon, J. A., & Yoder, D. S. (1998). The Community Service Self-Efficacy Scale: Evidence of reliability, construct validity, and pragmatic utility. *Michigan Journal of Community Service Learning, 5,* 48–57.

Savicki, V., Binder, F., & Heller, L. (2008). Contrasts, and changes in potential and actual psychological intercultural adjustment. In V. Savicki (Ed.), *Developing intercultural competence and transformation: Theory, research, and application in international education* (pp. 111–127). Sterling, VA: Stylus.

Shumer, R. (2000). Science or storytelling: How should we conduct and report service-learning research? *Michigan Journal of Community Service Learning* [Special issue], 76–83.

Snyder, M. (1974). Self-monitoring of expressive behavior. *Journal of Personality and Social Psychology, 30*(4), 526–537.

Sodowsky, G. R., Taffe, R. C., Gutkin, T. B., & Wise, S. L. (1994). Development of the Multicultural Counseling Inventory: A self-report measure of multicultural competencies. *Journal of Counseling Psychology, 41*(2), 137–148.

Steinke, P., & Buresh, S. (2002). Cognitive outcomes of service learning: Reviewing the past and glimpsing the future. *Michigan Journal of Community Service Learning, 8*(2), 5–14.

Transcultural C.A.R.E. Associates. (2009, July). *Inventory for Assessing the Process of Cultural Competence Among Healthcare Professionals-Revised (IAPCC-R)*. Retrieved July 6, 2009, from http://www.transculturalcare.net/iapcc-r.htm

Trochim, W. M. K., & Donnelly, J. P. (2007). *The researcher methods knowledge base* (3rd ed.). Manson, OH: Thomson.

Yanchar, S. C., Gantt, E. E., & Clay, S. L. (2005). On the nature of a critical methodology. *Theory & Psychology 15*(1), 27–50.

13

QUALITATIVE RESEARCH METHODOLOGY AND INTERNATIONAL SERVICE LEARNING

Concepts, Characteristics, Methods, Approaches, and Best Practices

Richard Kiely and Eric Hartman

P ublicly engaged universities, faculties, and students rarely have the luxury of fitting public problems to research methods. On the contrary, community-engaged and public-service researchers must be flexible and nimble with their methodological tools, able to systematically and rigorously analyze pressing questions in cooperation with community partners and in response to public problems. Whether the questions at hand involve the program factors in international service learning (ISL) that are most likely to invoke deep learning and reflection on the part of students, or how a community organization can demonstrate its effectiveness and articulate the work it does, the research problem, purpose, and questions must drive selection of methods. We begin with these three related assumptions: (a) choices and decisions about research design and methods should be informed by the purpose of the research; (b) quantitative, qualitative, and mixed method research approaches can generate important knowledge about programs, phenomena, problems, people, and policy but will always have specific limitations; and (c) given such limitations, criteria for assessing the quality of a particular research approach should be well understood and explicit throughout the research process.

Much of the discussion in the service learning field regarding research methodology, and qualitative research in particular, has centered on arguments and evidence related to advancing the rigor, credibility, and the technical aspects of research methods (Bringle & Hatcher, 2000, 2007; Bringle, Phillips, & Hudson, 2004; Shumer, 2000; Waldstein, 2003). This chapter will focus on the technical, conceptual, and pedagogical uses of qualitative research on ISL while indicating strategies for enhancing the quality of research on ISL. To meet these objectives, the chapter is divided into the following sections: (a) qualitative research: concepts, components, and characteristics; (b) ISL literature review and qualitative research approaches; (c) practice implications for faculty and students; (d) challenges, issues, and limitations; (e) recommendations for future use and research; (f) resources for qualitative research; and (g) summary and conclusions.

Qualitative Research Methodology: Concepts, Components, and Characteristics

Most scholars writing in the area of qualitative research find it difficult to capture a single, comprehensive definition for the field of qualitative inquiry (Denzin & Lincoln, 2005; Schwandt, 2001). Denzin and Lincoln (1994, 2000, 2005), who have edited three voluminous editions of the *Handbook for Qualitative Research*, focus on at least eight historical moments since 1900 and contend that each moment presents a different set of foundational concepts, categories, frameworks, issues, and challenges that define the field. Many writers impose definitional boundaries on the field by juxtaposing qualitative research with quantitative research and point out key methodological and epistemological differences (Creswell, 1994, 1998; Guba & Lincoln, 1989, 2000). Researchers with a more pragmatic bent emphasize practical issues related to what approaches work best under what conditions including research design, sampling rationale, analysis procedures, representation, and quality criteria for warranting knowledge claims (Greene & Caracelli, 1997; Mark, Henry, & Julnes, 1999; Merriam & Associates, 2002; Patton, 2002).

Despite various approaches to defining qualitative research, what is clear is that it has evolved from diverse philosophical and disciplinary traditions and practices including phenomenology, hermeneutics, symbolic interactionism, semiotics, sociology, psychology, and cultural anthropology (Denzin & Lincoln, 2000, 2005; Gall, Borg, & Gall, 1996; Lincoln & Guba, 1985; Merriam & Associates, 2002; Patton, 2002). Such an eclectic history has important epistemological and practical consequences for understanding and conducting qualitative research with human subjects involved with ISL programs (Merriam, 2002; Patton, 2002; Shumer, 2000). In the following section, we identify and summarize the concepts, components, and character-istics that are central features of qualitative research (Creswell, 1998; Denzin & Lincoln, 2005; Merriam & Associates, 2002; Patton, 2002).

Researcher as Instrument

Shifting from a detached social scientist who designs sophisticated non-human instruments and (quasi-) experimental methods, a fundamental distinguish-ing characteristic for all types of qualitative research is that the researcher is the main instrument for data gathering, analysis, interpretation, and repre-sentation (Merriam, 2002, p. 5). The qualitative researcher is more directly connected with the research participants and context and, as the research instrument, has the benefit of adjusting and responding in a timely fashion to changes in the environment, evolving program conditions, and participant is-sues and needs (Merriam, 2002; Patton, 2002). Qualitative researchers are in a unique position to document in the field the phenomena, events, conditions, human perceptions, meanings, and relations under study through observa-tions and interviews (Glesne, 1999; Merriam & Associates, 2002; Patton, 2002; Shumer, 2000).

Paradigmatic Lenses

From a practical and epistemological standpoint, being the research instru-ment who brings a particular worldview to the research process poses unique challenges that need to be addressed before, during, and after the qualitative research study (Merriam, 2002). For example, qualitative researchers typi-cally make an effort to clarify how their values, biases, and philosophical and paradigmatic assumptions guide their choices prior to undertaking a study and during the collection, analysis, interpretation, and representation of the data (Creswell, 1998; Guba & Lincoln, 2005; Merriam, 2002). As Glesne (1999) aptly points out, "the research methods you choose says something about your views on what qualifies as valuable knowledge and your perspec-tive on the nature of reality or ontology" (p. 4). Paradigms that structure and inform qualitative approaches, methods, and respective research activi-ties in the literature include post-positivistic, interpretive, critical, feminist, pragmatic, postmodern, and participatory approaches (Creswell, 1998; Guba & Lincoln, 2005; Merriam, 2002). Whether one is cognizant of it or not, each of these paradigmatic lenses frames the way in which researchers under-stand ontology (the nature and meaning of reality), epistemology (knowledge and the relationship of the researcher to what is under study), methodology (the research process and design), axiology (how values inform the research process), and rhetoric (how knowledge is represented and communicated) (see Creswell, 1998, pp. 75–78; Guba, 1990; Guba & Lincoln, 2005, pp. 191–212, for a detailed discussion of how paradigmatic assumptions inform the research process). A qualitative approach to research and writing should make the paradigmatic assumptions underlying the categories above explicit since, as Merriam (2002) points out, "your particular stance will determine the specific research design that you employ for carrying out your study" (p. 4).

Reflexivity

It is not unusual therefore to find qualitative researchers surfacing and clarifying the sets of epistemological assumptions that inform and shape the decisions they make throughout the research process (e.g., the problem focus and purpose, sampling rationale and choices regarding research design, methods, analysis procedures, reporting, and quality criteria) (Creswell, 1998; Glesne, 1999; Merriam, 2002). Qualitative researchers refer to this reflective process in research as *reflexivity* (Etherington, 2007; Glesne, 1999; Merriam, 2002). Etherington (2007) explains that "reflexivity is a tool whereby we can include our 'selves' at any stage, making transparent the values and beliefs we hold that almost certainly influence the research process and its outcomes" (p. 601). Reflexivity makes more visible and public how the ethical, practical, political, and theoretical dimensions of the research endeavor are filtered through our subjective lens into the research activities and decisions (Denzin, 1997; Ellis & Bochner, 2000; Etherington, 2007; Guillemin & Gillam, 2004; Patton, 2002). It is particularly important for practitioners working in resource-poor communities in diverse ISL contexts to incorporate reflexivity into the research process because the inquiry may have a direct impact on who benefits from the research, who participates in the research design and process, and how resources are allocated among diverse stakeholders involved in the ISL work (Kahn, chapter 6; Strand, Marullo, Cutforth, Stoecker, & Donohue, 2003).

Interpretivist/Constructivist

Although a number of paradigms can inform the choice of research design, the research process and results in qualitative inquiry tend to be *interpretivist* (see Glesne, 1999, p. 6) or *constructivist* (Guba & Lincoln, 1989). According to Glesne (1999),

> . . . since interpretivists assume that they deal with multiple, socially constructed realties or "qualities" that are complex and indivisible into discrete variables, they regard the research task as coming to understand and interpret how the various participants in a social setting construct the world around them. (p. 5)

Consequently, qualitative researchers aim their methods at discovering the multiple ways in which individuals perceive, interpret, and act within a particular time and place (Denzin & Lincoln, 2005; Glesne, 1999; Merriam, 2002). The notion that reality is socially constructed is particularly salient for researchers in ISL contexts where faculty and students interact with each other and with community members who maintain diverse perspectives on social problems, history, culture, gender, religion, and politics (see Kahn, chapter 6; Sutton, chapter 7, for ISL examples).

Naturalistic and Field-Based

According to Patton (2002), under real-world conditions in which programs are subject to change and redirection, naturalistic inquiry replaces the fixed treatment/outcome of the controlled experiment with the dynamic process orientation that documents actual operations and outcomes of a process, program, or intervention over a period of time (p. 42). In order to understand the meanings ISL participants attribute to a program, experience, event, or phenomena, it is necessary for qualitative researchers to conduct their studies with participants in natural settings (Patton, 2002). Qualitative research provides ISL researchers with a useful methodology to directly engage with study participants and their environment through interviews and observation in the field. This research can provide important knowledge on the value, impact, and/or effectiveness of ISL programs for campus and community participants.

Reporting and Representation

Qualitative researchers represent and communicate the results of data by providing rich, thick, in-depth descriptions of the people, program characteristics, sites, situations, events, and contexts through written and audiovisual media (Merriam, 2002; Patton, 2002). This includes words, images, stories, poems, video, music, pictures, performance, and dialogue (Kahn, chapter 6; Richardson, 2005). The variety of media in qualitative research allows ISL researchers to represent more effectively the myriad dimensions of a cross-cultural environment and capture the meaning that multiple stakeholders (community, student and faculty experiences) attribute to the quality and impact of the ISL program.

Inductive Process

Qualitative research does not typically follow a process of deduction by testing a set of predetermined hypotheses but rather attempts to discover, explore, develop, analyze, and uncover the themes, categories, patterns, tentative hypotheses, causal relationships, and theories that emerge from research with participants and/or in the field (Glesne, 1999; Merriam, 2002; Miles & Huberman, 1994; Patton, 2002). Patton (2002) explains that the "qualitative analyst seeks to understand the multiple interrelationships among the dimensions that emerge from the data without making prior assumptions or specifying hypotheses about the linear or correlative relationships among narrowly defined, operationalized variables" (p. 56). The inductive research and analysis process is iterative and the identification of meaningful conceptual patterns, themes, and categories relies heavily on the researcher's ability to engage in ongoing comparison of data being gathered from participants and in the field (Patton, 2002). See "quality criteria" section below for a more detailed discussion of data analysis procedures and criteria for warranting the quality of the qualitative research process and product.

Flexible, Dynamic, and Emergent

The qualitative research process is non-linear and recursive and needs to be flexible enough to adjust to, rather than control, naturally evolving events and situations (Glesne, 1999; Patton, 2002). It is good practice for researchers to modify a research design as a response to changing conditions if ongoing analysis of the data uncovers information that was not anticipated. However, changing a research design that has been approved by an Institutional Review Board or another entity raises ethical issues that should be addressed as amendments to the research protocol and their implications for the risk/benefit analysis (Wells, Warchal, Ruiz, & Chapdelaine, chapter 14). From a practical standpoint, ISL faculty and students have a variety of qualitative research designs, methods, processes, and quality criteria to choose from in any given context. This diversity, lack of control, and ambiguity might make the qualitative research process seem daunting or untenable to those not familiar with it. However, greater flexibility for responding to changing conditions in the field enhances the credibility, authenticity, and accuracy of the study's results by compelling researchers to be more careful and explicit about the choice of methods, foci, and questions most appropriate for addressing the study purpose, topic, and context, and by highlighting the importance of selecting suitable criteria for assessing the quality of the knowledge generated (Garratt & Hodkinson, 1998; Patton, 2002; Schwandt, 1996). In all qualitative research, the researcher is charged with maintaining copious records so that other interested researchers may discern the rationale for the methodological choices and decisions made.

An example from an ISL program illustrates the importance of flexibility well, and demonstrates the value of combining qualitative and quantitative methods. Through consultation with community partners in rural Tanzania, Hartman (2008) and his students were asked to conduct an evaluation of program impact for a Women's Rights group (WOMEDA) and an organization dedicated to local empowerment and appropriate technologies (FADECO). Representatives of those local organizations indicated there were no quantitative data available, but were open to investigating program outcomes through qualitative means. As students conducted interviews with clients, staff members, volunteers, and community members, they discovered the presence of a sign-in book from the previous four years at WOMEDA. Quantitative analysis of the sign-in book led to the conclusion that the average distance a woman walked to visit the nongovernmental organization was 20 miles, while qualitative interviews, home visits, and observation aided in clarifying the diversity of reasons behind those visits as well as the outcomes for the women involved. In hindsight, the process seemed quite logical, but it only emerged through a flexible and dynamic research process.

Purposes

Mark et al. (1999) point out that all research and evaluation is in some way a more systematic attempt to make sense of the world or assist others in making sense of the world. Their model suggests that there are four primary research and evaluation purposes: to assess merit and worth; provide oversight and compliance; improve programs; and advance knowledge or theory (p. 188). Fetterman (2000) and others in service learning research literature (Strand et al., 2003) would add empowerment as another important research purpose. To meet these purposes, researchers provide descriptions, make classifications, identify and explain causal mechanisms and relationships, and surface values (Mark et al., 1999). Maxwell (1996) claims that there are five research purposes that fit the inductive and phenomenological nature of qualitative research including

> 1. Understanding the meaning, for participants in the study, of the events, situations and actions they are involved with... 2. Understanding the particular context within which participants act, and the influence this context has on their actions... 3. Identifying unanticipated phenomena and influences, and generating new grounded theories about the latter... 4. Understanding the process by which events and actions take place... [and] 5. Developing causal explanations (pp. 17–20)

Maxwell (2004) provides a more detailed review regarding the substantial role of qualitative research in identifying and explaining causal mechanisms and relations, as well as a critique of the National Research Council report, *Scientific Research in Education,* for assuming a Humean regularity conception of causality.

Qualitative research can be undertaken to meet any of the above purposes and should be used when there is a need for studies that seek to go beyond the frequency and rate of a phenomenon and that provide deeper understanding and analysis of the meaning of participants' experience and the processes and contextual factors that lead to outcomes.

Qualitative Research Designs

In qualitative research, there are a number of research designs that have emerged from the diverse traditions above including case study, grounded theory, phenomenology, narrative analysis, ethnography, biography, and interpretive, critical, feminist, and postmodern research approaches (Creswell, 1998; Merriam & Associates, 2002). Each of these designs brings a set of assumptions that guide the process of collecting, describing, analyzing, interpreting, and representing data (Creswell, 1998; Merriam & Associates, 2002).

Methods. The primary methods for gathering qualitative data include: (a) interviews, (b) focus groups, (c) observation, and (d) document analysis (Creswell, 1994; Patton, 2002). Creswell (1994) also provides a summary of the advantages and disadvantages of each of the methods (pp. 151–152). Faculty, students, and community members can benefit from using a combination of different qualitative methods to gather information and generate important knowledge for understanding and addressing community problems and issues in ISL courses and programs. In addition, it is important to know when to end data collection. Gall et al. (1996) draw from Lincoln and Guba's (1985) original framework to determine when there is no need for further qualitative data collection: (a) *Exhaustion of sources* means that further analysis of existing information gathered from participants and other data sources will not affect study results; (b) *saturation of categories* means that new information does not substantially alter themes, patterns, and categories that have emerged from previous data; (c) *emergence of regularities* signifies that analysis of data consistently leads to patterns that are mutually exclusive but conceptually linked and any new data continues to be consistent with themes that have been identified; and (d) *overextension* means "that new information is far removed from the central core of viable categories that have emerged, and does not contribute usefully to the emergence of additional viable categories" (see Gall et al., pp. 561–562).

Purposeful sampling. Sampling in qualitative research is usually non-random, non-probabilistic, and intentional "because the initial definition of the universe is more limited . . . and because social processes have a logic and a coherence that random sampling can reduce to uninterpretable sawdust" (Miles & Huberman, 1994, p. 27). Qualitative sampling procedures are not completely predetermined and involve systematic, criterion-based, and contextually bound choices as fieldwork evolves (Miles & Huberman, 1994). In qualitative research, sampling procedures are purposely (as opposed to randomly) aimed at "information rich cases," including people, organizations, programs, cultures, and events that will offer insightful and essential knowledge about the phenomenon, topic, or focus of the study (Patton, 2002, p. 40). Qualitative researchers need to explicate the rationale and criteria for choosing a specific sample. Patton (2002) provides a useful summary of purposeful sampling strategies and rationales, some of which include extreme or deviant case, intensity sampling, homogenous sampling, snowball and chain sampling, typical case, critical case, confirming and disconfirming, stratified purposeful, and criterion-based sampling (pp. 243–244). Maximum variation (i.e., maximizing the diversity of the sample so that patterns are observed across a variety of sources) is a useful sampling strategy for enhancing study validity (Merriam, 2002; Patton, 2002).

Data analysis. There are many different procedures that qualitative researchers use to analyze data (Egan, 2002; Merriam, 1998; Miles & Huberman, 1994; Patton, 2002). Patton (2002) states that "the challenge of qualitative analysis lies in making sense of massive amounts of data. This involves reducing the volume of raw information, sifting trivia from significance, identifying significant patterns, and constructing a framework for communicating the essence of what the data reveal" (p. 432). Although all qualitative data analysis is inductive and begins once data gathering has been initiated, the most common data analysis strategy is the constant comparative approach which was developed by Glaser and Strauss (1967) as an analytical strategy for "grounding theory" from the data (Egan, 2002; Merriam, 1998, 2002; Patton, 2002). In general, the constant comparison method is an analytical process whereby researchers recursively sift through data to "continuously compare" experiences, incidents, comments, and other important meanings that emerge from data analysis (Merriam, 1998, p. 179). Constant comparison begins with data gathering and researchers attempt to identify through themes and categories, what each unit of data shares in common, meaningful differences, and/or what is salient to the phenomenon of research interest (Merriam, 1998, p. 179). As with all qualitative analyses, individual researchers are responsible for maintaining clear records (i.e., audit trail) of how they make decisions regarding constant comparison, coding, and their related conclusions (Patton, 2002).

Quality criteria. While qualitative research has often been marginalized and critiqued for its scientific "softness" and for lacking rigor (Smith & Hodkinson, 2005), the field has engaged in significant dialogue regarding issues of rigor, validity, and legitimacy of knowledge claims generated through qualitative research (Denzin & Lincoln, 2000; Guba & Lincoln, 2005). As Denzin and Lincoln (2000) point out, the fifth and sixth historical moments in the field of qualitative research signified a crisis of representation and legitimacy when many qualitative researchers called into question whether research could truly represent participants' authentic voices, meanings, experience, and reality. This crisis and subsequent critical examination of validity issues led to the development of a set of criteria, standards, and strategies for assessing the quality of the research product and process (Garratt & Hodkinson, 1998; Schwandt, 1996).

　　Guba and Lincoln (1989) introduced a robust set of epistemic criteria for warranting the *trustworthiness* knowledge claims and later developed non-epistemic criteria of *authenticity* for ensuring the quality of the qualitative research process. Guba and Lincoln's (1989) *trustworthiness* criteria largely "mirrored" positivist and post-positivist conceptions of criteria for warranting knowledge claims (e.g., objectivity, reliability, internal and external validity) but were meant to be more consistent with the inductive, naturalistic, and interpretive nature of qualitative research. We will discuss two types of quality criteria, trustworthiness and authenticity, as well as strategies for enhancing the credibility and rigor of knowledge generated through qualitative research in ISL below.

　　There are four parallel criteria that help establish the trustworthiness of the study findings: credibility, transferability, dependability, and confirmability (Guba & Lincoln, 1989, 2000). The credibility criterion, which mirrors internal validity in the empiricist research tradition (Bringle, Hatcher, & Williams, chapter 12), has to do with how well the researcher's findings, interpretations, and representations match study participant's experience and reality, and whether the study's findings make sense to participants and reader alike (Guba & Lincoln, 1989; Miles & Huberman, 1984). That is, credibility has to do with conventional notions of the "truth value" of the research findings (Miles & Huberman, 1984) or whether the researcher "got it right" (Wolcott, 1994). Guba and Lincoln (1989) outline a number of strategies that can be employed to enhance the credibility of the study findings including prolonged engagement; immersion and ongoing observation in the field; ongoing member checks to confirm emerging categories, patterns, and themes with study participants; peer debriefing to allow colleagues to review findings and provide feedback; triangulation of multiple researcher accounts, data sources, and methods; and progressive subjectivity in which the researcher engages in ongoing reflection on biases, expectations, and assumptions about the research process and product (Guba & Lincoln, 1989, pp. 238–239).

Transferability is another standard for ensuring the trustworthiness of knowledge claims in qualitative inquiry (Guba & Lincoln, 1989). The transferability criterion parallels the conventional social science standards for external validity (Bringle et al., chapter 12) or the generalizability of findings to other people, programs, cases, and contexts (Guba & Lincoln, 1989). Most qualitative researchers recognize the limits of generalizing findings taken from small (and large) samples across space and time in diverse and unique contexts and tend to place the onus for transfer and use of findings on both researcher and reader (Guba & Lincoln, 1989; Patton, 2002). Hence, the most common technique developed in the field for enhancing transferability is for the researcher to provide rich, thick, and nuanced descriptions of the context, people, programs, and phenomena under study so that the reader can determine what part of the findings might be useful in a different context (Guba & Lincoln, 1989; Patton, 2002).

The dependability standard is similar to the empiricist criterion of reliability (Bringle et al., chapter 12) in which other researchers can follow the research process, logic, and decisions and come up with similar conclusions (Guba & Lincoln, 1989). However, Merriam (1998) points out a key difference, "The question then is not whether findings will be found again, *but whether the results are consistent with the data collected*" (p. 206). Because qualitative research responds to changing conditions and circumstances in the field, the researcher must make ongoing decisions and adjustments related to the study design methods, sampling, questions, and foci (Merriam, 1998). Therefore, to enhance the dependability of the study researchers maintain an audit trail, which means keeping detailed reflections, records, and field notes that document technical, conceptual, and analytical decisions made throughout the research process (Guba & Lincoln, 1989; Merriam, 1998).

Confirmability is another criterion for warranting trustworthiness and parallels the positivist requirement of objectivity (Guba & Lincoln, 1989). Confirmability means that the reader can be reasonably confident in that the study data, categories, results, and interpretations "are not merely figments of the inquirer's imagination" and that each can be traced to their original source (Guba & Lincoln, 1989, p. 243). To fulfill confirmability, the researcher must document data analysis procedures and ensure that linkages among data, findings, and interpretations are easily discernable by the reader (Schwandt, 1997). In addition to an audit trail, the most effective strategy for ensuring a robust linkage among the data, analysis, findings, interpretation, and representation is to ground the findings in the voices of the study participants by including substantial direct quotations (Guba & Lincoln, 1989; Merriam, 1998; Patton, 2002).

To more adequately reflect the differences in the inquiry process that occur when the researcher becomes the research instrument, Guba and Lincoln (1989) developed authenticity criteria. Rather than parallel conventional quality criteria which rest on a distinct set of epistemological assumptions held within the empiricist tradition of social inquiry (e.g., objectivity, causality, generalizability, replication of instruments), Guba and Lincoln's (1989) authenticity criteria set standards for assessing how well researchers apply qualitative methods in the field; these entail a distinct set of inquiry processes and a different set of assumptions about what constitutes quality research and knowledge. Authenticity criteria (i.e., fairness, ontological, educative, catalytic, tactical authenticity) shift the emphasis of validity of knowledge claims to whether the research process embraced reciprocity, inclusivity, surfaced minority voices, empowered study participants, provided arenas for open dialogue, raised awareness, and was useful or stimulated action (Guba & Lincoln, 1989, 2000; Schwandt, 1997).

Combining epistemic trustworthiness criteria (i.e., assessing the quality of knowledge produced through qualitative inquiry) and dimensions of non-epistemic authenticity criteria (i.e., ensuring the quality of the inquiry process) can be a more effective strategy for warranting the quality of the knowledge claims made and for ensuring the moral and political integrity or "goodness" of the research process (Schwandt, 1997; 2001). This set of both epistemic and non-epistemic criteria makes sense in ISL contexts where students and faculty work directly with communities and organizations to address complex social problems. Garratt and Hodkinson (1998), Guba and Lincoln (1989), and Schwandt (1996) provide excellent review of criteria for warranting knowledge claims and ensuring the quality of the qualitative research process.

Review of ISL Literature and Qualitative Research Approaches

Although research on domestic service learning has provided substantial empirical documentation of its value to students, faculty, institutions, and communities (Eyler, chapter 10; Eyler, Giles, Stenson, & Gray, 2001), there is limited research on the theory, practice, value, and use of ISL programs and courses (Berry & Chisholm, 1999; Bringle & Tonkin, 2004; Crabtree, 2008; Grusky, 2000; Jones & Steinberg, chapter 5; Kiely, 2004, 2005; Tonkin, chapter 9). Much of the ISL literature is not empirical, cumulative, or theory-based while descriptions of programs, activities, nuts and bolts, and rationales for ISL are plentiful (Annette, 2003; Grusky, 2000; Hartman & Rola, 2000; Jones & Steinberg, chapter 5; Kadel, 2002; Kraft, 2002).

From the limited qualitative research that has been conducted on ISL, most studies provide very little explanation of the rationale behind the research methodology used for analysis and most focus their attention on course descriptions and student outcomes (Camacho, 2004; Crabtree, 1998; DiSpigno, Fallon, & Christen, 2001; Monard-Weissman, 2003b; Parker & Dautoff, 2007; Porter & Monard, 2001; Pusch, 2004; Tonkin, 2004; Simonelli, Earle, & Story, 2004; Tonkin & Quiroga, 2004). A small number of studies have examined how ISL courses or programs affect students and community partners (Monard-Weissman, 2003a, Tonkin, 2004) and agencies and institutions (Berry & Chisholm, 1999; Tonkin, 2004). A few studies are theory-based (Crabtree, 2008; Goodrich, 2005; Kiely, 2002, 2004, 2005; Monard-Weissman, 2002, 2003a, 2003b; Parker & Dautoff, 2007; Pusch, 2004). However, fewer studies draw from theories and/or recommendations in previous ISL research (see Goodrich, 2005, Kiely, 2002, 2004, 2005; Hartman, 2008; Monard-Weissman, 2002) and even fewer discuss the theoretical implications of their research (Crabtree, 1998, 2008; Kiely, 2002, 2004, 2005) for practitioners and/or the wider ISL, study abroad, or service learning communities. Further, the use of explicit research designs and multiple methods, programs, researchers, and sources in ISL is still very limited (Camacho, 2004; Hartman, 2008; Kiely, 2004, 2005; Kiely & Hartman, 2007; Jones & Steinberg, Chapter, 5; King, 2004; Monard-Weissman, 2002; Porter & Monard, 2001; Tonkin, 2004). See Jones and Steinberg (chapter 5) in this volume for a detailed analysis of the ISL research literature from the point of view of program design and research strategies.

From a methodological standpoint, among the patterns observed from a review of qualitative studies in ISL, there is very little consistency, cohesion, and collaboration within the ISL research community. Some studies employed specific research designs such as phenomenology (Maher, 2003), phenomenography (Inglis, Rolls, & Kristy, 1998), case study (Crabtree, 1998; Kiely, 2002, 2004, 2005; Kiely & Hartman, 2007; King, 2004; Simonelli et al., 2004), autoethnography (Goodrich, 2005), ethnography (Porter & Monard, 2001), and program evaluation (Tonkin, 2004). However, very few studies on ISL described in detail the rationale and dimensions of the research design, as well as the choice of methods and their value for the given research purpose (Goodrich, 2005; Kiely, 2002; Monard-Weissman, 2002; Porter & Monard, 2001). In addition, although some studies used data analysis procedures such as a constant comparative approach (Kiely, 2004, 2005; King, 2004), NUD*IST (Monard-Weissman, 2003b; Porter & Monard, 2001), and content analysis (Camacho, 2004; DiSpigno et al., 2001; Inglis et al., 1998; Parker & Dautoff, 2007), only a few discussed the specific analytical process for developing codes, categories, and conceptual linkages among themes (Kiely, 2002; King, 2004; Parker & Dautoff 2007; Porter & Monard, 2001).

Compared with research on domestic service learning, qualitative research studies on ISL are less valuable to ISL researchers and practitioners because there has been little effort aimed at explicating methodological choices, drawing from and/or generating theory, or building on existing ISL research and theory (Bringle & Tonkin, 2004; Crabtree, 1998, 2008; Jones & Steinberg, chapter 5; Kiely, 2005). As a result, ISL research, which is predominantly qualitative, has a limited knowledge or theory base from which to draw (Crabtree, 2008). From a methodological standpoint, most qualitative studies on ISL programs display a number of patterns that further limit the ISL practitioners' understanding of what works best under what conditions. Symbolic of the lack of consistency and cohesion across studies was the fact that there were no articles that evaluated the rationale, value, and limits of using qualitative methodology in ISL settings. In spite of this, the use of qualitative research methodology in ISL contexts has been growing in terms of foci, units of analysis, designs, methods, and theory development (Kiely, 2005; Tonkin, 2004) and the articles included in this volume serve as a promising sign that ISL research is becoming a more collaborative endeavor (e.g., Sutton, chapter 7; Tonkin, chapter 9).

Implications for Practice

As mentioned, the paucity of high-quality qualitative research and empirical research in general in ISL has important practical implications. First of all, there is little diversity of methods or robust analysis of the types of qualitative research designs and methods that have been used in ISL contexts. Second, qualitative research studies that have been conducted tend to ignore findings and recommendations from previous ISL research and as a result, there is little knowledge accumulation around best practices, effective programming and pedagogy, and useful theory to guide practice. To address this dilemma, a few examples are offered in this section of different types of qualitative designs and methods that we have drawn from our review of the literature and from our own research on different ISL programs.

Because ISL programs immerse participants in cross-cultural contexts where they work directly with community partners, qualitative research, which parallels ISL activities that place students and faculty in direct engagement with human subjects in their environment, can be of unique value to faculty, students, and community partners. We contend that qualitative research designs could improve the quality of ISL theory, practice, and impact; given space limitations, we will focus our attention on describing how case study and ethnography are particularly suited for future research on ISL courses and programs.

Case Study

A researcher using a case study approach "explores a single entity or phenomenon ("the case") bounded by time and activity (a program, an event, process, institution, or social group) and collects detailed information by using a variety of data collection procedures during a sustained period of time" (Creswell, 1994, p. 12). Case study designs allow ISL researchers to document in substantial detail diverse phenomena in a specific social and cultural context that might be of interest to multiple stakeholders including researchers, community members, practitioners, policymakers, and program staff (Kiely, 2002). Merriam (1998) states that researchers should use case study designs if they are "interested in insight, discovery and interpretation rather than hypothesis testing" and/or when "it is impossible to separate the phenomenon's variables from their context" (p. 29). Case studies are also useful for generating theory and providing deeper understanding of the relationship among contextual, programmatic factors, and outcomes because case studies typically incorporate into their design the use of multiple data sources including participant observation, interviewing, life histories, and document analysis allowing researchers greater flexibility and access to knowledge and information in a given social setting (Kiely, 2002; Patton, 2002; Stake, 1995, 2000). Jones and Steinberg (chapter 5) provide a discussion on limitations of the single-case study approaches to research.

In ISL immersion programs like those that the authors have facilitated in Nicaragua, Bolivia, and Tanzania, a case study approach was an effective design for understanding and explaining the transformational learning process and outcomes that participants experienced (Kiely, 2002, 2004, 2005). For example, Kiely (2002) found that using multiple methods and sources over time allowed for greater triangulation and for gaining a deeper understanding of the learning process students experienced that was unique to the ISL program and context in Nicaragua. Kiely's (2002) research took place in a context that was unfamiliar to the literature on study abroad or service learning, and focused on an ISL experience that was and still is in the process of developing through learning from community partners and a diverse population of second and fourth-year college students. Kiely (2002) used a number of qualitative methods to collect information from participants over time including journals, research papers, field observations, video footage, unstructured and structured interviews, and focus groups with students, which gave him an opportunity to explore the meanings students attributed to critical incidents, specific situations, and the quality and impact of ISL programming. As a result, Kiely's (2002) research provided a more holistic understanding of participants' learning over time and offered insights into how program components and contextual variables were related to participants' learning. Also, by interviewing students prior to the program, on-site, and over a 10-year period, he was able to develop a theoretical model for explaining how students learned from participation in this particular ISL setting and program (Kiely, 2002, 2004, 2005). Lastly, Kiely's (2002) study was informed by previous ISL research and a well-tested theoretical framework, Mezirow's (1991, 2000) transformational learning theory.

The results of the case study research had practical implications in terms of program improvement and contributed to theory by extending transformational and intercultural learning theories and expanded current understanding of ISL learning outcomes and processes. As a follow-up to Kiely's case study approach, Kiely and Hartman (2004, 2007) conducted comparative case study research that critically examined similar outcomes, processes, and factors across three different programs and ISL contexts. The results of this study shed light on how context and program factors influenced students' understanding of global citizenship as well as the quality of service and learning in three ISL contexts (Kiely & Hartman, 2004, 2007).

Ethnography

Although examples of case study approaches exist in ISL literature (Kiely, 2002; Kiely & Hartman, 2007; King, 2004), it is surprising that to date there are relatively few researchers (Kiely, 2002; Porter & Monard, 2001; Porter, 2003; Simonelli et al., 2004) who have used ethnography as a research approach for studying ISL courses or programs. Given that a major distinguishing factor of the ISL experience is that participants are situated and immersed in a dramatically different culture, ethnography, which was primarily developed in the field of anthropology as a way to examine culture, provides a particularly useful qualitative research design in ISL contexts (Keene & Colligan, 2004; Kiely, 2002; Simonelli et al., 2004; White, 2000). As Simonelli et al. (2004) point out,

> Ethnography is a field technique used to provide a qualitative picture of relationships, representing a well-rounded view that blends outsider observations with insider insights. The 'facts' recorded are interactions and statements, stressing people and their actions in social, spatial, temporal and historic context. (p. 46)

Ethnographic approaches offer a number of field-based observational strategies for gaining insight into multiple dimensions of the ISL experiences including their impact on students, faculty, communities, residents, non-governmental organizations, and institutions as well as the role of contextual factors in enhancing or hindering the quality of the ISL experience for these different constituencies (Kahn, chapter 6; Kiely, 2002; O'Donnell, 2000; Simonelli et al., 2004; Sutton, chapter 7; White, 2000). In ISL courses and programs, there are many elements that can be the foci of ethnographic observations of the culture of a particular group including, roles, power, relationships, critical incidents, responses, language, emotions, conversations, interactions, rituals, group dynamics, organization culture, community mapping, environmental conditions, physical characteristics, and spaces (Creswell, 1998; Denzin, 1997; Geertz, 1973; Lofland & Lofland, 1995; Patton, 2002; Tedlock, 2000; Van Mannen, 1988). We highlight below how ethnography and observation can be used as effective qualitative strategies for enhancing ISL research and pedagogy.

Qualitative Research as Pedagogy

Strand (2000) contends that community-based research (CBR) enhances the application and generation of knowledge toward addressing community problems, but also, for faculty and students, can contribute another useful dimension for learning through the service learning pedagogy. We concur with Strand's (2000) view and suggest that faculty embrace qualitative research, ethnography, and CBR as methods for improving pedagogy in ISL courses and programs. Structuring courses with opportunities to engage in qualitative research with the community has many benefits, not only for increasing students' understanding and abilities for conducting qualitative research in the field, but also in terms of creating knowledge with and for the community through CBR approaches (Strand, 2000; Strand et al., 2003). Based on our experience with ISL in several different countries in which we have incorporated CBR into coursework before, during, and after the ISL experience, students learn from the opportunity to conduct qualitative research that increases research skills and learning and, in the best case scenario, benefits the community.

There are several useful field-based strategies that can be used to enhance students' research skills in ISL contexts and, in particular, prepare them for crossing borders and the inevitable encounter with difference (Keene & Colligan, 2004; Porter, 2003; Simonelli et al., 2004; White, 2000). The contextual border crossing (Kiely, 2002; 2005, chapter 11) that occurs in ISL programs is not only physical (i.e., the environment) and cultural (i.e., beliefs, values, norms, rituals, and behaviors of a particular group) but includes direct encounters with asymmetrical relations of power and resources that are embedded in race, class, gender, language, education, and citizenship. These encounters across difference and power are often more pronounced, emotional, and traumatic in ISL programs in which service is at the forefront of the mission (Camacho, 2004; Kiely, 2004, 2005; Simonelli et al., 2004). Capturing through more systematic fieldwork the meaning of the experiences and relationships that emerge from contextual border crossing can lead to significant learning. The use of ethnographic and field-based strategies can foster students' learning through thoughtful and structured field-based observation, interviews, dialogue, relationship-building, and field notes (Keene & Colligan, 2004; Simonelli et al., 2004; White, 2000).

One of the most common ethnographic research strategies we have included in course assignments is observation and the practice of taking field notes (Clifford, 1990; Lofland & Lofland, 1984; Spradley, 1980). The use of ethnographic observation and writing field notes, we would argue, is a more systematic extension of the practice of journaling as a useful form of reflection, and helps meet different service and learning objectives (Kiely, 2005; O'Donnell, 2000; White, 2000; Whitney & Clayton, chapter 8).

Kiely has facilitated, with another faculty colleague, service learning programs in Nicaragua that focus on issues related to health care and access to health care. The primary purpose of the program is to provide students with opportunities for learning about health care and problems in a resource-poor village in Nicaragua while at the same time designing and implementing clinics, neighborhood health assessments, and health education materials to address health-care needs. North American students in Nicaragua are required to practice their participant observation skills and focus on critical incidents that occur in the field as well as reflect on their practice conducting clinics (Kiely, 2002). The results of structuring this qualitative approach to research into coursework has been important for students' learning but has also led to a fairly substantial impact on students' approach to identifying and solving community issues and problems (Kiely, 2002; Sutton, chapter 7).

Similar to other ISL educators, as part of our coursework, we introduce participant-observation to students as a useful ethnographic research method for focusing attention on important aspects of what is often a complex and unpredictable experience conducting service work in an unfamiliar place with people representing a different culture (also see Sutton, chapter 7). The first stage is providing structured guidelines for how to be a good participant-observer with suggestions on what to observe; how to negotiate insider–outsider dynamics; how to collect data through field notes; and how to describe, analyze, and interpret observations so that they capture the holistic meaning and importance of an experience or critical incident. We recommend students bring a notebook wherever they go and jot down brief descriptive notes on what one sees, feels, smells, tastes, and hears in a specific setting. We also encourage students to find a consistent time each day to analyze and interpret their notes from observations and interviews as part of their more in-depth journal entries. We encourage students to question, share, and explain what they believe to be the significance of specific observations with faculty and community members and/or daily group reflection seminars so that other students can share their insights and compare observations.

On rare occasions, students' observations during service work have led to specific interventions that have saved lives and improved community health. For example, one student observed a small infant who displayed symptoms of a potentially lethal staph infection, which led faculty to prescribe needed antibiotics as an effective treatment. Another student accompanied a child to the dentist to get a tooth pulled and began to focus her attention on dental hygiene in the health clinics where she consistently observed rotting and substantial tooth decay. This led her to search for local remedies and interventions in a situation where regular dental cleaning and toothbrushes were not available. She eventually identified various local remedies and materials that could be used to clean teeth and, after consultation with community members and the health professional affiliated with the program, introduced them to women and children during health clinics. Yet another student observed common skin infections and after interviews with community partners, focused her research on soap making using local resources. In each instance, students learned how to observe health and hygiene behavior and practices and then examine through interviews local knowledge and access to resources more systematically and in turn respond in ways that met and valued local knowledge, assets, needs, and concerns.

Challenges, Issues, and Recommendations for Future Research

Service learning scholars continue to express a desire for research that is theory-driven and methodologically rigorous in order to accumulate rigorous, useful, credible, and reliable knowledge on the quality and value of service learning in K-12 and higher education (Billig & Eyler, 2003; Bringle, 2003; Bringle & Hatcher, 2000; Bringle et al., chapter 12; Bringle, Hatcher, & Shumer, 2007; Eyler, chapter 10; Furco & Billig, 2002; Howard, Gelmon, & Giles, 2000; Kiely, chapter 11; Welch & Billig, 2004). Indeed, Ziegert and McGoldrick (2004) maintain that the service learning field is at a methodological cross-roads. This sentiment holds true in the case of qualitative research on the theory, practice, and value of ISL courses and programs (Kiely, 2005).

To continue to improve upon understanding ISL, broadly speaking, and to develop a deeper understanding of change, context, and processes important to participants and community partners in ISL, researchers should:

1. Increase the quantity of theoretically grounded, peer-reviewed qualitative ISL research situated within the existing literature;
2. Expand their use of diverse qualitative designs and paradigmatic lenses and more explicitly engage community partners, especially through CBR approaches that clearly address inequality, empowerment, and reciprocity through coinvestigated and co-created knowledge;
3. Draw on the insights and approach of critical, feminist, and multicultural theories to continuously ask practical, political, and normative questions about the relationship among research, social structures, context, knowledge, and power, such as—Who participates in the construction of knowledge in ISL programs and contexts? For whom is knowledge constructed? Who benefits? Whose reality counts? Who should benefit and participate in the construction of knowledge? (Chambers, 1998; Deshler & Grudens-Schuck, 2000). By doing this, as Camacho's (2004) study shows, students will gain a better understanding of asymmetrical relations of power between participants (server and served) in ISL programs and work more systematically to uncover and address the sources of unequal relations;
4. Provide better information regarding the rationale for choosing particular research designs;
5. Expand beyond student-focused studies to include community, institutional, and policy outcomes;
6. Clarify and further develop related but diverse concepts currently existing in the service learning, study abroad, international education, and

other literatures such as transformation, (global) citizenship, inter-cultural competence, culture shock, dissonance, community-driven, community partner, community development, sustainability, and others;

7. Focus on and further develop practitioners' use of qualitative research as methodology in the field and as part of courses; and

8. Continue to work with undergraduate and graduate students, community partners, service learning practitioners, and university colleagues to educate one another about the utility of research methodologies for specific questions and problems in particular ISL settings.

Ongoing activities to educate broadly as well as use and document best practices in qualitative research such as the techniques described above (i.e., triangulate by using multiple sources, researchers, methods, audit trails, reflexivity and transparency about the research process) are key elements to ensuring quality research and the accumulation of knowledge related to ISL courses and programs, theories, and outcomes. This is important because the distinctly emergent and dynamic processes involved in qualitative research do not lend themselves to ensuring conventional notions of reliability (Merriam, 1998). To read and evaluate research well, particularly in complex, unpredictable, and culturally unfamiliar ISL settings, peers must be proficient in the paradigms and methods employed. Given the breadth of questions, cultures, and contexts involved with ISL, we encourage our colleagues and institutions to challenge one another to engage our respective communities in continuously broader and deeper methodological discussions of all varieties. The social issues we address, after all, will refuse to conform to any singular methodological approach whenever we address them in their genuine complexity in the field.

References

Annette, J. (2003). Service-learning internationally: Developing a global civil society. In S. Billig & J. Eyler (Eds.), *Deconstructing service-learning: Research exploring context, participation and impacts* (pp. 241–249). Greenwich, CT: Information Age.

Berry, H. A., & Chisholm, L. A. (1999). *Service-learning in higher education around the world: An initial look.* New York, NY: The International Partnership for Service-Learning.

Billig, S., & Eyler, J. (2003). *Deconstructing service-learning: Research exploring context, participation, and impacts. Advances in service-learning research* (Vol. 3). Greenwich, CT: Information Age.

Bringle, R. (2003). Enhancing theory-based research in service-learning. In S. Billig & J. Eyler (Eds.), *Deconstructing service-learning: Research exploring context, participation, and impacts* (pp. 3–21). Greenwich, CT: Information Age.

Bringle, R. G., & Hatcher, J. A. (2000, Fall). Meaningful measurement of theory-based service-learning outcomes: Making the case with quantitative research. *Michigan Journal of Community Service Learning*, 68–75.

Bringle, R. G., & Hatcher, J. A. (2007, October). *Service learning research: Quantitative perspective*. Paper presented at the 7th Annual International Conference on Service-Learning Research and Community Engagement, Tampa, FL.

Bringle, R. G., Hatcher, J. A., & Shumer, R. (2007, October). *Competing paradigms: Quantitative and qualitative research methodology*. Paper presented at the 7th Annual International Research Conference on Service-Learning Research and Community Engagement, Tampa, FL.

Bringle, R. G., Phillips, M., & Hudson, M. (2004). *The measure of service learning: Research scales to assess student experiences*. Washington, DC: American Psychological Association.

Bringle, R. G., & Tonkin, H. (2004). International service learning: A research agenda. In H. Tonkin (Ed.), *Service-learning across cultures: Promise and achievement* (pp. 365–374). New York: International Partnership for Service-Learning and Leadership.

Camacho, M. M. (2004). Power and privilege: Community service learning in Tijuana. *Michigan Journal of Community Service Learning, 10*(3), 31–42.

Chambers, R. (1998). *Whose reality counts? Putting the first last*. London, UK: Intermediate Technology Publications.

Clifford, J. (1990). Notes on (field)notes. In R. Sanjek (Ed.), *Fieldnotes: The makings of anthropology* (pp. 47–70). Ithaca, NY: Cornell University Press.

Crabtree, R. D. (1998). Mutual empowerment in cross-cultural participatory development and service learning: Lessons in communication and social justice from projects in El Salvador and Nicaragua. *Journal of Applied Communication Research, 26*(2), 182–209.

Crabtree, R. D. (2008). Theoretical foundations for international service-learning. *Michigan Journal of Community Service Learning, 15*(1), 18–36.

Creswell, J. (1994). *Research design: Qualitative and quantitative approaches*. Thousand Oaks, CA: Sage.

Creswell, J. (1998). *Qualitative inquiry and research design: Choosing among five traditions*. Thousand Oaks, CA: Sage.

Denzin, N. (1997). *Interpretive ethnography: Ethnographic practices for the 21st century*. London, UK: Sage.

Denzin, N. K., & Lincoln, Y. S. (Eds.). (1994). *Handbook of qualitative research*. Thousand Oaks, CA: Sage.

Denzin, N. K., & Lincoln, Y. S. (Eds.). (2000). *Handbook of qualitative research* (2nd ed.). Thousand Oaks, CA: Sage.

Denzin, N., & Lincoln, Y. S. (2005). (Eds.). *Handbook of qualitative research.* (3rd ed.). Thousand Oaks, CA: Sage.

Deshler, D., & Grudens-Schuck, N. (2000). The politics of knowledge construction. In A. Wilson & E. Hayes (Eds.), *Handbook of adult and continuing education* (pp. 592–611). San Francisco, CA: Jossey-Bass.

DiSpigno, A., Fallon, M., & Christen, R. (2001). Combining volunteer work and study abroad: An international service-learning project. *NSEE Quarterly, 26*(4), 7–10.

Egan, T. M. (2002). Grounded theory research and theory building. *Advances in Developing Human Resources, 4,* 277–295.

Ellis, C., & Bochner, A. (2000). Autoethnography, personal narrative, reflexivity: Researcher as subject. In N. K. Denzin & Y. S. Lincoln (Eds.), *Handbook of qualitative research* (2nd ed., pp. 733–768). Thousand Oaks, CA: Sage.

Etherington, K. (2007). Ethical research in reflexive relationships. *Qualitative Inquiry, 13*(5), 599–616.

Eyler, J. S., Giles, D. E. Jr., Stenson, C. M., & Gray, C. J. (2001). *At a glance: What we know about the effects of service-learning on college students, faculty, institutions and communities, 1993–2000* (3rd ed.). Nashville, TN: Vanderbilt University.

Fetterman, D. (2000). *Foundations of empowerment evaluation: Step by step.* Thousand Oaks, CA: Sage.

Furco, A., & Billig, S. H. (2002). Establishing norms for scientific inquiry in service-learning. In S. H. Billig & A. Furco (Eds.), *Service-learning through a multidisciplinary lens. Advances in service-learning research,* vol. 2 (pp. 15–32). Greenwich, CT: Information Age.

Gall, M. D., Borg, W. P., & Gall, J. P. (1996). *Educational research* (6th ed.). New York, NY: Longman.

Garratt, D., & Hodkinson, P. (1998). Can there be criteria for selecting research criteria? A hermeneutical analysis of an inescapable dilemma. *Qualitative Inquiry, 4*(4), 515–539.

Geertz, C. (Ed.). (1973). *The interpretation of cultures.* New York, NY: Basic Books.

Glaser, B., & Strauss, A. (1967). *The discovery of grounded theory: Strategies for qualitative research.* New York, NY: Aldine.

Glesne, G. (1999). *Becoming qualitative researchers: An introduction* (2nd ed.). New York: Longman.

Goodrich, A. (2005). *International service-learning: Reevaluating the intention of multicultural teacher education.* Unpublished master's thesis, University of Georgia, Athens.

Greene, J. C., & Caracelli, V. J. (Eds.). (1997). *Advances in mixed-method evaluation: The challenges and benefits of integrating diverse paradigms: New directions for evaluation, No. 74.* San Francisco, CA: Jossey-Bass.

Grusky, S. (2000). International service-learning: A critical guide from an impassioned advocate. *American Behavioral Scientist, 43*(5), 858–867.

Guba, E. G. (Ed.). (1990). *The paradigm dialog*. London, UK: Sage.

Guba, E. G., & Lincoln, Y. S. (1989). *Fourth generation evaluation*. Newbury Park, CA: Sage.

Guba, E.G., & Lincoln, Y.S. (2000). Paradigmatic controversies, contradictions, and emerging confluences. In N. K. Denzin & Y. S. Lincoln, (Eds.), *Handbook of qualitative research* (2nd ed.; pp. 163–188). Thousand Oaks, CA: Sage.

Guba, E. G., & Lincoln, Y. S. (2005). Paradigmatic controversies, contradictions, and emerging confluences. In N. K. Denzin & Y. S. Lincoln (Eds.), *Handbook of qualitative research* (3rd ed.; pp. 191–215). Thousand Oaks, CA: Sage.

Guillemin, M., & Gillam, L. (2004). Ethics, reflexivity and "ethically important moments" in research. *Qualitative Inquiry, 10,* 261–280.

Hartman, E. (2008). *Educating for global citizenship through service-learning: A theoretical account and curricular evaluation*. Unpublished doctoral dissertation, University of Pittsburgh.

Hartman, D., & Rola, G. (2000). Going global with service learning. *Metropolitan Universities, 11*(1), 15–24.

Howard, J., Gelmon, S., & Giles, D. (2000, Fall) From yesterday to tomorrow: Strategic directions for service-learning research. *Michigan Journal of Community Service Learning,* 5–10.

Inglis, A., Rolls, C., & Kristy, S. (1998). The impact of participation in a study abroad programme on students' conceptual understanding of community health nursing in a developing country. *Journal of Advanced Nursing, 28,* 911–917.

Kadel, C. J. (2002). Service learning abroad. In R. M. Romano (Ed.), *Internationalizing the community college* (pp. 59–69). Washington, DC: Community College Press, American Association of Community Colleges.

Keene, A., & Colligan, S. (2004). Service-learning and anthropology. *Michigan Journal of Community Service Learning, 11,* 5–15.

Kiely, R. (2002). Toward an expanded conceptualization of transformational learning: A case study of international service-learning in Nicaragua (Doctoral dissertation, Cornell University), *Dissertation Abstracts International, 63* (09A), 3083.

Kiely, R. (2004). A chameleon with a complex: Searching for transformation in international service-learning. *Michigan Journal of Community Service Learning, 10*(2), 5–20.

Kiely, R. (2005). Transformative international service-learning. *Academic Exchange Quarterly, 9*(1), 275–281.

Kiely, R., & Hartman, E. (2004). *Developing a framework for assessing learning for global citizenship: A comparative case study analysis of three international service-learning programs*. Proceedings of the 4th Annual International Service-learning Research Conference, Clemson University, Clemson, SC.

Kiely, R., & Hartman, E. (2007). *The relationship among context, program factors and learning in global service-learning: A comparative case study of three programs in Nicaragua, Bolivia and Tanzania.* Paper presented at the 7th International Research Conference on Service-Learning and Community Engagement, Florida Campus Compact, Tampa Bay, FL.

King, J. (2004). Service-learning as a site for critical pedagogy: A case of collaboration, caring, and defamiliarization across borders. *Journal of Experiential Education, 26*(3), 121–137.

Kraft, R. J. (2002). International service-learning, University of Colorado, Boulder. In M. E. Kenny, K. Kiley-Brabeck, & R. M. Lerner (Eds.), *Learning to serve: Promoting civil society through service learning* (pp. 297–314). Norwells, MA: Kluwer Academic Publishers.

Lincoln, Y. S., & Guba, E. G. (1985). *Naturalistic inquiry.* Thousand Oaks, CA. Sage.

Lofland, J., & Lofland, L. (1984). *Analyzing social settings: A guide to qualitative observation and analysis* (2nd ed.). Belmont, CA: Wadsworth.

Lofland, J., & Lofland, L. (1995). *Analyzing social settings: A guide to qualitative observation and analysis* (3rd ed.). London, UK: Wadsworth.

Maher, M. (2003). Individual beliefs and cultural immersion in service-learning: Examination of a reflection process. *The Journal of Experiential Education, 26*(2), 88–96.

Mark, M. M., Henry, G. T., & Julnes, G. (1999). Toward an integrative framework for evaluation practice. *American Journal of Evaluation, 20*(2), 177–198.

Maxwell, J. A. (1996). *Qualitative research design: An interactive approach.* Thousand Oaks, CA: Sage.

Maxwell, J. A. (2004). Causal explanation, qualitative research and scientific inquiry in education. *Educational Researcher, 33*(2), 3–11.

Merriam, S. B. (1998). *Qualitative research and case study applications in education: Revised and expanded from case study research in education* (2nd ed.). San Francisco, CA: Jossey-Bass.

Merriam, S. (2002). Introduction to qualitative research. In S. Merriam & Associates (Eds.), *Qualitative research in practice: Examples for discussion and analysis* (pp. 3–17). San Francisco, CA: Jossey-Bass.

Merriam, S., & Associates. (2002). *Qualitative research in practice: Examples for discussion and analysis.* San Francisco, CA: Jossey-Bass.

Mezirow, J. (1991). *Transformative dimensions of adult learning.* San Francisco, CA: Jossey-Bass.

Mezirow, J. (2000). Learning to think like an adult: Core concepts in transformational learning theory. In J. Mezirow & Associates (Eds.), *Learning as transformation: critical perspectives on a theory in progress* (pp. 3–34). San Francisco, CA: Jossey-Bass.

Miles, M. M., & Huberman, A. M. (1984). *Qualitative data analysis: A sourcebook of new methods.* Newbury Park, CA: Sage.

Miles, M., & Huberman, M. (1994). *An expanded sourcebook: Qualitative data analysis.* Thousand Oaks, CA: Sage.

Monard-Weissman, K. (2002). Nurturing senses of care, justice, and reciprocity through service-learning: A case study of the international partnership for service-learning program in Ecuador (Doctoral dissertation, University of Pittsburgh, 2002). In K. Norvell (Ed.), *Recent dissertations on service and service-learning topics. Volume III. 2001–2003* (p. 78). Scotts Valley, CA: National Service-Learning Clearinghouse.

Monard-Weissman, K. (2003a). Fostering a sense of justice through international service-learning. *Academic Exchange Quarterly, 7*(2), 164–169.

Monard-Weissman, K. (2003b). Enhancing caring capacities: A case study. *Journal of Higher Education, Outreach & Engagement, 8*(2), 41–54.

O'Donnell, K. (2000). Building intercultural bridges. *Metropolitan Universities, 11*(1), 25–34.

Parker, B., & Dautoff, D. A. (2007). Service-learning and study abroad: Synergistic learning opportunities. *Michigan Journal of Community Service Learning, 13*(2), 40–53.

Patton, M. Q. (2002). *Qualitative evaluation and research methods* (3rd ed.; pp. 51–67). Thousand Oaks, CA: Sage.

Porter, M. (2003). Forging L.I.N.C.S. among educators: The role of international service-learning in fostering a community of practice. *Teacher Education Quarterly, 30*(4), 51–67.

Porter, M., & Monard, K. (2001). *Ayni* in the global village: Building relationships of reciprocity through international service-learning. *Michigan Journal of Community Service Learning, 8*(1), 5–17.

Pusch, M (2004). A cross-cultural perspective. In H. Tonkin (Ed.), *Service-learning across cultures: Promise and achievement* (pp. 103–130). New York, NY: The International Partnership for Service-Learning and Leadership.

Richardson, L. (2005). Writing: A method of inquiry. In N. K. Denzin & Y. S. Lincoln (Eds.), *Handbook of qualitative research* (2nd ed.; pp. 923–948). Thousand Oaks, CA: Sage.

Schwandt, T. (1996). Farewell to criteriology. *Qualitative Inquiry, 2*(1), 58–72.

Schwandt, T. (1997). *Dictionary of qualitative inquiry*. Thousand Oaks, CA: Sage.

Schwandt, T. (2001). *Dictionary of qualitative inquiry* (2nd ed.). Thousand Oaks, CA: Sage.

Shumer, R. (2000, Fall). Science or storytelling: How should we conduct and report service-learning research. *Michigan Journal of Community Service Learning,* 76–83.

Simonelli, J., Earle, D., & Story, E. (2004). Acompanar obediciendo: Learning to help in collaboration with Zapatista communities. *Michigan Journal of Community Service Learning, 10*(3), 43–56.

Smith, J.K. & Hodkinson, P. (2005). Relativism, criteria and politics. In N. K. Denzin & Y. S. Lincoln (Eds.), *The Sage handbook of qualitative research* (3rd ed.; pp. 915–932). Thousand Oaks, CA: Sage.

Spradley, J. (1980). *Participant observation*. Orlando, FL: Harcourt Brace Jovanovich College Publishers.

Stake, R. (1995). *The art of case study research.* Thousand Oaks, CA: Sage.

Stake, R. (2000). Case studies. In N. Denzin & Y. Lincoln (Eds.), *Handbook of qualitative research* (2nd ed.; pp. 435–454). Thousand Oaks, CA: Sage.

Strand, K. (2000). Community-based research as pedagogy. *Michigan Journal of Community Service Learning, 7*(1), 85–96.

Strand, K., Marullo, S., Cutforth, N., Stoecker, R., & Donohue, P. (2003). *Community-based research in higher education: Principles and practices.* San Francisco, CA: Jossey-Bass.

Tedlock, B. (2000). Ethnography and ethnographic representation. In N. K. Denzin & Y. S. Lincoln (Eds.), *Handbook of qualitative research* (2nd ed.; pp. 455–486). Thousand Oaks, CA: Sage.

Tonkin, H. (2004). *Service learning across cultures: Promise and achievement.* New York, NY: International Partnership for Service-Learning.

Tonkin, H., & Quiroga, D. (2004). A qualitative approach to the assessment of international service-learning. *Frontiers: The Interdisciplinary Journal of Study Abroad, 10,* 131–149.

Van Mannen, J. (1988). *Tales from the field: On writing ethnography.* Chicago: University of Chicago Press.

Waldstein, F. (2003). Epistemology and service-learning research. In S. Billig & A. Waterman (Eds.), *Studying service-learning: Innovations in education research methodology* (pp. 35–46). Mahwah, NJ: Lawrence Erlbaum Associates.

Welch, M., & Billig, S. (2004). *New perspectives in service-learning: Research to advance the field. Advances in service-learning research, vol. 4.* Greenwich, CT: Information Age.

White, T. J. (2000). Service learning and participant observation: Undergraduate field research. *Metropolitan Universities, 11*(1), 61–68.

Wolcott, H. F. (1994). *Transforming qualitative data: Description, analysis, and interpretation.* Thousand Oaks, CA: Sage.

Ziegert, A., & McGoldrick, K. (2004). Adding rigor to service-learning research: An armchair economists' approach. In M. Welch & S. Billig (Eds.), *New perspectives in service-learning: Research to advance the field. Advances in service-learning research, vol. 4* (pp. 23–36). Greenwich, CT. Information Age.

14

ETHICAL ISSUES IN RESEARCH ON INTERNATIONAL SERVICE LEARNING

Carole Wells, Judith Warchal, Ana Ruiz,
and Andrea Chapdelaine

E thical issues are a critical part of any research project. This chapter's purpose is not to review ethical issues involved in service learning projects (i.e., courses, programs), which have been discussed elsewhere (Chapdelaine, Ruiz, Warchal, & Wells, 2005; Tonkin, chapter 9). Instead, the focus is on providing a set of ethical guidelines for faculty and community partners as well as others to consider and use when conducting research on international service learning (ISL). Ethical considerations in ISL research are informed by a body of literature on international research ethics and another literature on community-based research that is explored in depth in this chapter.

Research on ISL is an ethical imperative in itself (Erasmus, chapter 15; Tonkin, chapter 9). It is critical that those involved in ISL demonstrate the outcomes of such work at the community, student, faculty, and institutional levels. Planned program assessments and research on outcomes for these constituencies should be an integral part of the service learning project from its onset. Moreover, such research must adhere to ethical standards to be effective in achieving this goal, which is the focus of this chapter.

Service Learning Ethics

The recent interest in ISL as a pedagogical tool to promote global sensitivity and understanding (Plater, Jones, Bringle, & Clayton, 2009), and to provide beneficial outcomes for international communities, highlights the need for a comprehensive research agenda to examine the effectiveness of service learning in achieving these goals (Tonkin, chapter 9). With an ever-shrinking global society, research on ISL will need to encompass not only the traditional Western world views of scientific investigation, but also multinational perspectives (Erasmus, chapter 15; Ferrell, Fraedrich, & Ferrell, 2002; Lowenberg & Conrad, 1998). Most work on research ethics is based on Western values, including guiding ethical principles, such as autonomy and individual rights, and the codes and techniques derived from such principles. For example, as discussed below, several research codes (e.g., The Nuremberg Code, 1949) and methods (e.g., informed consent) are predicated on the assumption that the primary concern is the individual's, as opposed to the group's, well being. Critical to this analysis, then, is an understanding that the multifaceted ethical issues involved in any ISL research project will be further complicated by conflicting worldviews, values, and beliefs with regard to "universal" ethical principles. Cultural differences may influence not only the design of the research, but also how the data are collected, the treatment of research participants, and the interpretation and dissemination of results (Bogolub & Thomas, 2005; Cohen, Pant, & Sharp, 1996; Punnett & Shenkar, 1996; Swaidan & Hayes, 2005).

Most importantly, all such initiatives must be premised on principles of mutuality and reciprocity, to ensure that the research will be of benefit to all involved parties. The ISL research project should be a collaborative, shared construction (Kiely & Hartman, chapter 13; Longo & Saltmarsh, chapter 4; Whitney & Clayton, chapter 8). Throughout the study, the process must be transparent and frequent communication between relevant constituencies must occur. The researchers must be flexible with regard to the research protocol and willing to alter plans to meet concerns of the community partners (Erasmus, chapter 15; Sutton, chapter 7).

That being said, a brief reminder of the necessity of developing an ethically sound service learning project may be helpful. Prior to any consideration of the ethical issues associated with a service learning research project, the risks versus benefits of the service learning project itself must be determined. The risk/benefit ratio, as it is commonly known, has been widely used by ethics review committees to determine if a particular project's anticipated benefits outweigh or justify any risks associated with the project. That is, to what extent will the service learning project benefit the community partners, the students, and other involved parties (e.g., sponsoring institutions)? For example, will the project have a short- and long-term positive impact on the quality of life for the community participants? Will the project increase student engagement and achieve the desired learning outcomes? Then, the researchers overseeing the service learning project must determine if those identified benefits outweigh any potential negative impact. Such risks include an inability for the positive impact of the project to be sustained over time; the resources of the community needed to execute the project are too demanding and thus deleterious to the community; and students encounter psychological, intellectual, or spiritual challenges that they are ill-equipped to handle or benefit from. Regardless of the specific questions a research project is designed to explore with regard to the service learning project, this careful assessment of the service learning project itself in terms of its benefits and risks must be answered first, prior to any research about the project.

To the extent that benefits outweigh risks and remaining risks are minimized, an ISL course or program is likely to be viewed as having met ethical standards (Rosenthal & Rosnow, 1984). However, it must be recognized that the weights assigned to identified benefits and risks are affected by individual and community values, backgrounds, and interests, resulting in different assessments of risk/benefit ratios. This is especially true in ISL, where the involved parties rarely share similar backgrounds and often there may be a perceived power imbalance between involved parties. For example, although the project may have significant, tangible benefits for the community, such as food or education, the project may also have costs to the community participants, including the extent to which their participation is voluntary.

Risk/Benefit of ISL Research

Once the risk/benefit assessment of the service learning course or program has been made, a systematic evaluation of the ethical considerations of the planned research must be conducted. This would involve a similar risk/benefit analysis as that described above. In an ISL context, examples of such benefits of research include increased knowledge, improved welfare of a particular population, greater cultural sensitivity of students, a clear demonstration of the anticipated positive outcomes of the project, and increased intercultural understanding for all involved parties.

Potential risks include taxing the time and resources of or causing psychological harm to the community partners, negative experiences for the students that increase their disquietude with persons from different cultures or nations, harmful perceptions of the community partners toward the educators and students or vice versa, potential faculty conflicts of interest, and long-term burdens on the community partners caused by the dissemination of the project results. Potential benefits and risks of conducting research on ISL are further explored below, along with ethical guidelines designed to maximize the risk/benefit ratio in a positive fashion.

International Research Ethics

A primary ethical consideration of any research is the protection of the research participants from harm. This mandate becomes increasingly more important and potentially difficult to achieve when research is conducted outside the United States by students, faculty, and community partners involved in ISL. Benatar and Singer (2000), for example, raise cautions about the "potentially exploitative nature of research in developed and developing countries" (p. 825) where "subjects" may be particularly vulnerable due to the economic disparities in goods and services. With regard to service learning, Chisholm (2004) cautions "The sad truth is that even ISL can be superficial, destructive or exploitive" (p. xi).

Typically, such protection is afforded research participants through the evaluation of the research by an Institutional Review Board (IRB) or Independent Ethics Committee (IEC). The IRB or IEC is an administrative body established and authorized by an institution such as a college, university, or medical facility to approve, require modification, or disapprove research activities that fall within its jurisdiction. The primary purpose of the review is the protection of the rights, safety, and welfare of research participants. In the United States, IRBs are governed by the National Research Act of 1974 that defines their purpose, function, and requirements. IRBs can act in coordination with other review boards, such as those that evaluate the quality of the research project, the methodology, protocol, or the financial efficacy of the research for the institution (see National Research Act of 1974, Pub. L. 93–348). But the IRB acts independently of the other review boards in its decision regarding the welfare of research participants.

An IRB review is especially important when research participants are members of vulnerable population groups, such as pregnant women, children, prisoners, the elderly, or persons with diminished comprehension. In ISL research, the term vulnerable population takes on new meaning. When research participants whose culture, economic conditions, political status, or language differ significantly from that of the researcher, then IRB members, sponsors, and others involved in the research should require special safeguards to protect participants' rights and welfare. Hence, it is critical that all ISL research be conducted as a mutual partnership and collaborative activity among all (i.e., faculty, students, and community partners), with particular attention to who might constitute a vulnerable group in the ISL context.

Although research that originates in the United States will be subject to a review by an appropriate IRB (from the college, university, or medical facility), a comparable review by the equivalent of an IRB/IEC in the host country would be ideal and highly recommended. This would be especially important for research initiated by the community partners or academics in the host country, which might not be subject to IRB review in the United States. The host country IRB/IEC, with full knowledge of the local laws and customs of the community, would have the authority to provide independent review of the research project, ensure protection of the local participants, and either authorize, require modification, or refuse to allow the research to proceed.

However, ISL researchers may face the nonexistence of IRBs in the countries in which they are performing their research. In this case, use of an IRB in the United States must be done with caution, as that board's evaluation will be influenced by Western values regarding research ethics. For example, informed consent (e.g., providing research participants with information regarding the purpose, procedures, and potential risks as well as benefits about the study prior to their participation) is considered critical to ensuring that a study meets ethical standards. Being fully informed presumes that a participant understands terms, procedures, and potential consequences in order to make a rational decision regarding participation. However, in some cultures or contexts, obtaining such consent, especially in written form, may be culturally inappropriate, difficult, or challenging in ways that North American researchers or IRB/IEC members are unfamiliar.

Rather than relying solely on an IRB not based in the host community, several possibilities may be considered. One possible approach is to have local constituencies become trained in IRB protocols and then have them review the proposed research, although such IRB training could still be influenced by American perspectives, since the training may be based in those values. Another approach would be to partner with a local organization or institution of higher education that has an IRB or equivalent, and request that they review the proposed study.

The need to establish IRBs to protect human research participants from harm occurred as a result of the many incidents of horrific abuses of power resulting in participant injury and death for the sake of research or other purposes. A review of the history of human research atrocities reveals all too clearly the need for ethical guidelines for international research, stemming primarily from the areas of medical and business research. Exploitation in the past (e.g., Nazi doctors in German concentration camps; the Tuskegee syphilis case; New Zealand's women with cervical cancer case; see Benatar &

Singer, 2000), which resulted in devastating harm to individual participants, fostered the development of significant efforts to monitor medical research practices to ensure that participants are protected. However, a systematic set of clear and universally accepted ethical guidelines for monitoring all research projects worldwide does not yet exist. The necessary knowledge and expertise needed to facilitate ethically sound research varies greatly across the world and the person or group primarily responsible for evaluating whether the project meets ethical standards is not clear. Should it be the IRB of the researcher's institution (when the researcher is not a member of the community in which the ISL takes place) or of the host community? What should be done when no such local IRB exists? How is the safety of the participants ensured?

In response to the above issues, specific guidelines for the protection of participants in biomedical research evolved. The Nuremberg Code (1949), the Universal Declaration of Human Rights (United Nations, 1948), the Declaration of Helsinki, which is a code for research and experimentation issued by the World Medical Association (2008), and the international research ethics guidelines produced by the Council for International Organizations of Medical Sciences (CIOMS) (2002) in collaboration with the World Health Organization, are examples of the international community's regulation of research practices to prevent further abuses. In the United States, The Belmont Report was released by the National Commission for the Protection of Human Subjects of Biomedical and Behavioral Research (1979) under the U.S. National Research Act.

The Nuremberg Code (1949), which carried no legally enforceable statute, was the first international call for the necessity of voluntary participation in research and informed consent. In 1948, the General Assembly of the United Nations adopted and proclaimed the Universal Declaration of Human Rights, an advisory document of 30 articles outlining the human rights guaranteed to all people. The Declaration of Helsinki, a document produced by the World Medical Association (2008) in 1964, established recommendations for medical doctors who conducted biomedical research with human participants. The key contribution of the Helsinki document was the concept that risks should not exceed benefits, as discussed previously. In response to rapidly changing factors in the medical research world, The Council for International Organizations of Medical Sciences (CIOMS) (2002) recognized "advances in medicine and biotechnology, changing research practices such as multinational field trials, experimentation involving vulnerable population groups, and also a changing view, in rich and poor countries, that research involving human subjects was largely beneficial and not threatening." The Council revised the *International Ethical Guidelines for Biomedical Research Involving Human*

Subjects three times in the past 30 years, most recently in 2002 when the Council affirmed:

> The challenge to international research ethics is to apply universal ethical principles to biomedical research in a multicultural world with a multiplicity of health-care systems and considerable variation in standards of health care. The Guidelines take the position that research involving human subjects must not violate any universally applicable ethical standards, but acknowledge that, in superficial aspects, the application of the ethical principles, e.g., in relation to individual autonomy and informed consent, needs to take account of cultural values, while respecting absolutely the ethical standards.

The Belmont Report declared three basic ethical principles: respect for persons, beneficence, and justice. The practical applications of these three principles involved informed consent, assessment of risks and benefits, and the selection of participants (The National Commission for the Protection of Human Subjects of Biomedical and Behavioral Research, 1979).

The revolution in the need and interest to protect human participants in research continues today. The United Nations Educational Scientific and Cultural Organization (UNESCO) is the leading United Nations organization working on ethics as applied to the sciences. In 1998, the World Commission on the Ethics of Scientific Knowledge and Technology (COMEST) was established as an intellectual forum and international advisory body responsible for the exchange of information among the scientific community to "examine fundamental ethical questions" (United Nations Educational Scientific and Cultural Organization, 2007). COMEST is responsible for ethics educational programs, conference series and the Global Observatory, an online database with coverage of bioethics and other areas of applied ethics in science and technology. This organization is also responsible for drafting the *Declaration on Science and the Use of Scientific Knowledge* and the *Science Agenda—Framework for Action.*

The United Nations is initiating these activities to discuss and develop an international perspective on research ethics, involving as many countries as are willing to participate. Following a recommendation by COMEST, the Division of Ethics of Science and Technology (2006) initiated a survey of science ethics and, in particular, is studying existing codes of conduct and codes of ethics for scientists. In an interim report published by UNESCO in fall 2006, 65 codes from three geographical areas (Asia and Pacific, Europe, and North America) were analyzed on several criteria. In terms of content of the codes, the analysis consisted of internal statements (those that refer to the scientist's ethical behavior) and external statements (those related to responsibility toward society). The most frequently mentioned internal statement for all disciplines surveyed was *confidentiality of information,* followed by *maintain/upgrade professional competence.* Due to the overrepresentation of codes from engineering, physics, and mathematics, *environmental responsibility* was the most frequently identified external statement. However, *public welfare and safety* were cited in all disciplines' codes (United Nations Educational Scientific and Cultural Organization, 2007).

Cross-Cultural/Community-Based Research

Cross-cultural research offers ISL researchers a wealth of information and expertise in conducting multinational and cross-cultural research. Cross-cultural researchers often perceive their values, cultural understanding, and ethical standards as universal and reflecting the larger global community. Involvement in quality social science research requires sensitivity to the culture and ethical standards of the host community and its research participants (Erasmus, chapter 15; Triandis, 1994). Therefore, Pollard (1992) and Fontes (1998) recommend that cross-cultural research, initiated by external researchers, involve (a) familiarity and knowledge about the host community and participants being studied; (b) effective and clear communication between visiting researchers and the host community; (c) a research purpose that serves the interests and needs of the host community and research participants; (d) a research agenda and research team that exhibits cultural sensitivity throughout the process; (e) research activities that are valuable and beneficial to not only the visiting researchers but also to the host community and the participants; (f) the appropriate dissemination of research results to the host community; and (g) the potential for collaboration with host community researchers. Fontes (1998) emphasizes that "extra care must be taken in the design, implementation, data analysis, and dissemination of the research to avoid disempowering the participants" (p. 55). Dalton and McVilly (2004) also raise concerns about the integrity of the research design. They suggest that careful attention be given to cultural diversity among participants and differing legal requirements across jurisdictions.

Similarly, extensive research and writing have been done on community-based research, which extends and adds complexity to basic principles of ethical research (Kiely & Hartman, chapter 13; Kimmel, 1988; Strand, Marullo, Cutforth, Stoecker, & Donohue, 2003). Traditional research has primarily focused on ensuring the well-being of individual participants, while community-based research must also consider the larger societal context and community in which that research takes place (Kimmel, 1988).

Thus, ethical considerations of community-based research are highly applicable to service learning research, both domestic and international, especially in the following two ways. First, research on service learning, although not yet extensive (Eyler, chapter 10), has demonstrated that such projects have a strong and lasting impact on the students as well as the community partners involved (Astin & Sax, 1998; Markus, Howard, & King, 1993; Osborne, Hammerich, & Hensley, 1998; Vogelgesang & Astin, 2000). Similar levels of impact have been found in community-based research (Kimmel, 1988). Given that potential impact, ethical issues such as voluntariness (i.e., coercion and deception), privacy, autonomy, information sharing, and control over dissemination of results, all become magnified in ISL research.

Second, the role of the researcher, who often plays an active part in the project, also is more complex than is the case in non-applied venues (Kiely & Hartman, chapter 13; Minkler, 2004; Quigley, 2007; Shore, 2007). In research on these ethical issues in community-based research, some potential problem areas that have been identified include (a) burdening and potentially exploiting the community due to the requirements of the project (e.g., IRB approval process, debriefing, demands on time due to students' presence); (b) failing to provide and obtain full informed consent; (c) not allowing community partners to choose their level of involvement; (d) designing and/or executing research with methodologies that lead to inaccurate or unusable results; and (e) promoting projects that do not reflect a real and mutually beneficial partnership between the researchers and the community (Kimmel, 1988; Quigley, 2007).

In sum, there are several bodies of work that provide some guidance when conducting research on ISL. Primarily, research from cross-cultural disciplines, national and international discussions of ethical issues, and community-based and international research provide ethical guidelines directly applicable to ISL research and highlight salient issues in meeting those guidelines. Based on a review of specific ethical issues, common themes, principles, declarations and international codes of research ethics (World Medical Association, UNESCO, International Institute of Health Studies, International School Psychologists Association, International Union of Psychological Science, World Council of Anthropological Associations, International Confederation of Midwives, International Nursing Council, International Sociological Association, International Society for Pharmacoeconomics and Outcomes Research, among others), we selected principles and developed the following ethical guidelines for research on ISL.

Introduction of Principles

In order to develop this set of ethical guidelines for research on ISL, principles upon which such standards are based must be delineated. The Belmont Report, prepared by the U.S. National Commission for the Protection of Human Subjects of Biomedical and Behavioral Research (1979), summarized existing practice into three basic ethical principles—autonomy/respect for persons, beneficence, and justice. Beauchamp and Childress (2001) added nonmaleficence. Chapdelaine, Ruiz, Warchal, and Wells (2005) offered ethical principles specific to service learning, which included fidelity and integrity in addition to the above list of principles. Together, the ethical principles of autonomy and respect for people's rights, beneficence, nonmaleficence, justice, fidelity, and integrity provide the basis against which all ISL research should be guided, in addition to prescribed guidelines of the IRB and the host country.

Prior to the delineation of these principles, we must recognize, as aforementioned, that the use of principles reflects a positivistic and individualistic approach to ethical standards. Even if universal principles are agreed upon, these would still be subject to different understandings and therefore must be applied grounded in the culture of the host community. For example, the researcher must recognize that impartiality is a western ideal that is perhaps not even desirable in certain contexts. Rather, being an active participant in the research process might facilitate better understanding of the project and its outcomes.

Autonomy, as a self-governing state, means that the individual has a moral responsibility for one's own actions. In research on ISL, autonomy implies that the researcher oversees the research process and allows the participants the freedom to decide on their involvement in the project. Both researcher and participants make informed, uncoerced decisions, while acknowledging that conflicts of interest may influence such decisions. Furthermore, the researcher must assure the right to privacy, confidentiality, and self-determination of the participants. The researcher should be aware and respect the participants in their cultural context.

Beneficence is the ethical principle of doing good and helping others. The researcher must safeguard the welfare and rights of the participants. However, this principle is based on how one defines good. Consequently, an important question is to determine "Who benefits from the research project?"

Nonmaleficence is the ethical principle of doing no harm. It is different from beneficence, because the obligation to not harm others is different from the obligation to help others. In research, a risk/benefit analysis should be performed prior to the process to determine the potential of harm. When harm occurs due to poor oversight of the consequences of the research project (the negative consequences could have been estimated or reasonable care was not taken), the duty to cause no harm was breached (whether the harm was intended or not).

Justice is the ethical principle that ensures impartiality, fair treatment of all persons, and fair representation of facts. Participants should be chosen based on the goals and design of the research project. The researcher must make sure that the information collected as well as the presentation of results and conclusions are representative of the participants' responses and intentions.

Fidelity is the loyalty to one's duty. The researcher must be aware of responsibility to the scientific community as well as the particular groups participating in the research. The researcher should also cooperate with other professionals and institutions and avoid conflicts of interest.

Integrity is the quality of being honest and consistently using a framework or set core of principles. The researcher must follow scientific guidelines, provide as much information as possible to the participants, avoid deception, and present results that are accurate and verifiable.

Ethical Standards for ISL

Based on our review of ethical guidelines for international research and the above principles, we propose aspirational ethical standards for research on ISL in the following four categories: (a) researchers' competency and responsibilities; (b) the rights of participants; (c) sponsorship; and (d) publication and dissemination of results (Table 14.1, p. 338.)

Researchers' Competency and Responsibilities

An ethical issue that takes on new relevance in research on ISL is the researcher's level of competency to design and implement the research study. When possible, the research should be reviewed for methodological and scientific standards, even prior to the delineation of procedures regarding participants. Bringle, Hatcher, and Williams (chapter 12) and Eyler (chapter 10) provide guidelines for evaluating quantitative research, while Kiely and Hartman (chapter 13) detail criteria for qualitative research. Under the competency sphere, the following questions should be addressed: Does the researcher understand the context (e.g., legal, social, political, cultural) within which the research will be conducted (see Erasmus, chapter 15; Sutton, chapter 7)? Is the research conducted by a team including members of the culture and language group to assure effective communication, trust, and genuine consent involving members of the local community in the research process (Kahn, chapter 6; Kiely & Hartman, chapter 13; Tonkin, chapter 9)? Is the research applicable to the culture? Does the research project apply knowledge of current, standard research practice and scientific principles?

The researcher is ultimately responsible for ensuring the ethical and scientific integrity of the project. The design should be reviewed and approved by an ethics committee in the United States, the host country, or both, to consider information about potential risks and benefits, as mentioned earlier. Other aspects of research, such as deception, debriefing, consent, funding, sponsorship, institutional affiliations, other potential conflicts of interest, and incentives for participants, should be reviewed. Moreover, laws and regulations of the country in which the research is performed need to be understood and followed. Under the researcher's responsibility is also the issue of identifying who benefits from the research project. Is the researcher studying what is in the best interests of the participants (whether they are students, colleges or universities, agencies or communities, or faculty)?

There can be circumstances in which adhering to "best research practices" according to one set of criteria may cause other ethical concerns. For example, an often-used technique in field research to isolate the impact of a program (in this case, the service learning project) is to employ the use of a control group, that is, a community group similar to the target population that would not benefit from the service learning project, for comparison purposes. Given community needs, is it appropriate to deny the service learning project to particular community members? Other complicating factors include potential power imbalances, the use of deception, informed consent, and other methodological techniques (e.g., random assignment). Those engaging in research on ISL must carefully consider such ethical implications of all selected research protocols and seek external review.

Another methodological issue that must be carefully considered in ISL research is language barriers. For any written research materials, the researchers should follow recommended practices of appropriate translation, including back translation (i.e., after the document is translated, have someone translate it back to the original language to determine if intention has been maintained). Written and oral language translators should be part of the host community. However, to the greatest extent possible, they should be independent from the research project itself, such that their role is not influenced by their own interests in the project. For example, if a participant is criticizing the project, the translator may be hesitant to give that feedback without censure to the researcher for fear of losing the benefits associated with the project.

With these issues in mind, we propose the following set of ethical guidelines related to the researcher's responsibilities and competency at the beginning of research on ISL:

- **Overall Responsibilities of Researchers**
  - ○ Researchers will treat all involved in the ISL research process with respect and dignity.
  - ○ Researchers will be sensitive to and knowledgeable about differences in culture, values, attitudes, and opinions.
  - ○ Researchers will be adequately trained for carrying out and conducting the ISL research.
  - ○ Researchers will follow laws and regulations of the researchers' home country and those of the host country.
  - ○ Researchers will follow professional codes of ethics throughout the ISL research.
  - ○ Researchers will conduct the ISL research as outlined in the proposal and approved by the review committees. Any methodological or ethical issues that arise should be identified and dealt with during the process and reported to the respective committees.
  - ○ Researchers will provide accurate information about the ISL research to the host community.
  - ○ Researchers will maintain trust in the ISL research process among participants and/or those involved in the host community.
  - ○ Researchers will provide periodic progress reports to representatives of the host community on the status of the ISL research.
- **Competency of Researchers**
  - ○ If not a member of the host community, researchers will be familiar with the cultural, political, and social history of the host community.
  - ○ Researchers will use only those methodologies for which the researchers have the appropriate training, qualifications, experience, and expertise.
- **Research Design**
  - ○ In planning the ISL research, the feasibility of the proposed research will be determined. The risks and benefits should be clearly identified and solutions or contingency plans should be proposed for potential problems.
  - ○ Standards of sound scientific and ethical investigation in the evaluation of the ISL research design will be followed (e.g., sample, sources of data, consent, meeting professional ethical standards).

- ○ The value and merit of the proposed ISL research will be of utmost importance (e.g., to ISL scholars and to the citizens of the host community).
- ○ The safety and protection of participants and those affected by the proposed ISL research will be determined by the researchers as they address potential harm and the proposed project is reviewed by relevant groups.
- ○ Language that is reasonably understandable to relevant constituencies will be used throughout the ISL research process.
- ○ The method of data collection will be identified in the development of the ISL research design.
- **Methodological and Ethical Review**
  - ○ The ISL research project will be presented for methodological review.
  - ○ The ISL research project will be presented to an established international institutional review board, local ethics committee, and the involved host country ethical review process.

Rights of Participants

As discussed previously, the protection and rights of participants in multinational research is a primary area of concern for international research organizations and should receive equal attention when planning ISL projects. In regard to participants' rights, the researcher should assure, first and foremost, protection from harm. The researcher should have rigorous safeguards in place to protect the health, welfare, and safety of participants.

The issue of informed consent takes on new challenges when international participants are involved. The researcher should provide enough information for the participant to make an educated decision about participation in the research project. The information should educate participants on the nature and purpose of the research, who is responsible for the implementation of the research project, the right of voluntary participation, the right to withdraw from the project at any time with no negative consequences, and the potential risks and benefits to the participants and the community. Complicating the matter of informed consent is the requirement that the information be provided in a manner that the participants can understand. This may involve using an advocate who can interpret the consent form and obtain verbal approval from participants who may not be able to read and/or write. Several researchers (Brown, 1994; Dalton & McVilly 2004) suggest that fully informed consent may not be possible at the beginning of a project and that "process consent" may be necessary, where participants' involvement is renegotiated at regular intervals throughout the project, providing the participants the opportunity to withdraw without penalty at each new phase of the research. Brown (1994) recommends using the term "empowered consent" as it more accurately reflects the intent of the process by providing participants with complete and meaningful disclosure that supports their freedom to engage fully in the research (therapy) process, not merely have the process presented to them. This will require a statement in the research proposal and IRB application reflecting this regular review process. In addition, there may be a need to expand the traditional definition of informed consent, which emphasizes individual choice, to one that is more collectivistic in nature; that is, community consent. Achieving these ethical objectives requires continual reevaluation and consultation throughout the research process, and willingness to adapt the research plan to meet changing community needs and concerns.

Another issue in the protection of the participants is the assurance of confidentiality of information. When possible, information should also be kept anonymous in order to protect the participants' privacy, unless the participants are informed, understand the consequences, and approve the use of identifying information. If participants agree to disclose their identity or are easily identifiable (e.g., through photos, demographic information), they should be warned about potential consequences upon presentation and publication of the research. When the participants are students, there should be an alternative to participation in the research project. And when compensation is available, it should not be excessive to the point of coercing participants. We propose the following ethical guidelines related to the protection and rights of participants in ISL research:

- **Protection from Harm**
  - Participants will be protected from any unacceptable harm or costs they might incur as a result of participating in the research project.
- **Informed Consent**
  - Participants will be provided with enough information to make an educated decision about their participation in the ISL research project.
  - Participation in the ISL research project will be voluntary.
  - Participants will have the right to withdraw from the ISL research project at any time without negative consequences.
  - Participants will be provided with a description of potential risks and benefits of the ISL research project to help inform their decision.
  - Informed consent will be provided in the native language of the participants and in a manner that can be easily understood by the participants.

   ◦ Information about the ISL research will be provided as needed throughout the project and participants' voluntary agreement renegotiated as necessary.
- **Confidentiality**
   ◦ Information about participants will be kept confidential and, whenever possible, anonymous.
   ◦ When personal information about participants is used, participants will be fully informed about the potential consequences, including publication of the ISL research.

Sponsorship

Another important aspect to consider in research on ISL is sponsorship. A critical issue is the ownership of the research and its outcomes, especially with regard to the access of the sponsor to the research project during the process, proprietary issues related to the information collected during the research, and how the credits will be presented in any publications. Traditionally, the researcher is responsible for all aspects of the research process: content, methodology, selection of participants, analysis, conclusions, publication format, printing, copyright, distribution, and promotion. However, when the research has a sponsor, questions of conflict of interest, confidentiality of research participants, allocation of research funds, independence, and objectivity can arise. Such questions should be clarified prior to the onset of the research project in order to ensure the credibility of the research project and the interests of those involved.

Moreover, the sponsoring organization must be willing to assume full responsibility for the project, such that they must fully commit to providing needed resources. Especially relevant in this regard is the issue of sustainability. That is, consideration of the long-term consequences of the project and how the sponsoring institution can maintain its support for the international learning community are especially critical.

In participatory community-based research in which community residents become coresearchers and, in effect, sponsors (i.e., supporters) of the research, these issues become inherently more complex. As Kiely and Hartman (chapter 13) discuss, qualitative research paradigms rely on the participants to authenticate the research enterprise and establishing the basis for credit and recognition of various roles warrants attention by the primary researcher. These issues are also made salient by the norm of reciprocity that accompanies the design of service learning experiences (Longo & Saltmarsh, chapter 4).

Consequently, the following ethical guidelines are recommended concerning sponsorship:

- **Ownership**
  - In order to maintain professional autonomy and objectivity, the researchers will determine the respective roles and responsibilities of the researchers and the sponsors, including a discussion of ownership and decisions about proprietary issues.
- **Risks and Benefits**
  - Researchers will determine the risks and benefits of the sponsorship in accordance with university policy and IRB guidelines.
  - Researchers will inform sponsors of scientific procedures and the potential risks of conclusions that do not match expectations.
- **Conflict of Interest**
  - Researchers will identify, mitigate, and/or clarify any conflicts of interest.
- **Confidentiality Related to Sponsorship**
  - Researchers will protect the confidentiality of the research participants from sponsors.
  - Researchers will provide only summary data to sponsors, unless other arrangements have been negotiated ahead of time and are understood by all relevant constituencies.
  - Researchers will not release survey responses without the consent of respondents.
- **Research Funds**
  - Researchers will use funds for agreed-upon purposes.

Publication and Dissemination of Results

Ethical issues related to ISL research extend to the very end of the research process: publication and dissemination of the results. There are two types of dissemination, both of which raise ethical issues. First, the research team has an ethical obligation to share the results of the project with those involved in the service learning project—other educators, students, and community partners. Second, the researcher frequently will also wish to publicize the results of the ISL project, so that others might benefit from the information gained as a result of the research project. For both types of dissemination, the aforementioned ethical principles must be adhered to, as improper dissemination could cause harm to ISL constituents, compromise the integrity of the work, or erode benefits gained from the service learning project.

Ownership of the results should be viewed from the lens of mutuality and reciprocity (Longo & Saltmarsh, chapter 4). To some extent, all those involved in service learning—community partners, faculty, and students—have some ownership of the results. All these voices must be considered when decisions regarding dissemination and publication are made. Results must be shared with the ISL community in a manner that is accessible and allows for review and feedback. Prior to the onset of the research project, possible outcomes of the research should be discussed with all involved parties, including the potential negative consequences of the results. At that time, decisions regarding how such results will be shared should be made. We, therefore, recommend the following ethical guidelines concerning the publication and dissemination of results related to ISL research:

- **Authorship**
  - Sponsors of the research will be identified along with an explanation of their relationship to the research, especially if such relationships may have affected the nature and scope of the project.
  - All individuals who contributed significantly to the research will be recognized as coauthors or listed in the acknowledgments section of the publication. When appropriate, such acknowledgment of contributions will include the instructors, student participants, and the community partners.
  - All references to others' work will be referenced and cited appropriately.
- **Accuracy of Reporting and Accessibility**
  - All data will be accurate and verifiable. If significant errors are found after publication of the results, researchers will take steps to correct such errors by issuing retractions or corrections in appropriate venues.
  - When sharing the results of the project, researchers will ensure that the information is accessible and understandable to the community partners. For example, results might be summarized in a brief letter or executive summary that is translated into the native language of the community for dissemination to the participants.
  - When the ISL research results are shared with the community partners, this information will include recommendations on how the results might be used to benefit the community through education or application.

- **Confidentiality and Consent**
  - ○ Any sharing of ISL research will be done in such a manner that the anonymity and confidentiality of the research participants are maintained. Any potentially identifying information such as demographics will only be included to the extent that it does not identify individuals in the study, unless consent has been obtained.
  - ○ Any qualitative data such as narratives from those involved in the ISL research will only be included in the published results if consent from the participant to include such narrative data has been obtained.
  - ○ If other researchers request data for continuing research purposes, such data will only be released if confidentiality and/or anonymity of the research participants are preserved or unless additional consent has been obtained.
- **Minimizing Risk due to Dissemination**
  - ○ Prior to dissemination and publication of the ISL study's outcomes, a careful assessment of potential consequences of the research results in terms of what they reveal about the efficacy of the service learning project will be made.
  - ○ Researchers and community partners will assess and discuss anticipated negative consequences prior to publication.

Conclusion

Even though the ethical standards proposed above are relevant to all aspects of an ISL research project, some types of ISL research require special consideration of particular standards. For instance, when the researcher is investigating a population that cannot provide consent on their own, the guidelines regarding the protection of participants requires even more attention, compared to projects in which participants are faculty and/or students. When the participants are from a different culture or country than the researcher, the ethical guidelines concerning the researcher's responsibility to understand the language, cultural, social, economic, and political issues may have a considerable impact on the project. When the dissemination of research results may bring harm to the participants, the researcher and community partners need to consider those standards regarding publication and dissemination of the ISL research results more cautiously.

These guidelines, as aspirational ethical standards, should be applied prior to beginning the research on an ISL course or program. The standards by themselves may not be sufficient to address all ethical dilemmas. For some

TABLE 14.1
Ethical Guidelines for Research on International Service Learning

Researcher's Competency and Responsibilities

- **Overall Responsibilities of Researchers**
  - Researchers will treat all involved in the ISL research process with respect and dignity.
  - Researchers will be sensitive to and knowledgeable about differences in culture,
  - values, attitudes, and opinions.
  - Researchers will be adequately trained for carrying out and conducting the ISL research.
  - Researchers will follow laws and regulations of the researchers' home country and those of the host country.
  - Researchers will follow the professional code of ethics throughout the ISL research.
  - Researchers will conduct the ISL research as outlined in the proposal and approved by the review committees. Any methodological or ethical issues that arise should be identified and dealt with during the process and reported to the respective committees.
  - Researchers will provide accurate information about the ISL research to the host community.
  - Researchers will maintain trust in the ISL research process among participants and/or those involved in the host community.
  - Researchers will provide periodic progress reports to representatives of the host community on the status of the ISL research.
- **Competency of Researchers**
  - If not a member of the host community, researchers will be familiar with the cultural, political, and social history of the host community.
  - Researchers will use only those methodologies for which the researchers have the appropriate training, qualifications, and expertise.
- **Research Design**
  - In planning the ISL research, the feasibility of the proposed research will be determined. The risks and benefits should be clearly identified and solutions or contingency plans should be proposed for potential problems.
  - Standards of sound scientific and ethical investigation in the evaluation of the ISL research design will be followed (e.g., sample, sources of data, consent, meeting professional ethical standards).
  - The value and merit of the proposed ISL research will be of utmost importance (e.g., to ISL scholars and to the citizens of the host community).
  - The safety and protection of participants and those affected by the proposed ISL research will be determined by the researchers as they address potential harm and the proposed project is reviewed by relevant groups.
  - Language that is reasonably understandable to relevant constituencies will be used throughout the ISL research process.
  - The method of data collection will be identified in the development of the ISL research design.

TABLE 14.1
(*Continued*)

- **Methodological and Ethical Review**
  - ○ The ISL research project will be presented for methodological review.
  - ○ The ISL research project will be presented to an established international institutional review board, local ethics committee, and the involved host country ethical review process.

Rights of Participants

- **Protection from Harm**
  - ○ Participants will be protected from any unacceptable harm or costs they might incur as a result of participating in the research project.
- **Informed Consent**
  - ○ Participants will be provided with enough information to make an educated decision about their participation in the ISL research project.
  - ○ Participation in the ISL research project will be voluntary.
  - ○ Participants will have the right to withdraw from the ISL research project at any time without negative consequences.
  - ○ Participants will be provided with a description of potential risks and benefits of the ISL research project to help inform their decision.
  - ○ Informed consent will be provided in the native language of the participants and in a manner that can be easily understood by the participants.
  - ○ Information about the ISL research will be provided as needed throughout the project and participants' voluntary agreement renegotiated as necessary.
- **Confidentiality**
  - ○ Information about participants will be kept confidential and, whenever possible, anonymous.
  - ○ When personal information about participants is used, participants will be fully informed about the potential consequences, including publication of the ISL research.

Sponsorship

- **Ownership**
  - ○ In order to maintain professional autonomy and objectivity, the researchers will determine the respective roles and responsibilities of the researchers and the sponsors, including a discussion of ownership and decisions about proprietary issues.
- **Risks and Benefits**
  - ○ Researchers will determine the risks and benefits of the sponsorship in accordance with university policy and IRB guidelines.
  - ○ Researchers will inform sponsors of scientific procedures and the potential risks of conclusions that do not match expectations.

(*continued*)

TABLE 14.1
(*Continued*)

- **Conflict of Interest**
  - ○ Researchers will identify, mitigate, and/or clarify any conflicts of interest.
- **Confidentiality Related to Sponsorship**
  - ○ Researchers will protect the confidentiality of the research participants from sponsors.
  - ○ Researchers will provide only summary data to sponsors, unless other arrangements have been negotiated ahead of time and are understood by all relevant constituencies.
  - ○ Researchers will not release survey responses without the consent of respondents.
- **Research Funds**
  - ○ Researchers will use funds for agreed-upon purposes.

Publication and Dissemination

- **Authorship**
  - ○ Sponsors of the research will be identified along with an explanation of their relationship to the research, especially if such relationships may have affected the nature and scope of the project.
  - ○ All individuals who contributed significantly to the research will be recognized as coauthors or listed in the acknowledgments section of the publication. When appropriate, such acknowledgment of contributions will include the instructors, student participants, and the community partners.
  - ○ All references to others' work will be referenced and cited appropriately.
- **Accuracy of Reporting and Accessibility**
  - ○ All data will be accurate and verifiable. If significant errors are found after publication of the results, researchers will take steps to correct such errors by issuing retractions or corrections in appropriate venues.
  - ○ When sharing the results of the project, researchers will ensure that the information is accessible and understandable to the community partners. For example, results might be summarized in a brief letter or executive summary that is translated into the native language of the community for dissemination to the participants.
  - ○ When the ISL research results are shared with the community partners, this information will include recommendations on how results might be used to benefit the community through education or application.
- **Confidentiality and Consent**
  - ○ Any sharing of ISL research will be done in such a manner that the anonymity and confidentiality of the research participants are maintained. Any potentially identifying information such as demographics will only be included to the extent that it does not identify individuals in the study, unless consent has been obtained.

TABLE 14.1
(Continued)

○ Any qualitative data such as narratives from those involved in the ISL research will only be included in the published results if consent from the participant to include such narrative data has been obtained.

○ If other researchers request data for continuing research purposes, such data will only be released if confidentiality and/or anonymity of the research participants are/is preserved or unless consent has been obtained.

- **Minimizing Risk due to Dissemination**

○ Prior to dissemination and publication of the ISL study's outcomes, a careful assessment of potential consequences of the research results in terms of what they reveal about the efficacy of the service learning project will be made.

○ Researchers and community partners will assess and discuss anticipated negative consequences prior to publication.

---

dilemmas, the guidelines may conflict, making adherence to the code more challenging and review by disinterested parties more central prior to final decisions about the design of the research project. When such cases occur, the next step should be to consider the ethical principles, which are the foundation of the standards. In any case, consultation with other experts may be necessary. Such experts might include members of the community, those having expertise with regard to cultural or methodological issues and content knowledge, and IRB members. The ISL researcher should consider several possible solutions to each issue or dilemma and evaluate the risk and benefit of such solutions. Consequently, the researcher, hopefully in conjunction with community partners or other participants, should select the action that would result in the best outcome for all parties involved, which may include not conducting the research. Hopefully, these ethical guidelines will enable researchers to conduct research on ISL that benefits community partners and future service learning and ISL initiatives.

References

Astin, A. W., & Sax, L. J. (1998). How undergraduates are affected by service participation. *Journal of College Student Development, 39,* 251–263.

Beauchamp, T. L., & Childress, J. F. (2001). *Principles of biomedical ethics* (5th ed.). New York, NY: Oxford University Press.

Benatar, S. R., & Singer P. A. (2000). A new look at international research ethics. *British Journal of Medicine, 321,* 824–826.

Bogolub, E. G., & Thomas, N. (2005). Parental consent and the ethics of research with foster children: Beginning a cross-cultural dialogue. *Qualitative Social Work: Research and Practice, 4,* 271–292.

Brown, L. S. (1994). *Subversive dialogues: Theory in feminist therapy*. New York, NY: Basic.

Chapdelaine, A., Ruiz, A., Warchal, J., & Wells, C. (2005). *Service-learning code of ethics*. Bolton, MA: Anker.

Chisholm, L. A. (2004). Foreword. In H. Tonkin (Ed.), *Service-learning across cultures: Promise & achievement* (pp. ix–xi). New York, NY: The International Partnership for Service-learning and Leadership.

Cohen, J. R., Pant, L.W., & Sharp, D. J. (1996). A methodological note on cross-cultural accounting ethics research. *International Journal of Accounting, 31,* 55–66.

Council for International Organizations of Medical Sciences (CIOMS). (2002). *International ethical guidelines for biomedical research involving human subjects.* Geneva, Switzerland: World Health Organization. Retrieved July 21, 2009, from http://www. cioms.ch/frame_guidelines_nov_2002.htm

Dalton, A. J., & McVilly, K. R. (2004). Ethics guidelines for international, multicenter research involving people with intellectual disabilities. *Journal of Policy and Practice in Intellectual Disabilities, 1,* 57–70.

Division of Ethics of Science and Technology. (2006). *Interim analysis of codes of conduct and codes of ethics* (UNESCO Report No. SHS/20 06/PI/H/5). Retrieved July 21, 2009, from http://unesdoc.unesco.org/images/0014/001473/147335E.pdf

Ferrell, O. C., Fraedrich, J., & Ferrell, L. (2002). *Business ethics. Ethical decision making and cases* (5th ed.). Boston, MA: Houghton Mifflin.

Fontes, L.S. (1998). Ethics in family violence research: Cross-cultural issues. *Family Relations, 47,* 53–61.

Kimmel, A. J. (1988). *Ethics and values in applied social research. Applied social research methods series* (Vol. 12). Newbury Park, CA: Sage.

Lowenberg, G., & Conrad, K. A. (1998). *Current perspectives in industrial/ organizational psychology*. Needham Heights, MA: Allyn & Bacon.

Markus, G., Howard, J., & King, D. (1993). Integrating community service and classroom instruction enhances learning: Results from an experiment. *Educational Evaluation and Policy Analysis, 15,* 410–419.

Minkler, M. (2004). Ethical challenges for the "outside" researcher in community-based participatory research. *Health Education and Behavior, 31,* 684–697.

National Commission for the Protection of Human Subjects of Biomedical and Behavioral Research. (1979). *The Belmont Report: Ethical principles and guidelines for the protection of human subjects of research.* Retrieved July 21, 2009, from http://ohsr.od.nih.gov/guidelines/belmont.html

National Research Act of 1974, Pub. L. 93–348 (1974). Retrieved July 21, 2009, from http://thomas.loc.gov/cgi-bin/bdquery/z?d093:HR07724:@@@L|TOM:/bss/d093 query.html

Nuremberg Code. (1949). In *Trials of war criminals before the Nuremberg Military Tribunals under Control Council Law No. 10, Vol. 2* (pp. 181–182). Washington, DC: U.S. Government Printing Office. Retrieved July 21, 2009, from http://ohsr.od.nih.gov/guidelines/nuremberg.html

Osborne, R. E., Hammerich, S., & Hensley, C. (1998). Student effects of service learning: Tracking change across a semester. *Michigan Journal of Community Service learning, 5,* 5–13.

Plater, W. M., Jones, S. G., Bringle, R. G., & Clayton, P. H. (2009). Educating globally competent citizens through international service learning. In R. Lewin (Ed.), *The handbook of practice and research in study abroad: Higher education and the quest for global citizenship* (pp. 485–505). New York, NY: Routledge.

Pollard, R. Q. (1992). Cross-cultural ethics in the conduct of deafness research. *Rehabilitation Psychology, 37,* 87–101.

Punnett, B. J., & Shenkar, O. (1996). Ethics in international management research. In B. J. Punnett & O. Shenkar (Eds.), *Handbook for international management research* (pp. 145–154). Cambridge, MA: Blackwell.

Quigley, D. (2007). *Teaching research ethics for community-based participatory research*. Retrieved July 21, 2009, from http://www.researchethics.org/uploads/pdf/teaching%20research%20ethics_001.pdf

Rosenthal, R., & Rosnow, R. L. (1984). Applying Hamlet's question to the ethical conduct of research: A conceptual addendum. *American Psychologist, 39,* 561–563.

Shore, N. (2007). Community-based participatory research and the ethics review process. *Journal of Empirical Research on Human Research Ethics, 2,* 31–41.

Strand, K., Marullo, S., Cutforth, N., Stoecker, R., & Donohue, P. (2003). *Community-based research and higher education: Principles and practices.* San Francisco, CA: Jossey-Bass.

Swaidan, Z., & Hayes, L. A. (2005). Hofstede theory and cross cultural ethics conceptualization, review, and research agenda. *Journal of American Academy of Business, 6,* 10–15.

Triandis, H. C. (1994). Cross-cultural industrial and organizational psychology. In H. C. Triandis, M. D. Dunnette, & L. M. Hough (Eds.), *Handbook of industrial and organizational psychology* (2nd ed., vol. 4, pp. 103–172). Palo Alto, CA: Consulting Psychologists.

United Nations. (1948). *Universal declaration of human rights.* Retrieved July 21, 2009, from http://www.un.org/en/documents/udhr/

United Nations Educational, Scientific and Cultural Organization (UNESCO). (2007, August). *An overview of scientific programmes and initiatives in the United Nations system* (34 C/INF.13). Retrieved July 21, 2009, from http://unesdoc.unesco.org/images/0015/001521 /152140e.pdf

Vogelgesang, L. J., & Astin, A. W. (2000). Comparing the effects of service-learning and community service. *Michigan Journal of Community Service learning, 7,* 25–34.

World Medical Association. (2008). *World Medical Association Declaration of Helsinki: Ethical principles for medical research involving human subjects.* Retrieved July 21, 2009, from http://www.wma.net/e/policy/pdf/17c.pdf

PART FOUR

AN INTERNATIONAL PERSPECTIVE

15

A SOUTH AFRICAN PERSPECTIVE ON NORTH AMERICAN INTERNATIONAL SERVICE LEARNING

Mabel Erasmus

O ver the past decade, I have been involved in hosting both study abroad students and service learning students at the University of the Free State in South Africa. While I was serving as project manager of a language empowerment initiative, funded by the Flemish Community Government in Belgium, we hosted, inter alia, a Dutch student doing the work experience section of a Language Practice course and a French Ph.D. student conducting research for a dissertation on linguistic empowerment in South Africa. Since my appointment within the Community Service initiatives at the University of the Free State, and later the service learning section of the University, several groups of students from the United States, accompanied by faculty members, have visited for shorter periods. Some of the groups came for the purpose of "doing good" and "helping" "poor" South Africans, bringing with them gifts of toys, boxes of crayons, and clothes. Those who came as international service learning (ISL) students had an entirely different approach; and we were able to experience and learn how service learning differs from traditional community service approaches.

Sixty service learning courses (referred to as "modules" within academic programs in South Africa) are currently listed at the University of the Free State; we also have several key sites for multidisciplinary engagement (or flagship sites) in community settings, where service learning and community-based research take place within established partnership formations. It thus occurs more and more often that students from abroad, and some from other African countries, take part in service learning, study abroad, or community-based research activities. For me personally, and for our university with its growing emphasis on internationalization, it is thus a most opportune time to engage in a research collaborative that specifically focuses on ISL, in all its variations and myriad implications for a highly diverse set of possible participants and contexts.

Reflecting on North American ISL from a South African perspective is like holding up a mirror. The concept of service learning was fairly recently brought to South Africa from the United States; and thus, our understanding of ISL is influenced by U.S. conceptualizations and practice. In response to the call of the South African government to increase the social responsibility of higher education institutions and their students, there has recently been increasing support for the pedagogy of service learning as a valuable form of community engagement involving the active participation of higher education staff, students, and external stakeholders. The growing support largely came about as a result of the national Community—Higher Education—Service Partnerships (CHESP) initiative of the Joint Education Trust (which later became the JET Education Services section of the Trust). The CHESP initiative was launched in 1999 in partnership with the Ford Foundation and the W.K. Kellogg Foundation (Lazarus, 2001). CHESP's strong link to donor organizations and universities of the United States naturally resulted in the introduction into the South African agenda of service learning as a well-established mechanism for integrating service with the learning programs of students, and also as a preferred form of civic engagement in the United States (Thomson, Smith-Tolken, Naidoo, & Bringle, 2008). Among the myriad possibilities relating to how community engagement could be integrated with academic work through teaching and learning, service learning appeared on the South African horizon as a well-defined, well-considered pedagogy with committed advocates from the United States who were flown in regularly with U.S. donor funding through the CHESP initiative. All along, these experts have been able and willing to guide South African colleagues in exploring, investigating, and investing in service learning. Subsequently, the notion of service learning found its way into important national documents such as those produced by the Higher Education Quality Committee (HEQC, 2004a, 2004b) in preparation for the first round of institutional audits.

Misgivings about the wisdom behind importing an educational approach from the United States have increased over the past five years or so. What previously amounted mainly to a frustration with the "McDonaldization" of the world, deepened considerably after the invasion of Iraq. The persistent holding of people in detention without trial at Guantanamo Bay, and evidence of widespread torture (horrible images from the Abu Ghraib Prison; terms such as *renditions* and *water-boarding*), remind South Africans of the worst days of Apartheid, but in this case these human rights violations are/were executed overtly and on a grand, international scale. When the word "democracy" is used by the present U.S. government, many fear the worst. . . .[1] Will Iran be invaded next?

By the time we realized how unacceptable we found the actions of the United States (especially in view of our own sad and terrible past), many of us who had been participating in the CHESP initiatives had already decided that service learning could add immense value to the training of our students and to the ways in which higher education institutions are engaged with communities. In addition, the trust and appreciation we had developed for the U.S. proponents of service learning and what they stand for could not be eradicated by our apprehension about the current role of the United States in the world. In view of the persistence of the wide gap between what is stipulated by the South African Constitution, on the one hand, and the harsh realities of the lives of the majority of people in the country, on the other, we also realize that we need to work closely with colleagues in the United States and other countries in our efforts to find more effective ways to prepare students for their future roles as responsible citizens and leaders of their countries and the world. What I value, above all, in respect to what we have gained from the example of our U.S. colleagues is their willingness to validate our initiatives, almost in the spirit of Appreciative Inquiry (see Cooperrider, Whitney, & Stavros, 2008), and to listen and share without being judgmental or prescriptive, thus enabling us to believe wholeheartedly in what we can achieve through service learning.

In view of the above, the aim of my contribution to the present project will be to reflect on how I understand North American ISL, and more particularly research on North American ISL, as presented in the chapters in this volume as well as some other sources. The reflective surface (mirror) that I shall hold up will include (mainly service learning) perspectives from the South African context, as an example of a (potential) host country—the only one I know well.

Conceptualizing ISL—Opportunities for a Constructive Dialogue

According to Plater (chapter 2), ISL finds its context within the notions of internationalization and global awareness, as two of the leading issues that drive the engagement of North American higher education institutions in international activities. Plater points out that some of the many threads that are woven together in this regard include divergent motivations such as, "global economics and competition," "humanitarian concerns," "global philanthropy," and "the press for democratic societies." With a view to ISL, Plater frames the response of North American higher education to the growing internationalization movement in terms of "a new insight regarding the way in which globally competent citizenship might be defined and developed as a conceptual model" (chapter 2). My contention is that perspectives from host countries of ISL students could and should add to these insights.

To me, it seems as if there is still a need to find a more balanced approach (Furco, 1996) to potential ISL outcomes, namely, between (a) learning and development outcomes for students (e.g., globally competent citizenship), and (b) service or other outcomes for host country community participants (not to be referred to as "beneficiaries" or "recipients"). This is underscored by the question posed by Tonkin (chapter 9) as to whether the roots of ISL are more deeply embedded in community service or in study abroad. The key to the search for a more balanced conceptualization lies in the recognition that ISL involves a multiplicity of actors, perspectives, policies, and the like, broadly represented by the service learners themselves and the population with which they interact (Tonkin, chapter 9). The chapters in this publication, and my personal experience with U.S. ISL students, leads me to concur with Tonkin's contention that the North American ISL agenda (my term) is currently determined largely by the U.S. higher education structures, ideologies of service and engagement, and concepts of experiential learning. The following statement also seems valid: "American models of ISL stress [the] impact on [the] student—sometimes to an unsettling degree" (Tonkin, chapter 9). This leaves us with the following question: To what extent does the ISL enterprise exist to serve a North American purpose?

Ironically, or perhaps typically, the above reminds me of our more painful local service learning experiences; that is, those wake-up calls that occur when community partners have the courage to warn the university that the latter is perceived to be mainly serving its own purposes through its service learning agenda. It is therefore from a critical, self-reflective vantage point that I present my South African-based perspectives, as tentative contributions to future dialogue with a (potential) host country. This is also in response to Tonkin's question: "How can service, learning, and service learning be defined and redefined from multiple (non-United States) perspectives?" (chapter 9). This question in itself opens up opportunities for collaborative research, including comparative studies that could be mutually enriching. For example, working with Julie Hatcher (Hatcher & Erasmus, 2008), we draw comparisons between the U.S. approach to service learning as it relates to John Dewey's theory of the role of education in a democracy, and the South African approach, with reference to an African perspective (i.e., "education for self-definition and self-reliance," as proposed by Nyerere [Assié-Lumumba, 2005, pp. 51–52]). Nyerere's educational philosophy contributed valuable insight in terms of the contention that developing countries should be wary of situations in which they are forced into juxtaposition with external ideas and realities, but should rather be pro-active and strive toward "fusion by choice" (Assié-Lumumba, 2005, pp. 38–53) from a position of self-affirmation when faced by strong external influences. I saw this as a constructive way of looking at how service learning is finding its South African space; it might also be an appropriate way for ISL host countries to deal with this form of U.S. involvement.

Service learning, the primary lens through which I currently view ISL, is brand new in South Africa compared to the United States and, thus, still needs to find its academic space and an authentic, local voice. In South African publications (Bender, Daniels, Lazarus, Naudé, & Sattar, 2006, p. 24; HEQC/JET, 2006, p. 16), the definition of service learning by Bringle and Hatcher (2004, p. 127) is cited. In addition, theoretical and conceptual frameworks are based on experiential learning (e.g., Dewey, 1916, 1933; Kolb, 1984) and the well-known typology of student engagement put forward by Furco (1996). From the South African experience of working in the field of service learning, however, it has become clear that our circumstances demand that we add indigenous conceptualizations and emphasize aspects that will reflect our context more effectively (Hatcher & Erasmus, 2008; Thomson et al., 2008). The definition of service learning that we work with at the University of the Free State thus includes the following explicit reference to the nature of the partnerships required:

> [Service learning] requires a collaborative partnership context that enhances mutual, reciprocal teaching and learning among all members of the partnership (lecturers and students, members of the communities and representatives of the service sector). (University of the Free State, 2006)

It is encouraging to read U.S. problematizations of the conceptualization of service learning, which would naturally also, at least in part, be applicable in the case of ISL. One example is Beilke's (2005) argument that the educational ideas of Boyer (1990, 1994), an important impetus behind civic engagement and service learning in America, are deeply elitist, essentially contending that the world is to be "acted upon" by academic elites. Another example is Butin's (2006) warning that service learning has taken on the status of a "grand narrative" in the United States. He argues that "there may be a fundamental and unbridgeable gap between the rhetoric and reality of the aspirations of the present-day service learning movement" (Butin, 2006, p. 474). In South Africa, service learning proponents also find themselves grappling with philosophical, paradigmatic, and epistemological issues—owing to the highly politicized environment in which higher education is attempting to reposition itself and redefine its role while being pulled in many directions. This situation is aggravated by a range of "morbid symptoms" (to quote the Marxist, Antonio Gramsci, 1971) resulting from the recent consecutive interregnums—previously between Apartheid and democracy; more recently between the more elitist Mbeki-era and the Zuma or populist era. One such challenge lies in finding a disciplinary home and/or departmental positioning for service learning in the current South African context, including, inter alia, adult education, development centers, and higher education studies. Colleagues (comfortably) based in disciplines such as sociology, philosophy, anthropology, and development studies, have challenged service learning proponents about the use of concepts such as "community," "sustainability," and "development," bringing to mind Kahn's (chapter 6) warning about "succumbing to colonialist models of development." During the Community Service policy review process at the University of the Free State, much time and effort went into finding a broadly acceptable response to the questions: Who is the "community" in "community engagement"? Do terms like "service" and "development" denote a paternalistic positioning of the University? U.S. faculty and their ISL students who wish to become involved in an environment where stakeholders are engaged in trying to work out these tricky matters could make valuable contributions, and at the same time learn much about the practical challenges posed by living and working in highly diverse societies.

In South Africa, the overworked notion of higher education "transformation" has almost become devoid of meaning by now. The fact remains, however, that higher education institutions all over the world are bound to become irrelevant if they forget that serving the public interest (or the public good), in a knowledge-based way, is their raison d'être. The rapid pace of change everywhere thus forces higher education to place itself at the forefront of transformative thinking, and engaging deeply with the world at a local, national, international, and global level is a prerequisite for this (Plater, chapter 2; Tonkin, chapter 9). In the Preamble of the Community Service Policy of the University of the Free State, the challenge of transformation is explicitly linked to the repositioning of the University within the African context:

> The Policy acknowledges the concurrent challenge of operating in a truly African reality and reflecting an African consciousness and identity, and undertakes to champion the contextualisation of the University of the Free State as a university of excellence in, and for, Africa. The Community Service Policy thus envisions community engagement in the form of a pioneering approach that is increasingly integrated with teaching, learning and research. (University of the Free State, 2006)

Spurred on by U.S. colleagues (Bringle & Hatcher, 2005) to advance the scholarly agenda of service learning through theory-based research, I have utilized a theoretical framework for thinking about service learning's potential role in preparing students to engage with our highly complex world in the spirit of "Mode 2" knowledge production (Erasmus, 2007), which seems relevant to ISL as well. Gibbons' (2006) notion of engagement as a core value in a Mode 2 society currently serves as a metaphor by which to live and work, as I strive to balance the exciting possibilities with the potential disasters inherent in service learning.

During the past decade, the South African higher education arena was influenced by, or rather exposed to, the Mode 2 knowledge debate initiated by Gibbons and several others. Kraak (2000, pp. 2, 10) succinctly distinguishes the new Mode 2 from traditional Mode 1 knowledge production by describing the former as open, intrinsically transdisciplinary, trans-institutional, and heterogeneous, and adds: "In short, Mode 2 is problem-solving knowledge" (Kraak, 2000, p. 2). Some hoped that this debate would cause a stir in the comfort zones of academics with an elitist orientation. Higher education's community engagement and even service learning were also featured in that debate (Subotzky, 2000). During the past three years, Gibbons has taken the Mode 2 argument to a subsequent level, inter alia in a presentation in Queensland, Australia, where he contended that a new social contract between science and society was required, which would radically change the way in which higher education institutions go about their business (Gibbons, 2005). More recently (and locally), he was a keynote speaker at the broadly representative national Community Engagement conference that was held in Cape Town in September 2006—a source of irritation to some; but for others, including myself, his persuasive argumentation serves as an extended metaphor that can, inter alia, add to our understanding of service learning, and potentially also of ISL. In short, Gibbons (2006) argues that higher education institutions all over the world should face the fact that they live and work in a Mode 2 society, both locally and globally. According to him, the emergence of a Mode 2 world is a response to the growing complexity of problems and issues that need to be addressed, as well as to the increasing uncertainty in respect thereof. This collective Mode 2 response contributes, in its turn, to the blurring, infringement, and permeability of traditional boundaries between the various institutions of society—the state, market, industry, culture, and science. Both higher education staff and students are thus forced out into the *agora* or marketplace where knowledge-related issues are negotiated, within myriad transaction spaces, for the production of socially robust knowledge.

In an article about the role of service learning in preparing a new generation of scientists for a Mode 2 society and world (Erasmus, 2007), I have argued that both higher education staff and students are afforded an opportunity to develop skills that are required for such a world through the more open, participatory knowledge-generation ethos of service learning. To my mind, it may be useful to conceptualize ISL within the Mode 2 paradigm as well. How can this theoretical framework be employed for research into service learning and ISL? Perhaps it could be useful in deliberations about critical aspects of partnerships, participation, reciprocity, and mutuality that are inherent in both these forms of engagement. Chapters by Kahn (chapter 6), Sutton (chapter 7), Kiely and Hartman (chapter 13), Whitney and Clayton (chapter 8), and Longo and Saltmarsh (chapter 4) illustrate how collaborative, participatory, and community-focused ISL can reflect some of the thinking contained in Gibbon's Mode 2 approach.

Partnerships, Participation, and Reciprocity—An Evidence-Based Approach

In my opinion, the three most noteworthy contributions that the North American conceptualization of service learning has made to South African higher education are the following:

1. An understanding of how the academic curriculum can be utilized to foster a sense of responsible citizenship in students;
2. An appreciation of the value of thoughtfully structured critical reflection during the community-based (service) learning experience; and
3. Renewed interest in and commitment to the cultivation of reciprocal relationships within partnership formations.

It is especially in respect of the third point that much interest has arisen among those in South Africa who regard service learning with a good measure of skepticism. Moreover, it seems that service learning and ISL colleagues in the United States are currently also paying special attention to this matter, as evidenced, for example, by the fact that the theme of the Eighth International Research Conference on Service Learning and Community Engagement, held in New Orleans in 2008, was: *The Scholarship of Engagement: Dimensions of Reciprocal Partnerships*. Longo and Saltmarsh (chapter 4) point out that many questions about reciprocity in an international context still remain unanswered and are in need of investigation. They also point out that ISL students should be prepared "not to assume the onus of contributing to community change," but should be willing and ready to participate in reflective inquiry into matters concerning the local context that need critical interrogation. I suggest that ISL students should specifically be prepared for, and guided in, reflecting with others in the host environment, in order to allow for non-judgmental "connecting" (Kiely, 2005, p. 8; see also Whitney & Clayton, chapter 8) and mutuality through the joint construction and reciprocal flow of knowledge.

In South Africa, misgivings about the possibility of achieving reciprocity in service learning partnerships were expressed as early as 2000, at the very inception of the CHESP initiative. In a publication that introduced the Gibbons debate on "new knowledge production and its implications for higher education in South Africa," under the title *Changing Modes* (Kraak, 2000), Subotzky (2000, p. 114) refers to the "politics of partnerships" and points out that service learning is prone to unequal power relations as a result of the fact that the interests of one partner (especially the academy) easily become dominant. According to him, the ideal is "to recognize and mediate the partners' differences in identities, roles, capacities and interests through relations of mutuality and reciprocity" (Subotzky, 2000, p. 114), which implies building capacity toward the joint ownership, design, control, and evaluation of community engagement endeavors. In accordance with Gibbons' notion of a Mode 2 society, Subotzky (2000, p. 103) points out that transdisciplinary, multisectoral, and inter-institutional approaches are required when complex challenges are addressed; and in the developing country context, this reality can be expressed by a slogan such as: "partnerships or perish." Higher education institutions in South Africa increasingly have to account for the quality and depth of their engagement with communities in negotiating a sound balance between the higher education's agenda and the developmental and other goals of these communities. It is not always possible to hold service agencies responsible for facilitating such engagements. Owing to a shortage of financially strong service agencies (nongovernmental organizations, nonprofit organizations, and community-based organizations) who can speak on behalf of local communities in the Free State province, faculty involved in service learning at the University of the Free State strive toward the formation of triad partnerships (including the voices and participation of service agencies, the service sector, and community residents) that would/could/should be more conducive to reciprocity and mutuality.

It can be assumed that partnership formation in the *agora*, as Gibbons (2006) suggests, will bring about a profound change in the rules of engagement between higher education and society. In such an environment, where boundaries have become blurred, knowledge is contextualized as a result of the "reverse communication" that takes place when society "speaks back" to science (Gibbons, 2006, p. 22). In the South African development context this would mean that local communities become increasingly emancipated and that they therefore insist on participating in knowledge-production on their own terms. This implies that their voices must be heard when agendas and rules are set for engaging in joint projects and programs. For both service learning and ISL, this entails increased possibilities for achieving the rather elusive ideals of reciprocity and mutuality (Bringle, Hatcher, & Williams, chapter 12; Longo & Saltmarsh, chapter 4; Whitney & Clayton, chapter 8).

In the Preamble of the University of the Free State Community Service Policy (University of the Free State, 2006), the university undertakes to become "a model of a truly robust and responsive university that uses its teaching, research and community service capacities to make a significant contribution to the development of its province and also that of its wider region, South Africa and Africa." Providing evidence of such a significant contribution poses a considerable challenge for those engaged in community engagement and service learning. Where ISL students are involved, U.S. faculty could assist in shouldering this burden of proof through international collaboration and participatory research projects in the field. In addition, involvement of international participants could play a significant role in facilitating partnership relations across various divides and in dissipating some of the tensions that exist in local transaction spaces.

For example, Robert Bringle has been present in South Africa and has mediated in instances where community constituencies felt compelled to speak back to managers, administrators, and faculty at the University of the Free State about the purpose and outcomes of service learning and other forms of community engagement. Questions such as the following were asked at various stages: "Where is the sustainability in service learning?" and "Who will do the development [i.e., after the students have left and obtained their degrees]?" In instances where training was provided as part of a service learn-ing initiative, the following was pointed out by a spokesperson, "Community members say they cannot eat books." After having attended several service learning partnership meetings (during the early days of CHESP), community members informed us that they could not return home after a day's deliber-ations without food to put on the table for their family. Another response to service learning involvement at a specific site was: "Your students get their degrees, but we are still 'volunteers' without jobs." Incidentally, these "vol-unteer" youths were called upon several times to "entertain" ISL and study abroad students from the United States. The fact of the matter is that the sheer physical distance from some ISL sites, coupled with the perceptions of the United States as an exceptionally privileged society, inevitably limits the possibilities for hearing the voices of community members. My contention is that sustained collaboration with community sites where higher education institutions of host countries are involved in long-term partnerships is bound to create spaces that are more conducive to dialogue and the two-way flow of various forms of knowledge.

In my view, such a flow of knowledge(s) facilitates reciprocity in the form of mutual learning and collaborative knowledge construction. Thus, an evidence-based approach to reciprocity in service learning and ISL could entail, inter alia, the obligation to provide evidence of curriculum development (for both service learning and ISL courses) through contextualization and enrichment of course content and through capturing and including relevant forms of local knowledge, experiential understanding, skills, and constructive, hopeful attitudes.

In an effort to create transaction spaces for knowledge flows, the Uni-versity of the Free State focuses its collaboration with the communities that it serves on several "flagship" sites, referred to as "key sites for multi-disciplinary engagement" in the 2006 Community Service Policy (University of the Free State, 2006). The first urban partnership site that was developed, the Mangaung-University of the Free State Community Partnership Program (MUCPP), was initially funded by the W.K. Kellogg Foundation. The rural partnership site (Khula Xhariep Partnership, 2009) is situated in the sparsely populated, resource-scarce, and totally under-serviced southern part of the Free State province; and, situated in a former "homeland" or "Bantustan," the QwaQwa campus of the university has also been identified as a key engage-ment site. The QwaQwa region has been identified as a Presidential nodal point for development initiatives and thus holds the promise of the availability of national and international funding earmarked for development projects. In these and many other transaction spaces various sectors of society need to find ways to work together in addressing the many challenges that they face. According to the Gibbons metaphor that I have referred to above, one could consider service learning and ISL faculty and students as "boundary objects" (Gibbons, 2006, pp. 25–26), or rather boundary subjects/agents/actors, who will increase the permeability of boundaries by moving across these boundaries many times. Ideally, in the process, they will assist the various local actors in finding a common language for action that should eventually be reflected in the contextualization of curricula.

By facilitating collaborative knowledge (re)construction across boundaries, service learning and ISL agents promote what Fourie (2003, p. 37) refers to as utilization of local epistemologies and cosmologies. A systematic inquiry into this matter needs to be undertaken, building on the seminal work done by McMillan (2002), who focuses on "knowledge reproduction processes in a service learning curriculum" (p. 55), and O'Brien (2005), who argues for the specific grounding of service learning in the South African context. Such an investigation should build on the conviction that the "knowledge society" is currently infused with "possibilities to explore alternative, innovative knowledge flows in order to enable the political empowerment of communities to foster their entry into the knowledge era on their own terms, as knowledge producers and users," as Bawa (2003, p. 50) so eloquently puts it. This obviously opens up exciting possibilities for collaborative research (e.g., El Ansari, Phillips, & Zwi, 2002).

The foregoing resonates with the argument of Longo and Saltmarsh (chapter 4), who advocate the development of long-term partnerships and the selection of sites on the basis of academic learning objectives that would enable community members to fulfill a meaningful role as coeducators (see also Whitney & Clayton, chapter 8). The authors point out that it seems easier to make the epistemological argument about the value of knowledge being created outside the confines of the classroom in respect of international experiences, than in respect to education on the home campus, and add: "Yet, it is essential that as with any service learning experience, the service is set up in a way that really does value the contributions of the local community" (Longo & Saltmarsh, Chapter.4). In my view, the following research question arises from this statement: What forms of evidence of local community contributions have been valued and how can they be collected and presented?

The University of the Free State's strategies for advancing faculty involvement in endeavors of joint knowledge construction in the *agora* through service learning might be relevant for ISL as well. These have included the following: (a) linking service learning with personal scholarship agendas of faculty; and (b) including engaged scholarship in performance (promotion and tenure) incentives for faculty. As far as the second strategy is concerned, the implication is that faculty should endeavor to connect their own "scholarly service to the community," as it is referred to in the performance management document of the University of the Free State, directly to the service learning placement sites where their students are placed. The fact is that service learning activities of students are not always as meaningful for communities as might be hoped; and thus, by connecting faculty as subject specialists to these communities, a second level of more sustained intervention can be created that also promotes understanding and mutual learning, with the ultimate aim of increasingly grounding course content in the communities. In a similar vein, promoting direct engagement of ISL administrators and faculty with host-country faculty members and their local partners should further strengthen research collaboration and ensure that ISL initiatives are relevant and contextualized.

Impressions of and Reflections on ISL Research

The deliberate increase in emphasis on service learning research in the United States would also influence scholarly approaches to and research on ISL. In her contribution regarding what ISL can learn from research on service learning, Eyler outlines what now constitutes a cumulative body of research and evaluation studies that has yielded, in her words, "a fairly consistent pattern of small but significant impact on adolescents' and college students' personal, social/citizenship and academic outcomes" (chapter 10). Over recent years, U.S. research on the various types of student outcomes associated with service learning has grown in sophistication and rigor to the point that ISL proponents, as well as practitioners and researchers in other countries embarking on service learning initiatives, can learn from the wealth of experience in the field. Through my work with faculty who are engaged in service learning at the University of the Free State, I know and appreciate that the first, almost instinctive urge of faculty is to establish whether all the extra effort is worthwhile in terms of what their students gain. Subsequent questions that arise are: Why? or Why not? and How can it be improved? Quantitative research approaches followed by U.S. scholars (Bringle & Hatcher, 2000; Bringle, Phillips, & Hudson, 2004; Bringle et al., chapter 12) thus provide a benchmark—we need not try to reinvent the wheel in this regard. A key service learning faculty member and colleague (Naudé, 2008) at the University of the Free State recently completed a Ph.D. dissertation, with Professor Bringle as her main supervisor, in which she investigated the role of reflection in service learning for psychology students. Her study helped to place us in a position of considerable strength regarding the use of quantitative methodologies in service learning research.

More light is shed on aspects of ISL student outcomes in the contribution by Kiely (chapter 11), in which he provides a brief history of various forms of international learning, as well as an informative literature review on various theories of intercultural and transformative learning that would also be of great value in studying local service learning experiences in South Africa. From a host-country perspective, one would wish to investigate the other side of the coin as well; that is, the effects that the presence of ISL students have on individuals and communities at the placement site. This effect could include some measure of "culture shock" and various "disorienting dilemmas" brought about by these encounters with strangers. Since transformative intercultural learning involves tacit, visceral elements inherent in the personal, emotional, and spiritual impact of ISL experiences, it seems evident that qualitative (Kiely & Hartman, chapter 13) and mixed-method approaches, as well as the triangulation of results, would be required in order to allow for the emergence of clearer patterns of outcomes and responses.

A possible gap that I have discerned, in terms of the impact of ISL on students, is that investigations do not reflect awareness, on the part of faculty, of the fact that ISL student development provides an ideal opportunity to foster critical awareness of the contentious position of the United States in the world. U.S. perspectives regarding what global citizenship entails are bound to be intrinsically linked with critical reflections on the role that the United States plays on the world stage; for ISL students, their interactions with host-country people provide unique opportunities to gain broader, more nuanced perspectives on developing a new generation of American citizens with a view to ensuring the future of democracy (Levine, 2007).

In alignment with the special attention to student outcomes, the responsibility toward students needs to be counterbalanced by accountability to other participants, as Whitney and Clayton point out (chapter 8). In a developing country it might be more important to convince our local community partners of the validity and value of the research than our academic peers, some of whom might never be convinced anyway. Garlick (2003) points out the importance of first benchmarking higher education engagement endeavors with regard to legitimate expectations of regional partners and then with other higher education institutions. Such a refocus of attention on local constituencies (which would be situated in the host country in the case of ISL) would require that monitoring, evaluation, and research should be undertaken in collaboration with participants directly involved in the experiences. To an increasing degree, such participants insist on being given a full say in higher education's engagement activities to ensure that such involvement will be responsive and relevant to both local and global issues. We are directly accountable and have to go on living and working with the "victims" of our service learning (and your ISL) endeavors. A colleague from the University of KwaZulu-Natal is of the opinion that higher education institutions in actual fact "inflict" their students on communities if good service learning practices are not followed.

In the following statement, Tonkin emphasizes the broad accountability that is required, and posits ISL (and service learning) research as an ethical imperative:

> ... we need to know whether present [ISL] practices are achieving their objectives, or indeed achieving any objectives at all. Not only are we accountable to our funders, our institutions, and our students; we are also accountable to our hosts and the public good. Thus research is more than an academic exercise: it is an ethical imperative. (chapter 9)

Providing scholarship-based evidence of accountability, good practices, and quality management (Erasmus, 2009) is especially important in developing countries (typically "targeted" as host countries for ISL) where higher education funding and other resources are very scarce. In view thereof, any higher education intervention always needs to be carefully scrutinized. It is crucial to structure ISL partnerships in such a way that transaction spaces are created for addressing mutual challenges in participatory ways. This will also require rethinking research topics and strategies for ISL, and refocusing attention to achieve a more equitable, balanced research agenda that is aimed at benefiting all the main stakeholders.

One of the main gaps that currently exists in ISL research, as identified by several U.S. scholars and chapters in this volume (Kiely & Hartman, chapter 13; Longo & Saltmarsh, chapter 4; Tonkin, chapter 9; Whitney & Clayton, chapter 8), is that there is a need to focus more attention on host community impact studies. Some questions arise in this regard: To what extent are community voices heeded by sending institutions? Do these institutions rely heavily on community agency intervention and representation? Is this philanthropic? Is it good service learning and ISL? As emphasized by Kiely (chapter 11) and Whitney and Clayton (chapter 8), deeper exploration of these issues through intentional reflection and participatory, collaborative research paradigms is required; and data should be collected from various sources of information, leading to joint interpretation of results to inform action. The challenge is that all of these activities are essentially time-consuming undertakings, including ongoing negotiations to build trust; getting a representative group of stakeholders on board; managing unequal power-relations; and coping with disappointment. In our context we sometimes have to accept that we can only hope to "fail forward," nonetheless remaining committed to the journey—even if we are not always focused on a specific destination.

A mutual challenge that both sending- and host-country faculty have to tackle head-on relates to the need to provide convincing evidence of outcomes of service learning and ISL initiatives. This would entail negotiating the question as to what will be regarded as indicators of progress and of the achievement of goals that have been jointly determined. We need to find ways to make what we have achieved and built together through joint ISL courses and programs to be visible. I would therefore argue in favor of having written agreements, such as Memorandums of Understanding, between universities and community partners that include stated goals, specify procedures for joint governance, and outline some form of visible, measurable evidence of outcomes, whether for project-based or more process-oriented ISL and service learning (for an example of such measurable service learning outcomes, see Krause, 2007). A Memorandum of Understanding fits in the South African context for supporting the arrangements for community engagement and the following is an example of what could be included, based on the template, Guidelines for Service Learning Collaboration (University of the Free State, n.d.) of the University of the Free State: The pre-implementation agreement will include, inter alia, joint formulation of "a collective vision and goals," "expectations and anticipated benefits for each partner," and "the partnership's anticipated products and any copyright or ownership issues." Evaluative, impact-related questions in a post-implementation interview with partners would then include the following:

- *How do you understand the purpose of this service learning project?*
- *How did you/your organization benefit from being involved in it?*
- *Were the benefits different from those you expected at the beginning of the service learning project? Please explain.*
- *In what ways do you believe that you influenced the University as a result of your connection with one of its courses/projects?*
- *What suggestions do you have for improving the service learning project in the future?*

(Evaluation Instruments available at UFS, online)

Reflective questions in a South African publication containing a self-evaluation instrument for faculty are, however, intended to probe deeper for examples of evidence than the above questions (HEQC/JET, 2006, pp. 67–79). One such question is: "To what degree were the explicit goals of the partnership attained?" (HEQC/JET, 2006, p. 79). In my opinion it remains for the participants to decide collaboratively on what would constitute success for the service learning or ISL partnership, and for each constituency involved. And, it is in negotiating, monitoring, and evaluating such explicit indicators of success that the challenge of and opportunities for reciprocity, mutuality, and balancing of benefits (and risks) become evident.

In addition to making outcomes measurable, even visible, the real challenge is to do more than merely paying lip service to reciprocity, as pointed out before. I believe that innovative research will be required to prove that service learning and ISL actually do involve reciprocal teaching and learning—that is, that they facilitate a two-way flow of knowledge, understanding, wisdom, skills, and constructive dispositions. A key strategy might be to involve local researchers, community agencies, and organizations—who may be assumed to have gained "experiential understanding"—in endeavors of joint knowledge construction. What, then, will constitute proof of the inclusion of and recognition of local knowledge(s)?[2] As mentioned above, evidence could be provided by including such knowledge in course content through curriculum development. How can such a process be facilitated? At the University of the Free State we have included data collection questions for faculty and students, through which we hope to stimulate, activate, and capture the knowledge that is reproduced, created, and constructed jointly. The questions incorporated into our web-based course portfolio for faculty, include the following, "What did you and the students learn from partners?" and "How will the knowledge mentioned above be utilized to enrich and contextualize the curriculum content?" (University of the Free State, 2008, pp. 23–25).

In addition to the above, we have recently added a new assignment to our faculty service learning training program that involves several hours of observation (listening and learning) at the intended placement sites for students; faculty members have to produce a site report in which they specifically reflect on the question as to what knowledge, wisdom, and skills can potentially be contributed by the community and other external partners. The post-implementation course evaluation instrument for students (UFS, online) also contains questions aimed at collecting evidence of knowledge gained from external partners and fellow students. Under the heading, learning from others (reciprocity), the following questions are asked:

- What did you learn from community members?
- What did you learn from the service sector staff?
- What did you learn from your fellow students?

Another gap in research seems to exist in both the service learning and ISL fields in the area of program evaluation studies. Again, one should take into consideration that interactions are highly complex, necessitating the utilization of a variety of research methodologies, as well as the inclusion of various stakeholders and interested parties in the evaluation research teams. In South Africa, the program evaluation research linked to the CHESP initiative (see Mouton & Wildschut, 2005) was structured in a way that included various sets of instruments (e.g., questionnaires, interview schedules, focus-group protocols) for the different constituencies. U.S. experts involved in developing the instruments included Sherrill Gelmon, Robert Bringle, Tim Stanton, and others. In cases where ISL student placements are linked with host-country service learning, such longitudinal program evaluation studies will have the added benefit of also including research expertise from the United States. This will involve closer collaboration with host-country faculty and other participants in recording, analyzing, and representing data about the impact and outcomes of service learning and ISL engagements for stakeholders, including funders of community agencies; the latter often request such assistance owing to the fact that they themselves are almost invariably understaffed and lack the necessary funding to pay external consultants to conduct the impact studies required by sponsors. As part of a more inclusive approach of this type, students (both service learning and ISL) and community members should be involved as coresearchers. I am convinced that there are considerable benefits involved in equipping students and community members with skills to conduct baseline studies, as well as project evaluation, which will, of necessity, include an understanding of participatory, community-based research methodologies.

In addition to the above focus on program evaluation studies, there is considerable value to be added to service learning and ISL by establishing a link with community-based research. Even though the book by Strand, Marullo, Cutforth, Stoecker, and Donohue (2003) seems to present community-based research as "a blueprint for life after service learning" (Phil Nyden's statement on the jacket of the book, thus not the position of the authors), the two types of community engagement are more likely to be complementary to each other. Including community-based research in service learning and ISL where relevant could strengthen both, while service learning and ISL could also be embedded in larger community-based research projects in the host country, where possible and appropriate. The following are three examples of such multidisciplinary, inter-sectoral, intercommunity research projects involving University of the Free State faculty, researchers, students, and the occasional ISL student; local service sector and private sector partners; international scholars and donor organizations; and local community people with firsthand experience:

- The "Agricultural Research for Development" initiative, with funding and expertise provided from the Netherlands.
- The "Hand-in-Hand" program focusing on the development of small businesses and entrepreneurship—an initiative based in India and currently partly funded by a German donor organization.
- The "Assuring Health for All" (AHA) rural community-based project that is largely funded by the South African government.

In South Africa, those working in the field of service learning have many fine ideas about research that should be undertaken; but we have only started focusing serious scholarly attention on some of the myriad aspects that need investigation. A recent impact assessment of the CHESP initiative by a research evaluation agency, presented in the form of high-level findings, delivered the verdict that "[c]urrent scholarship in the country is on average (still) weak and thin," adding that "[t]his may change in the future as the field matures and more (established) scholars enter the domain" (Mouton & Wildschut, 2007, p. 11). At this stage, there is certainly no lack of enthusiasm and innovative ideas among service learning faculty, friends—and even former foes who have recently entered the field or intend to do so. Aspects that are relevant to such scholarship-based activities include the following:

- Studies of constructs relating to student outcomes that include investigations into emotional intelligence (EQ) and (from the fields of salutogenesis and psychofortology) resiliency, wisdom, hope, and a sense of coherence. The notion of "nothing about us without us" bears relevance in these cases as well, since students have to be openly and deliberately involved in, and informed about, the investigations into these personal outcomes that are to be achieved.
- Theory-based approaches (as advocated by Bringle & Hatcher, 2005) that include invoking, for example, grounded theory (O'Brien, 2005), critical theory, and social justice approaches (e.g., a Ph.D. study in which Petersen, 2007, applied critical discourse analysis within a social justice framework).
- Participatory, constructivist approaches for more holistic, inclusive studies based on participatory action research where long-term involvement is required; and action research approaches that have developed

as a result of Australian and British influences (e.g., the *Living Theory* approach of Whitehead and McNiff, 2006).

- Philosophical and paradigmatic shifts, as exemplified by a phenomenological inquiry into the role of the service sector in service learning by Bruzas (2004).
- Evidence of an epistemological shift (i.e., toward more open systems of knowledge generation) including contextualization of curricula and course content (Erasmus, 2007).
- Ethical aspects related to service learning: In response to the excellent ethical guidelines for service learning research provided by Chapdelaine, Ruiz, Warchal, and Wells (2005) and Wells, Warchal, Ruiz, & Chapdelaine (chapter 14), some colleagues suggested that direct inclusion of external partners in the process of ethical decision making would more often than not be required in our context.

To me, it seems clear that there is almost unlimited scope for research in these fields, and that it is, in fact, an ethical imperative to conduct such research, since good service learning and ISL practice would invariably be based on information acquired through systematic inquiry, especially in collaboration with host-country faculty, service agencies, and community members.

Conclusions and Suggestions for Further Action

From a host-country perspective, the typology of ISL possibilities provided by Jones and Steinberg (chapter 5) is particularly useful in terms of understanding and taking into account the broad range of varieties and variables that these possibilities create. From personal experience, I know that the obligation to set up special service learning experiences for international students causes much additional work for all involved from the host country. I therefore tend to agree with my colleague from the University of Stellenbosch[3] that it is preferable to link ISL students with service learning in the host country, where possible. In addition, reciprocity in the form of exchanges of faculty, students, and community agency staff will prevent these engagements from amounting to one-way traffic. Through mutual internationalization and exchange programs, global citizenship should be extended to include those who are traditionally regarded as potential recipients of service.

As I understand the current U.S. situation regarding ISL, it seems evident that U.S. ISL faculty are concerned with issues similar to those that service learning faculty are struggling with in South Africa, which could imply that these issues would be relevant for other countries as well. Entering into dialogue and setting up research collaboration would be a constructive way to address our mutual interests and challenges. Owing to the fact that service learning has now taken root in South Africa, it could increasingly become a valuable ISL destination and partner. I believe that it would be mutually rewarding for faculty and partners to enter into an ongoing, long-term dialogue and collaboration, both face-to-face and online, about options regarding the nature, purposes, challenges, and value of service learning and ISL.

In South Africa, with its high unemployment rate, devastating HIV/AIDS and tuberculosis figures, shocking crime statistics, and poor service delivery, we do not have time to reinvent the service learning wheel. We urgently need to facilitate the kind of learning for our students that will help them become productive, resilient, involved, and optimistic citizens and professionals in their future work environments. To achieve this, we will need all the assistance we can get. I see an important role for both service learning and ISL in this regard. Most of our challenges will be with us for a very long time, and our best community engagement efforts might not make as big a difference as we would hope, but through your involvement we shall know that we are not alone in striving for a better life for all. Together, we will achieve better quality training for students, in the spirit of "Yes, we can!" U.S. faculty have and can continue to help us appreciate our service learning strengths and build on them; and hopefully you, in turn, will gain a new understanding of how your ISL initiatives could be enhanced. Through collaborative research endeavors, all of us will be able to demonstrate how serious we are about the work.

Notes

1. It was reported in January 2008 that an estimated total of 200,000 Iraqis had been killed in the name of democracy; many more have been maimed and/or disabled, and several thousands have been displaced.

2. Intellectual property rights might come into play where indigenous knowledge is involved.

3. An excellent South African example of an ISL opportunity is the well-structured course offered at the University of Stellenbosch as part of a certificate program in Community Development; see A. Smith-Tolken, mail to: asmi@sun.ac.za.

References

Assié-Lumumba, N. T. (2005). African higher education: From compulsory juxtaposition to fusion by choice—forging a new philosophy of education for social progress. In Y. Waghid & B. van Wyk (Eds.), *African(a) philosophy of education: Reconstructions and deconstructions* (pp. 19–53). Stellenbosch, South Africa: Stellenbosch University, Department of Education Policy Studies.

Bawa, A. C. (2003). Rethinking community-based learning in the context of globalisation. In H. Perold, S. Stroud, & M. Sherraden (Eds.), *Service enquiry. Service in the 21st century* (1st ed.; pp. 47–58). Cape Town, South Africa: CommPress.

Beilke, J. R. (2005). Whose world is this? Towards critical multicultural consciousness through community engagement. In M. Bellner & J. Pomery (Eds.), *Service-learning: Intercommunity & interdisciplinary explorations* (pp. 129–141). Indianapolis, IN: University of Indianapolis.

Bender, C. J., Daniels, P., Lazarus, J., Naudé L., & Sattar, K. (2006, June). *Service-learning in the curriculum. A resource for higher education institutions.* Higher Education Quality Committee in collaboration with JET Education Services [HEQC/JET]. Pretoria, South Africa: Council on Higher Education.

Boyer, E. L. (1990). *Scholarship reconsidered: Priorities of the professorate.* San Francisco, CA: Jossey-Bass.

Boyer, E. L. (1994). Creating the new American college. *Chronicle of Higher Education,* A48.

Bringle, R. G., & Hatcher, J. A. (2000, Fall). Meaningful measurement of theory-based service-learning outcomes: Making the case with quantitative research. *Michigan Journal of Community Service Learning, 68–75.*

Bringle, R. G., & Hatcher, J. A. (2004). Advancing civic engagement through service-learning. In M. Langseth & W. M. Plater (Eds.), *Public work and the academy: An academic administrator's guide to civic engagement and service-learning* (pp. 125–145). Boston, MA: Anker Press.

Bringle, R. G. & Hatcher, J. A. (2005). Service-learning as scholarship: Why theory-based research is critical to service-learning. *Acta Academica Supplementum, 3,* 24–44.

Bringle, R. G., Phillips, M., & Hudson, M. (2004). *The measure of service learning: Research scales to assess student experiences.* Washington, DC: American Psychological Association.

Bruzas, C. (2004). *The hand is the cutting edge of the mind. The role of the service partner in service learning.* Unpublished doctorial dissertation, University of KwaZulu-Natal.

Butin, D. W. (2006). The limits of service-learning in higher education. *The Review of Higher Education, 29,* 473–498.

Chapdelaine, A., Ruiz, A., Warchal, J., & Wells, C. (2005). *Service-learning code of ethics.* Bolton, MA: Anker Publishing Company.

Cooperrider, D. L., Whitney, D., & Stavros, J. M. (2008). *The appreciative inquiry handbook: For leaders of change* (2nd ed.). Brunswick, OH: Crown Custom Publishing.

Dewey, J. (1916). *Democracy and education.* New York, NY: MacMillan.

Dewey, J. (1933). *How we think: A restatement of the relation of reflective thinking to the educative process.* Boston, MA: D. C. Heath and Company.

El Ansari, W., Phillips, C. J., & Zwi, A. B. (2002). Narrowing the gap between academic professional wisdom and community lay knowledge: Perceptions from partnerships. *Public Health, 116*(3), 151–159.

Erasmus, M. A. (2007). Service learning: Preparing a new generation of scientists for a Mode 2 society. *Journal for New Generation Sciences, 5*(2), 26–40.

Erasmus, M. A. (2009). Embedding service-learning in South African higher education through good practices and quality management. In M. Moore, & P. L. Lin (Eds.), *Service-learning in higher education: Paradigms and challenges.* Indianapolis, IN: University of Indianapolis.

Fourie, M. (2003). Beyond the ivory tower: Service-learning for sustainable community development. *South African Journal of Higher Education. SAJHE/SATHO, 17*(1), 31–38.

Furco, A. (1996). Service-learning: A balanced approach to experiential education. In *Expanding boundaries: Service and learning* (pp. 2–6). Washington DC: Corporation for National Service.

Garlick, S. (2003, July). *Benchmarking "good practice" university-region engagement efficiency.* Paper presented at the InsideOut Conference on Higher Education and Community Engagement, University of Queensland, Australia.

Gibbons, M. (2005, March). *Engagement with the community: The emergence of a new social contract between society and science.* Keynote address presented at the Griffith University Community Engagement Workshop, Queensland, Australia. Retrieved June 25, 2009, from http://www.irua.edu.au/policy/policy-20050304.doc

Gibbons, M. (2006, September). *Engagement as a core value in a mode 2 society.* Paper presented at the CHE-HEQC/JET-CHESP Conference on Community Engagement in Higher Education, Cape Town, South Africa. Retrieved June 25, 2009, from http://www.chesp.org.za/HomePage/HEQC-CHESP%20Conference%20Proceedings.pdf

Gramsci, A. (1971). Selections from the prison notebooks of Antonio Gramsci. In Q. Hoare & G. N. Smith (Translators and Eds.), *Selections from prison notebooks* (pp. 77–83). London, UK: Lawrence & Wishart.

Hatcher, J. A., & Erasmus, M. A. (2008, Fall). Service-Learning in the United States and South Africa: A Comparative analysis informed by John Dewey and Julius Nyerere. *Michigan Journal of Community Service Learning 15*(1), 49–61.

Higher Education Quality Committee, South Africa [HEQC]. (2004a). *Criteria for institutional audits.* Pretoria, South Africa: Council on Higher Education.

Higher Education Quality Committee, South Africa [HEQC]. (2004b). *Framework for institutional audits.* Pretoria, South Africa: Council on Higher Education.

Higher Education Quality Committee/JET Education Services, South Africa [HEQC/JET]. (2006). *A good practice guide and self-evaluation instruments for managing the quality of service-learning.* Pretoria, South Africa: Council on Higher Education.

Khula Xhariep Partnership. (2009). *Khula Xhariep Partnership.* Retrieved June 29, 2009, from http://khulaxhariep.co.za

Kiely, R. (2005). A transformative learning model for service-learning: A longitudinal case study. *Michigan Journal of Community Service Learning, 12*(1), 5–22.

Kolb, D. A. (1984). *Experiential learning: Experience as the source of learning and development.* Englewood Cliffs, NJ: Prentice-Hall.

Kraak, A. (Ed). (2000). *Changing modes: New knowledge production and its implications for higher education in South Africa.* Pretoria, South Africa: Human Sciences Research Council.

Krause, M.W. (2007). Service learning in physiotherapy taken to a new level: Experiences in South Africa. *Physical Therapy Reviews, 12,* 277–284.

Lazarus J. (2001, November). *A new contract between higher education and society: Responsiveness through a scholarship of engagement.* Paper presented at the 3rd Consultative Conference of the Council on Higher Education, Benoni, South Africa.

Levine, P. (2007). *The future of democracy: Developing the next generation of American citizens.* Medford, MA: Tufts University.

McMillan, J. (2002). The sacred and profane: Theorising knowledge reproduction processes in a service-learning curriculum. In S. H. Billig, & A. Furco (Eds.), *Service-learning through a multidisciplinary lens* (pp. 55–70). Greenwich, CT: Information Age Publishing.

Mouton, J. & Wildschut, L. (2005). Service learning in South Africa: Lessons learnt through systematic evaluation. *Acta Academica Supplementum, 3,* 116–150.

Mouton, J., & Wildschut, L. (2007). *An impact assessment of the CHESP initiative. High-level findings.* Stellenbosch, South Africa: Evaluation Research Agency.

Naudé, L. (2008). *Service-learning and student development: The role of critical reflection.* Unpublished doctorial thesis. University of the Free State.

O'Brien, F. (2005). Grounding service-learning in South Africa. *Acta Academica Supplementum, 3,* 64–98.

Petersen, N. 2007. *Community service learning in teacher education: About 'otherness' and locating the self.* Unpublished doctoral thesis University of Johannesburg.

Strand, K., Marullo, S., Cutforth, N., Stoecker, R., & Donohue, P. (2003). *Community-based research and higher education: Principles and practices.* San Francisco, CA: Jossey-Bass.

Subotzky, G. (2000). Complementing the marketisation of higher education: New modes of knowledge production in community-higher education partnerships. In A. Kraak (Ed.), *Changing modes: New knowledge production and its implications for higher education in South Africa* (pp. 88–127). Pretoria, South Africa: Human Sciences Research Council.

Thomson, A. M., Smith-Tolken, A., Naidoo, T., & Bringle, R. G. (2008). *Service learning and community engagement: A cross cultural perspective.* Retrieved July 28, 2009, from http://www.istr.org/conferences/barcelona/WPVolume/Thomson .Smith-Tolken.Naidoo.Bringle.pdf

University of the Free State. (n.d.). Service Learning Website: http://www.ufs.ac.za/ servicelearning

University of the Free State. (2006). *Community service policy of the University of the Free State.* Retrieved June 25, 2009, from http://www.ufs.ac.za/faculties/ content.php?id=3790&FCode=Z1

University of the Free State. (2008). *User guide: Webbased service learning database.* Available online via http://ufs.ac.za/servicelearning

Whitehead A. J. & McNiff J. (2006). *Action research: Living theory.* London, UK: SAGE Publications.

Robert G. Bringle has been involved in the development, implementation, and evaluation of educational programs directed at talented undergraduate psychology majors, high school psychology teachers, first-year students, and the introductory psychology course. As a social psychologist, he is widely known for his research on jealousy and close relationships. His work as Director of the IUPUI Center for Service and Learning has resulted in numerous national recognitions for his campus and himself. He has published *With Service in Mind: Concepts and Models for Service Learning in Psychology* (edited with D. Duffy), *Colleges and Universities as Citizens* (edited with R. Games & E. Malloy), *and The Measure of Service Learning: Research Scales to Assess Student Experiences* (with M. Phillips and M. Hudson). For his accomplishments and scholarship on service learning, Dr. Bringle was awarded the Ehrlich Faculty Award for Service Learning and he was recognized at the International Service Learning Research Conference for his outstanding contributions. He was the Volunteer of the Year in 2001 for Boys and Girls Clubs of Indianapolis. The University of the Free State, South Africa, awarded him an honorary doctorate for his scholarly work on civic engagement and service learning. Dr. Bringle received his Ph.D. in social psychology from the University of Massachusetts-Amherst and he is currently Chancellor's Professor of Psychology and Philanthropic Studies at Indiana University-Purdue University Indianapolis.

Nevin C. Brown, a historian by academic training, has spent most of his professional career working in the areas of urban policy and the engagement of urban universities with their surrounding communities. Brown is currently Senior Fellow, Postsecondary Engagement at Achieve in Washington, DC. In this capacity, he is responsible for developing and strengthening partnerships with national higher education organizations to advance Achieve's college- and career-ready policy agenda, as well as overseeing the development of advocacy tools and materials aimed at higher education audiences. Before joining Achieve, Mr. Brown was president of the International Partnership for Service Learning and Leadership, which provides study abroad opportunities for undergraduate and graduate students in several nations worldwide. Brown has also served during the past three decades in various staff roles with the Education Trust, the American Association for Higher Education, the National Association of State Universities and Land-Grant Colleges (now the Association of Public and Land-Grant Universities), the District of Columbia Public Schools, the American Association of State Colleges and Universities, the University of Houston, and the Southern Regional Council's Southern Governmental Monitoring Project. He also cochaired the European Links Committee for UAA from 1995 to 2003, through which he was involved in the creation of the European Urban Research Association.

Andrea Chapdelaine is the Provost and Vice President for Academic Affairs at Albright College, Reading, PA. She earned a B.A. in Psychology from the University of New Hampshire and an M.A. and Ph.D. in Social Psychology from the University of Connecticut. Together, with Ruiz, Warchal, and Wells, she has done extensive work on ethical issues in service learning including publishing *Service learning Code of Ethics*; she has also presented at numerous national and international conferences and workshops.

Patti H. Clayton is an Independent Consultant and Scholar (PHC Ventures, www.curricularengagement.com), a Senior Scholar with the IUPUI Center for Service and Learning, and a Visiting Fellow with the New England Resource Center for Higher Education. Previously, she has 10 years of experience leading community-engaged teaching, learning, and scholarship initiatives at North Carolina State University, where she was founding Director of the Center for Excellence in Curricular Engagement. Her interests include critical reflection and assessment, student and faculty learning, instructional design and curriculum development, transformational partnerships, and democratic civic engagement. Her work has appeared in *Students as Colleagues, Higher Education and Civic Engagement —International Perspectives, Advances in Service Learning Research, Innovative Higher Education, To Improve the Academy*, and the *Michigan Journal for Community Service Learning*. She serves as co-editor with Bringle and Hatcher of the forthcoming book *Research on Service Learning: Conceptual Frameworks and Assessment* and is on the editorial board of the *Journal for Applied Learning in Higher Education*. She was a Finalist for Campus Compact's Thomas Ehrlich Faculty Award for Service Learning and its Leadership Award for Campus and Community Engagement. Clayton has integrated service learning into all of her courses for the past 10 years, and has mentored several students in designing and implementing international service learning capstone projects. In all aspects of her work she seeks to support intellectual, personal, and civic development through cocreating opportunities for reflective practice, leadership, scholarship, and mentoring.

Mabel Erasmus is Associate Professor in Higher Education Studies at the University of the Free State (UFS), South Africa. Her community engagement-related work and experience at the UFS have included the development of a training program for community interpreters and the management of an extensive language empowerment initiative at local government level, funded by the Flemish Community Government, Belgium. She was appointed in the UFS Chief Directorate: Community Service in 2001. In 2004, she was awarded a Centenary Medal by the UFS, "for her central role in developing the UFS's community service policy and the establishment of integrated community service learning modules, as well as her contribution to the establishment of multilingualism at local government level." Dr. Erasmus has participated in several projects and programs of the national Community-Higher Education–Service Partnerships (CHESP) initiative in South Africa. She has presented papers at national and international conferences, and has authored publications on various topics, including community interpreting, linguistic empowerment, sustainable development, and, more recently, academic service learning. In 2005, together with R. Bringle, she acted as coeditor of a special volume of the South African journal *Acta Academica*, titled *Research and (Community) Service Learning in South African Higher Education Institutions*. In January 2007, she was appointed as Head of the Division: Service Learning within UFS's Centre for Higher Education Studies and Development. Her responsibilities include facilitating the various aspects of institutionalizing service learning, with specific focus on policy development, quality management, staff development, and collaborative research initiatives. She has been invited on a regular basis to facilitate workshops, assist with policy development, and present at forums on community engagement and service learning at other higher education institutions.

Janet Eyler is Professor of the Practice of Education, Peabody College of Vanderbilt University. Her scholarly work has focused on various forms of experiential learning, including a number of publications on internships and service learning. She codirected a national FIPSE-funded service learning research project "Comparing Models of Service Learning" and a Corporation for National Service research project on learning outcomes for college students, which were the basis for the book, *Where's the Learning in Service Learning* coauthored with D. Giles, Jr. She received the Outstanding Research Award of the National Society for Experiential Education in 1998 and 2008, the Ehrlich

Faculty Award (a national award honoring contributions in service learning leadership) in 2003, and Annual Research Award of the International Association for Research in Service Learning and Community Engagement in 2007.

Eric Hartman serves as a Lecturer in Global Studies at Arizona State University and is an active member of the Board of Directors for Amizade Global Service-Learning, where he served as Executive Director from 2007–2010. Hartman has cooperated with scores of community organizations on successful locally designed and driven development projects on four continents. He contributed a chapter to *Learning to Serve: Promoting Civil Society through Service Learning*, in addition to writing on related themes for popular publications. Hartman's dissertation at the University of Pittsburgh focused on considering global citizenship through global service learning. He has presented and consulted on that topic at numerous universities and at the annual conferences of the American Political Science Association and The International Association for Research on Service-Learning and Community Engagement, among others. He has taught courses on global citizenship, international development, and regional history in Bolivia, Ghana, Jamaica, Peru, Pittsburgh, and Tanzania.

Julie A. Hatcher is Associate Professor in Philanthropic Studies, in the School of Liberal Arts at IUPUI. She is the Director of Undergraduate Programs for the Center on Philanthropy and a Senior Scholar with the Center for Service and Learning. Research, scholarship, and formal presentations focus on civic learning outcomes, civic engagement and service learning in higher education, implications of John Dewey's philosophy for higher education, philanthropic motivations, and reflective practice for students and faculty. Julie was instrumental in integrating service into the educational culture at IUPUI and supporting civic engagement as a distinct aspect of campus mission. She began the Office of Service Learning in 1993 and served as the Associate Director of the Center for Service Learning until 2010. She has consulted with faculty and campuses on designing philanthropic studies curriculum, integrating service into academic study, and assessment of civic engagement. Julie has collaborated on many international projects with faculty from China, Egypt, Kenya, Macedonia, Mexico, and South Africa. She received the first International Association for Research on Service Learning and Community Engagement Dissertation Award, the Indiana Campus Compact Brian Hiltunen Faculty Award, and the first IUPUI award for Outstanding Woman Leadership for part-time employees.

Steven G. Jones is Associate Provost for Civic Engagement and Academic Mission at the University of Scranton. Previously, he served as coordinator in the Office of Service Learning, IUPUI Center for Service and Learning, where he was responsible for coordinating faculty development and support activities regarding service learning, supervising the Service Learning Assistant Scholarship program, building support for service learning among campus constituencies, and supporting Commitment to Excellence in Civic Engagement grantees. He was previously project associate for the Integrating Service and Academic Studies project at Campus Compact. He edited the second edition of Campus Compact's *Introduction to Service Learning Toolkit* and is a coauthor of two other Campus Compact monographs, *The Community's College: Indicators of Engagement at Two-Year Institutions* and *The Promise of Partnerships: Tapping into the Campus as a Community Asset*. He is also coeditor, with Jim Perry, of *Quick Hits for Educating Citizens*. Steven received a Ph.D. in political science from the University of Utah and was an associate professor of political science at the University of Charleston from 1995 to 2002, where he also served as the Director of the Robert C. Byrd Institute for Government Studies.

Hilary E. Kahn, Associate Director for the Center for the Study of Global Change at Indiana University, Bloomington, has been teaching within the Indiana University system since 1997 and has been involved in the internationalization of higher education since 2004. She is also the Director of the Ph.D. Minor in Global Studies, the Director of "Voices and Visions: Islam and Muslims from a Global Perspective," and an adjunct professor of anthropology. She has taught numerous courses on topics such as anthropological theory, ethnographic methods, visual anthropology, intercultural communication, the anthropology of religion, and indigenous cultures of Central America and Mexico. She currently teaches about "Human Rights and the Arts," and leads multidisciplinary graduate seminars and reading courses as part of the Global Studies Minor. She also directs an international service learning program in Bluefields, Jamaica. Her topical and regional areas of interest and expertise include international education, intercultural teaching and learning, visual anthropology, human rights, social advocacy and art, and global studies. She has presented at national and international conferences and published numerous peer review articles, book chapters, book and film reviews, and a book, *Seeing and Being Seen: The Q'eqchi' Maya of Guatemala and Beyond*.

Richard Kiely currently serves as the Associate Director of the Center for Teaching Excellence at Cornell University. He also serves as the Faculty Fellow at Cornell University's Public Service Center. He was the former Faculty Director of the Cornell Urban Scholars Program and the Cornell Urban Mentor Initiative—two university-wide, interdisciplinary service learning programs. In 2002, he received his Ph.D., from the Department of Education at Cornell University and in 2005, he was recognized nationally as a John Glenn Scholar in Service Learning for his longitudinal research that led to the development of a transformative model of (global) service learning. From 2002 to 2006, he was an Assistant Professor in the Department of Lifelong Education, Policy, and Administration at the University of Georgia and taught graduate courses in the areas of learning theory, instructional design, program planning, community development, service learning, and qualitative research. His current research and teaching interests focus on the scholarship of teaching and learning and (global) service learning as an approach to pedagogy, research, organizational learning, and community development.

Nicholas V. Longo is director of Global Studies and Assistant Professor of Public and Community Service Studies at Providence College. From 2006 to 2008, he served as the director of the Harry T. Wilks Leadership Institute, an endowed civic leadership center at Miami University in Ohio. He also served as a program officer at the Charles F. Kettering Foundation in the area of civic education and directed Campus Compact's national youth civic engagement initiative, Raise Your Voice. Nick is author of *Why Community Matters: Connecting Education with Civic Life* and has written and edited several books and articles on service learning and civic engagement.

William M. Plater served for 19 years as the chief academic officer of IUPUI, until July 2006, a period spanning more than half of its existence as a campus of Indiana University. Earlier, Plater served as Dean of the School of Liberal Arts at IUPUI and as Associate Director of the School of Humanities at the University of Illinois at Urban-Champaign. At IUPUI, Plater played a major role in developing the civic mission of the campus, in addressing the conditions of faculty work, in expanding international programs, in creating new fields of interdisciplinary inquiry, and in establishing a habit of innovation in undergraduate learning. More recently, as Chancellor's Professor and Director of International Community Development, Plater has worked with the Center on Philanthropy, the Public Policy Institute, and International Affairs to extend IUPUI's civic engagement work into international dimensions with the principal objective of aligning community and university interests to help make the Indianapolis region one of the world's best places to live, to work, and to learn by the midpoint of the century. He has worked with a number of national associations on projects and programs related to internationalization and civic engagement, including serving on the advisory panel for the Carnegie Foundation's development of its voluntary classification in civic engagement.

Ana Ruiz is Professor of Psychology at Alvernia University, Reading, PA. She earned her bachelor's degree at Catholic University of Pernambuco. She completed her master's in cognitive development at Federal University of Pernambuco and obtained a doctoral degree in developmental psychology from Cornell University. Her experience with service learning extends from teaching to publications and workshops focused on identifying and resolving ethical dilemmas.

John Saltmarsh is the Director of the New England Resource Center for Higher Education (NERCHE) at the University of Massachusetts, Boston, as well as a faculty member in the Higher Education Administration Doctoral Program in the Department of Leadership in Education in the Graduate College of Education. He is the author of numerous book chapters and articles on civic engagement, service learning, and experiential education, and the coauthor of the *Democratic Engagement White Paper* (NERCHE, 2009). He serves as the chair of the board of the International Association for Research on Service Learning and Community Engagement, as a member of the Board of The Democracy Imperative, as well as on the editorial board of the *Michigan Journal of Community Service Learning*, the editorial board of the *Journal of Higher Education Outreach and Engagement*, and on the board of the Association of American Colleges and Universities Core Commitments Project. He is a member of the National Review Board for the Scholarship of Engagement, a National Scholar with Imagining America's Tenure Team Initiative, and member of the Advisory Committee for the Carnegie Foundation's Community Engagement Classification. From 1998 through 2005, he directed the national Project on Integrating Service with Academic Study at Campus Compact. He holds a Ph.D. in American History from Boston University and taught for over a decade at Northeastern University and as a Visiting Research Fellow at the Feinstein Institute for Public Service at Providence College.

Kathryn S. Steinberg has a Ph.D. in Educational Psychology, and an M.S. in Clinical Psychology, both from Purdue University. She is currently the Assessment Specialist for the IUPUI Center for Service and Learning. Dr.

Steinberg also teaches on an adjunct basis in the Psychology Department at IUPUI. She previously served for nine years as the Assistant Director of Research at the IU Center on Philanthropy. In that capacity she was involved in research on the measurement of giving and volunteering in the United States. Kathy's current research focus involves assessment of student civic learning outcomes.

Susan Buck Sutton is Associate Vice President of International Affairs for Indiana University, with specific responsibility for the Office of International Affairs at Indiana University-Purdue University Indianapolis, where she leads campus internationalization through a distinctive philosophy of dialogue and collaboration that was honored with the 2009 Andrew Heiskell Award for International Partnership from the Institute for International Education. Sutton is also Chancellor's Professor of Anthropology with research interests in migration, tourism, and community in contemporary Greece. She has published four books and over 50 articles.

Humphrey Tonkin, President Emeritus and University Professor of the Humanities at the University of Hartford, has chaired the Canadian Fulbright Commission, the Council for International Exchange of Scholars, and the board of the International Partnership for Service Learning and Leadership. He edited the study *Service Learning Across Cultures* and was author, with Jane Edwards, of *The World in the Curriculum*.

Judith Warchal is a Professor of Psychology and Program Coordinator for the Master's Degree in Community Counseling at Alvernia University, Reading, PA. She earned a B.A. in Elementary/Special Education from King's College, an M.S. in Rehabilitation Counseling from the University of Scranton, and a Ph.D. in Counseling Psychology from Lehigh University. Together, with Chapdelaine, Ruiz, and Wells, she has done extensive work on ethical issues in service learning, including publishing *Service learning Code of Ethics* and presenting at numerous national and international conferences and workshops.

Carole Wells is the Vice Provost for Academic Affairs and Dean of Graduate Studies at Kutztown University, Kutztown, PA. She earned a B.A. in Psychology from LaSalle University, an M.A. in Counseling Psychology from Kutztown University, and an M.S. and Ph.D. in Social Psychology from Temple University. Together, the authors (Chapdelaine, Ruiz, Warchal, and Wells) have done extensive work on ethical issues in service learning including publishing *Service learning Code of Ethics* and have presented at numerous national and international conferences and workshops.

Brandon C. Whitney, MESc., is co-founder and Director of Operations of ioby.org, a NYC-based nonprofit dedicated to fostering local environmental knowledge and action in urban spaces. He is also an Associate with the Center for Humans and Nature, an interdisciplinary think-tank that explores and promotes civic responsibilities for the environment, as well as a Visiting Fellow with the New England Resource Center for Higher Education (NERCHE) at UMass-Boston, collaborating on the Next Generation Engagement project. Brandon served as a Research Associate with the Center for Excellence in Curricular Engagement at North Carolina State University for several years, collaborating on scholarship projects aimed at adapting the service learning pedagogy to a variety of contexts including curricular development, international education, and civic engagement in higher education. As an undergraduate, he designed his own international service learning capstone project and launched the development of a mentoring process and guidebook as part of his scholarship associated with international service learning. He coauthored an invited article on student leadership in service learning, published in *Higher Education and Civic Engagement—International Perspectives*, and has presented on ISL at a variety of national and international conferences. Brandon holds undergraduate degrees in Biology and Political Science from North Carolina State University and a Master of Environmental Science from Yale University.

Matthew J. Williams received a B.S. in Psychology (with a concentration in Industrial/Organizational Psychology) from IUPUI in 2006, and received his M.A. in Philosophy (with a concentration in Bioethics) from IUPUI in 2009. During his studies, he completed a Graduate Assistantship at the IUPUI Center for Service and Learning, followed by supporting the Center's Signature Center activities as a Research Associate. He is currently a Research Assistant at the IU Center for Health Policy. His bioethical interests include egalitarianism as it relates to health care and health care reform policies.

INDEX